Principles and Practices of Management and Organizational Behaviour

Principles and Practices of Management and Organizational Behaviour

Chandrani Singh

Joint Director, MCA, Sinhgad Institute of Business Administration and Research, Pune

Aditi Khatri

Freelance HR Consultant and Soft Skills Trainer, Pune

SAGE | TEXTS

Los Angeles | London | New Delhi
Singapore | Washington DC | Melbourne

First published in 2016 by

SAGE | TEXTS

SAGE Publications India Pvt Ltd
B1/I-1 Mohan Cooperative Industrial Area
Mathura Road, New Delhi 110 044, India
www.sagepub.in

SAGE Publications Inc
2455 Teller Road
Thousand Oaks, California 91320, USA

SAGE Publications Ltd
1 Oliver's Yard, 55 City Road
London EC1Y 1SP, United Kingdom

SAGE Publications Asia-Pacific Pte Ltd
3 Church Street
#10-04 Samsung Hub
Singapore 049483

Published by Vivek Mehra for SAGE Publications India Pvt Ltd, typeset in 9.5/11 pt ITC Stone Serif by Diligent Typesetter India Pvt Ltd, Delhi and printed at Saurabh Printers Pvt Ltd, Greater Noida.

Library of Congress Cataloging-in-Publication Data

Names: Singh, Chandrani, author. | Khatri, Aditi, author.
Title: Principles and practices of management and organizational behaviour / Chandrani Singh, Joint Director, MCA and Placement Head, Sinhgad Institute of Business Administration and Research, Pune, and Aditi Khatri, Freelance HR trainer and consultant, Pune.
Description: Thousand Oaks : SAGE Publications India Pvt Ltd, 2016. | Includes bibliographical references and index.
Identifiers: LCCN 2016001968 | ISBN 9789351508953 (pbk. : alk. paper)
Subjects: LCSH: Industrial management. | Organizational change. | Decision making. | Conflict management. | Teams in the workplace. | Leadership.
Classification: LCC HD30.28 .S474 2016 | DDC 658—dc23 LC record available at http://lccn.loc.gov/2016001968

ISBN: 978-93-515-0895-3 (PB)

The SAGE Team: Amit Kumar, Indrani Dutta, Vandana Gupta and Rajinder Kaur

I would like to dedicate this book to my parents and sibling, who have nurtured me with great care and commitment, helped and supported me during my formative years, and bestowed unconditional love upon me. I am privileged to be born to such wonderful parents.

To my life partner, for providing me with a robust support system.

To my in-laws for their constant encouragement and support.

And last but certainly not the least, my pious indebtedness to my kids Shaurya and Shreya, who adore their mother for her intellectual contributions.

Chandrani Singh

This book is dedicated to my parents, Meera and Dilip Chavan, who have always been my pillar of support and have inspired me in my endeavour to learn and disseminate knowledge for societal benefits.

To my husband Mahesh Khatri for his constant support and motivation.

To my dear sister Nikita for making me believe that nothing is impossible.

To my sweet little distracting daughter Aarvi and my entire family.

And last but not the least, to my teachers who have always guided me to work towards excellence.

Aditi Khatri

Brief Contents

Detailed Contents

List of Figures

List of Tables

Preface

This book is written for the students and the professional community with the objective of providing a unique blend of management practices and contemporary approaches to organizational behaviour in ever-changing business and market scenarios of an era largely dominated by competition and antagonism. In today's world, business organizations are provided with a wider scope to operate, execute, strategize, and diversify, which ultimately calls for new and dynamic strategies and concepts of management practices, to help organizations evolve and grow in a superior manner and increase their sustenance. The exemplary and case-based approach of the book is vital for the readers who aim at exploring the correlation between the two broad topics and the impact they create on each other.

From the students' perspective, this comprehensive textbook helps management students obtain a complete and packaged solution on the management practices and organizational behaviour. The chapters have been meticulously planned with multiple case studies and numerous examples. To date, no book addresses the above two broad topics in entirety. Emphasis of this book lies mainly on clarifying the concepts of management with a detailed coverage of various management functions like planning, directing, decision-making, controlling, and staffing and their application to leadership and motivation strategies, which are very crucial to the formation of organizational culture and have a huge impact on the organizational environment.

This book consists of 16 chapters, of which the first 7 chapters deal with the management trends and functions ranging from the traditional era to the contemporary world and the remaining 9 chapters explore behavioural trends of organizations and managing the organizations across several domains for better sustainability and productivity.

Chapters 1 and 2 deal with the introduction and evolution of management over a period of time, with inputs and guidelines from the management gurus of the yesteryears and of modern age as well.

Chapters 3 to 7 emphasize on individual management functions with detailed coverage on the benefits, characteristics, importance, processes, and models to give the reader clarity and visibility about the functional approaches to management.

Chapter 8 revolves around organizational behaviour accompanied by its nature, scope, dimensions, approaches, and related models.

The later chapters mainly cover the behavioural aspects of an organization from people's perspectives. Since people are the main assets of the organization, the chapters suggest that there is a dire need to understand human psychology and supporting disciplines, which provide insights into human behaviour, their adaptability, and congruence to many behavioural theories. Chapter 13 talks about motivation of employees from organizational perspective. The chapter on stress and conflict expresses the need to address them for improved organizational benefit and productivity. Since an organization comprises human beings, who are key assets of a company, a substantial chunk of information on behavioural trends projects issues related to people. For example, if stress is being addressed, it is because of the people factor; if the conflict is being resolved, it is again because of the people with difference in views, ideas, and opinions; if leaders are being created, then also the focus is on the people aspect of the organization; and, needless to say, this task is being carried out devotedly with new concepts, ideas, and models emerging only to help organizations thrive well in this competitive world. Groups and teams formed within an organization always work towards organizational goals; therefore, the dynamics have to be very proper for consensus in all organizational activities. Two chapters extensively deal with the same.

Chapter 15 deals with organizational change in continuums, which have significant impact on culture, climate, and the organizational environment, improvising on the robustness of organization for a better future.

The Chapter at a Glance feature appended at the end of each chapter has been designed with an aim to provide a concise content repository for student groups for effective and efficient coverage of the course and to the interested readers who can, using abridged versions of the chapters, let their knowledge, rationale, and imagination work wonders in creating their own perspectives for particular topic and content.

The instructors are also encouraged to use the complementary material available on the companion website to the book—chapter-wise PPT slides, instructors' manual, and answer keys to the objective questions (provided in the book). The companion website can be accessed at https://study.sagepub.in/singh_PPMOB.

Acknowledgements

First and foremost, we would like to thank God for giving us the strength and fortitude it took to complete this project holistically.

We are highly indebted to the management and behavioural scientists whose contributions to this literature in the past and the present enabled us to explore the depths of this science and helped us put forth to the audience a readily interpretable version of the complex theories, concepts, and practices of management and behavioural sciences.

We have been the most fortunate in getting the patronage of spiritual and professional mentors from all quarters, with special mention of Dr Subodh Jagdale, an eminent soft skills trainer and astro-ayurveda specialist who helped us improve our literary skills by providing insights into the topics discussed.

We are indebted to SAGE for having made the book available to the critics who helped us by providing prized inputs to improve the quality of this literature from various aspects.

We would also like to thank the reviewers, whose crucial suggestions and comments helped us in developing the content of the book, especially Dr Durba Pal, Department of Management Studies, National Institute of Technology (NIT), Durgapur; Dr Monika Srivastava; Dr Gauri Hari Singhania, Institute of Management and Research, Kanpur; and Dr J. Sathyakumar, Thiagarajar School of Management, Madurai.

We applaud the efforts and contributions of Diwakar Garg (IOS Developer), Saloni Ranka (working with Eaton Group), Amritha Anand (our wise pupil), and Mitesh Dedhia (working with Accenture) for having the drive and motivation to perform the technical edit of this book. We sincerely convey heartfelt gratitude to all these personalities, specifically the staff of our institution, who have been a source of constant motivation and inspiration to us. The publication of this book would not have been possible without their constant support.

We acknowledge each other's contributions and the effort we put forth. We acknowledge the fact that we stood strongly by each other at times when path to completion seemed to be complex and unachievable.

Thank you all!

About the Authors

Chandrani Singh, currently working in the capacity of Joint Director (MCA) and Placement Head at the Sinhgad Institute of Business Administration and Research, Pune, is an academician of significant stature. Apart from her current administrative and academic role, she also handles the recruitment processes of the techno-management students under the Sinhgad Group of Institutions, Pune. She is also the Cofounder and Director of i-Teknika Services and Solutions, an organization catering information technology (IT)-enabled services to customers. She is instrumental in developing a web-enabled rapid recruitment assessment and training-software abbreviated as WERRAT, which has found its significance amongst the stakeholders.

Formerly an alumnus of NIT Rourkela, where she pursued Masters in Engineering and Masters in Computer Applications, Dr Singh has been actively involved in the research and development initiatives and is on the Advisory Board of National and International Conferences and Journals. She has published and presented multiple research papers in international journals and conferences of repute. She has authored *Software Project Management* and co-authored *e-World: Emerging Trends in Information Technology* and edited AITIS Conference proceeding in the year 2008.

She also chairs the responsibility of paper setting and central assessment processes under the University of Pune and has also acted as a liaison for various industry–academia initiatives with Tata Consultancy Services, Zensar Technologies, and so on.

She had been a very active sports persona in her yesteryears and set the national record in a track event in the mid-1980s. In personal, she is a fun-loving person with a very optimistic mindset in every walk of life.

Aditi Khatri is a freelance Human Resource (HR) Consultant and a Soft Skills Trainer and has worked with TACO Composites Ltd (a Tata Enterprise), Pune, as Assistant Manager-HR and Tricon Infra Buildtech Pvt Ltd, Pune, as Head-HR, where she has been instrumental in developing HR policies and processes.

She joined the Sinhgad Institute of Business Administration and Research, Pune, in the year 2012, in the capacity of Assistant Professor and Training Placement Officer and served the institute for a year-and-half and had carried out during this tenure several academia–industry interaction initiatives.

Ms Khatri then went on to set up her own venture by the name of Focus Consultants, through which she has imparted trainings to 2,000+ students and professionals and has earned the repute of a proactive trainer and a public speaker.

She has presented a number of papers at national-level conferences and successfully coordinated various induction and training programmes across the country.

Ms Khatri has a very optimistic approach towards life and has a go-getter attitude. She is a very creative person, and her creativity reflects in both her hobbies and work.

CHAPTER 1

Introduction to Management

Learning Objectives

- Understanding the term 'management' from various perspectives such as a process, activity, discipline, and so on.
- Enlightening the students on the organizational, personal, and social objectives to be achieved through management within an organization.
- Understanding the importance of management, since effective management in an organization leads to optimal utilization of resources and cost reduction for every process and project within an organization.
- Understanding the important functions of management using an exemplary approach and the reader's takeaway would be the added precision in understanding their necessity from management perspective.
- Connecting and correlating between business, management, and organizational procedures and the various external and internal factors influencing all of them.

An Opening Vignette

Although great deeds of human accomplishment, such as the Egyptian pyramids, the Great Wall of China, the Colosseum in Rome, and the Taj Mahal in India, show evidence of expert management in primeval times, the research on management as a scientific concept began in the late 19th century.

Considering the example of Henry Ford and his car model by the name of T, which saw huge customer acceptance in a period of 12–15 years with Henry Ford sitting on a capital of $600 million in a very short tenure. It was said that at that point of time, the T model had become the symbol of wealth and luxury and Ford saw to it that greater volumes of production of model T at low/reasonable cost helped him reach out to mass and amass wealth from them. When workers started to grumble, he showered them with rewards and high compensation, but the success was short-lived because soon came General Motors who strategized to satisfy the customers in a different manner. It is said as Ford focused on low-cost models and timely delivery of the same, he was more of a technology persona who put emphasis more on the construction part of the car rather than on analysing the acceptance of the same across various segments. Therefore, when GE Motor came out with different alternatives for different segments of customers, the T model started losing its sheen to its rival, and Ford's management ideas and theories were stamped as imperfect. Concentrating more on producing the T model, which he thought would be the best, without actually understanding the needs of various customer segments, his way of managing business had a flaw in it. From there on, many management theories and concepts by experts started acquiring prominence, which led to the formulation of management as a field of study and research. In this chapter, the reader gets a generic view about management before exploring it in depth at a later stage.

Introduction

Every individual is a member of several groups like family, school, college, military, some sports team, corporate firm, and so on. This is because every individual has numerous needs and wants that cannot be satisfied individually. Hence they prefer to operate in groups. Also man is a social animal and likes to live with other people. It is by living and working together in organized groups and establishments that people satisfy their financial and societal needs.

When people are operating in a group, their efforts have to be controlled, coordinated, and directed towards a common goal. This is nothing but management. Like the brain controls the entire functioning of the human body, management controls the functioning of an organization.

Definitions

> *Management is defined as the process by which a cooperative group directs action towards common goals.*
>
> Joseph Massie

The above definition of management can be better explained as a team of employees/ departmental unit who work in collaboration towards a specified departmental/organizational goal, such as improving the quality of services/goods, reducing operational cost, and achieving targets in terms of revenue and sales.

> *To manage is to forecast and to plan, to organize, to command, to co-ordinate and to control.*
>
> Henri Fayol

> *Management is a distinct process consisting of planning, organizing, actuating and controlling performed to determine and accomplish the objectives by the use of people and resources.*
>
> George R. Terry

The definitions by Fayol and Terry on management revolve around its functional aspects. For example, if a small event, whether it is business or general, has to be managed, then the first step requires a plan to be drafted for the same, followed by the organization of the event, executing it, and during execution controlling it to accomplish specific objectives. The same set of steps is applicable to any project (software, construction, insurance and so on) undertaken by any firm.

Management is a multi-purpose organ that manages a business and manages managers and manages worker and work.

Peter Drucker

Peter Drucker's definition of management is both people- and task-centric.

Management is defined as the creation and maintenance of an internal environment in an enterprise where individuals working together in groups can perform efficiently and effectively towards the attainment of group goals.

Koontz and O'Donnel

This definition puts emphasis on the fact that management is a goal-oriented process where people in a team/department/organization work towards designing and creating new products/services, improving productivity of people, reducing time and cost, and adhering to quality.

Nature of Management

The term 'management' is viewed from different perspectives and holds various features or characteristics, discussed in the following subsections.

Management As a Process

Management is seen as a process as it involves performing a series of interrelated functions to achieve the desired result. Some of the major functions involved in management are planning, organizing, directing, coordinating, and controlling. As a process, management has the following implications:

- **Continuous process:** Management is not a one-time process. It is an ongoing process. It deals with recognizing the problem and taking suitable steps to solve it. Thus, it is never-ending process.
- **Social process:** Management consists of interactions among people. For an organization to achieve its goals, the management has to develop and maintain cordial relations among the people in the organization.
- **Integrated process:** Management plays an important role in bringing financial, human, and physical resources to achieve the centralized organizational goals.

For example, if we consider management as a process, then we can readily take the example of a project management process within an organization which starts with initiating the project, planning for the project in terms of schedule, cost, and resources, executing the project in accordance with the plan, and finally initiating the closure for the project. Management as a process is continuous because it deals chiefly with the resolution of issues and is integrated since it involves balancing three key aspects—people, time, and cost—to achieve the project/organizational goals.

Management As an Activity

Like several other activities performed by humans, like walking, reading, listening, cooking and so on, management is also an activity. Management as an activity helps the managers to get the things done and includes the following:

- **Informative activities:** These include collection and dissemination of information and so on. For example, collecting information on the products'/services' market value or the growth chart of its competitors.
- **Interpersonal activities:** These include activities like employee performance feedback, training, and so on.
- **Decisional activities:** These include taking decisions on production plans, advertising campaigns, and so on.

Management As an Art and Science

There is always an argument on whether management is an art or science. However, the fact is that management is both an art and science. It is considered to be an art since it requires that a person possesses various managerial skills, which can be categorized as conceptual (understanding the cause and effect to a particular problem), human (to lead and control groups), and technical skills (to be adept in some technology/platform). In addition, it is considered to be science because various laws and principles are framed and followed where and whenever required when group activities are being coordinated. It consists of simulating flight paths to managing satellite transmissions to simpler tasks such as managing the flow of water in dams.

Management As a Group

Management as a group signifies a group of people responsible to plan, guide, and coordinate the efforts of other individuals working in the organization. Individuals in this group are referred to as managers, and they function at different levels of organizational hierarchy, like top, middle, and lower/operating levels. Management as a group can be viewed in two different ways:

- **Group of all managers taken together:** These managers can be anybody from a chief executive officer (CEO), chief technology officer (CTO), and chief operating officer (COO), who are involved in setting long-term goals, to those who are at the operational level and are entrusted with minor decision-making authority like sanctioning a leave or scheduling an employee for a shift, and so on.
- **Group of only the top-level managers:** These managers are involved in strategic decision-making and are commonly termed as the board of management or the management body of the organization.

Management As a Discipline

Management has developed as a specialized branch of knowledge. It encompasses principles and practices for the efficient and effective management of establishments. Management has become a very widespread arena of study; this is evident from the increase in the number of individuals opting for specialization in management studies. For example, during the initial years a business school graduate gets a generic view of the various subjects under management and then goes on to specialize in areas such as HR, IT, sales, finance, and marketing management.

Management As a Resource

Organizations attempt to achieve their set objectives with the help of various resources, such as materials, money, manpower, machinery, and so on. All the efforts would go in vain if these resources are not coordinated and managed effectively. Thus, we can say that management is a crucial resource that plays an important role in the success of an organization.

Management Orients towards Organizational Goals

Every managerial activity is directed towards the achievement of the predetermined goals and objectives of the organization. For example, an organization has set its long-term goal to cross a billion dollar revenue by 2020, or suppose India, as per Hon'ble Dr A.P.J. Abdul Kalam, had set its goal to double the food production and agriculture products by 2020, resulting in improved food security for people by that time. To set a goal and working towards achieving it is what management is all about, because all factors such as people, resources, budget, schedules, costs, and core competence have to be managed to achieve the goal.

Management Is a Universal Process

Management is an indispensable constituent of every organization irrespective of its size or nature of operation. In fact, management exists everywhere in the universe and in all types of activities whether social, political, commercial, and so on. For example, managing poverty, illiteracy, political turbulence to managing the economy of a nation depicts how management can be a universal process.

Objectives of Management

Consider the case of the company QUITO. The organization has set as its objective to increase its profit margin by 4% year on year so that it can have a 20% margin by the end of five years. It is aggressively trying to increase sales of its IT-enabled insurance services and has made a five-year plan to be the largest market player of this sector. QUITO is also looking to diversify in such business areas as outsourcing, infrastructure management services in the Asia Pacific region in addition to its existing IT and IT-enabled services, for growth and expansion. The employees of QUITO, from its debut years, have actively been involved in seeking customers' faith and trust while doing business by providing them with quality services. Now suppose we want to decipher the organizational objectives of QUITO, then the following objectives are brought into limelight.

Organizational Objectives

Every organization exists to achieve certain objectives. Thus, it is essential that every managerial activity be directed in such a manner that it facilitates the accomplishment of these predefined organizational objectives. Some of the organizational objectives are as under:

- Profit maximization
- Growth and expansion
- Goodwill of customers

It was said that the employees of QUITO harboured a culture of aligning their personal goals with the organizational goals. They had individual performance and productivity targets to attain which a majority of the employees solicitously did since their expectations of receiving performance rewards/bonuses were taken care by the HR section of QUITO. Biannual appraisals were done to provide the employees with the feedback on their performance, at the same time providing more growth opportunities to employees with strong feedback.

Personal Objectives

Several people are working in the organization to achieve the organizational objectives but, at the same time, these people also have their own objectives as follows:

- Fair remuneration with rewards and bonus for employees
- Unbiased and healthy working conditions with a transparent communication process across the management levels
- Growth opportunities to the staff of the organization
- Job security for the employees with continuous projects in pipeline

Social Objectives

Along with the organizational and personal objectives, management also has to take care of the social objectives. These could be

- providing quality goods and services to the consumers.
- conservation of environment and natural resources as a part of corporate social responsibility.
- timely payment of taxes, such as sales tax, income tax, service tax, value-added tax, professional tax, and so on.
- honesty in dealings with customers, suppliers, or vendors.

Importance of Management

Optimum Utilization of Resources

Managers identify the requirement for various factors of production like workforce, money, machinery, and material. They then ensure that these resources are available in an adequate amount for the accomplishment of the organizational goals. They also ensure that the resources do not exceed the requirement as this may lead to losses. Managers also train and guide employees so that they can complete the work effectively and efficiently, leading to optimum utilization of resources.

Achievement of Group Goals

A number of people work in an organization. Every individual may work on a specific task or function. However, to achieve the desired organizational goals, it is necessary that all the efforts should be directed in one direction. This can happen only when managers create a conducive environment wherein people in the organization work as a team.

Cost Reduction

In the modern times of intense competition, none of the business firms can prosper unless it is capable of supplying the necessary goods and services at the lowest possible price. Management guides the routine actions in such a way that all wastages are shunned. By decreasing prices and improving efficiency, managers empower an enterprise to be capable of dealing with competitors and thus to make profits

Growth and Survival

These days the business environment changes rapidly. There is a constant change in the demands of the market and society. Management forecasts these changes and enables the organization to face the challenges of the changing environment. The changes in the business environment may create opportunities or threats. It is efficient management that helps to identify the opportunities, leading to not only survival and stability but also growth of the enterprise.

Having stressed on the importance of management, now the prime focus will be in distinguishing administration from management since functionally management focuses on the execution of tasks, whereas administration focuses on decision-making. The strategic, tactical, and operational decisions taken by management come under the administration function, whereas plans designed after taking decisions and executing the design as per the plan is management. For example, a decision is taken (administrative aspect) by the defence sector of the Government of India to build roads across the borders, for which an extensive plan is designed by the civil engineers of the defence sector or it is outsourced to some roadway construction company. They design the plan, constituting of material, manpower, and cost required to build the road across the terrains. If the plan is approved, then the construction company executes it and that becomes the management aspect of the decision taken. Hence, the reader has to be quite clear about the distinction between administration and management and the illustrations in the next section bring out more differences between them.

Difference between Administration and Management

The differences between administration and management are given in Table 1.1.

Table 1.1 Differences between Administration and Management

S. No.	*Points*	*Administration*	*Management*
1	Definition	'Administration as a function is concerned with the determination of the corporate policy, the coordination of finance, production and distribution, the settlement of the compass (i.e., structure) of the organisation, under the ultimate control of the executive.' (Sheldon)	'Management is concerned with the execution of the policy, within the limits setup by administration and the employment of the organisation for the particular objects before it.' (Sheldon)
2	Nature	Determinative or thinking function	Executive function
3	Type of work	Concerned with determination of policies and procedures	Concerned with implementation of policies
4	Level	Top-level function	Mostly middle- and lower level function

(Table 1.1 Continued)

(Table 1.1 Continued)

S. No.	Points	Administration	Management
5	Decision-making	Decision-making is influenced by external forces like public opinion, government, and so on.	Decision-making is influenced by organizational policies and procedures
6	Functions	Major administrative functions include planning and controlling	Directing and controlling are the prime functions incorporated in it
7	Skills	Human and conceptual skills	Human and technical skills
8	Process	Administration decides on what is to be done and when it is to be done	Management decides on who should do it and how should he/she do it
9	Applicability	Government and public sector	Business firms
10	Direction of human efforts	Not directly concerned with direction of human efforts	Concerned with direction of human efforts in execution of plans

Figure 1.1 Extent of Administration Across Various Management Levels

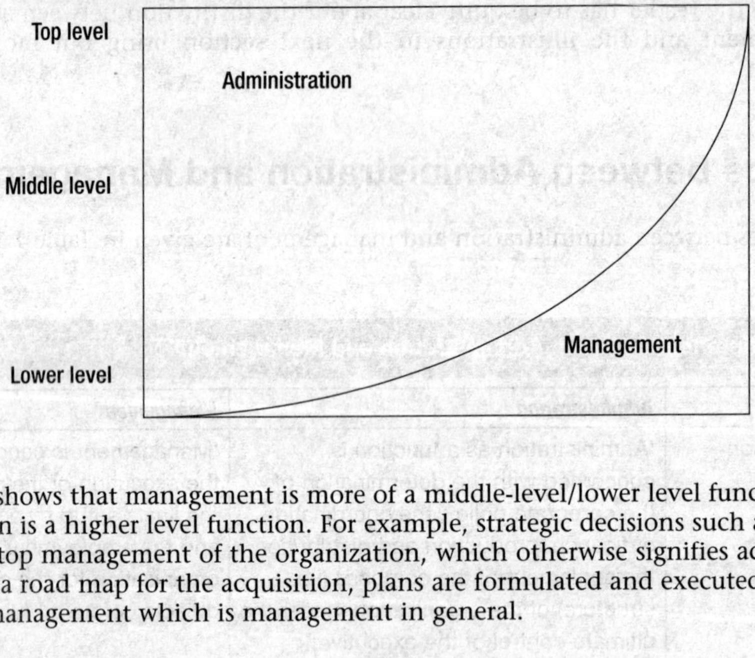

Figure 1.1 shows that management is more of a middle-level/lower level function, whereas administration is a higher level function. For example, strategic decisions such as mergers are taken by the top management of the organization, which otherwise signifies administration, and to create a road map for the acquisition, plans are formulated and executed by the lower and middle management which is management in general.

Levels of Management

Levels of management denote the line of separation among the various managerial positions within an organization. The number of levels in the managerial hierarchy largely depends on the number of people employed in the organization, nature and scale of business operations, and size of the business firm. Each level of management enjoys different amount of authority and status. Also, each level holds different amount of responsibility and has specific roles, functions, and relationships with the other levels.

The levels of management can be classified into three broad categories (discussed in the following subsections).

Top-level/Strategic-level Management

The top-level management includes board of directors, CEO, CFO, CTO, and so on. This level of hierarchy has the highest authority and responsibility. Some of the key functions of top management are as follows:

- To prepare a business-level plan for the organization, including all areas of operation.
- To identify the matters that are important for the existence, growth, and profitability of the organization, such as using advanced technology, setting up a new unit, and so on.
- To set up the organizational goals and objectives.
- To design strategies to achieve the predefined organizational goals.
- To decide on the organizational structure, hierarchy, various positions to be created and relation between these positions.
- To control and coordinate activities of all the functional departments.
- To select people to fit into the vital positions in the organizational structure.
- To act as liaison between various external stakeholders and the organization.

Middle-level Management

The middle-level management acts as a link between the top-level management and the operational-level management. This level includes departmental managers, deputy managers, assistant managers, and so on. Some of the major functions of the middle-level management are as follows:

- To prepare the departmental plan aligned with the organizational plan.
- To identify the department-level goals and objectives and frame strategies to achieve the same.
- To carry out all the managerial activities for smooth functioning of the department.
- To issue orders and guidelines to the operational level of management and also control and coordinate their activities.
- To act as liaison between the top-level and lower level management, for example, explaining the policies and procedures prepared by top-level management to the lower level management.
- To report to the top-level management.

Lower/Supervisory/Operative-level Management

According to R.C. Davis, 'Supervisory management refers to those executives whose work has to be largely with personal oversight and direction of operative employees.' It consists of supervisors, foremen, and so on. This level of management is responsible for issuing guidelines to perform routine activities. The people in this level guide, control, and coordinate efforts of the line workers. The lower level of management performs the following functions:

- Planning the routine activities
- Assigning tasks and issuing orders to workforce
- Supervising and guiding to workforce

Table 1.2 Major Functions Across Levels of Management

Major Functions	*Levels*	*Designations/Positions*
• Set objectives • Scan environment • Plan and make decisions	Top level	• Board of Directors • CEO, CFO, CTO • President • Vice-President
• Develop and implement activities • Supervise first-line managers • Report to top management • Allocate resources	Middle level	• Functional Manager • Deputy Manager • Assistant Manager
• Carry out routine work • Supervise employees • Coordinate activities of line managers	Lower level	• Foreman • Supervisor

- Creating and maintaining a cohesive environment among workers for teamwork
- Reporting to the middle management
- Evaluating performance of the workers
- Managing the grievances among workers

Table 1.2 shows the functions based on the levels of management and the positions accorded to the employees based on the level they are working in and their associated roles and responsibilities based on the functions allotted to the specific levels. The table clarifies the complexity of tasks allocated to managers at all levels and sums up whether they are to be carried out daily as routine activities at the operational level or monthly, quarterly, comprising of budget or resource allocation, half-yearly, yearly, or whether they are tasks that accrue to a five-year plan generally undertaken by the top-level.

Types of Managers

Managers are categorized into three types on the basis of level or position in the hierarchy, role—direct or indirect—specialization, and functions (Figure 1.2).

On the Basis of Level or Position in the Organization

Top Managers

The top-level managers fall in the top level of management. They decide the organizational goals and formulate strategies to achieve them; hence, they are also called strategic managers, for example, president, vice-president, CEO, and so on.

Middle Managers

The middle-level managers act as a link between the top-level management and the operational-level management. The middle-level managers are responsible for communicating the organizational policies and procedures and ensuring that those are implemented. For example, manager, deputy manager, assistant manager, and so on.

Figure 1.2 Types of Managers

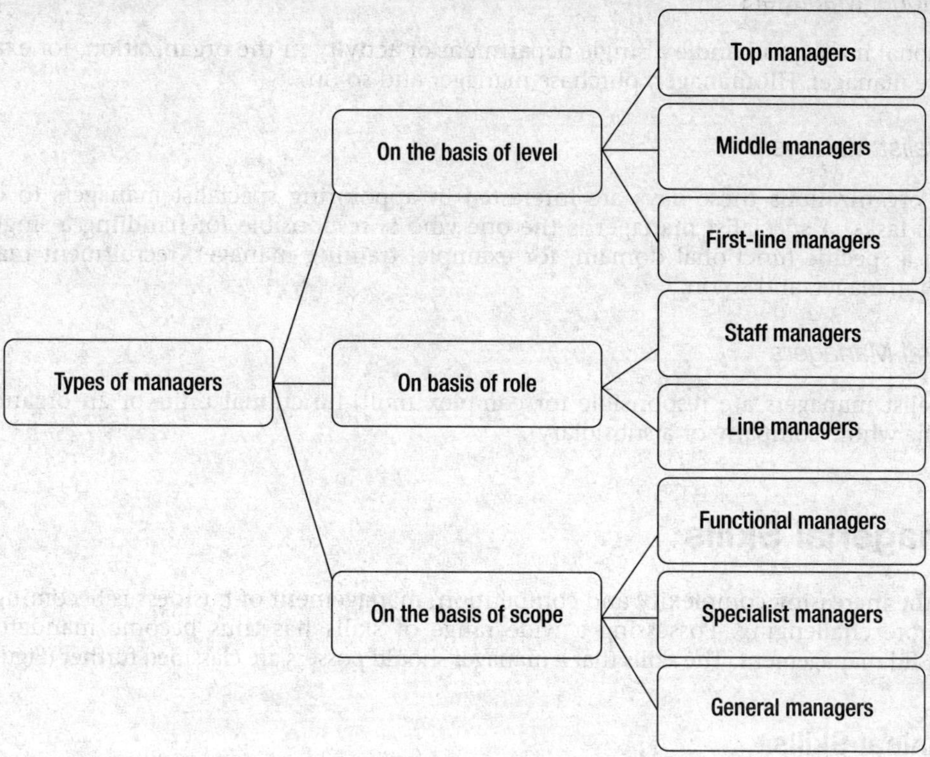

First-line Managers

Individuals at the lowest level of management who are accountable for the work done by others are called line managers. The duties of first-line managers are to guide, control, and supervise the workforce. First-line managers are responsible for the routine work carried out in the organization. The examples of first-line managers are supervisor and foreman. The reader can also refer to Sections 1.7 and 1.10.

On the Basis of Role: Direct or Indirect

Staff Managers

Staff managers utilize special technical/subject knowledge to guide and support the efforts of workforce. Staff managers are not directly concerned with revenue generation. The examples are HR and finance managers, who have staff responsibilities.

Line Managers

Line managers are accountable for activities that lead to direct influence on the output of the organization. The organization's profitability will have a negative effect if the managers fail to fulfil their responsibilities. The examples are vice-president (operations) and manager (marketing).

On the Basis of Scope of Activities Managed

Functional Managers

Functional managers handle a single department or activity in the organization, for example, finance manager, HR manager, purchase manager and so on.

Specialist Managers

Many organizations these days are interested in appointing specialist managers to handle various tasks. A specialist manager is the one who is responsible for handling a single area within a specific functional domain, for example, training manager, recruitment manager, payroll manager, and so on.

General Managers

Generalist managers are responsible for complex multi-functional units of an organization (i.e., the whole company or a subsidiary).

Managerial Skills

With the increasing complexity and competition, management of business is becoming more and more challenging. Possessing a wide range of skills has thus become mandatory for successful management. The skills that a manager should possess are classified further (Figure 1.3).

Technical Skills

Technical skills refer to an individual's aptitude, knowledge, and understanding about handling equipment, procedures, and techniques involved in carrying out any activity. In short, this skill relates to expertise in technicalities of a specific job. The ability to handle computer numerical control (CNC) machines is an example of technical skill.

Figure 1.3 Managerial Skills

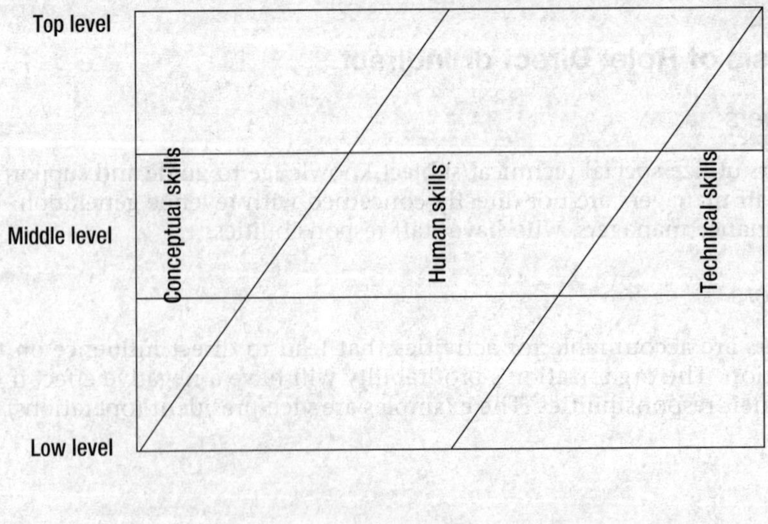

Technical skills are most important for the lower- or supervisory-level management since this level works closely with the workforce and is also responsible for guiding and supervising them in operational tasks. The importance of this skill decreases as we climb the hierarchy.

Human Skills

Human skills refer to an individual's ability to work with people. Having human skills is very essential as it fosters teamwork and helps in the accomplishment of organizational goals in an effective manner. Having human skills help the managers to communicate and understand their subordinates and find out effective ways of motivating them.

Unlike the technical and conceptual skills, the importance of human skills remains the same throughout all the levels of management as one has to deal with people irrespective of the position in the hierarchy.

Conceptual Skills

Possessing conceptual skills enables one to view organization as a whole unit. It refers to the ability to view the entire situation in totality. It helps to analyse the environment and factors governing the situation. Thus, an individual can come up with an appropriate solution to the problem.

For example, consider the marketing and production departments of the same company. Although both the departments belong to the same firm, their individual goals are different. However, the top-level managers see these individuals in a manner wherein the individual goals of the departments are directed towards achieving the goals set by the company as a whole.

Conceptual skills include the ability to think creatively, forecast, strategize, communicate, and debate on different pursuits. Conceptual skills are important for the top level of management since this level is responsible for planning, policymaking, and formulating strategies. The importance of conceptual skills decreases as we move down the hierarchy.

Managerial Competencies

Over the years, management researchers, studying the behaviour of managers at various levels of the organization and in organizations of diverse types, have come to the conclusion that successful managers possess the following competencies.

Effective Communication Skills

Managers who can communicate clearly and precisely either verbally or in writing and disseminate information according to the needs and characteristics of the audience are said to be effective managers. These managers mould themselves with regard to the employees' style and personality and listen and respond to each of them.

Conflict Management and Resolution

Managerial competency aims at resolving conflicts amongst teams or individuals by creating common agreements and settling disputes.

Implementing Strong Feedback Mechanism

Successful managers believe that to keep employee performance high, there should be a mechanism to monitor employee performance on a continuous basis in order to motivate them and to instil in them a sense of responsibility and ownership for every task they undertake.

Aligning Organizational Goal to Performance-oriented Goal

This is done by managers through effective planning, organizing, and allocating roles and responsibilities to people for smooth execution of tasks.

Remake of Organizational Structure for Employee Retention Across Levels

A manager is said to be competent if he can change the structure of the organization from time to time in order to retain the best talent across the industry.

Focus on Employees' Growth

A manager's competency can be emphasizing and implementing career development plan for his employees, which paves the way for growth and learning opportunities of an individual within an organization.

Strategic Planning and Decision-making

A competent manager is a great visionary who can see the prospects and future of the organization from a long-term perspective, along with issues that his organization can face in the future. He also ensures that his departmental goal becomes a key constituent of the organizational goal, which is in general a summation of the individual unit's goal. The manager knows how to get things done through the formal channels and the informal network.

Focus on Relationship Building and Diversifying

A competent manager accomplishes the work goals through collaborative relationships, appreciates the insights of other employees, and takes appropriate actions to increase diversity in the workplace.

Here goes the story of a general manager of a manufacturing firm who, after patiently hearing to the issues faced by the marketing and sales head, production head, and research head, went on to implement an integrated planning system across all the units in order to ramp up sales, promote productivity, and increase research and development activity within the organization. For this purpose, he directed the engineering support group to help the sales unit by actually assisting in demonstration of the products to prospective customers. He also addressed the need for more budget for the marketing of the product. He, on production head's verbatim, obtained the sanction from the finance department for two new assembling units which had undergone substantial wear and tear and was taking a lot of time to finish assembling the television sets. Within three months, the sales of the television sets soared up and demand from the customers could be met with continuous supply of models with reference to customer segments. The research unit, after having heard to a motivation lecture from the general manager, became extremely eager to try out with new features for the light-emitting diode (LED) and plasma display panels.

Scope/Functional Areas of Management

The functional areas of management can be categorized as follows (Figure 1,4).

Financial Management

Financial management deals with procurement and utilization of funds of the business firm. Some of the activities included in financial management are listed below:

- Estimating the amount of funds required to run the business
- Ensuring the availability of funds at right time
- Deciding on the most appropriate sources of funds
- Ensuring optimum utilization of the financial resources
- Maintaining the financial records
- Managing the earnings

Figure 1.4 Scope of Management

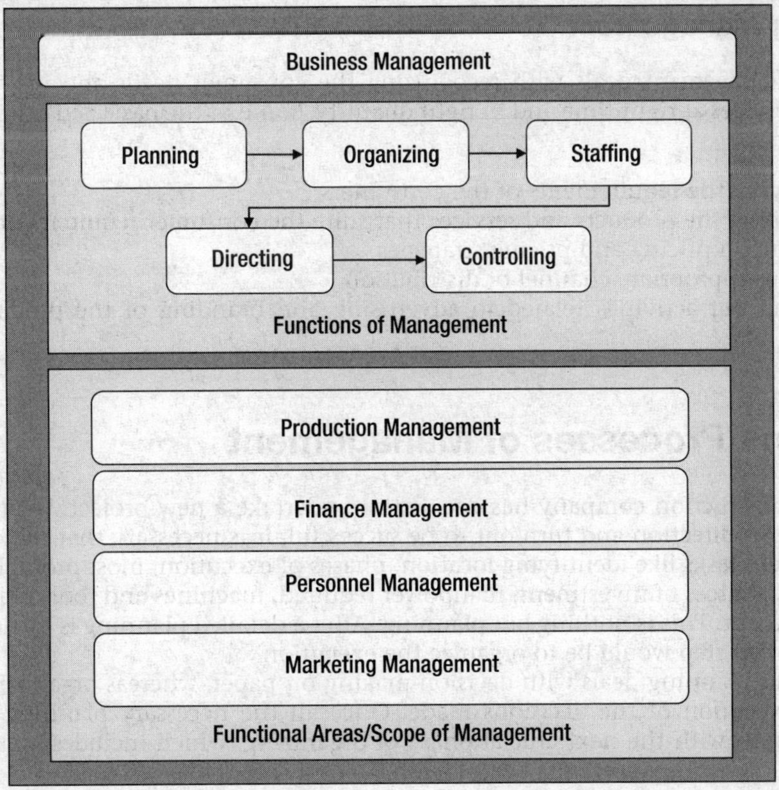

Human Resource Management

Personnel management revolves around managing the human resource employed in the organization. Some of the key functions of personnel department include:

- Human resource planning
- Recruitment and selection
- Training and development
- Performance appraisal
- Career planning
- Promotions and transfers
- Compensation and benefits
- Maintaining employee records
- Employee separation

Production Management

Production management includes all the activities, right from forecasting the requirement of raw material to producing the finished goods. The major activities include:

- Deciding on the layout of the plant
- Forecasting the raw material needs
- Timely maintenance
- Inventory management
- Design and development of product

Marketing Management

Marketing management deals with recognizing the consumer needs and providing quality goods and services at right time and in right quantity. Some of the basic activities included are as follows:

- Identifying the requirements of the consumers
- Developing the products and services that suite the consumer requirements
- Deciding on pricing and pricing strategies
- Selecting appropriate channel of distribution
- Carrying out activities related to advertising and branding of the product or service offered

Functions/Processes of Management

Suppose a construction company has decided to undertake a new project. For the project to move in a right direction and turn out to be successful, it is necessary that the company has a plan, wherein tasks like identifying location, phases of execution, most profitable sources of raw material, sources of investment, manpower required, machines and tools required, and so on are carried out. This is nothing but planning. After a detailed planning is carried out in this respect, the next step would be to organize the execution.

Simply put, planning deals with decision-making on paper, whereas organizing deals with the actual execution of the decisions made. Once all the necessary planning is done, the company begins with the next crucial phase of organizing, which includes making the land

Figure 1.5 Process of Management

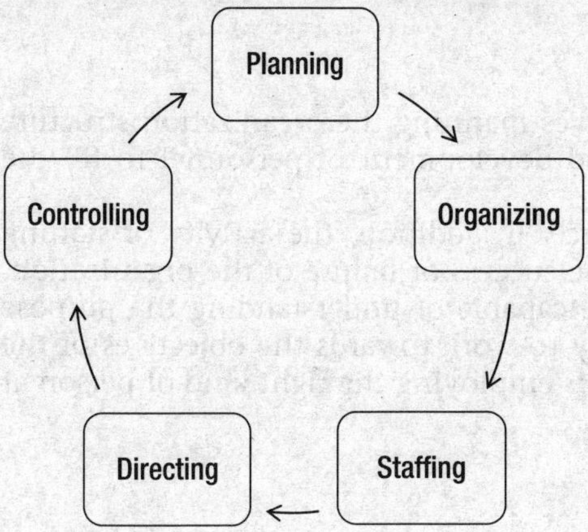

available for the project, arranging for the funds, purchasing the required machinery, tools and equipment, arranging for the raw material, and so on. All these resources must be made available at the right time so that the things move as per plan. If in any case things do not move as per plan, adjustments are made so that the final outcome is not affected.

After providing the 3Ms, which include machines, methods, and money, the next challenging step for the company would be to employ the required manpower to complete the project. First, the company would begin to identify how many internal people can be shifted to take care of the new project, after which if there is any shortfall, the company would recruit people external to the organization. Staffing deals with employment of not only permanent employees but also the contract labour.

Once the human and non-human resources are made available, the company starts training and providing instructions to its employees regarding how the work is to be executed. However, the task does not end here. In order to complete the work as per the plan, the employees need to be supervised and motivated continuously. All the methods and techniques to be followed are presented to the employees so that there is no discrepancy in the execution. All this is nothing but directing.

The company has put in a huge investment, and a single work step or unforeseen event can result into huge losses. Therefore, the company sees to it that the actual work and the plans are compared from time to time, and in case of any discrepancy, timely corrective actions are taken. This is called controlling.

Whether it is a huge project or the same party, management can be seen everywhere and in the order as mentioned below.

The process of management involves carrying out a series of functions as stated in Figure 1.5.

Planning

According to Koontz and O' Donnell, 'Planning is an intellectual process, conscious determination of course of action, the basing of decision on purpose, facts and considered estimates'.

Planning is basically anticipating the future and deciding the future course of action. This function also deals with systematic planning of the various human and non-human resources required by the organization to accomplish the predetermined objectives. Without planning, all the efforts go in vain.

Organizing

According to Henri Fayol, 'To organize a business is to provide it with everything useful or its functioning i.e. raw material, tools, capital and personnel's'.

Once the entire planning has been done, the next step is organizing, which means making available all the resources that would help in achieving the organizational goals. Organizing involves the process of recognizing and grouping the activities to be executed, defining, and allotting responsibility and authority, and establishing relationships among various positions so that the objectives can be achieved.

Staffing

According to Koontz and O' Donnell, 'Staffing involves manning the organization structure through proper and effective selection; appraisal and development of personnel to fill the roles designed on the structure'.

No organization can work without human resource. In addition, the activity of staffing needs to be performed very carefully as it decides the success or failure of the organization. The people employed in the organization should be capable of understanding the purpose why the organization exists and also have the ability to work towards the objectives of the organization. To summarize, we can say that staffing is employing the right kind of person at the right time and in right position.

Directing

According to Human, 'Directing consists of process or technique by which instruction can be issued and operations can be carried out as originally planned'.

Directing is considered to be one of the most important functions of the management since it enables realization of the plans. Directing includes supervising, motivating, and providing leadership to people to accomplish the desired result.

Controlling

According to Theo Haimann, 'Controlling is the process of checking whether or not proper progress is being made towards the objectives and goals and acting if necessary, to correct any deviation'.

Controlling refers to measuring the actual output to the desired output and taking corrective actions if there are any discrepancies. Controlling is performed through a series of activities like

- Setting the standards
- Measuring the actual performance
- Comparing the actual performance with the established standards
- Taking corrective actions
- Providing feedback

Types of Environment and Their Influence on Business

Every organization operates within an environment. No organization can exist independently. All the organizations depend on the external environment for inputs, that is, resources required to carry out various functions. All these forces, which influence the operations and are external to the organization, are called external factors. These factors are also referred to as uncontrollable factors as they are beyond the control of the organization. The other environment is internal, which can be defined as all the forces and conditions within the organization that influence its behaviour. Thus, environment can be broadly classified into internal environment and external environment (Figure 1.6).

Figure 1.6 Environmental Factors Affecting Business

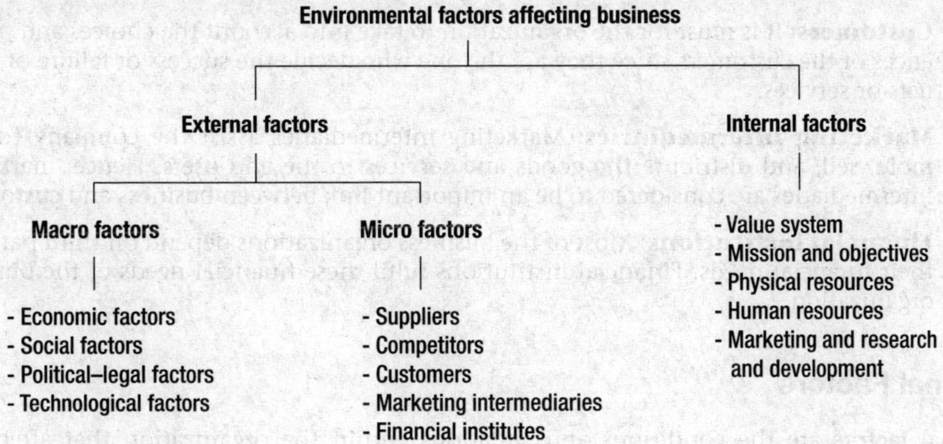

External Factors

All the forces and conditions that influence the operations of the organization and are external to the organization are referred to as external factors. These factors are said to be uncontrollable factors as they are beyond the control of the organization. The external environment is further categorized into macro and micro-environment.

Macro Environment

Macro environment includes the following factors:

Economic factors: Economic factors include economic conditions and economic policies that have an impact on the business operations; for example, inflation, recession, growth rate, and so on.

Social factors: Social factors have a considerable impact on the working of the business. Thus, it is very essential for every organization to study these factors carefully. Social factors include customs, traditions, preferences, values, demographics, level of education, and so on.

Political–legal factors: Political factors include government rules and regulations, policies, legal framework, and so no that largely affect the functioning of the business.

Technological factors: It is very essential for an organization to keep up with the technology for long-term survival. Technological factors basically deal with the use of modern machine and equipment, Internet, ecommerce, social media, electronic media, and so on to carry out the business operations.

Microenvironment

Microenvironment includes the following factors:

Suppliers: The success of an organization depends largely on its ability to provide timely and quality goods and services to the customers. For this purpose, the organizations depend on the suppliers who provide them with necessary inputs.

Competitors: In order to outsmart its competitors and be ahead in the competition, organizations are required to keep a close eye on the market situation and formulate their plans accordingly.

Customers: It is must for the organization to take into account the choices and preferences of the customers since they are the one who decide the success or failure of products or services.

Marketing intermediaries: Marketing intermediaries assist the company to promote, sell, and distribute the goods and services to the end users. Hence, marketing intermediaries are considered to be an important link between business and customers.

Financial institutions: Most of the business organizations depend on third party for their financial needs. Financial institutions fulfil these financial needs of the business organization.

Internal Factors

Internal factors are the conditions and situations within the organization that affect the business operations. These factors are also referred to as controllable factors. Internal factors include the following:

Value system: It refers to the internal cultural framework of the organization. Every business decides plans and policies and expects its employees to act within this framework.

Mission and objectives: Businesses decide their operational strategies depending on the mission and objectives.

Physical resources: Physical resources like money, materials, and machines also influence the functioning of the business to a large extent.

Human resources: If the employees of the organization are skilled and qualified, it would benefit the organization; else it would have a negative impact. Also, the decision-making ability plays a crucial role in the success of the organization.

Marketing and research and development: If an organization is good at its marketing strategies and has a strong research and development department, it ensures longevity of the business.

Summary

This chapter gives the reader an overview of the concepts, principles, practices of management, functions of management, and types of management skills required to operate the business processes within the organization, and also elaborates on the environmental factors affecting the business processes and how effective management can resolve the turmoil and turbulence in businesses. The chapter focuses on the following:

- Definitions of management by management gurus
- Perspectives of management and its nature
- Importance of management
- Functional approach to management
- Management levels
- Environmental factors affecting business in an organization

Exercise

Objective Questions

1. Management is
   - Ongoing process
   - Social process
   - Integrated process
   - All of the above
2. Which of the following approach is used to study management?
   - Art
   - Process
   - Science
   - Profession
3. Which objective of management takes care of conservation of environment and natural resources?
   - Organizational objectives
   - Personal objectives
   - Social objectives
   - None of the above
4. Which level of management includes departmental managers, deputy managers, and assistant managers?
   - Strategic-level management
   - Middle-level management
   - Operative-level management
   - None of the above
5. Which is the correct order for the process of management?
   - Planning, organizing, staffing, directing, controlling
   - Planning, organizing, directing, staffing, controlling
   - Planning, organizing, staffing, controlling, directing
   - None of the above
6. Which managerial skill refers to the ability to view the entire situation in totality?
   - Technical skills
   - Human skills
   - Conceptual skills
   - None of the above
7. Line managers are accountable for activities that lead to the direct influence on the organization's output?
   - True
   - False
8. Who among these come under specialist manager?
   - Training manager
   - Finance manager

- Purchase manager
- HR manager

9. Which of the following are the environmental factors affecting business?
   - Suppliers
   - Customers
   - Physical resources
   - All of the above

10. Planning is
   - a social process
   - an intellectual process
   - an integrated process
   - none of the above

Discussion Questions

1. What are the different skills and functions of a manager?
2. Define management. List its functions. What is meant by management process?
3. Explain the basic functions of management. Do they differ from industry to industry? Discuss.
4. Define management and explain the functions involved in the process of management.
5. Explain meaning, need, and scope of management.
6. Explain nature of management.
7. What do you understand by the systems approach? Explain the management information system (MIS) contingency approach of management.
8. Management is not administration. Discuss using an exemplary approach.

CASE STUDY

In the year 1998, Nokia became the world's number one mobile maker by giving a tough competition to the telecom company Motorola. It produced high-quality and user-friendly mobile phones along with the efforts concentrating on wireless Bluetooth and wireless technology.

The company's products were primarily further divided into four major divisions: mobile phones (data devices for business and personal use and wireless voice), multimedia (mobile gaming devices and home satellite systems), networks (wireless switching), and enterprise solutions (wireless systems for business). Nokia was the best in market, which had really very good technology, and value for money products. It was the best until the launch of first iPhone. Later, Samsung realized the power of Google Android and it started with the move to adopt Android OS.

Nokia had failed to adopt this environmental change and truly capitalize the market. Nokia started losing its customers and failed to attract them. Later, to have more market capture, Samsung launched a variety of smartphone segments with different prices and also launched tablets to attract the customer.

By the first quarter of 2012, Samsung became the world's number one mobile maker and Nokia was completely out of market.

Questions

1. Which environmental factors played a major role in losing business for Nokia?
2. What strategy should Nokia come up with to return to the phone market?

Critical Thinking Questions

1. How much open-minded are you to the ideas of other team members?
2. What are the steps that you have taken to get the work done from your subordinates?
3. Give an example where social factors have influenced businesses?
4. How do you keep yourself and your team motivated as a manager?

Chapter at a Glance

Introduction to Management

When people are operating in a group, their efforts have to be controlled, coordinated, and directed towards a common goal. This is nothing but management.

Features of Management

- Management as a process (continuous process, social process, integrated process).
- Management as an activity (informative activities, interpersonal activities, decisional activities).
- Management as an art and science.
- Management as a group.
- Management as a discipline.
- Management as a resource.
- Management is goal-oriented.
- Management is a universal process.

Objectives of Management

- Organizational objectives
- Personal objectives
- Social objectives

Importance of Management

- Optimum utilization of resources
- Achievement of group goals
- Cost reduction
- Growth and survival

Levels of Management

- Top-level/strategic-level management
- Middle-level management
- Lower/supervisory/operative-level management

Functional Areas of Management

- Financial management
- Personnel management

(Continued)

(Continued)

- Production management
- Marketing management

Functions/Process of Management

- Planning
- Organizing
- Staffing
- Directing
- Controlling

Managerial Skills

- Technical skills
- Human skills
- Conceptual skills

Types of Managers

Managers are categorized three types as follows:

On the Basis of Level

- Top managers
- Middle managers
- First-line managers

On the Basis of Role

- Staff managers
- Line managers

On the Basis of Scope of Activities Managed

- Functional managers
- Specialist
- General managers

Environmental Factors Affecting Business

- External factors
    - Macro Factors
        - Economic, legal, political, social, and technological factors
    - Micro factors
        - Suppliers, customers, competitors, marketing intermediaries, and financial institutes
- Internal factors
    - Value system, human resources, physical resources, marketing research and development, and mission and objectives.

CHAPTER 2

Evolution of Management Thought

Learning Objectives

- Evolution of early management principles and practices in the Indian context.
- Adoption of evolutionary management concepts and practices by the management gurus of the western world.
- Research findings and conclusions of management best practices and human behavioural trends by the experts.
- Current trends in management and their application in organizations.

An Opening Vignette

The evolution of management came into existence in the days of Chandragupta Maurya. In his book *Arthashastra*, Kautilya, minister during the king's regime, stressed on the need for good governance and stated that the book is an ideal repository for those entrusted with power to govern.

Surprisingly, the current trends of management practices are also described in this famous book in the form of organizational vision, mission, and objectives, which were incorporated by the 20th-century management guru Peter F. Drucker. Kautilya insisted that Chandragupta, the founder of the Maurya dynasty, should acquire more power by conquering the states of India one after the other and should unify most of states. The emperor's acquisition of the Indian subcontinent extended from Pakistan in the west to Bengal in the east and the Himalayas in the north to the Deccan Plateau in the south, except Tamil Nadu and Orissa. As per Kautilya's directives, Chandragupta acquired power and authority over the entire Indian subcontinent, which by common management principles align to setting the objectives and working towards its effectiveness by identifying the potential. On the execution front, Kautilya believed that running such a vast territory required excellent leadership skills, improved resource capital, and a sound organization hierarchy with king as the head, prime minister, who looks after the operational aspect of the state machinery using ministers of state legislature down to the leaders who are allotted responsibility at a microlevel. Alignment in the thought of Kautilya and 20th-century management guru Peter Drucker with respect to organization being a 'social dimension with business and economic objective and with a proper hierarchy, exuding power and authority' is very evident from their work considering the above citations. Kautilya also focused heavily on the human resource unit of the organization and advised Chandragupta to lay out plans for the resource, motivation, development, and satisfaction, which form the basis of organizational development, and also identify resource potential across levels. The other aspects of management approaches, as instilled by Kautilya and aligned with Drucker's principles, are as follows:

- Studying the impact of external factors affecting the organization, that is, the strength of other kingdoms, their ambitions, and threats anticipated from these arenas.
- Setting up realistic targets, that is, modernization of cities, acquisition of states, and effective administration of the same.
- Diversification of economy, that is, forest reserves, mines, agriculture, trade, fisheries, land and water, minerals and metals, and so on.
- Formulation of policies and procedures which are lawful and justified for the organization.
- Investment provision for the sustainable growth of any organization, that is, the kingdom of Chandragupta Maurya.
- Decentralization of power by appointing state heads to rule their own states, as is being done in modern-day organizations.

The other areas of management on which Kautilya laid emphasis on were as follows: crisis management, risk management, strategic management, acquisition and mergers, establishing connects, developing a network, and creating an information system framework, which have been instilled in modern management approaches of today.

Introduction

Since the early days, the concept of management had come into existence. Whenever effort had to be expended by a team, it was extremely important that the team had to be managed. Therefore, a group of two or more individuals had to be managed by an entity in the early days. The principles of management were first laid down by Kautilya in his book *Arthashastra*, which emphasized on the fact that no person can single handedly achieve something. It always requires that there be alliance, route, and control to achieve certain goals and objectives; hence, the art of management has come into existence.

Historical Perspective

Management has been considered a formal discipline since the late 19th century. Most of the modern management thoughts evolved during the 20th century. The use of management principles had surfaced from 2900 BC in Egypt, where more than a hundred thousand men were utilized for 20 years in continuum to build the pyramids. Other famous ancient structures which heavily evoke and implement managerial concepts and practices are the Middle Eastern Ziggurats, the Great Wall of China, the Persian roads, and so on. Management concepts were implemented from the time of Moses and through the Greek and Roman eras to usage of assembly-line techniques for fitting warships in a 10-hour duration in the 15th century in Venice. This was the period of dictatorship, punishment, fear of god weighed by human management. In the 16th century, management principles and terms started evolving, such as mass approval, leadership ability, power and authority, and so on. The power and authority were allotted to an individual, organization, or group for administering their responsibility towards others from managerial perspective. These crude approaches were later refined by designing theoretical and conceptual frameworks to be called management principles. Further, the Enlightenment and Renaissance Age brought massive changes with respect to managerial skills, abilities, and perceptions. With the advent of the Industrial era, with setting up of warehouses and factories in the early 19th century, evolved other concepts such as costing, management, production lines, schedules, and so on.

Approaches to Management

Classical Approaches

Classical management theory evolved as a result of the Industrial Revolution and constituted of the traditional school of management approaches such as scientific management, administrative principles, and bureaucratic organization with special emphasis on the economic rationality of management, that is, maximization of monetary rewards, implying that employees work for monetary benefit, and to get hard work out of employees, managers should entice them with rewards. Classical theorists felt that these emotions could be controlled using logical and rational structuring of jobs. The classical approach to management emphasizes on the fact that employees do have physical and financial needs and do not possess social needs or needs of job satisfaction. It is characterized by centralized decision-making and profit maximization. The classical approach had existence from 1900 to 1920 with a strong focus on economic efficiencies. The major contributors to the classical approach were Frederick Winslow, Frank Gilbreth, Henry Fayol, and Max Weber. This approach comprises scientific, administrative, and bureaucratic management. Scientific management entails the best way of doing a job, whereas administrative management focuses on basic managerial functions and bureaucratic management focuses on forming rules, procedures, and workload distribution.

Scientific Management

Frederick Winslow Taylor (1856–1915), the father of scientific management, had many followers, such as Henry Gantt, Frank Bunker Gilbreth, Lillian Gilbreth, Harrington, and Emerson, who became management gurus later and were innovators of various management concepts and principles. Together with Taylor, they revolutionized management thinking. Scientific management emphasizes on proficiency and systematization in management.

Administrative Management

While scientific management theorists tried to determine the best work practices, administrative management theorists explored the ways of executing the jobs together and operating an organization efficiently. This school of thought is also called administrative management. Henri Fayol (1841–1925), a French industrialist and architect, found the administrative management theory. The other experts were Chester Barnard and Colonel Lyndall Urwick.

Bureaucratic Organization

Organizations grow in size with increased functional specialization resulting in strategic, tactical, and operational layers of management coordinating the organizational effort. The result is a bureaucratic approach to organizational structure. With emphasis on the removal of managerial discrepancies and usage of unwanted power, Max Weber advocated some strategies to provide a solid base for systematizing group efforts. It is stated that an organization's cultural values align mostly to the application of bureaucracy. For example, Japanese managers put much emphasis on communication processes, interdepartmental relation, and paternalistic approach, whereas American organizations highlight managerial styles, decision-making, and control machinery. The Japanese perspective increases employees' commitment by producing a legitimate order with illogical power of authority, whereas the American perspective leads to the formation of in-house labour market in which managers can divide and exploit workers.

Human/Behavioural Approach

According to this approach, management is the process of getting things done by people, and the crucial aspect of it is to understand human psychology. The two important factors which play a key role in increasing productivity is motivation and good employee relation. Further, the approach states that apart from the impact of organizational factors such as attitude, changes in cultural environment and pressure also have a major impact on an individual and hence should be taken into account considerably. Behavioural management emphasizes on individual attitudes, behaviour, and group processes and recognized the importance of behavioural processes in the workplace. Major contributors to this approach are Elton Mayo, Mary Follettt, Douglas McGregor, Chris Argyris, and Abraham Maslow. Theories by Douglas McGregor and Abraham have been discussed in detail in Chapter 13.

Contingency/Situational Approach

The contingency approach, which describes organizing of the 21st century, has two prominent models: the Burns and Stalker model and the Lorsch and Lawrence model. Burn and Stalker talked about mechanistic organization, that is, the rigid form of organization and organic organization which is flexible in structure and adaptable to change, and concluded that successful organization in stable situations was mechanistic in design, and in unstable situations those organizations which were successful were organic in design. Lorsch and Lawrence state that every organization should attain equilibrium between differentiating forces and integration factors, that is, tendency among managers to think and act differently, and strong collaboration between different subunits to achieve a common goal. The Lorsch and Lawrence model concluded that organizations fail under complex environmental conditions due to high differentiation and lesser integration, and organizational integration can be achieved through formal hierarchy, departmentalization, organizational policies and rules, and cross-functional culture.

The contingency approach explores the optimal ways of doing things where the performance of one subunit is reliant on its surroundings and has direct or indirect association with other units or subunits.

Thus, performance within an organisation is dependent on situation, and if a change is anticipated within the organization then the manager must try to change the situation influencing it.

In other words, contingency theory states that there is no single best way to manage an organization because what suits an organization may not suit the other organization.

Contingency approaches are framed to depict organizational design situations. Contingency design adapts an organization and its units to situations which describe environmental uncertainty. Environmental uncertainty comprises of social, political, and economic pressures on the organization, on technological breakthroughs, resource and supplier consistency, and consistency in demand of products and services of the organization.

Features

- Managers should present the objectives and prepare strategies, formulate organizations, and must instil mechanisms to adjust to changes in the surroundings.
- Managers should have adequate human relations skill and leadership styles to incorporate changes and bring steadiness.

Impact

- This approach does not adhere to strict management principles and practices and mostly follows what the environment (political, social, economic, and technological) requires.
- The management of the organization is more creative than being mechanistic.
- Contingency approach could be considered a practice-based approach.

An example of the contingency aspect a manager is facing is the non-availability of a web designer till the end of October for his a six-month project scheduled to be over by the end of December. The manager now has to inform his unit head either to allocate him a resource from other teams or to reschedule the project by adding a month extra to his project calendar. This decision can be taken by the manager on the basis of additional cost incurred in the project due to delay in schedule and resource feasibility, that is, commitment of the substitute in other projects.

Operational Approach

The operational approach to management emphasizes on management functions and principles involved in performing these functions. The emphasis on several management functions changes from organization to organization and from level to level. The operational approach to management focuses mainly on planning, directing, organizing, staffing, and controlling. These functions cannot have a static form as an organization has to function in a dynamic mode.

This approach, also known as the management process approach, views management as a social process where actions are initiated to accomplish objectives.

- Operational approach offers a broader scope of management across organization levels and types.
- This approach suggests that management is a universal phenomenon irrespective of the type of organizations or levels of an organization.
- The approach gives a practical perspective by providing classification of managerial functions at the first level into planning, organizing, staffing, directing, and controlling. However, the operational approach has been criticized on the following grounds.

Criticisms

In this approach, there is no universal acceptance of management functions, expressions used are not usually shared, and every approach has some shortcoming or the other.

Systems Approach

This approach came into existence around the year 1950, and the pioneer for the systems approach was Wiener, followed by many systems theory specialists. Basically this approach helps in studying the functions of complex organizations and correlates planning, organizing, directing, staffing, and controlling with each other and also the problems associated with the same. The approach in itself cannot be applied to any type of organization to a deeper extent as there are no specific tools and techniques for implementing this approach.

In 1960, a unified approach evolved, which was known as the 'systems approach'. Its early contributors include Ludwing Von Bertalanffy, Lawrence J. Henderson, W.G. Scott, Deniel Katz, Robert L. Kahn, W. Buckley, and J.D. Thompson.

The system theorists believed an organization to be a flexible and open system, constituting of subsystems as a whole, where every unit is working in sync with every other unit. The system might comprise a hierarchy of subsystems such as the Indian government system/machinery, which comprises the state government machinery, or Indian economy comprising various industries such as agriculture, construction, oil, pharmaceuticals, metals, and minerals, and so on, which constitute various companies who have various units such as manufacturing, production, IT, accounting, and sales and marketing machineries.

Features of Systems Approach

This system has the following features:

- A system acts as a single unit consisting of subcomponents and inputs, output, processing, feedback, and so on.
- The various subsystems within the system should not be studied in isolation.
- The system is defined by an appropriate boundary.
- An organization is susceptible to changes in the environment.

In the systems approach, the focus is on overall effectiveness of the system. If an organization is considered to be a system, then all its functional units are the subsystems of the organization.

The systems approach is considered both general and specialized systems. The general systems approach is the concept related to sociology, psychology, and philosophy, and a specific management system includes the investigation of administrative structure, information, planning and control mechanism, job design, and so on.

The systems approach considers the quantitative and behavioural approaches as subsystems and may succeed where the process approach to management has failed and where the organization is considered to be an open system. Chester Barnard used the system concept of management for organization and stressed on the need of effective leadership by balancing conflicting forces.

Evaluation of the Systems Approach

The systems approach supports modern types of organizations, such as project management organization, where planning, organizing, directing, and controlling are interrelated.

This approach is not concrete as it is not applied to big and complex organizations. Moreover, it does not offer any tool and method for managers.

Examples of the Systems Approach to Management

The systems approach to management states that organizations are flexible and open systems, consisting of subsystems as a whole, where every unit is working in sync with every other unit, and the system has to adapt to changes in the political, economic, and social environment. In addition, the systems approach to management considers a system as a unit with input, output, process, and feedback. We consider some examples which describe the systems approach better.

A healthcare system consists of several levels of care or subsystems as follows:

- Intensive care unit (ICU)
- Extended care unit
- Normal care unit
- Outpatient care unit
- Homecare unit

The above subsystem can also be treated as levels of healthcare, and based on the status of patients' health they are shifted across the levels. If a patient is ill but does not require hospitalization, then he is given treatment through the outpatient department, else he is admitted in the normal care unit. From the normal care unit, he can be shifted back and forth to the ICU based on the criticality of his condition.

The other subsystems of healthcare are as follows:

- State legislation of health (under the influence of political environment).
- Health insurance, mediclaims, accidental insurance (under the influence of economic environment).
- Management as a subsystem of healthcare organizations (autocratic, collaborative, and so on).
- Organization as a subsystem, that is, primary and secondary healthcare or individual, group, health centres as organizational entities of healthcare.
- Healthcare infrastructure as a subsystem comprising of health and hygiene institutes, hospitals, blood donation camps, emergency service units, mobile healthcare, and so on.
- Support systems comprise of medical institutions where training for health cure is imparted and industries which manufacture drugs to cure health.

Whether these subsystems interact with each other? Yes, they do. When a patient's status changes from ill to critically ill, then he is transferred to the ICU. The output of normal care unit in the form of medical reports and diagnosis of that individual becomes input to the critical care, which is a subsystem in itself. If healthcare is considered as a system in whole, then the input to the system are the patients whose health has to be taken care of and the output should be patients who have been cured and feedback would be the standard or the quality of healthcare rendered to the patient. The boundary of the healthcare system can also be defined, such as funding for healthcare organizations, and where an institute is not set up within the operational boundaries of the healthcare system, the funding for setting up an institute should be taken care of by financial institutions. Another example can be Pizza Hut and Domino's Pizza, who operate within their own boundaries, though they are the same businesses. The healthcare system is an open system and has to operate within its boundaries and has to follow government rules and policies related to insurance schemes, mediclaims, drug directives, and so on. Closed systems can be attributed to organizations that operated way back in the 1960s, where external factors were ignored by managers while making decisions with regard to regulatory compliances, market trends, and political and economic issues.

Mathematical/Quantitative Approach

The mathematical/quantitative approach gives a basis for decision-making and believes that management consists of mathematical models and processes. This discipline is called 'operations research.' It uses scientific techniques for providing quantitative base for managerial decisions. The exponents of this school view management as a system of logical process.

Different mathematical and quantitative techniques or tools, such as linear programming, non-linear programming, transportation, job scheduling, and queuing, have found applicability in all the areas of management. The quantitative approach paved way for the mathematical approach.

The mathematical approach has imbibed a culture of critical thinking amongst managers and can only be treated as an analytical tool in managerial practice.

Limitations

This approach provides solutions only for problems which can be solved mathematically and analytically.

- Human behavioural aspect is not computationally solvable.
- This approach is not realistic because decision-making is not always model based.
- Management has many other functions than decision-making, such as planning, directing, controlling, and so on.
- Mathematical models most often do not contain the entire knowledge base; hence, these might not help in accurate decision-making.

Harold Koontz also observed that 'it is too hard to see mathematics as a separate approach to management theory. Mathematics is a tool rather than a school.'

Example of Quantitative Approach to Management

This approach applies mathematical models and statistical techniques to management decision-making. Some examples are as follows:

- Determining the critical path for the development of the web-enabled food waste management system, including the delays which have been accounted for.
- Determining the percentage of wheel-and-axle alignment errors that have been accounted for the specific vehicle company.
- In the area of operations management, the quantitative approaches reduce delivery timelines, streamline production processes, and assist in forecasting inventory and raw material for future needs.

Contribution by Different Theorists

F.W. Taylor's Theory of Scientific Management (1856–1916)

Source: https://en.wikipedia.org/wiki/Frederick_Winslow_Taylor

F.W. Taylor started his career with a US-based steel company and rose till the position of chief engineer in a span of 10 years. During his days with the steel company, he continuously monitored the performance of managers and workers. Taylor observed that these managers and workers did not understand nor implement systematic workload distribution or task execution, though he could feel that such type was highly required for improved productivity and consistency in growth. His ideas and observations proved to be very effective in areas such as production planning, task breakdown, allocation of task, cost–benefit analysis, and so on.

Concept

Taylor invented the concept of scientific management, in which he described mathematical methods to select and train professionals, distribute workload, map task allocation to skill using the techniques, introduce the concept of wage system, and award for those who performed well. Taylor stressed on the need for appropriate working conditions, like well lit-up areas, adequate ventilation, hygienic sanitation, canteen facility, and recreation areas. He could clearly distinguish planning from execution and emphasized that a manager should plan, schedule, guide, and control his staff. He firmly believed that efficient management can cater to employer getting the highest returns and employee getting a good wage.

Principles

- **Scientific methods outweigh rule of thumb:** Clear definition of roles and responsibilities. Fair workload distribution, following appropriate work standards, and implementation of appropriate compensation schemes.
- **Creating group harmony:** Incorporating scientific approach in employee selection, training, and mapping role and responsibility can bring harmony within the team or group.
- **Cooperation:** Workers and management should facilitate each other by working in unison and aligning them to organizational goals.
- **Maximum output:** Maximum output is achieved through appropriate workload distribution and undertaking responsibility and execution of the responsibility by both the management and the employees. From the employer's side, there should be rightful delegation of task, and from the employee's side the task should be executed ideally.
- **Improved work procedures:** The management should see to it that workers get the opportunity to improve in their work area not only for their self-development but also for the growth of the company and bring in required productivity and output.

Key Features

- **Separation of planning and execution functions:** Taylor observed that planning for any task or activity should be done by an individual who is not involved in executing that task. The best way to manage task is that an individual, usually a manager, does the planning and his team members execute that task.
- **Scientific structuring of task:** Taylor emphasized that task allocation and day-to-day distribution of task should be such that an average worker under normal conditions should be able to complete the task in a stipulated time period and on working days.
- **Scientific categorization across work, methods, motion, and time:** Taylor refers to the categorization of work in relation to efficiency required to perform the work, and the efficiency required for the type of job varies from one to the other.

In terms of the methods, Taylor observed that different methods were used to perform different types of tasks, so he distinctly felt the need for improving and refining the methods. For example, Walmart, an established chain of stores, lost millions in business due to server downtime for an hour a few years ago, so it improved its method of scientifically replicating the database on to some other servers so that in case of emergency during a particular server's downtime, the others are up and working.

In terms of motion, if the job involving man and machine is scientifically sequenced, then unnecessary movements are eliminated and time required to perform the job is optimally reduced, and it can be performed more efficiently.

In terms of time, Taylor observed that different jobs required different time periods; hence, it was extremely necessary to categorize jobs as per time and schedule.

In terms of fatigue or stress, Taylor observed that employees needed relaxation time to preserve their health and efficiency after performing their duties and responsibilities, so the concept of leave and holidays was taken into consideration under scientific management.

- **Scientific wage allocation:** Taylor observed that wages should be given to the workers according to the task description and complexity. In addition, a differential piece-rate wage system was formulated by Taylor, which acted as an incentive to lazy workers.
- **Standardization of work:** Standard procedures related to work should be made with respect to tools, working hours and conditions, production cost, and so on.

- **Scientific selection and training:** Taylor observed that the workers should be selected based on skill sets, experience, and qualifications. Moreover, workers who do not have the required skill sets should undergo required training for the task assigned to them.
- **Pay incentives:** Pay and reward schemes motivate workers to work productively, and Taylor observed that with a rise in efficiency, wage of the workers should also rise, which further motivates them.
- **Economy:** Taylor observed that profit making from a product could be earned if resources used are optimum and the cost is controlled.
- **Mindset transformation:** To implement the concept of scientific management, Taylor observed that it required the management and the employees to change their mindset with responsibility towards producing the largest possible surplus and substituting the old rule of thumb with scientific justifications.

For example, McDonald's applies the scientific management principles in their operations by establishing performance-oriented incentives and rewards to employees, and it has also come up with scientific training methods for which a special worldwide management training centre by the name of Hamburger University has been set up at Illinois.

Critics

The concept of scientific management was well received immediately after it was laid down by Taylor, but later it was criticized during the first quarter of the 20th century.

The assessment was that Taylor had formulated a scientific approach to management rather than embedding science into it.

- It was concluded that scientific management principles did not consider the physical, mental and emotional well-being of the worker.
- Critics observed that Taylor laid more emphasis on production management than on other verticals.
- Another observation was that with the aid of tools, equipment, and material, a worker had to perform the task, and for the task execution he was instructed by the foreman or supervisor at every step, which, according to the expert's opinion, constrained the thought process of the workers and did not give them chance to utilize their own brains.
- Critics' study of scientific management suggested that the concept emphasized the need of excellent workers for highest productivity but the reality was something different.
- Another point raised was that increased productivity of workers increased the yield of the company but the wages did not increase proportionately as per the increased yield.
- This approach was also criticized for time, fatigue, and motion studies, which could not be scientifically measured.
- Critics observed that implementation of scientific management required a considerable amount of time; hence, it disrupted the smooth functioning of the organization.

Henry Gantt's Ideology on Management

Source: https://en.wikipedia.org/wiki/Henry_Gantt

Henry Gantt was a US citizen, originally a mechanical engineer by profession, and was a pioneer of scientific management since he was an associate of F.W. Taylor. Henry Gantt was the inventor of the famous progress tracking tool known as the Gantt chart. Gantt wrote several books, such as *Work, Wages and Profits* and *Industrial Leadership,* and published research papers on various concepts of organizational management. He founded the Gantt Task and Bonus Plan, wherein reward was given to those who were highly productive, a refinement of

Taylor's differential system of wage payment. Implementing his concept, the wage of an individual was calculated as follows:

- Substandard productivity—wages based on time rates
- Productivity as per the standard norms—accorded 20% bonus
- Productivity above standards—high differential rates

Henry Gantt paid special attention to the person in general engaged in work and also imbibed the concept of motivation among individuals.

F. Gilbreth and L. Gilbreth

Frank and Lillian Gilbreth not focused on time-and-motion study to perform tasks in the best possible time frame. Time-and-motion study and piece-rate incentives were developed by scientific management theorists and are used even today. The piece-rate incentive system defines that income is proportionate to the productivity of an individual. Scientific management theorists focussed on scientific selection and training of employees, proper design of work, and its sub-tasks, introducing work's best practices, development of a holistic approach to solving organization problems, and a professional approach to management. F. Gilbreth formulated 18 basic tasks and spent a considerable amount of time analysing the best and quickest methods of performing a task. His wife, L. Gilbreth, a psychologist and a management expert by profession, continued preaching her husband's management dictions and even penned down books such as *The First Ambassador of Management* 1960. Workers at Monsanto use time-and-motion study to perform tasks in the best possible time frame.

Henri Fayol's Thoughts on Management (1841–1925)

Henri Fayol's principle states that all the business activities can be categorized into six functions:

- Production
- Sales and purchase
- Finance
- Security
- Accounting and
- Management

Source: https://en.wikipedia.org/wiki/Henri_Fayol

The activities of management as stated by Fayol include:

- Planning
- Organizing
- Directing
- Coordinating
- Controlling

Managerial Traits

As identified by Henri Fayol, the traits of a manager should be as follows:

- The individual should possess the right vigour.
- The individual should possess the ability to make decisions, learn, and understand.
- The individual should be willing to take responsibility and also take initiatives as and when required.

- The manager should possess more awareness and his general knowledge should also be good.
- The function performed by the manager should be aptly known by him, whether it is the production function or accounting function.
- The manager should have appropriate work experience in the domain which he handles.
- Fayol was a French industrialist of the 20th century who coined down the 'Principles of Management' in French, which was later translated to English.

Fayol's Principles of Management

Fayol has set forth the following principles:

- **Division of work:** The total workload should not be allocated to a single individual. Work, whether technical or managerial, should be distributed so that a person specializes and produces output reasonably.
- **Authority and responsibility:** The most important of aspect of management is allocating work to others. Whoever allocates work has the authority over others and simultaneously shoulders responsibility to get the work done.
- **Discipline:** Discipline is mandatory at all levels of management and is obtained by applying stringent rules and regulations.
- **Unity of command:** Command is exhibited by only one individual over others across levels.
- **Unity of direction:** A manager of any unit or group is expected to look after the activity of that group.
- **Alignment of individual interest to group interest:** On no account should an individual's interest be over the organization's interest.
- **Employee wage and compensation:** An employee should be given some amount of remuneration for the task carried out by him and the wage should be directly proportional to the task allocated.
- **Centralization:** Control of decision-making should be in the hands of top management. In other words, centralization is where top management retains decision-making power.
- **Scalar chain:** Every organization should follow a scalar chain which relates to the chain of superiors from top to bottom within an organization and communication flow should happen via the scalar chain.
- **Order:** There should be a proper order or rule by which the resources are allocated the right place and the right job.
- **Equity:** All members of the organization should be treated equally by the managers, so that there exists harmony in relationship between the boss and the subordinate.
- **Job security:** Security of job brings stability for an individual and also for the organization. Therefore, unless an employee is not performing properly he should not be terminated from the job.
- **Initiative:** The second nature of the manager is to take initiatives. While doing that the manager should actively take suggestions from the subordinates and execute those initiatives.
- **Esprit de corps:** All the employees within the organization should be grouped together to work for a common cause and achieve the desired objectives.

Incorporating Fayol's principles of management, it is seen that many call centre agents are authorized to perform one-time fee reversals without taking permission from the supervisor, companies are paying a percentage of salary as performance bonus to employees on a yearly basis and are absorbing in-house employees with an objective to retain employees with specific skill set and thereby cutting on training and recruitment cost, and appointing human interface between compliance unit and other business units for effective communication.

Chester Barnard

Chester Barnard (1971), who had served as the President of New Jersey Bell Telephone, has laid down his ideas in the book *The Functions of the Executive* about the management theory concepts and practices. His focus was mainly on team collaboration and cooperation of employees, and he believed that with effective cooperation and contribution from each employee and with rewards to each employee, a manager could easily attain the organizational goals.

Max Weber's Principles of Management

Weber framed rigid management rules to eliminate inconsistencies and stressed the need of bureaucratic form of management, which is based on a rationale, order, and lawful ability and accrues to public benefits. The features of bureaucratic form of management are the following:

Source: https://en.wikipedia.org/wiki/Max_Weber

- **Work breakdown structure:** A work is divided into tasks, and each task is assigned to separate personnel who are proficient in that task.
- **Levels of authority:** Levels of authority should be maintained to closely monitor and supervise the employees whether they are performing the tasks properly and as per the directions laid down.
- **Policies and procedures:** Weber believed that organization's policies and procedures had to be in place to govern the work behaviour and maintain consistency amongst the employees.
- **Rights and responsibilities:** Weber believed that every employee should be allocated rights and responsibilities of the organization and proper guidelines should be laid down for performing the job regularly.
- **Technical expertise:** As per Weber, the candidate with the right skill set and expertise should be allocated a job and the appraisal of that candidate should happen subject to his performance in that job.
- **Content management:** Weber stressed on the need of an effective content management System pertaining to databases and documents and other written records of the organization.
- **Impartial assessment:** Weber stressed on the need for an impartial assessment of employees where their family relations or having kith or kin does not influence the assessment or even functioning of the organization.

Weber's Notion of Bureaucracy

Weber favoured bureaucratic form of organizational structure, which has many layers of management, right from senior executives to supervisors who work alongside frontline employees. A decision taken by a bureaucratic organization has to pass through many management layers for approval. Refund decisions, for example, may have to pass from frontline employees, through shift supervisors, to store managers for a retail outlet in a bureaucratic company.

Advantages of Bureaucratic Form of Organization

- Division of work and labour
- Allocation of appropriate roles and responsibilities
- Approved policies and procedures
- Greater exercise of control over organizational strategic decisions

- Standardization and work best practices aptly followed
- Democratic form of ruling
- Optimally utilized resources

Disadvantages of Bureaucratic Form of Organization

- **Alignment to market triggers is slow:** A stringent series of authority with built-in controls slows down decision-making.
- **Loss of communication both internal and external to organization:** Internally, since a group is addressed with their decision-making, the group as a whole resists to change. Externally, customer feedback never reaches top management; hence, operational changes in the organization are slow.
- **Loss of creativity:** Employees down the lower level might lose their creative or innovative attitude as they become increasingly aware that their opinions are not heard of by the top management.
- **Loss of competitive advantage:** The firms having a bureaucratic form of organization have to go through the long formal process of supplier selection and assessment, purchase, and sales approvals, which directly affects the organization, resulting in the loss of competitive edge against others.

George Elton Mayo's Principles

Elton Mayo, during his tenure as a researcher at The Wharton School of the University of Pennsylvania in the United States, laid down certain principles which emphasized human relations and importance of desires, attitudes, and feelings of workers. Elton Mayo, in later years, conducted several experiments on Hawthorne Plant workers of Western Electric Company, the results of which are published under six volumes, such as *Human and Social Problems of Industrial Civilization*, *Expectations of Industrial Worker*, *Leadership in Industrial Civilization*, and *Management and Morale*. The experiments were conducted from years 1924 to 1932 in the following phases:

Source: https://en.wikipedia.org/wiki/Elton_Mayo

- **Experiments on effect of changes in illumination in the production environment:** Two groups were formed: a group that worked under constant lighting situations and the other where lighting conditions were varied at time intervals. The observations were recorded, and the results showed that productivity was affected when lighting was not adequate, else the productivity remained the same.
- **Experiments on effect of changing work conditions:** In this, changes with regard to employee suggestions were implemented. Changes were made in the following areas:
    - Group bonus incentive scheme
    - Change in employee relaxation time
    - Start of refreshment schemes to employees
    - Elimination of Saturday as the working day
    - The other changes were abolished, and only the fourth one remained.

The main results derived from the study were that productivity increased due to socio-psychological factors such as employee getting the desired attention, recognition, encouragement to participate, formation of small workgroups, and supervision with minimal directives.

- **Interviews:** This programme was conducted to understand the behavioural pattern of employees towards company benefits, insurance options, compensation, and salaries.

Because the number of employees interviewed was large, the implementation of an unstructured form of interview gave many interesting insights into understanding people's behavioural pattern. Some of the most interesting observations were as follows:

- Supervisors knew about the workers' expectations.
- Alignment of male workers towards the financials was significant.
- Lack of cooperation was the key to variance in emotional attitude.
- Employee satisfaction bore a direct correlation to his expectations from the company.
- Group behaviour actually influenced individual behaviour.
- It was found that a worker rose in status when he gained both internal and external experience.
- An important revelation with regard to the management of an organization was that it always had its objective set on cost optimization and increase of efficiency while workers' objective revolved around the logic and sentiment.

- Experiments on group influence versus conducive financial offerings
  - Conducted between 1931 and May 1932.
  - A group of 14 male workers was identified for performing the experiment.
  - The main aim was to analyse how a group could influence a worker to restrict his output even if he was paid more incentive/bonus for larger output.
  - Hourly rate of wages was fixed, and overall group additional benefit depended upon the average output of each worker and that of the entire group.
  - It was assumed that workers would produce more output, and in addition to that they would help each other.
  - The companies had not improved its working condition for this experiment and were not responsible for the analysis of the results derived from the experiment.
  - However, a general observation was made about an entity's behaviour and impact of group behaviour on the entity.
  - Under this experiment, it was found that workers failed to achieve the company's target due to the following reasons:
    - **Job loss:** Workers felt that if they generate more, a few workers among them would be put out of employment.
    - **High performance standard:** Most of the workers did not want the management to set higher work standards iteratively.
    - **Protection of less-skilled employees:** Workers had maintained coordination among themselves to protect the less-skilled employees.
    - **Approval of executives:** Workers were confident that management would accept lower production and not take any punitive measure for the same.

Conclusions from the Experiment

- Decisive factor for human behaviour–informal relationship.
- Resolution of management–employee conflicts was achieved through counselling.
- Common amongst all organizations was the existence of informal organization.
- The group had fixed average productivity of their own only because of public demands.
- The productivity could not increase even if they were paid more incentives/bonus.

Major Findings and Conclusions of Hawthorne Experiments

- **Communal factors:** Communal factors are accountable for deciding the level of productivity. According to Elton Mayo, 'a business organization is a social system, a system of rituals and a mixture of logical, non-logical and illogical behavior'.
- **Group influence:** Employees created their own groups which were dissimilar from official group to beat the inadequacy of official relationship. Norms of a particular group

were different and workers were free to change their group according to the norms. Therefore, management could not deal with workers independently as group behaviour influenced individual behaviour.

- **Production level:** There was no direct association between manufacturing level and operational environment.
- **Motivation:** Workers are merely motivated by financial benefits.
- **Conflicts:** Goal of management differed from those of workers' objective.
- **Leadership:** Superior is accepted as head if his method is in agreement with human relations approach. The essence of leadership was to direct group behaviour and not exert pressure for production.
- **Cordial relationship**: Employees believed in sustaining good association with others at the cost of their own incentive or bonus due to which production got hit often.
- **Behaviour of workers:** More often workers exuded group behaviour.
- **Supervision:** It was found that productivity was not affected because of the existence of friendly relationship between superiors and workers.
- **Communication:** Workers could clarify their views and feelings related to a particular action. Problems faced by workers could be simply identified and solved as they were open to converse with each other.
- **Reaction of workers:** Complaints and disapproval by workers were indication of deeper contentment.

Criticism of Hawthorne Experiments

- **De-recognition:** The researchers did not give credit to forces accountable for output in the workplace.
- **Workers' bias:** Elton Mayo concluded that management always used logic, whereas workers were largely driven by an emotion which was not the ultimate truth.
- **No logical enquiry:** Hawthorne experiment lacked scientific enquiry.
- **Absence of universalism:** Research was conducted on The Western Electric Company only.
- **Negligible consideration of social factors:** Elton Mayo omitted impact of social factors on workers' behaviour and organizations' environment.
- **Research constraints:** Experiments were not conducted in accordance with labour laws and trade union activities.
- **Treatment of employees:** Employees were forced to accept management goals.
- **Less importance on observation:** Valid results were not arrived at due to fewer observations.
- **No proper validation:** Small experiment set gave inconsistent result.
- **Excessive weightage to employee satisfaction:** Researchers gave much importance to workers' satisfaction, which if measured was more than their productivity.
- **Nil origination of new facts:** Findings were not new and Mayo did not unearth any new point regarding the significance of group in communal life.

Evaluation of the Hawthorne Experiment

The Hawthorne experiment proves to be a milestone in the domain of behavioural findings and has made important contribution towards human interest in the arena of industrial psychology and individual sociology.

Mary Follett's Management Principles

Mary Follett was thought to be a pioneer in the field of HR management. She believed that human psychology played an important role in management and nurtured the passion to study the human characters at various levels of the organization. Mary Follett wrote several books on areas such as business management, dynamic administration, and so on. Follett's views on management were as follows:

Source: https://en.wikipedia.org/wiki/Mary_Parker_Follett

- **Conflict resolution:** Follett stated that resolution to a conflict does not happen by dominating others who have different views on that issue or by compromise. It is best resolved by integrating the opinions of both the teams.
- **Authority:** Follett stated that authority should be of the role and not designated to a person as it spoils the relationship when the concept of subordination comes into play. Moreover, the employee and employer relationship should be based on cooperation rather than on status.
- **Group formation and member participation:** Follett stated that apart from a group's behavioural impact on individual, it is the motivation created by group leaders and management which inspires every member within the group to participate and take ownership in executing tasks.
- **Leadership:** Follett believed that enhanced leadership abilities enhances the power of guiding and also be guided by the group, thereby formulating decisions accordingly.
- **Coordination:** She believed that proper coordination accrued through better planning, decision-making, and is a continuous process.

Chris Argyris's Theory of Adult Personality

Chris Argyris believed that if managers treat the employees of their team as adults or as mature individuals and believe that the individual will take up the responsibility, then the organization can surely proceed towards its goals quickly. Also, Chris explored management practices and needs and capabilities of adults. He could show a sharp contrast between mature and immature theory and believed that people needed less structure because it created more limits. He stressed on the need of the following:

- Clearly defined task for better productivity
- Boss–subordinate relation should be sober
- Allocation of more responsibility ensured better productivity
- Friendly environment in organizations ensured rapid growth

Chris also talked about human behavioural transitions from the stage of immaturity to a mature adult state, which consisted of the following traits:

- Passive to active
- Dependence to independence
- Transition to multiple ways of behaving
- Shallow interest to deeper interests
- Short-term perspective to long-term perspective
- Lack of self-awareness to be aware and be in control
- Subordinate to superordinate position

Peter F. Drucker and His Principles of Management (1909–1974)

Peter F. Drucker laid down certain management principles and was never a staunch supporter of scientific management and its rationale for the same. Peter Drucker was a management guru of the early 20th century and his contributions were as follows:

Source: https://en.wikipedia.org/wiki/Peter_Drucker

- According to Drucker, management encompasses the concept of innovation, which includes development of new ideas, adoption of ideas from various domains, and so on. As a discipline, management has separate tools, techniques, approaches, and skills which are used for innovation.
- Drucker stated that management has no existence of its own and starts with an institution or an organization. The existence and functions of management are concurrent with the existence and functions of a manager.
- Drucker's principle emphasizes on effective organizational structure having the following three characteristics:
    - Should have smooth performance
    - Contains a minimum number of managerial positions
    - Provides the youth with a platform to prove their worth
- The Drucker principle emphasizes a hybrid of centralization and decentralization process followed by top- and middle-level management, which includes decisions taken for the department were shared mutually between two parties.
- Drucker introduced the concept of management by objectives, which includes planning methods, setting standards and procedures, appraising performances, and providing motivation to employees to achieve specific objectives.
- Drucker envisaged continuous changes in the society and stressed that human attitude should be open towards change and further developments.

Management by Objectives (MBO) by Peter Drucker

The above concept underlines organizational objectives and enforces that employees should align themselves to the said objectives. The essence of the above concept lies in setting goals, choosing course of action, and making decisions.

Characteristics of MBO

- It is said that there should be adequate involvement of senior- and middle-level management in decision-making, implementation of decisions, and incorporating required changes for organizational effectiveness.
- The goals set should be in accordance with all the members of the group and the organization should work towards attaining maximum result from available resources. It is also seen that short- and long-term goals are realistic and attainable.
- The main feature of management by objective is that both superior and subordinate focus more on what has to be accomplished rather than how it has to be done.
- Support from the superior to his subordinate in achieving realistic short-time goals is one of the key points which is focused on using this framework.

Steps in MBO Planning

- **Setting of goals:** The first step is to set the organizational objectives and making these objectives known to everybody within the organization. Once these goals are established, they should be made known to all the members along with the results which have to be obtained.

- **Superior–subordinate participation:** At this phase, the goals of the individual units and employees are finalized.
- **Matching goals and resources:** The management must make certain that the subsidiaries are provided with the required instruments and resources to accomplish these goals.
- **Implementation of the plan:** After establishment of objectives and allocation of necessary resources, the subordinates can implement the plan.
- **Performance appraisal:** Reviews on the progress of the manager and the subordinates are done at this stage. Such reviews would unearth the favourable or the problematic situation occurring then and there. Performance appraisals are based on rational and measurable standards.

Advantages of MBO

- **Result-centric philosophy:** MBO is characterized by result-centric philosophy. It provides support to staff in terms of opportunities, tools, and resources to achieve those goals.
- **Formulation of realistic goals:** MBO facilitates speedy progress of an organization by achieving attainable goals.
- **Facilitates objective appraisal:** MBO promotes management by self-control, replacing management by domination, thus resulting in appraisals becoming more intentional and impartial.
- **Employee morale boost:** Employee involvement, participative decision-making and two-way handshake between employees encourage honest communication.
- **Effectuating organizational planning process:** MBO helps in developing action plans, allocating resources as per plan, envisaging the risks, and taking preventive actions for the attainment of goals.
- **Provides motivation to employees:** MBO gives employees occasion to use imagination and inspiration to achieve the mission.
- **Facilitates effective control:** Continuous assessment is a crucial characteristic of MBO which helps in exercising control over employees and processes within an organization. Performance is measured against the standards and deviations are calculated.
- **Facilitates leadership:** Leadership skills can get accentuated and are useful for the efficient management of activities of a business unit. Therefore, a manager has a better chance to climb up the corporate ladder.

Limitations of MBO

- **Time-consuming:** MBO is a time-consuming process with clearly defined roles at each level and reviews of progress happening at regular intervals.
- **Promotion/demotion technique:** MBO punishes employee with substandard performance and rewards one who has exuded superior performance.
- **Increases documentation:** The MBO programme introduces extensive documentation in the form of training manuals, newsletters, instruction booklets, questionnaires, performance analytics, and reporting to the organization to have a rigid control and status track of the organizational activities.
- **Creates organizational problems:** MBO can create an absolute mismatch in the targets created by the subordinates and superiors of the organization. Added to this, the programme excessively controls employee performance.
- **Intra-organizational conflicts:** Sometimes, departmental goals and objectives might be totally different wherein every unit will work towards accomplishing its own goals and fail to align itself with the organizational goals.
- **Lack of coordination:** Difficulties are encountered while coordinating organizational objectives with individual and the departmental objectives.
- **Lacks consistency:** The marginal benefits often diminish year on year and opportunities are lost because individuals stick to conventional goals.

- **Common problems with goal setting:** (a) Absence of measurable goals, (b) inflexible and rigid goals, (c) greater weightage to quantifiable and easily calculable results, and (d) emphasis on short-term goals rather than long-term goals.
- **Lack of appreciation:** Occasional failure of the top management to communicate the principles of MBO to the entire staff and motivation across all levels is inadequate since managers and subordinates are always working under pressure environments. This creates difficulties in the execution of the MBO programme.

Essential Conditions for Successful Implementation of MBO

- Support from all employees of the organization
- Acceptance of the MBO programme by managers
- Training of managers on MBO philosophy
- Organizational commitment
- Allotment of time and resources
- Provision of a continuous feedback system

Pyramid Concept by C.K. Pralahad

C.K. Pralahad, along with Stuart L. Hart, introduced the bottom of the pyramid concept, which states that billions of people live at less than $2 per day, in line with what the theory in economics states. They stressed on the idea of fortune at the bottom of the pyramid. The pyramid concept states how large corporations can serve low-income group profitably. The gurus further state that there is accessibility as well as money in bottom of the pyramid markets and the consumers accept advanced technologies readily. Only the capacity to consume has to be created along with the need. There is a huge market potential with four to five billion underserved people and an economy of $13 trillion. C.K. Pralahad and Stuart stated that the philosophy for developing products and services would be based on:

- Small unit packages
- Low margin per unit
- High volume and high return on capital employed

The principles around which bottom of the pyramid should revolve for economic growth opportunities are as follows:

- Competitive prices
- Operational scalability
- Innovations
- Eco-friendliness
- Functionality identification
- Process conceptualization
- Customer education
- Customer accessibility
- Infrastructure and interface design
- Innovative product delivery process

Recent Trends in Management

The management and the managers have to keep themselves adept with the changing times, technology, innovation, development, increased globalization of markets and competitors, changing demographics, new political environment leading to increased complexities, short product lifecycles, market fragmentation forcing the companies to be decentralized, downsized, boundaryless and flat. Along with the changing trends, an organization has to deal with radical changes and inventions in processes and concepts in the management domain as a whole. A few of the recent trends have been discussed in the following subsections.

Six Sigma

Six Sigma is an approach to better the quality of process output by recognizing and eliminating the causes of faults and to reduce inconsistency in manufacturing and business processes. It uses quality management techniques and crafts a unique infrastructure of employees within the business (Black Belts and Green Belts) who are specialists in these methods. Each Six Sigma venture follows a defined succession of steps and has targets such as price reduction or revenue increase. The term 'Six Sigma' originated from the statistical modelling of manufacturing processes. The maturity of a manufacturing process can be described by the percentage of defect-free products it creates. A Six Sigma process is one in which almost 100% of the products manufactured are statistically free of defects (3.4 defects per million). Motorola aimed at obtaining 'Six Sigmas' for all of its manufacturing operations, which has now become a buzzword for every organization.

Knowledge Management

An organization's competitive benefit gyrates around its most advanced ability, that is, the knowledge workers who resolve difficult problems, build up novel products, and set new directions for business and organizations that want to protect these assets. Hence, knowledge management is all about capturing, storing, and sharing expertise across organizations, which revolves around a specific lifecycle comprising of the following:

- Create
- Store
- Find
- Acquire
- Use
- Learn

The ultimate gain through knowledge management is that when experts collaborate, progress can be made much faster than any one employee working alone. There are various knowledge management tools and techniques and a specific architecture for managing knowledge effectively.

Knowledge Process Outsourcing

It is a concept in which knowledge- and information-related work is performed by employees working in the subsidiary of a parent organization either in the same state or in a different state and is focused more on knowledge-intensive business processes catering to business expertise. It is a major industry shift where instead of standardized processes, implementation of highly complex and customized processes happen requiring skilled analytical, technical, and judgmental capability. Some knowledge process outsourcing services are data analytics and market research; these services aim mainly at cost reduction.

Retail Management

Retail management aims at bringing customers to the stores to fulfil their buying needs. It revolves around substantial time consumption and gives accessibility to customers to locate the product they desire. The hype of retailing in India is due to its ability to provide infrastructures such as post offices, public distribution system, the khadi and village industries, and canteen stores department.

What the Management Gurus Have to Say about the Current Trends in Management

Globalization

Reduced boundaries between nations and their increasing flow of resources and knowledge have led to a change in the world order that has had a great impact on global business.

Management gurus have concluded that the rising expectations from business and society with global competencies, combined with the increasing complexity, command the attention of business organizations around the world.

Technology

If the profound flow of globalization has been the potential force behind the far-reaching and dynamic changes in business, then the prominence of information technology cannot be denied. In most innovative companies, businesses are technology driven, customers are courted, and supply chains are managed via websites, social media, and email; marketing, manufacturing, and distribution processes are managed by information systems.

Sustainability and Corporate Social Responsibility

Along with good and profitable business, our planet has to be sustainable. Businesses have realized this need and have taken this responsibility in recent times, and now there is an increasing focus on solutions of multifaceted social issues, such as ecological sustainability, power security, and access to healthcare. This also underlines the need for an increased knowledge interaction and impact on business management.

The Study of Psychology

The impact of technology and globalization on business and the study of human psychology—coming into cognition, motivation, behaviour and performance—has become an important part of organizational management.

Business Ecosystems

The most prominent trends in management have been the rise of business ecosystems. The key focus areas of modern management are: working knowledge and experience, creativity in ecosystems, cross-organization knowledge flows, modular architectures, and good support for legacy systems.

Summary

This chapter revolves around the evolutionary stages of management and has collated perspectives of various management gurus on the genre of management studies. It also addresses the recent trends in management.

Exercise

Objective Questions

1. Classical management theory evolved as a result of
    - Industrial Revolution
    - Socioeconomic revolution
    - Political revolution
    - None of the above
2. Scientific management was led by
    - Henri Fayol
    - Henry Gantt
    - F.W. Taylor
    - Max Weber
3. Frank and Lillian Gilbreth focussed on time-and-motion study.
    - True
    - False
4. Which of the following is a disadvantage of bureaucratic form of organization?
    - Approved policies and procedures
    - Democratic form of ruling
    - Work's best practices aptly followed
    - Alignment to market triggers is slow
5. Mary Follett was thought to be a pioneer in the field of
    - Market analysis
    - Human psychology
    - HR management
    - Finance
6. Which approach acts as a single unit constituting of subcomponents, inputs, output, processing, and feedback?
    - Quantitative approach
    - Contingency approach
    - Operational approach
    - Systems approach
7. MBO was introduced by
    - Peter F. Drucker
    - Elton Mayo
    - Henry Gantt
    - Max Weber
8. Which of these helps us to get better the quality of process output by recognizing and eliminating the causes of faults and reduce inconsistency in manufacturing and business processes?
    - Knowledge process outsourcing
    - Retail management

- Six Sigma
- Knowledge management

9. Who conducted several experiments on Hawthorne Plant workers?
   - Peter F. Drucker
   - Elton Mayo
   - Henry Gantt
   - Max Weber

10. Which approach explores the optimal ways of doing things where performance of one subunit is reliant on its surroundings?
    - Contingency approach
    - Quantitative approach
    - Operational approach
    - Systems approach

CASE STUDY

Zenibeth Factory, which manufactured Quasar television sets, was took over by a Japanese company in the United States in the 1980s. After overtaking the company, it was decided to make changes in the way the factory operated, which resulted into drastic changes. The company implemented the Sig Sigma business practices to improve its environmental footprint and sales. After the implementation of Six Sigma, the factory sensed a decrease in waste generation. The company now had more improved processes, it became productive by reducing the waste, and therefore it doubled the revenue.

Questions

1. What is your opinion on how did Six Sigma help the company to reduce the defects?
2. Justify how the company may have doubled its profit by implementing Sig Sigma.

Critical Thinking Questions

1. Describe your experience where you have developed a good rapport with your peers and supervisors.
2. Describe your experience where you have used creative ways to solve a problem?
3. Tell about a time when you had to implement a change in your area of work as you had the responsibility for it.

Chapter at a Glance

Evolution of Management Thought

Whenever efforts had to be expended by a team, it was extremely important that the team had to be managed. Therefore, a group of two or more individuals had to be managed by an entity in the early days.

Approaches to Management

- Classical approach
- Scientific management—entails the best way of doing a job
- Administrative management—focuses on basic managerial functions
- Bureaucratic management—focuses on forming rules, procedures, and workload distribution.
- Behavioural approach
- HR approach
- Contingency approach
- Operational approach
- Systems approach

Taylor's Principles of Scientific Management

- Scientific methods outweigh rule of thumb
- Creating group harmony
- Cooperation
- Maximum output
- Improved work procedures

Fayol's Principles of Management

- Division of work
- Authority and responsibility
- Discipline
- Unity of command
- Unity of direction
- Alignment of individual interest to group interest
- Employee wage and compensation
- Centralization
- Scalar chain
- Order
- Equity
- Job security
- Initiative
- Esprit de corps

Major Findings and Conclusions of Hawthorne Experiments

- Communal factors
- Group influence
- Production level
- Motivation
- Conflicts
- Leadership
- Cordial relationship
- Behaviour of workers
- Supervision

(Continued)

(Continued)

- Communication
- Reaction of workers

Bureaucratic Organization

Organizations grow in size with increased functional specialization, resulting in strategic, tactical, and operational layers of management coordinating the organizational effort. The result is a bureaucratic approach to organizational structure.

Features of Bureaucratic Form of Management

- Work breakdown structure
- Levels of authority
- Policies and procedures
- Rights and responsibilities
- Technical expertise
- Content management
- Impartial assessment

Mary Follett's Management Principles

- Conflict resolution
- Authority
- Group formation and member participation
- Leadership
- Coordination

Modern Approaches of Management

- Contingency/situational approach
- Operational approach
- Systems approach
- Mathematical/quantitative approach

Peter F. Drucker and His Principles of Management

- Setting of goals
- Superior–subordinate participation
- Matching goals and resources
- Implementation of plan
- Performance appraisal

Recent Trends in Management

- **Six Sigma:** Six Sigma is an approach to better the quality of process output by recognizing and eliminating the causes of faults and to reduce inconsistency in manufacturing and business processes.

- **Knowledge management:** Knowledge management is all about capturing, storing, and sharing expertise across organizations and revolves around a specific lifecycle that comprises the following: create, store, find, acquire, use, and learn.
- **Knowledge process outsourcing:** It is a concept in which knowledge- and information-related work is performed by employees working in the subsidiary of a parent organization either in the same state or in a different state and is focused more on knowledge-intensive business processes catering to business expertise.
- **Retail management:** Retail management aims at bringing customers to the stores to fulfil their buying needs.

Current Trends in Management by Management Gurus

- **Globalization:** Rising expectations from business and society with global competencies, combined with increasing complexity, command the attention of business organizations around the world.
- **Technology:** In most innovative companies, business is technology driven, customers are courted, and supply chains are managed via websites, social media, and email; marketing, manufacturing, and distribution processes are managed by information systems.
- **Sustainability and corporate social responsibility:** Along with good and profitable business, our planet has to be sustainable. Businesses have realized this need and have taken this responsibility in recent times, and now there is an increasing focus on solutions of multifaceted social issues, such as ecological sustainability, power security, and access to healthcare.
- **The study of psychology:** The impact of technology and globalization on business and the study of human psychology—coming into cognition, motivation, behaviour, and performance—have become an important part of organizational management.
- **Business ecosystems:** The most prominent trends in management have been the rise of business ecosystems. The key focus areas of the modern management include working knowledge and experience, creativity in ecosystems, cross-organization knowledge flows, modular architectures, and good support for legacy systems.

CHAPTER 3

Planning

Learning Objectives

- Studying the importance of planning and how effective planning can help in optimization of different types of resources and thereby reducing the cost.
- Understanding the planning process and its significance in relation to business scenarios and environment.
- Aligning the execution of a task, series of tasks to the project or business plan in order to track the status, progress made in any business activity which narrows down to the principle that planning helps in effective progress reporting.
- Studying various planning tools and utilize them for business decisions.

An Opening Vignette

Business Plan for a Manufacturing Company—Executive Summary

Himalayan Cycles, keeping in view road conditions, manufactures normal and mountain bikes for the Indian and Himalayan roads. The Indian population in the last few years has shown strong enthusiasm in mountain and sports biking, and with the Government of India taking better initiatives for excellent road conditions and roadways interlinking cities, there is more and more enthusiasm amongst the common mass to travel using this mode of transport. Based on market projections, Himalayan Cycles concluded that the increased enthusiasm was also due to growing traffic congestion and rising fuel prices.

To meet this demand, Himalayan Cycles is trying to set up two more manufacturing units with 7% rise in the current employee strength. Its sales are expected to grow 7% year on year with a revenue growth of 12% by the end of the second financial year.

Overview of the Business

Himalayan Cycles was started in the year 2008 by two friends Hiren and Naren in a small workshop in the outskirts of Faridabad, very close to Nainital. Initially, they started

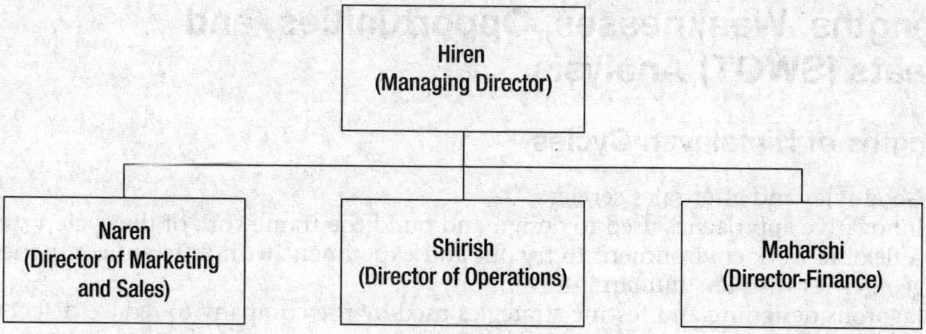

manufacturing small parts of the bicycle, such as brake pad, seat saddle, and so on, and then within two years they started with the customization of normal cycles. Initially, they appointed three people and bought two second-hand machineries to start with the production, but as the demand grew, they employed 10 more people to design, build, and test each new bicycle frame. In 2010, they obtained a contract from a team of mountain cyclists to build light, rigid, responsive, and racing cycles and came upon an industry survey that the sale of mountain bikes is expected to increase by 12% every year over the next five years.

Organizational Structure

Market Data (Author's Assumptions on Figures)

According to a study carried out by the Department of Transportation, approximately 2.5 million bicycles are purchased every year, of which 2% are high-end custom-built bicycles that cost an average of ₹25,000. As per the industry survey, sales of sports cycles after the Commonwealth Games in 2010 rose by 4.5%. The bicycle enthusiasts were mostly from the towns of North India, in the age range of 24 to 35, with male enthusiasts surpassing the female. At the same time, there was significant rise in the sale of women's cycles in comparison to the previous years.

Currently, five eminent manufacturers of bicycles in India—Hero, Hercules, BSA, Atlas, and Firefox—have 75% of the market share, and Himalayan Cycles is not one of them. However, if the company can expand production to meet the current demand, the projected sales indicate that Himalayan Cycles will also experience an increase in sales of mountain bikes within the next three years. This increase in sales is attributed to the fact that Himalayan Cycles is customizing cycles with regard to road conditions in plains and hilly areas of the country.

Marketing Strategy

Himalayan Cycles is currently selling its bicycles through distributors and retailers, and now it plans to do it through electronic media as well. Therefore, it is planning to do effective Internet marketing and is aggressively designing a website to display its products, which is estimated to cost ₹75,000. However, at the same time, Himalayan Cycles is targeting typical Internet users and is anticipating that it will get an additional 5% growth in sales and revenues. In addition, it will promote the brand by sponsoring three racing events in the Himalayan region.

Strengths, Weaknesses, Opportunities, and Threats (SWOT) Analysis

Strengths of Himalayan Cycles

- Good sales and after-sales services
- Innovative approaches used to design and build the framework of the cycle
- A flexible work environment to try out and experiment with different components and geometries with less human intervention
- Rigorous designing and testing strategies used by the company to reduce defect density
- Very less production and throughput delays

Weaknesses of Himalayan Cycles

- Not a large-scale organization
- Absence of a brand name
- Constrained resource availability and chances of scalability

Threats

- Competition with eminent market players
- Growth of the industry is subject to government's initiative to plan for good roadways and road connectivity across cities
- Threat can be perceived from external players as well for exclusive product range since manufacturing such items (high-end ones) incurs more expense and less profit.

Opportunities

- With the government focusing on smart cities, the scope of growth of better roadways with a control on the environmental pollution is limitless.
- With increased resource availability in terms of infrastructure, machinery, and financials, Himalayan Cycles has a chance to grow exponentially.
- With the professional cyclists consenting to test ride their bikes, it can be an easy climb for Himalayan Cycles towards promising business activities.
- Also, with so many firms like Infosys starting intra-campus commute using bicycles, Himalayan Cycles has opportunities to tie up with these corporate honchos for mass dealings.
- Himalayan Cycles can also encash on tourism opportunities and tie up with the tourism industry for cycle tour offers as well.
- It can also connect with the healthcare industry for better prospects.

Inventory and Construction Costs and Capital Expenditures

Unit Price

The price listing for normal bikes is in the range of ₹7,000 to 30,000. Mountain bike costs are in the range of ₹20,000 to 115,000, and the prices are not expected to change year on year.

Production Cost

The following are the components of the production cost:

- Computer-aided design
- Cast iron, mould, and graphite composite for the frame
- Shaping and painting the frame
- Assembling the parts, packing, and shipping

They together cost on an average ₹10,000 for the two categories of bikes is about 12% of the total revenue.

Inventory Costs

The inventory costs of finished goods, raw material, and parts accrue per annum to 10% of the revenue.

Labour, Machinery, and Maintenance Costs

The labour, capital, and maintenance costs to date sum up to 27% of the Himalayan Cycles revenue. Therefore, if the company starts two other units, then the cost would go as high as 50% in the initial year.

Infrastructure Cost

The current infrastructure cost on lease mode is 15% of the total revenue and additional investment would upscale it to 25%, and Himalayan Cycles has to consider the possible scenarios of

- leasing additional space nearby.
- moving the whole workshop to a larger but remote facility.

Leasing the unit that is adjacent to the present workshop is a favourable option, because it will be relatively easy for Himalayan Cycles to transport designer-builders and material between the adjacent units. Also, moving the graphite inventory from the warehouse to the adjacent workshop, which was larger and cost effective, because the construction was temporary though robust, was a big cost-saving option.

The second alternative was quickly dismissed because of the indirect costs associated. Accordingly, the first option was the best, because it would not disrupt the builder-designers workflow for the Himalayan Cycles and was available at a cheap price.

Introduction

Planning is a vital activity of the management of an organization. Planning is necessary not only for an organization but also in every walk of life of an individual. Once an event or an activity is planned, many aspects of the said event or activity become discrete. First of all, with planning in process the objectives become clear, and it can be determined how best to achieve these objectives.

Meaning

Planning, as can be simplistically defined, is a type of activity which encompasses what, when, where, how, and by whom an activity is to be done. It is an approach which helps one to decide on the path to achieve the set of objectives an individual or an organization or a group of people have. It is a trait possessed by an intellectual characterized by thinking before doing. From organizational perspectives, it should be a process followed by every manager to achieve better performance.

Definition

The definitions by some management gurus are as follows:

> *Planning is the selecting and relating of facts, and the making and using of assumptions regarding the future, in the visualization and formulation of proposed activities, believed necessary to achieve desired result.*
>
> —George Terry

> *Planning is deciding in advance what is to be done. It involves selection of objectives, policies, procedures and programs from amongst the alternatives.*
>
> —M.S. Hurley

> *Planning is that function of the manager in which he decides in advance what he will do. It is an interactive process in which creative thinking and imagination are essential.*
>
> —Haynes and Massie

> *Planning is an intellectual process, conscious determination of course of action, the basing of decision on purpose, facts and considered estimates.*
>
> —Koontz and Donnell

> *Planning is an attempt to anticipate the future in order to achieve better performance.*
>
> —Hodge and Johnson

Features of Planning

Centralized Authority

Planning means determining the future course of action; this is what makes the entire planning process complex and difficult. This requires not only centralized efforts but also a centralized authority. A centralized authority is considered to be the essence of effective and successful planning. The two prime responsibilities of this authority include formulating a plan and preparing blueprint.

For example, in a manufacturing firm, it is not the marketing department that sets the target but the centralized planning department that does this task and also suggests the measures to achieve the set target.

Goals and Objectives

Setting the goals and objectives is the first task before planning begins, just like planning is the first task before execution of any task. Planning without defining the goals and objectives would be just like driving a car without knowing the destination. Thus, every plan has to be built on the foundation of predefined objectives set by the central authority. The plan may have single or multiple objectives; prioritization of objectives becomes essential if the plan has multiple objectives. The objectives can be bifurcated into short term and long term depending on the time frame in which they need to be achieved. Objectives could be economic, social, or political.

For example, if a company strives to increase the market share, it is an economic objective, whereas if it is carrying out various awareness programmes for common mass, it is a social objective.

Deterministic Time Schedules

Planning is accompanied by fixed time schedules. If there is a plan, then it is accompanied by a timeline by which the plan has to be implemented. A plan can be any of the three types: short-term, medium-term and long-term plans. Because organizations' goals also fall in these categories, plans are designed and put into action for reaching the goals.

Comprehensive and Social

Planning can be looked at from a bigger dimension and can go to the level in which the entire government of a country is involved in planning to bridge down economic inequalities for achieving a socio-economic objective. Planning, when done by the government, should be comprehensive in the sense that it should address all the sectors like finance, production, economic resources, and so on for the entire nation to accrue the benefits.

Regulations and Controls

Regulations and controls comprise a vital element of planning. If a country has a planned economy, which is continuously regulated and controlled by proper controls on production, consumption, exchange (export and import), and labour wages, it is less impacted by economic downturns.

Nature of Planning

The chief characteristics or nature of planning are as follows.

Planning is a Creative Process

If followed, this process enables an individual to think about the future and plan the required course of action to be taken. There can be many alternatives available for the course but using experience, intuition, and knowledge the best possible course of action has to be taken.

Planning Helps in Fulfilment of Objectives

An organization sets its own goals and objectives. To help achieve the goals and objectives, the top management and the middle-level managers have to formulate plans. For example, when Tata Consultancy Services (TCS) developed ORCA Financial Software, a standalone product, its chief objective was to establish the company as the best global organization for the large-scale deployment of financial management software solutions on the Caché platform.

- To establish a fully object-oriented, component-based application, which will enable us to deliver robust software quicker and more efficiently than any competitor.
- To ensure that customers can operate their business software solutions on infrastructures that match their needs.

In order to fulfil the above objectives, quality planning for the large-scale flexible manufacturing system, human resource planning (for developing and maintaining the software), risk planning, and planning for the commercials had to be done by the senior managers. Similarly, large-scale implementation plan had to be made by the concerned project head to achieve the desired objective.

Planning Is the Core Function of Any Organization

Planning is succeeded by other management functions, such as organizing, controlling, and directing. These functions are interconnected and interlinked. For example, a mobile company wants to improve the sale of its products. In order to do so, the manager has to focus on the increase in advertisement and marketing of the product, competitive pricing of the product, and quality of the product, for which a detailed plan engulfing all of the above areas has to be formulated. After the plan, the manager needs to organize the team so that tasks are allocated and authority is granted to achieve the objective. To achieve an increase in sales the manager might need to recruit, select, train, and develop employees. This function of management is otherwise known as staffing. Along with the task of staffing comes the task of motivating, communicating, guiding, and solving people's problems. Controlling being the last step, a manager should necessarily monitor the output with respect to the goals set. Having set the objectives for OCRA financials, the TCS business head should monitor whether alignment to the specified objectives is happening or not.

Planning Helps to Improve Organization's Efficiency

Planning leads to maximum output with minimum expenditure, and proper planning helps allocation of appropriate task and authority to the individuals and keeps the individual or the group motivated.

Planning Is an Ongoing Process and Helps to Identify Constraints

Planning is a continuous activity, and plans made by managers have to be revisited time and again for modifications to the same. It involves incessant collation, evaluation and choice of data, scientific exploration and investigation of the probable courses of action, and the selection of the best option.

Planning Is Always Accompanied by Implementation

A plan which has been designed has no significance until and unless it has been put into action. For example, until a budget is formulated and expenditures are planned and expenses are done according to the plan, there is no significance of the plan. Therefore, a plan should be accompanied by action.

Planning also Promotes Unity and Consistency

Planning involves unity of employees in the organization, because it forces employees to assist in decision-making and give valued suggestions while the plan is made, and once made the plan is effective uniformly for every individual within an organization.

Plans should be prepared, reviewed, updated and presented to the concerned authority for implementation. Plans change and get revised frequently or are merged with other subplans and appraised for their effectiveness under changing business scenarios.

Importance of Planning

- Planning greatly helps in the reduction of uncertainty in the future. This is because of continuous advancements in the field of science and technology, changes in government rules and regulations, changes in habits and habitat of people, and so on.
- With proper planning, material and human resources are not optimally procured and utilized. Delegation of tasks, roles, and responsibilities happens effectively, there is no duplication of effort, and the assigned work gets completed in the allocated time.
- With proper planning, organizations' goals and objectives are also achieved, thus increasing organizational effectiveness.
- Planning helps in selecting the best solution or alternative for a particular problem attainable at minimum cost.
- Planning and implementation of any plan enable a manager to monitor whether a project is going according to the plan or not. Effective planning ensures proper control, which means to understand the deviations encountered while implementing the plan.
- Planning enables the managers to come up with innovative ideas and also have an appropriate mechanism for facing emergency situations.
- Effective planning can give a competitive edge to any industry/organization, because it involves expansion in the scope and capacity of the services rendered by the organization, changes in the working culture, changes in the quality of services delivered, and also the technological changes which the organization goes through with proper planning.

Limitations of Planning

Planning Does Not Render Flexibility

With predetermined rules, regulations, policies, and procedures, freedom to do some task in a different way is not possible. Planning does not encourage experimentation to be an individual.

Planning Is a Time-taking Process

To plan for something, one needs the required information. After having collected the information, it is required to analyse the same, derive results, and then narrow down to a certain alternative. For example, planning for the cost which will be incurred for a business tour for a project team, an organization should collect information pertaining to flight fare and flight details, available accommodation option and accommodation rates, local transport facilities and rates, and then narrow down to the best possible alternative. All these require quite a lot of time.

Planning Is Not Deterministic

Planning is futuristic and incurs risk because future is not known. Hence, with the change of time the plan might become obsolete, since it is an estimation process or an activity. If an organization or an individual is totally dependent on a plan, then it can be dangerous because nobody can be certain about the future.

Planning can Secure Future in a Deceptive Form

Detailed planning can make a manager rely excessively on the plan and give him a sense of satisfaction or having followed the plan closely. In this case, if the results in following the plan are negative, then it becomes disastrous.

Planning Is Costly

Collation and analysis of information are costly in terms of money, effort, and time.

Susceptibility of Planning

Planning is also susceptible to the following:

- Political scenario
- Changes in science and technology
- Competitive environment
- Natural disasters
- Price fluctuations
- Trend change

Types of Planning

Long-term Plans

These are formulated by the senior management. To formulate long-term plans, a manager has to see through the future and best forecast the futuristic estimates keeping in mind the current scenarios—financial, social, economic, political, and technological—of his organization and the country. For example, a fashion designer has to formulate long-term plans up to a tenure of two to three years because trends in fashion change inevitably by that time, whereas for a technology industry, it might span a duration of five to seven years to develop, promote, and market a new product. For any individual, a long-term plan is an investment plan. Long-term plans can also be expanding the business across the globe. Initially, long-term plans could look impossible to achieve.

Short-term Plans

Short-term plans are made to achieve objectives within a short tenure. Examples of short-term plan are to design a website for any organization within a span of two weeks or publishing a bi-yearly research journal planned by the research cell of any university or college. Short-term plans are devised by the managers who work at the operational or tactical level of the organization.

Medium-term Plans

These plans are made keeping in mind the tenure of one to a maximum of three years. These plans are devised by the senior management with a strong focus on organizational growth and include increasing the product line with a few new products to be released into the market in a span of two to three years or diversifying to bring out a complete solution for the product being used. For example, Fuji earlier used to develop film rolls but later it started developing the photography paper instead of procuring it from third parties.

Operational Planning

Operational planning is planning the day-to-day activities or schedules. For example, the departmental head took a meeting to state that until the budget for the next financial year is released, an employee has to plan for his upgradation by participating in the forthcoming training programme.

Steps in Planning

The various stages of the planning process have been discussed in the following subsections (Figure 3.1).

Set the Target

An organization works towards achieving certain targets. For example, Accenture had been helping Unilever to meet its growth targets by establishing global systems, applications, products (SAP) platform for doubling the revenue and size of the company. The target of any organization should be clear, concise, and measurable in terms of schedule, budget, or resources. The targets are set based on the opportunities visualized by managers and are influenced by organization's mission, values, and beliefs. Once a target is set, then plan can be worked out to accomplish it. Target can be from the perspective of an organization, a department, or a unit.

Figure 3.1 Steps in Planning

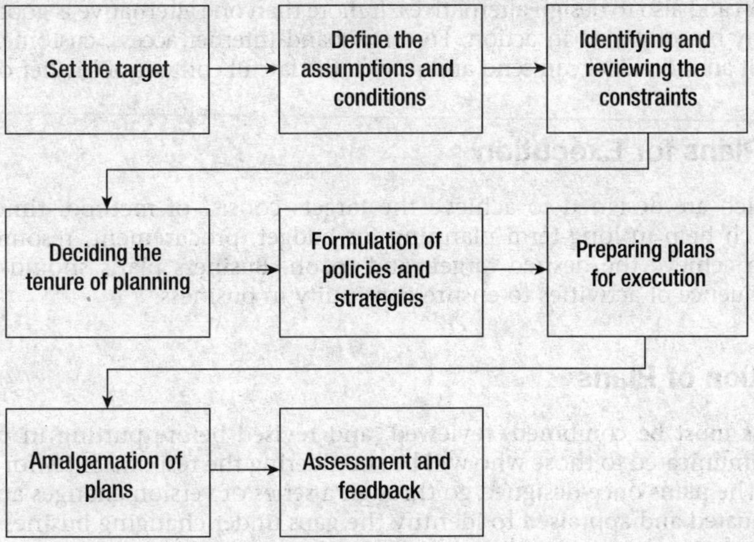

Define the Assumptions and Conditions

There should be clearly defined assumptions and conditions before a plan is finalized. For example, a production company is laying down plans to produce specialized product, then the assumption made is that it will require extensive training sessions for its staff to produce that product. Another consecutive assumption can be that for training the resources, duration and funding will be required appropriately. Assumptions can be indirectly seen as forecasts, which are events or activities that will happen in the future and are factual in nature. Assumptions are vital to the success of planning and are revised with changes in the business situations. Alternate plans may be prepared as fallback if some set of plans do not work with the set of assumptions.

Identifying and Reviewing Constraints

Constraints act as a barrier and restrict the smooth execution of a plan. For example, a production company can have as constraints building and machinery capacity, labour quality, adequate supply of parts and raw material, optimum production schedule, and healthy cash flows with change in demands. Hence, SWOT analysis has to be performed before actually designing a plan.

Deciding the Tenure for Planning

Once the targets, assumptions, and constraints are laid down, the next step is to decide the tenure of planning. The tenure depends on time to obtain the capital for the business venture, the future availability of raw or semi-finished products, and time taken to develop, market and sell the product.

Formulation of Policies and Strategies

After the target is defined and assumptions are identified, management can formulate policies and strategies to achieve the target along with the involvement, views, and ideas of middle management. Intuitiveness, far-sightedness, and experience are required amongst the top- and middle-management employees of the organization to formulate the most appropriate policy of the organization and also to design alternatives. If more than one alternative is good, then various alternatives may be combined in action. For broadband Internet access, customers of Verizon's policy state that an individual can send and receive the lawful content of his/her choice.

Preparing Plans for Execution

The plans which are designed to achieve the targets consist of method, time, and capital planning, which help in long-term planning for budget, procurement, resources, schedule, and quality to achieve the desired target, and so on. Business plans should also envisage timing and sequence of activities to ensure continuity in business.

Amalgamation of Plans

Different plans must be combined, reviewed, and revised before putting in operation and should be communicated to those who will be shouldering the responsibility for putting them into practice. The plans once designed go through a series of version changes and these plans should be evaluated and appraised to identify the gaps under changing business scenarios.

Planning Tools and Techniques

Forecasting

Forecasting is an essential concept in business as it is based on the business activity happening in the present and that has happened in the past and for which expectations for the future is set. Once the expectations for the future are set, plans are devised to satisfy the business needs.

According to Henri Fayol, 'Business forecasting includes assessing the future and making provisions for it', while Neter and Wasserman state that 'Business forecasting refers to the statistical analysis of past and current events in given time series to obtain clues about future pattern of movements'.

Forecasting as a Process

Accurate forecasting is possible if any business has strong financials and foundations. This means that any business is assessed over a period of time. Its strengths and weaknesses are identified and then the estimation for the future is done. If the estimate varies or deviates more from the actual, then the forecast has to be refined.

For example, Airbus' Global Market Forecast stresses the need for aircrafts ranging from 100-seat aircraft to the largest A380 based on factors such as demographic and economic growth across countries and continents, tourism trends, oil prices, and development of new and existing routes and destinations.

Benefits of Forecasting

Forecasting helps in growth of the business. As it is based on forecasts, business plans are devised and executed, ensuring better productivity, optimized usage of resources, and effective cost.

Forecasting Techniques

There are broadly two methods of forecasting, that is, the qualitative and quantitative method.

Qualitative Method of Forecasting

The method is based on human judgement or opinion and is non-mathematical, and also can instil bias, which can make the forecast inaccurate. This method can take into account latest changes in the environment. The methods consist of executive methods, market research, and Delphi method.

Quantitative Method of Forecasting

This method is mathematical, consistent, and data driven. Accuracy of the forecast is based on the data quality. The methods consist of extrapolation, regression, time series, and causal/ econometric models.

Application Areas of Forecasting

The application areas of forecasting range from political, social, technological, economic to market prominence, and labour supply.

EXAMPLE

The simplest type of forecast is the naive forecast, which uses the actual demand from the past as the demand for the future, ensuring that the past will repeat. For example, sales forecast represented using naive forecast for the month of May will be 45 metric ton since it is anticipated that the pattern will repeat. Using the averaging concept it will be (25 + 35 + 56 + 45)/4 = 40.25.

Month	*Actual (Metric Ton)*	*Forecast (Metric Ton)*
January	25	
February	35	25
March	56	35
April	45	56
May		45

Benchmarking

Benchmarking is the process of identifying the industry's best practices across various businesses, which may be operational, procedural, or product specific, and is a measure to improve performance of any business or industry by cross-referencing the indicators. A comparative study of the product and internal and external processes to the organization is done by managers to understand their own strengths and weaknesses in relation to the above dimensions. The objective of benchmarking is to identify best performances or practices and incorporating the best practices into their own by innovating rather than imitating.

Benchmarking Process

The benchmarking process has been shown in Figure 3.2.

Use of Benchmarking

Companies use benchmarking to achieve the objectives shown in Figure 3.3.

Figure 3.2 Process of Benchmarking

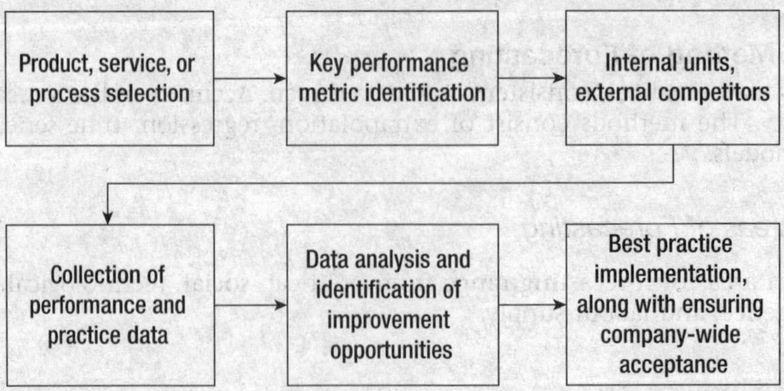

Figure 3.3 Reasons for Implementation of Benchmarking

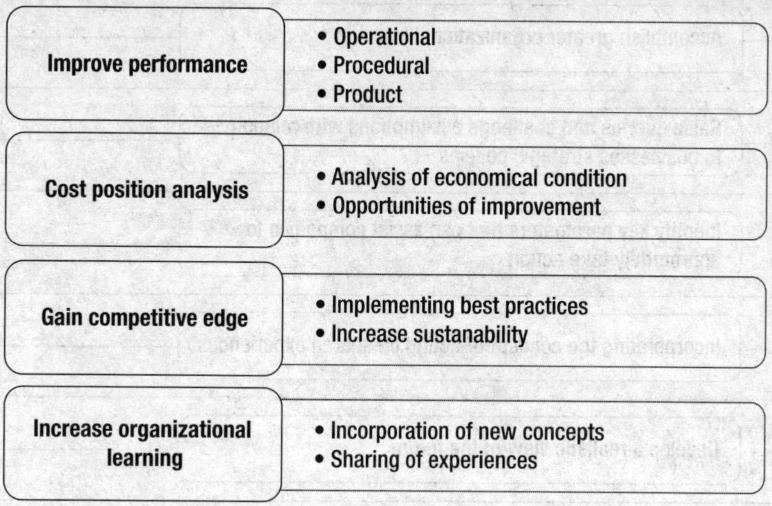

Scenario and Contingency Planning

Scenario planning compels the executives to examine various courses of action based on a variety of operating policies and financial conditions as envisaged by the company. Contingency or situation planning is based on monitoring the impact of sudden changes in market scenarios or disruption in trade. Scenario and contingency plans do not encourage one-dimensional thinking, and by testing a variety of situations and doing causal analysis, managers can challenge the assumptions and then decide the course of action. Plans are put on pressure test so that the company can handle any situation.

Scenario and Contingency Planning Process

The steps of the process are shown in Figure 3.4.

Figure 3.4 Scenario and Contingency Planning Overview

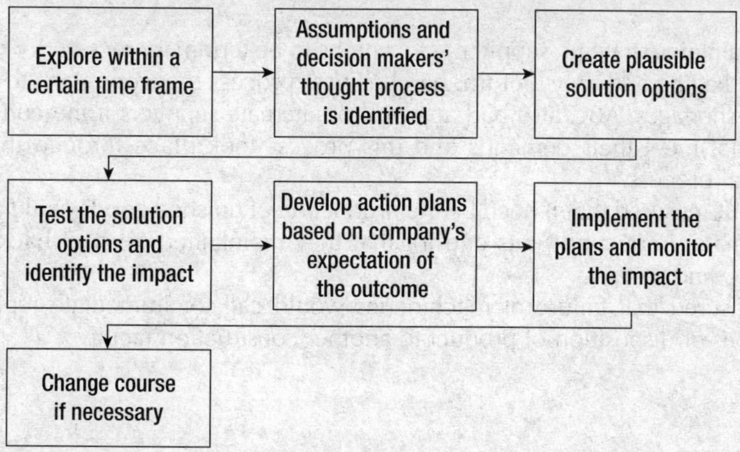

Figure 3.5 Use of Scenario and Contingency Planning

- Accomplish greater organizational learning
- Raise queries and challenge assumptions with relation to businesses strategic policies
- Identify key parameters that can assist companies to appropritely take action
- Incorporating the concept of acting on shared experiences
- Develop a realistic view of the future
- Strategic analysis should encompass global aspects and change management

Use of Scenario and Contingency Planning

Companies use scenario and contingency planning to achieve the goals enumerated in Figure 3.5.

EXAMPLE

ABC's initiative to meet customer demands is through a consistent product supply. This supply ensures through invocation of proper contingency plans, which include backup manufacturing plans based on the level of inventory and the production schedules.

Process

- ABC maintains strategic supplier associations to be a primary receiver of raw material and packaging and they, in turn, had business process recovery plans to diminish or reduce shortages. ABC also had approval of alternate suppliers if the current supplier could not meet their demands and this process took place through their supplier approval process.
- Also, ABC ensured that if need be the production of finished goods could also happen at alternate production units and for that they maintained a list of backup contract builders, and so on.
- ABC ensured that failure of machineries would call for immediate replacement of machines or disposition of product to another construction facility.

Use of Staff Planners

Staff planners plan for the organization as it starts growing in size by units, employees, resources, and assets, and these experts are skilled in incorporating planning processes and using effective planning tools and techniques for streamlined planning. However, it has been perceived that there is a communication gap between staff planners and line managers. They should collaborate very often to implement the plan, which may lose effectiveness.

Essentials of a Good Plan

- A plan if designed should assist in better utilization of the resources whether material or human resources. With planning, allocation of tasks, roles, and responsibilities to the required resources happens effectively, duplication of effort is reduced, and resource operations become smoother and faster.
- A good plan should help achieve organizations' goals and objectives if the plans made are realistic and enable every employee of the organization to have a direction for the same.
- A good plan should optimally utilize resources, inventory, and produce the right quantity of products at right time and remove any redundant or ineffective activities carried out in the organization.
- A good plan helps in locating and identifying future uncertainties, which can be avoided by a minimal percentage with the help of a good plan.
- A robust plan helps in growth of an organization. Planning to launch a new line of products or adding new products into a product family, bringing changes in the quality of products, or services can help the organization to be more competitive.
- A good plan encourages appropriate control measures to be taken to see whether the activities are going according to the plan or not.
- A good plan motivates the employees because they are also involved in making decisions and giving suggestions for making improvements in the plan. Employee cooperation also enhances with effective planning.
- A good plan initiates innovation and creative thinking amongst senior management, because after a lot of rational brainstorming a plan shapes up and is put up as a blueprint.
- A good plan reduces a lot of effort and time of operational people because for a plan being in place they need only to execute according to the plan.
- Planning helps managers cope with the changing scenarios; therefore, a good plan should closely align with the future events such as changes in political, economic, social, and technical scenarios.
- A good plan can brave bad weather, that is, anticipate risks and can help in using effective business continuity planning approaches despite the turbulent market and political conditions.

Planning Made Exemplary

Planning, an essential function of management, involves mapping tasks to goals. The term 'planning' can be better explained with the help of an example.

EXAMPLE

An organization wants to ramp up its sales. The sales manager first needs to decide the steps necessary to accomplish that goal. The steps are converted to a plan. When the plan is in place, the manager can follow it to accomplish the goal of improving company sales.

Company: Bactrac
Financial year: 2012–2013
Short-term goal: To improve sales of the company for this financial year
Tasks to be accomplished to achieve the goals:

- **To establish a network:** Bactrac has tapped Syncap Corp. which will use its platform to create integrated social-marketing programmes across Facebook, Twitter, and Google+ for more than 20 Reckitt Bactrac brands, including Garment Cleansing Agent, Kitchen Cleaners, and Toilet Cleaners, and so on.
- **To increase marketing and advertising of the product:** To lift sales, Bactrac is investing an additional £100 million in main brands such as toilet cleaners, and shifting more of its marketing spending from television ads to digital media and consumer education campaigns.
- **Product innovation:** Bactrac's first-quarter sales growth was driven by 'continued excellent performance' in emerging markets and product innovations as various categories of cleansing agents.
- **To increase inventory of the finished good:** Bactrac's inventory process, which always maps supplies with demand.
- **Increase in marketing and sales staff.** To promote business, Bactrac increased its marketing and sales staff by 2% across geographies.
- **Tapping emerging markets.** Bactrac announced its strong growth in emerging markets and reiterating its full year financial targets. Total second-quarter net revenue,

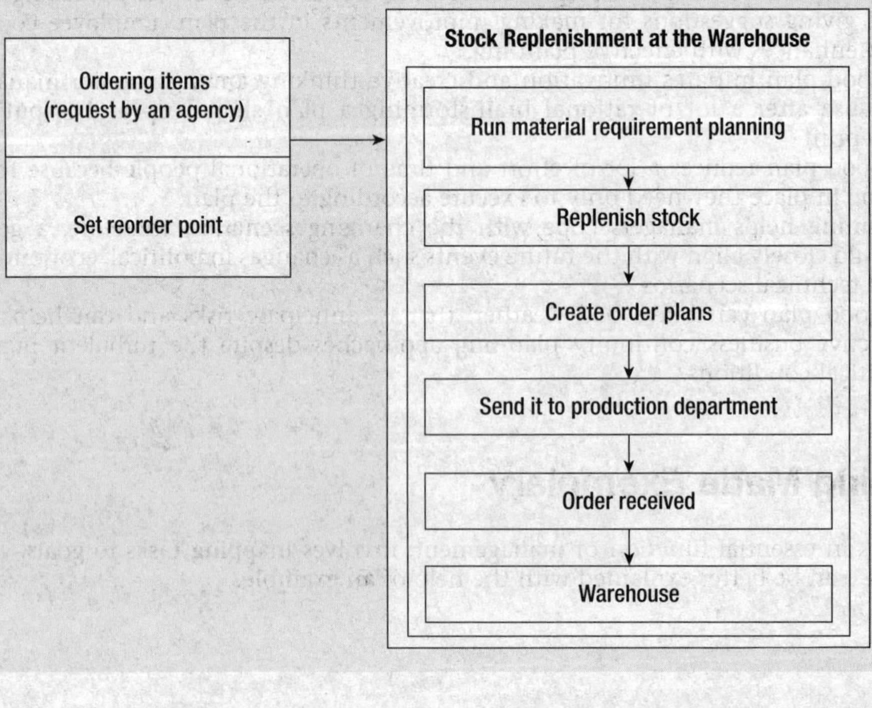

at constant rates, increased by 3%. Growth trends in both developed and emerging markets were similar to those in the first quarter of 2012. There was an improving trend in health, while the hygiene power brands of antiseptic lotions and cleansing agents. For six months, total net revenue, at constant rates, increased by 4%. Growth was driven by a very strong performance in America except North America, most of the northern and southern regions of Asia and Russia, the Middle East and Africa, with subdued results in Europe. Here, weak market conditions and consumer sentiment continued to prevail. The company's performance was largely due to major non-seasonal health power brands and from hygiene power brands.

- **Promote activities** such as upselling, discount offers, customer rewards, and free samples.
- **Excerpts from Bactrac for advertisement of free samples.** Bactrac India has been offering price discount on its liquid soap brand and also upselling its cleaning agent with a small antiseptic soap pack. To be eligible for the free sample kit, you must be (i) an Indian citizen and (ii) 18 years of age or older at the time of registration. Registration will be exclusively online at www.bactracdettolproductcat.com, and must include first and last names, complete mailing address, email, and 10-digit mobile numbers. Limit is one sample per person per household. Offer is subject to availability.
- **Track cold calls, appointments, and identify prospects.** Bactrac is trying to enhance its prospects through mergers and acquisitions to build better business. It has the required resources to fund such acquisitions and has the management capability to absorb, integrate, and manage such acquisitions within its existing structure.
- **Track sales pipeline,** sales cycle time, time required for closing sales with prospect, received, and closed referral

ID	Customer	Emp	Title	Category	Rating	Est. Closed Date	Probability (%)	Est. Revenue (in $)	Forecast Value (in $)
1	Adinath Chopra	A. Jai	Sales rep	(1) Category	Warm	3 Nov 2012	80%	10,000	8,000
2	Ashotosh V.	T. Suri	Sales manager	(1) Category	Cold	15 Nov 2012	80%	5,000	4,000
3	C. Singh	A. Jai	Sales head	(2) Category	Hot	23 Nov 2012	80%	50,000	40,000
	Total							**65,000**	**52,000**

- **Soften and resolve internal and external cause:** Bractac's strategy during recession time accompanied with economic downturn was to use media extensively to announce their products, categories, and their prices to a bigger customer base at deflated media costs for achieving long-term goals.
- **Keeping a track of non-sales task** such as documenting or report writing: Along with the activities undertaken for sales to become effective, Bactrac's strategy was to also indulge a certain portion of their time in documentation of the activities and the reporting of the effectiveness of planning strategy undertaken to ramp up the sales. This was done to archive in the knowledge base, the sales strategy adopted for future references.

EXAMPLE: MANPOWER PLANNING BY BLAZE STAR

Blaze Star Company set an expansion agenda intended to double its product output within five years. For this, the company faced manpower issues:

- Organization which was originally designed to operate one asset and had not evolved to handle two.
- Maintaining the high performance record and low-cost structure currently in place.

An agency was engaged to assess the impact of the growth on the manpower needs and a roadmap to achieve the manpower plan.

Planning for manpower required execution of three steps:

- Creating a baseline using current manpower and attrition rate.
- Understanding level of business, expansion/contraction, and market condition.
- Mapping action drivers, trade standards, and top-down estimates against these parameters and elements to approximate existing and potential manpower demand.

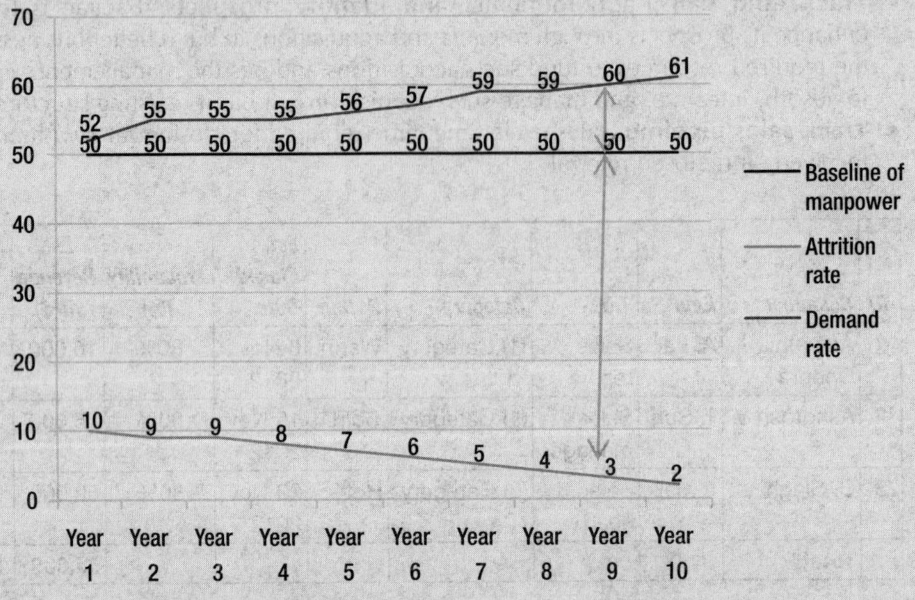

The agency established manpower demand for the current business and also projected future requirements on the basis of

- calculation of resources per activity or task in line with industry standards.
- project-team structure or format.
- estimation of resources top-down per organizational entity.

Also, current and expected future gaps in manpower requirements were identified. The analysis highlighted significant understaffing in core functions, though there was strong sharing and utilization of resources. Then, with the agency's recommendation the company formulated task-based and event-based manpower planning which rendered several benefits, such as

- increase in production through closing its gaps in manpower demand.
- enabling the company to maintain its low-cost structure and standards.

This chapter underlines the importance in relevance to the management and highlights the essentials of a good plan, justifies that good management requires concrete planning and goes on to exemplify planning to give the readers more clarity on it being the first and the most important function of management.

Global Implications

Lidl, a German grocer, with big US expansion plans is planning for massive expansion by opening 100 stores in the United States by 2018 and thereby posing great threat to US grocer giant Publix. Lidl's stores are based in Germany, similar to Aldi, and have strong chances of capturing the US market. The stores offer select grocery items, the majority of which are its private label offered at a discount to most other grocers. The recent trends show customers' inclination to buy more restaurant food and meal-kit delivery services offered by Lidl, which also has the potential to take in the market share of the other grocers.

Bilcare Research Plans Capacity Expansion in Germany: Bilcare Research AG, a part of the Pune-based Bilcare Ltd based out of Maharashtra, India, and a global producer of rigid films and foils, is venturing for extensive capacity planning in Botzingen, Germany, to meet the growing demand of pharmaceutical packaging films in the European market. Bilcare is simultaneously trying to strengthen its presence in the Asian market. For that, Bilcare Research is investing approximately €50 million and visualizes that this expansion will greatly change the quality aspect of films and foils, such as it will enhance work safety, hygiene, and environmental protection worldwide.

Bilcare Research, with a focus on research and development, operates in seven sites across the globe. Besides, polyvinyl chloride film production, the company is also involved in coating, stenting, and lamination of films.

CASE STUDY

The team structuring given below will depict the resource plan required for assigning roles and responsibilities for developing the Employee Administration System Project for a company named QUITO, which will look after employee satisfaction, grievances, and mitigation mechanisms through the software.

Employee Administration System Project Team of QUITO

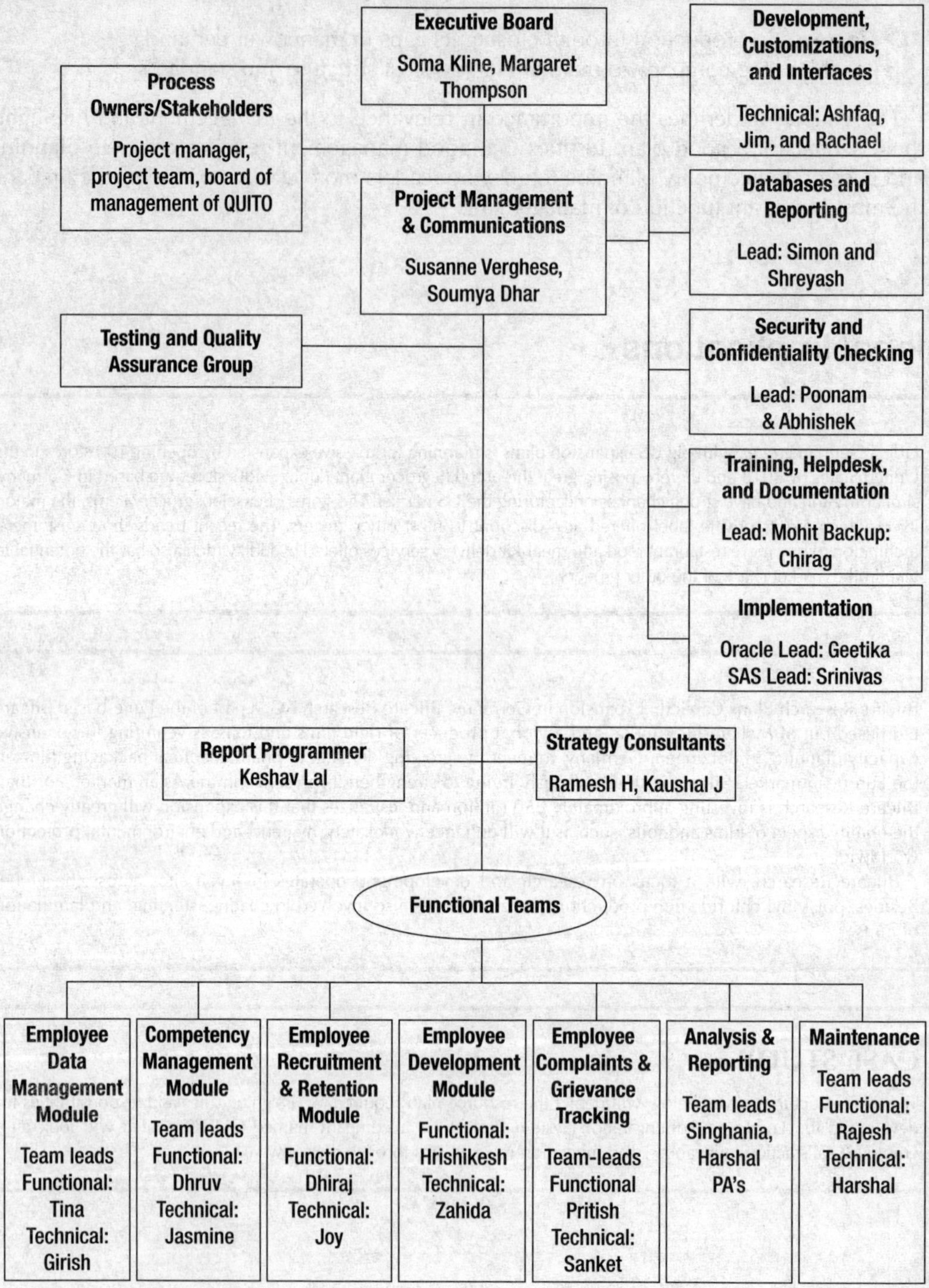

EMPLOYEE ADMINISTRATION SYSTEM PROJECT SCHEDULE PLAN (2008–2009)

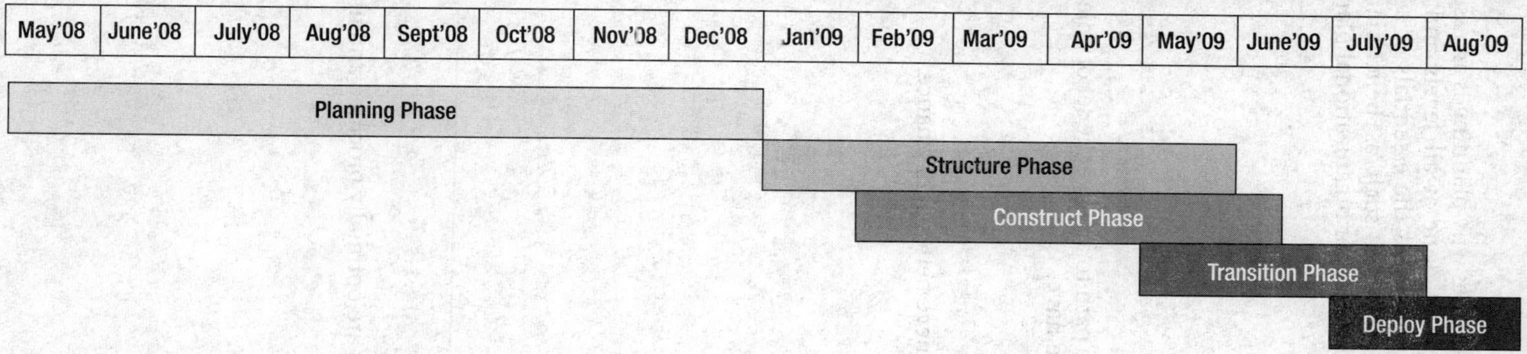

Phase 1: Planning Major Activities

- Define project objectives, scope, approach, and schedule
- Establish project team, roles, responsibilities, and budget
- Define project standards and administration processes
- Develop project communications, testing, training, and quality assurance plans
- Monitor and track project schedule, issues, change, cost, progress, results, and quality

Phase 2: Structure Major Activities

- Analyse the system
- Design the system
- Code the system
- Evaluate business and technical process changes and its relevant codification

Phase 3: Construct Major Activities

- Functional staff assesses, refines, and validates package functional setup and configuration
- Technical staff assesses, refines, recodes, and tests package data access and application code
- Security staff assesses, refines, and validates application security
- Technical staff assesses, refines, tests, and validates custom functionality and third-party interfaces
- Finalize testing plans, approach, and test cases for all levels of testing
- Install and set up end-user training tools and environment
- Freeze upgraded database and refresh with current employee administration system data

Phase 4: Transition Major Activities

- Perform full system testing in the month of July 2009
- Correct all system test issues and problems
- Perform second move to production test
- Perform full integration testing
- Correct all integration test issues and problems
- Perform third move to production test
- Perform parallel testing
- Correct all parallel test issues and problems
- Perform fourth move to production test (as needed)
- Develop and conduct end user demos and training

Phase 5: Deploy Major Activities

- Conduct end-user demos and training
- Freeze EAS access
- Perform move to production (end of July)
- Perform go-live testing, 5 August 2009
- Correct all issues and problems
- Employee administration system access resumed, 5 August 2009
- Provide post go-live support

Summary

The chapter focuses on the importance of planning and justifies why planning is an essential management function, which is continuous in nature and done at all levels and from various organizational perspectives. The chapter also summarizes the essentials of a good plan and portrays the robust features of the planning tools, such as benchmarking, forecasting, and contingency planning, which are very effective for organizational planning and decision-making.

Exercise

Objective Questions

1. Planning is an approach which helps us decide on the path to achieve the set of objectives an individual or an organization or a group of people have.
   - True
   - False
2. Planning is a process followed by every ______ to achieve better performance.
   - Employee
   - Manager
   - All
   - None
3. Planning is an ______ process.
   - Ongoing
   - One time
   - Autocratic
   - None of the above
4. Which of these are being devised by the managers?
   - Long-term plans
   - Short-term plans
   - Medium-term plans
   - None of the above
5. With proper planning material and human resources are optimally procured and utilized.
   - True
   - False
6. Planning is accompanied by _______ schedules.
   - Flexible time
   - Fixed time
   - Both
   - None of the above
7. Planning does not render flexibility.
   - True
   - False

8. Planning is also susceptible to
   - Political scenario
   - Changes in science and technology
   - Price fluctuations
   - All of the above
9. Executive methods, market research, and Delphi method are examples for
   - Quantitative method of forecasting
   - Qualitative method of forecasting
   - Benchmarking
   - None of the above
10. Contingency planning assesses what effect sudden market changes or business disruptions might have on a company and devises strategies to deal with them
    - True
    - False

CASE STUDY

Tevica Private Limited was the largest company being set- up for selling of packed food items. It was involved into variety of food packets like chips, butter cookies, breads, and many more. Mr Somesh is the CEO of this company and says that the company has a very good brand value and is among the first five players of packed food market. He keeps a close eye on the market trends and environmental changes happening around.

There are various food-packaging units coming up in the market these days. To maintain the same brand value, Mr Somesh plans that he comes up with following ideas:

- Expand his unit to various other locations.
- Provide promotional offers during festive season.
- Go global on the market by selling the food packets online.

Questions

1. Discuss the opportunities, strengths, and weaknesses available for the company.
2. What strategy would you suggest to Mr Somesh to continue with its brand value in the market?

Critical Thinking Questions

1. Planning is an intellectual process. Comment.
2. What could be the barriers for planning?
3. How can a plan be made effective?
4. Suggest some practices to implement effective planning.

Chapter at a Glance

Planning

Planning is an approach which helps us decide on the path to achieve the set of objectives an individual or an organization or a group of people have. From organizational perspectives, it should be a process followed by every manager to achieve better performance.

(Continued)

(Continued)

Features of Planning

- Centralized authority
- Goals and objectives
- Deterministic time schedules
- Comprehensive and social
- Regulations and controls

Nature of Planning

- Planning is a creative process.
- Planning helps in fulfilment of objectives.
- Planning is the core function of any organization.
- Planning helps to improve organization's efficiency.
- Planning is an ongoing process and helps to identify constraints.
- Planning is always accompanied by implementation.
- Planning also promotes unity and consistency.

Importance of Planning

- Planning greatly helps in reduction of uncertainty in the future.
- With proper planning, material and human resources are optimally procured and utilized.
- With proper planning, organizations' goals and objectives are achieved, thus increasing organizational effectiveness.
- Planning helps in selecting the best solution or alternative for a particular problem attainable at minimum cost.
- Planning and implementation of any plan enables a manager to monitor whether a project of any kind is going according to the plan or not.
- Planning enables the managers to come up with innovative ideas and also have an appropriate mechanism for facing emergency situations.
- Effective planning can give a competitive edge to any industry/organization.

Limitations of Planning

- Planning does not render flexibility.
- Planning is a time-taking process.
- Planning is not deterministic.
- Planning can secure the future in a deceptive form.
- Planning is costly.

Types of Planning

- **Long-term plans:** These are formulated by the senior management. To formulate long-term plans a manager has to see through the future best forecast, and the futuristic estimates keeping in mind the current scenarios—financial, social, economic, political, and technological—of his organization and also the country.

- **Short-term plans:** These are made to achieve objectives within a short tenure. Short-term plans are being devised by the managers who work at the operational or tactical level of the organization.
- **Medium-term plans:** These are the plans made keeping in mind tenure of one to a maximum of three years. These plans are devised by the senior management with a strong focus on organizational growth.
- **Operational planning:** Planning the day-to-day activities or schedules.

Steps in Planning

- Set the target.
- Define the assumptions and conditions.
- Identify and review the constraints.
- Decide the tenure of planning.
- Formulate policies and strategies.
- Prepare plans for execution.
- Amalgamate plans.
- Assess and provide feedback.

Planning Tools and Techniques

- **Forecasting:** This includes assessing the future and making provisions for it.
- **Benchmarking:** This improves performance by identifying and applying best demonstrated practices to operations and sales.
- **Scenario and contingency planning:** Scenario Planning allows executives to explore and prepare for several alternative futures.
- **Use of staff planners:** As organizations grow there is corresponding need to increase the sophistication of the planning system itself.

Essentials of a Good Plan

- A plan if designed should assist in better utilization of the resources, whether material or human.
- A good plan should help achieve organizations goals and objectives.
- A good plan should optimally utilize resources, inventory, and produce the right quantity of products at right time and remove any redundant or ineffective activities carried out in the organization.
- A good plan helps in locating and identifying future uncertainties, which can be avoided by a minimal percentage with the help of a good plan.
- A robust plan helps in growth of an organization.
- A good plan encourages appropriate control measures to be taken to see whether the activities are going according to the plan or not.
- A good plan motivates the employees.
- A good plan initiates innovation and creative thinking amongst senior management.
- A good plan reduces a lot of effort and time of operational people.
- Planning helps managers to cope with the changing scenarios.
- A good plan can brave bad weather, that is, anticipate risks and can help in using effective business continuity planning approaches.

CHAPTER 4

Organization

Learning Objectives

- Getting a broader idea of the concept of organizing, principles and processes of organizing, organization structure, and its concepts.
- Obtaining a fairly deep insight into the functional aspect of organizing.
- Correlating the alignment of an organization's mission, vision, objectives to the organization structure, and its impact on business.
- Getting a holistic view on the centralization and decentralization concepts and their impact on the organizational growth.

An Opening Vignette

McDonald's as an organization is a global player in fast food category with the mantra of enhancing 'quality', 'service', 'cleanliness', and 'value'. The organization since its inception has been engaging in massive product promotion and aligning the customers' preferences and experience to their organizational goal for quick growth, turnover, and scalability.

As an organization, it is focused on keeping its key assets, the employees, satisfied by providing opportunities, nurturing talent, delegating authority, enhancing leadership abilities, and forming diverse groups for experiential learning.

The business model of McDonald's comprises contributions from owners, suppliers, and employees and is a robust and balanced model.

Inculcating the right business ethics, making profit in business, and giving back better living to the customers are the main mantras of McDonald's. Organizational structure has a crucial impact on the organization's ability to handle contingencies, provide competitive edge, manage diversity, and indulge in continuous innovation, which as an organization McDonald's has been highly successful in attaining. How as an organization McDonald's survived the changes in the environment and how the various factors affected the business of the organization is a very interesting study in itself. Given below are some of the macro factors which affected the organization in some way or the other. In times of turbulence, McDonald's was able to handle contingencies and manage diversities largely due to the matrix structure of the organization. McDonald's organizational structure is a hybrid of functional structure for corporate, divisional structure for restaurants, and geographic structure for the global market.

Political Factor

Depending on business rules, regulations, and laws of various nations, McDonald's has to tune its operations, services, products, and strategies accordingly since it is a global player. At one time, the management of McDonald's decided to reduce the salt content in its products by 14% (Food Service Agency, 2005) in the UK following a report from SACN UK, which established facts confirming that a high level of salt intake leads to rise in the frequency of occurrence of heart disease.

Economic Factor

Headquartered in the United States, a country having a strong economic background, McDonald's has to keep a very competitive pricing strategy to win its way through greater customer base across nations. In Russia, Big Macs are sold at the cheapest price and, in India, a burger has been ordained even as a Mac *Aloo Tikki* at a very low price.

Sociological Factor

Because McDonald's products are said to enhance cholesterol level, which once upon a time had affected a large base of health-conscious customers, its management immediately introduced many healthy supplements with its existing product range.

Technological Factor

With the advent of technology and Internet, McDonald's could reach out to millions through online presence, marketing, and advertisement. With the advent of the Internet, even a small incident goes viral in no time, and McDonald's had in the past confronted such issues and solved them.

Environmental Factor

Hazards to the environment due to slaughter of animals and birds or imbalance is a criminal offence and McDonald's had to fight against such issues in the past.

Legal Factors

As an organization, it has to abide by health, legal, and safety framework of various nations along with strong labour and employment laws. For McDonald's, a safe product means a check of the product across 70 points and then only the health of that food product is ascertained by the organization as a good.

Introduction

Organization is a social unit of people, systematically structured, and managed to accomplish a task or to achieve collective goals on a continuous basis.

Organization is the basis upon which the whole structure of management is built. Organization is associated with developing a framework where the overall work is divided into manageable constituents in order to enable the accomplishment of objectives or goals. Thus, organization is the structure that enables living things to work collectively. In a static sense, an organization is an arrangement staffed by a group of individuals who are working towards a common goal.

Examples: Corporations, governments, non-government organizations, armed forces, non-profit organizations, and so on.

The term 'organization' is used in four different senses:

- **Organization as framework of relationships:** Organization refers to the structure and interactions among various job positions which are created to realize certain objectives.
- **Organization as a process:** Organization is viewed as an active process and a management activity which is essential for forecasting the utilization of company's resources.
- **Organization as a system:** Organization is also viewed as a system. System concepts diagnose that organizations are made up of constituents, each of which has exclusive properties, abilities, and reciprocated associations. The constituent elements of a system are linked together in such a complicated manner that actions executed by one individual have far-reaching effects on others.
- **Organization as a group of persons:** Organization is very often viewed as a group of persons contributing their efforts towards certain goals.

Definitions

Organizations may be defined as a group of individuals large or small that are cooperating under the direction of executive leadership in accomplishment of certain common object.

Keith Davis

Organization is a system of cooperative activities of two or more persons.

Chester Barnard

Organization is the form of every human association for the attainment of a common purpose.

Mooney and Reily

Organization is a harmonious adjustment of specialized parts for the accomplishment of some common purpose or purposes.

Haney

In its broadest sense, organization refers to the relationship between the various factors present in the given endeavor. Factory organization concerns itself primarily with the internal relationships within the factory such as responsibilities of personnel arrangement and grouping of machines and material control. From the standpoint of enterprise as a whole, organization is the structural relationship between various factors in an enterprise.

Spriegel

Need/Importance of Organization

Andrew Carnegie, a renowned industrialist of United States, when sold his company United States Steel Corporation, showed his confidence in organization by saying, 'Take away our factories, take away our plants, our avenues of transportation, our money, leave nothing but our organization and we shall establish better factories'. Since ages and all walks of life, organization has been playing a significant role. The importance of organization is as stated below:

A tool for achieving objectives: Organization is an important tool in the hands of management for accomplishing the objectives of an enterprise.

Facilitates administration and management: A sound organization increases efficiency, avoids duplication of work, avoids delay in work, improves managerial skills, and motivates employees to perform their duties.

Ensures optimum use of human resource: Good organization establishes individuals with interests, knowledge, skills, abilities, and viewpoints.

Enhances creativity: A well-conceived and comprehensive organization is the source of creative thinking and origination of new thoughts.

Prevents corruption: Enterprises which lack sound organization most of the times have problem of corruption. Sound organization helps to prevent corruption by raising morale of the employees. As a result, employees are encouraged to work with higher efficiency, commitment, and honesty.

Fosters growth of enterprise: Good organization plays a key role not only in growth but also in the expansion and diversification of an enterprise.

Eliminates overlapping and duplication of efforts: In a situation where the distribution of work is not visibly identified and the work is done in a disorganized manner, there will be duplication and overlapping of efforts. As a good organization requires that the work be clearly assigned amongst employees, such overlapping and duplication is to be eliminated.

Coordination: Various jobs and positions are linked together by a structural relationship of the organization. The organizational process exercises its due and balanced emphasis on the coordination of different activities.

Principles of Organizing

For timely and systematic completion of work, it is must for every organization to adopt some techniques or principles. Thus, these principles would be the deciding factor for the success or failure of an organization.

Principle of Objective

All the enterprises, whether large or small, set certain central objectives. Every element of the organization and organization as a whole should be geared to the central objectives identified by the enterprise.

Principle of Specialization

A clear-cut division of labour enables specialization. According to this principle, division of work among the employees should be based on their knowledge, skills, abilities, capabilities, and interests. This would lead to specialization, which would in turn lead to efficiency, quality, and elimination of wastage of resources.

Scalar Principle

This principle is sometimes referred to as the chain command. There must be clear lines of authority running from the top to bottom of the organization and linking all the individuals in the organization.

Principle of Authority

Authority is an important ingredient of the organizational structure. It is a tool by which a manager can create an environment where an individual can perform with greater efficiency.

Principle of Span of Control

This principle states that there is a limit to the number of subordinates who report to one superior. Supervision of too many people can lead to trouble and confusion. Also, the superior will not be able to spare time to supervise each of his subordinates. It will also lead to increased complexity of the organizational structure.

The span of control depends upon a number of considerations. It is easy to supervise a large number of subordinates involved in routine jobs and working in the same room, whereas it is difficult to supervise highly diverse and specialized personnel scattered widely. The ability of the employees, their willingness to assume responsibility, and the attitude of the management towards delegating and decentralization should also be analysed in detail while making a decision on the span of control.

Principle of Unity of Command

This principle is basically about avoiding dual reporting. It states that every employee working in the organization should be kept in the supervision of only one boss. This principle eliminates the possibility of conflicts in instructions and fosters a feeling of personal responsibility for work.

Principle of Definition

Each individual in the organization should be made aware about his/her responsibilities, duties, authorities, and relations with the other job positions in the organizational structure.

Principle of Unity of Direction

The basic motive for the existence of organization is the attainment of certain objectives. Major objectives should be split into functional activities and there should be one objective and one plan for each group of people.

Principle of Parity of Authority and Responsibility

The responsibility for execution of work must be accompanied by the authority to control and direct the means of doing the work.

Principle of Supremacy of Organizational Objectives

The organizational goals and objectives should be given wide publicity within the organization. The people contributing to it should be made to understand that an enterprise's objectives are more valuable and significant and one should give higher priority to the organization's objectives in comparison to personal motives.

The Process of Organizing

From Figure 4.1 it is clear that organizing is a process involving multiple activities. The details of all these have been discussed in the following subsections.

Fixing the Objectives of the Organization

The top-level management holds the responsibility of fixing the overall objectives of the organization, whereas the middle-level management fixes the departmental objectives and lower level management fixes the day-to-day objectives. The objectives decided by each level of management should be both specific and realistic.

Finding Activities Must for Achieving Objectives

Once the objectives are fixed, the strategic level of management determines different activities that are required to be performed in order to accomplish the set objectives. This is a crucial stage as it helps to eliminate duplication, overlapping, and wastage of efforts.

Figure 4.1 Steps in Organizing

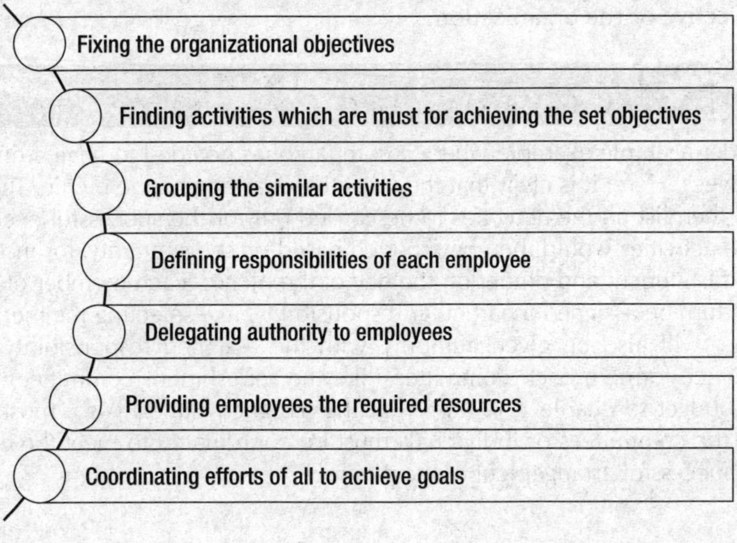

Grouping the Similar Activities

All the activities which are similar in nature are grouped together to form departments. This is also termed as departmentalization. This leads to specialization.

EXAMPLE

All the activities that are directly or indirectly related to management or development of the human resource like training, performance appraisal, and recruitment are grouped together and form the HR department.

Defining Responsibilities of Each Employee

In this step, the responsibilities of all the individuals working in the organization are clearly defined. This would ultimately lead to selection of the right candidate for the right job. This brings about efficiency since each individual is aware about what he/she has to do.

Delegating Authority to Employees

In a situation where two or more individuals are working together for a common purpose, it becomes necessary to clearly define the authority relationship among them. Each subordinate should know whom he has to report. Also, each superior should be aware of the authority he has over his subordinates.

Providing Employees with Required Resources

After defining authority relationships, the employees must be provided with all the resources required for achieving the objectives of the organization.

Coordinating Efforts of All to Achieve Goals

This is the last and most important step in the process of organizing. Here, the efforts of all individual employees, groups, and departments are fetched together and coordinated towards the mutual objective of the organization.

EXAMPLE

Let us consider a simple example where a company has decided to have a one-day picnic for its employees. Here, it is clear that the objective is arranging the picnic. The HR department would then list all the activities to be carried out for the successful execution of the picnic. These activities would then be grouped based on the similarity, for instance arranging for breakfast, lunch, and dinner on the day of the picnic. Each member of this committee would in turn be assigned a particular responsibility, like selecting the menu and so on. Each member will also be given authority with the assigned responsibility for efficient execution. Once formed, each committee (like the refreshment committee) will then be allocated a budget to enable it to carry out the assigned duties. Also, most importantly, efforts of all the committees or individuals must be coordinated to meet the central objective, that is, successful arrangement of the picnic.

Organization Structure

CASE STUDY: AN ORGANIZATION WITH NO STRUCTURE

Four classmates started a tours and travels service for senior citizens and women. Their objective was to do something good for the weaker section of the society, and profit was not their main motto. They used to work in collaboration with each other, and every member monitored every task right from taking in customers to making their travel plans to booking accommodations, tickets to visa processing, and also into the food habits of these customers since they were all senior citizens.

Within the first few months, they could win 40 customers as they carefully customized the tours as per the requirements of the citizens at an affordable cost. Since they were new in the business, they designed the tours according to customer preferences to the minutest detail. They even provided customers with useful information like nearby hospitals, clinics, and medical stores available in and around the location while on a tour. The four friends made it a point to meet once a week to discuss the issues they were facing and areas in which they could improve.

They continued putting the same amount of effort and started thinking of new ways to expand their business. After a year or so, they took on lease a small office and appointed a helpdesk person to receive calls and take in customer requirements. Initially they used to plan tours for citizens within India, but as their business grew they started providing services out of India. However, as they started overseas operations, they realized that things were getting out of control. They needed additional manpower to handle the activities and tasks with relation to tour planning customization, visa processing, ticket booking, accounting and finance, auditing, and so on.

With the induction of additional manpower, including persons in the finance and administration departments, there arose a requirement to create an organizational structure with proper organizational objectives, allocation of roles, responsibilities and tasks to every individual. At the same time the task of structuring information flow, designing extensive growth plans for the organization, setting up discrete lines of authority and decision-making, was being carried out. Even roles were being allocated to some employees on the customer side, comprising of marketing, sales, and customer service, and some on the supplier side for the negotiation of deals and partnerships. Every member within the organization worked as a team, collaborating, cooperating, and encouraging the implementation of new ideas to steer the organization to success.

In other words, it is evident from the case that as an organization grows, there arises an increased need for a proper organizational structure with clearly defined authority and effective team dynamics to support the organization.

An organizational structure specifies the various job positions and depicts how the same are formally divided, grouped, and coordinated. It provides an appropriate framework for authority relationships. It is a means to help the management to achieve the organizational objectives. It can also be considered as the viewing glass or perspective through which individuals see their organization and its environment. An organization can be structured in many different ways, depending on their objectives. The structure of an organization will define the ways in which it functions and executes. Organizational structure allows the expressed allocation of duties for different functions and processes to different entities, such as branch, department, workgroup, and individual.

Organizational structure affects organizational action in two major ways. First, it provides a basis on which the standard operating procedures and routines rest. Second, it determines which individuals get to participate in which decision-making process and thus to what degree their views shape the organization's actions.

There are several reasons why designing an organizational structure is such an important aspect. Organizational structure has a crucial impact on the organizations ability to

- deal with contingencies.
- achieve a competitive advantage.
- effectively manage diversity.
- increase its efficiency and ability to innovate new goods and services.

Formal Organization

The formal organization refers to the structure that is designed and prescribed by the management of the enterprise. It is defined as a 'hierarchical concept of subordination of entities that collaborate and contribute to serve a common goal'. A formal organization has its own set of rules and regulations that are to be followed by each individual in the organization. It depicts clear lines of authority and the superior–subordinate relationship, also each of the individual is assigned specific duties and responsibilities. In a formal structure, there are predefined objectives and the individual efforts are diverted towards achieving these objectives.

According to Barnard, 'Any organization shall be considered formal at the stage when the activities of two or more persons are coordinated consciously to achieve the definite objective'.

Example: College, hospital, company, and so on.

Features of Formal Organization

- Authorities and responsibilities are clearly defined.
- It does not consider the emotional aspect.
- It is predetermined and purposefully created.
- It is based on delegation of authority.
- It provides for division of labour.
- Organizational charts are followed.

Advantages

- It promotes discipline in the organization.
- It provides a basic structure of division of work and responsibility. Without such a structure, it becomes very difficult for employees to agree between themselves on the duties and responsibilities of every individual.
- It gives a clear-cut idea about the authority and responsibility of the individuals. Thus, a formal structure reduces confusions and brings clarity in working.
- The dependency is not on a single person.
- It decreases the possibilities and occasions of conflict.
- The formal organization helps to keep the firm operating despite the changes in the workforce.
- It eliminates duplication of work, which in turn leads to effective utilization of resources.

Disadvantages

- At times, the formal organization causes reduction in initiatives of the person working in the organization.
- It does not consider the emotional aspect.
- It may cause delay in work.

Informal Structures

This is a shadow organization made up of the informal, but often critical, relationships between members of the organization. The informal structure has its presence in all the formal structures. Informal structure depicts the way in which individuals communicate and relate themselves with others beyond the formal structure. The informal structure develops through various frequent instances like having regular interaction, lunch, coffee with colleagues. For example, most IT companies have an informal organization to promote innovation amongst the employees.

According to J.L. Massie, 'Informal organization is any human group interactions that occur spontaneously and naturally over long period of time.'

Features of Informal Organization

- The informal organizations are not depicted in the organizational chart.
- The informal organizations do not have any particular structure.

- It denotes human relationships beyond the formal organizational structure.
- Informal organizations are outcome of voluntary associations.
- The informal organizations develop out of personal preferences, beliefs, habits, and understanding.

Advantages

- It is an effective channel of communication in certain cases.
- It develops a sense of belongingness among the individuals.
- The gaps and deficiencies that exist in the formal organizations can be filled up by the informal organization.
- The members of informal organizations help each other in case of unforeseen events or emergencies.
- Informal group forces the manager to plan and act more carefully than he would otherwise.
- Informal organization is a check and balance on unlimited use of authority by a manager.

Disadvantages

- It operates based on the group psychology.
- The interests of the formal and informal groups may clash, leading to conflict making the job of managers difficult.
- The informal organizations may fall prey to rumours.
- It may cause problems by resisting changing at certain occasions.

Difference between Formal and Informal Organizations

The difference between formal and informal organizations is presented in Table 4.1 and Figure 4.2.

Mechanistic Structure

A mechanistic structure, also known as a bureaucratic structure, is based on an official, centralized network. The structure is ideal for organizations that function in a steady and consistent atmosphere. A mechanistic structure is very rarely changed since this type of structure acquires stability.

Table 4.1 Formal and Informal Organizations

S. No.	Basis	Informal Organization	Formal Organization
1	Structure	Undefined	Predefined
2	Relations	Personal relations	Formal relations
3	Purpose	For social satisfaction	To achieve organizational objective
4	Dynamism	Flexible	Rigid
5	Leader	Voluntarily chosen	Manager
6	Communication	Fast	Slow
7	Nature	Sentimental	Official
8	Example	Group of trekkers	Departments in the organization

Figure 4.2 Formal and Informal Organizations

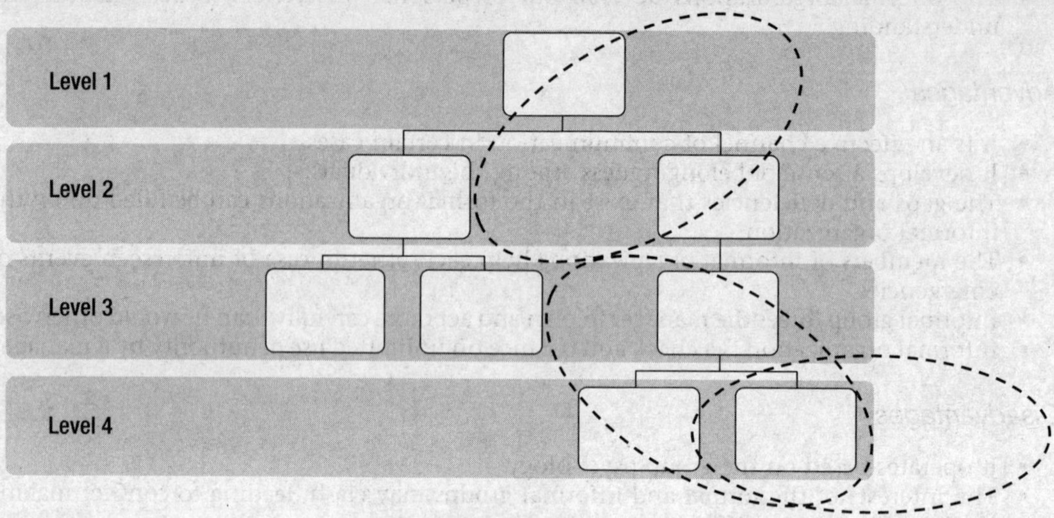

There is a well-defined hierarchy and the strategic decisions are taken by the top management of the organization. Subordinates work under the direction of the management and communication follows a top-down approach.

The mechanistic form of organization ensures that there is allocation of task to each individual, which is stable in nature, and integration between various functional units is less since the organization has achieved a desired level of stability. The mechanized structure is characterized by

- decisions taken by management.
- information flow through a chain of command.
- highly specialized tasks.
- low level of integration between departments.
- characterized by low degree of change or change over the years is very slow.

Examples of mechanistic structures include healthcare, universities, and governmental organizations.

Organic Structure

Organic structures are characterized by unstable and dynamic environments and are subjected to frequent changes. When the situation changes, the organization must be able to congregate, process, and distribute information at a very fast pace, else it might lose its competitive edge. Communication is quick and does not follow a top-down hierarchy. Because there is a high level of integration between functions and departments, the information flow is effortless. The rapid pace at which information flows helps the organization to quickly adapt to the changes in the external and internal environment.

Organic organizations exercise dual specialization, and employees work in unison and execute and coordinate complex tasks of large projects.

Decision-making in organic structures is a complex process. It involves many teams from all the levels of the organization. For organic structures, as there are no standardized processes, authority can also be allocated to lower level employees. For example, a team may contain

Table 4.2 Mechanistic and Organic Organizations

Mechanistic	*Organic*
Individual specialization with employees working on only one task and specialize in that task only	Dual specialization with employees working together on multiple tasks
Integration amongst units low and hierarchy structurally defined	High level of integration with authority allotted to task teams as well
Decision-making is done by the top management and mechanistic organization follows a centralized approach with vertical lines of communication	Decision-making is done by teams across the hierarchy with communication being lateral and decentralization of power and authority
Use of standard operating procedures	There are no standard operating procedures
Communication is mostly penned down	Evidence of verbal communication
Status accorded as per the size of the organization	Status based on perceived ability
Organization is a collation of tasks and people who perform a specific task	Organization is the collation of teams with people working in different capacities together over a period of time

sales, accounting, research and development, and production representatives. When decisions have to be taken, it is the responsibility of one of these members, as there are no clearly defined roles and responsibilities allocated to the members, to decide on any point, and see that it is complied with by other members of the team and subordinates beneath them. A comparative analysis of mechanistic and organic structures of the organization.

Difference between Mechanistic and Organic Organization

The difference between mechanistic and organic organization is shown in Table 4.2.

Types of Organization Structures

Functional Structure

The concept of functional organization was proposed by F.W. Taylor. In functional structures (Figures 4.3–4.5), individuals having identical skills and performing similar tasks are grouped together into formal work units, generally called departments. Members of functional departments share technical know-how, interests, and responsibilities. Employees within the functional division of an organization tend to perform in areas of their expertise. The functional structure may differ according to the major functions of a business.

Advantages

- **Specialization:** The organizational efficiency increases as each employee performs the task as per their specialization.
- **Reduced workload:** As each of the functional head is responsible for only one function, workload is reduced.

Figure 4.3 Functional Structure for Business Entity

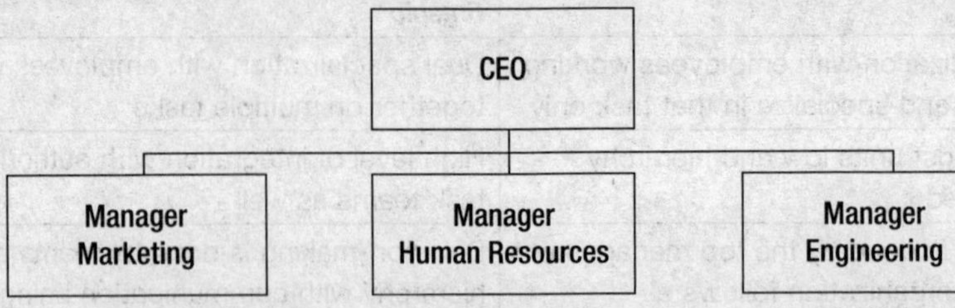

Figure 4.4 Functional Structure for a Hotel

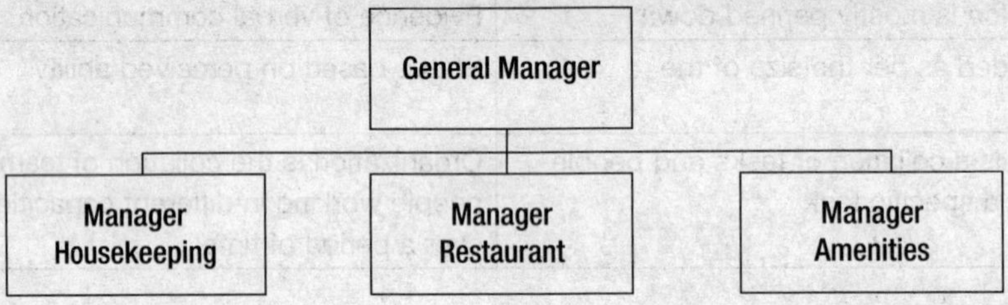

Figure 4.5 Functional Structure for a College

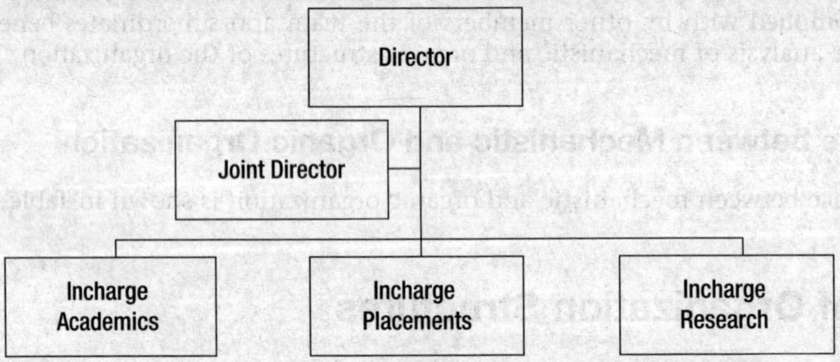

- **Flexibility:** It is easier to accommodate a change with little or no difficulty.
- **Improved control:** As each employee is in charge of only one function, it is easier to spare time to supervise all his/her subordinates.
- **Mass production:** Due to specialization and standardization it becomes feasible to go for large-scale production.

Disadvantages

- **Complex relationships:** An individual has several superiors due to which accountability for results cannot be easily fixed. In addition, cross-functional relationships create confusion.
- **Inefficient administration:** As the same groups are controlled by various specialists, there is inefficient administration.

- **Expensive:** As a large number of specialists need to be hired, it leads to an increase in cost.
- **Ineffective coordination:** Each of the functional managers is bound to think only from the perspective of his/her department rather than from the perspective of the whole organization.
- **Delay in decision-making:** Because several functional specialists are involved in the process of decision-making, decisions may be delayed.

Divisional Structure

In the divisional structure, the organization is organized into various divisions based on four criteria product, market, process, and location (Table 4.3). Thus, divisional structure is most suited for the organizations having a wide range of products, area of operation, work processes, or customers. Each of the divisions is self-contained and has its own set of functional units like marketing, manufacturing, finance, HR, and so on.

Advantages

- **Highly flexible:** Divisional structure can respond more quickly to the changing environment.
- **Specific:** Expertise is focused on specific product, market, process, or location.
- **Coordination:** The divisional structure leads to better coordination across functional departments.
- **Clear accountability:** Divisional structuring provides a clear correlation between the expense and profit of the individual divisions. Business objectives of the divisions can be formulated more objectively and expectations can be better agreed.
- **Ease of operation:** Greater ease to modify the size by adding or deleting divisions.

Disadvantages

- **Reduced economies of scale:** Duplication of efforts across divisions leads to increase in the operating and administrative cost.
- **Rivalry:** Divisional structures may also result into rivalry as the divisions compete for resources.

Table 4.3 Divisional Structure Based on Product, Market, Location, and Process

Type	*Emphasis*	*Example*
Product	Goods provided/services catered	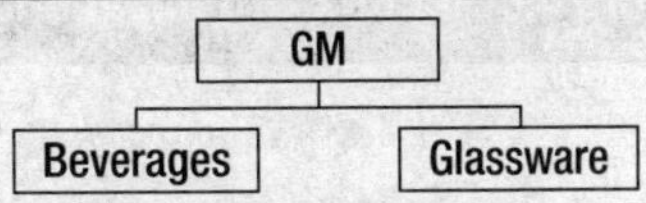
Market	Target customers/clients	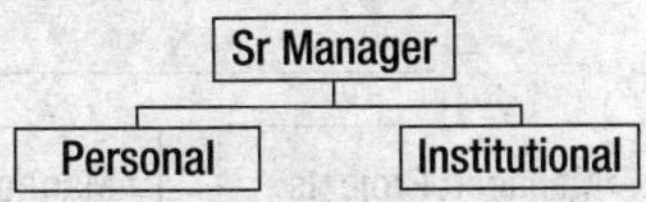
Location	At which activities are carried out	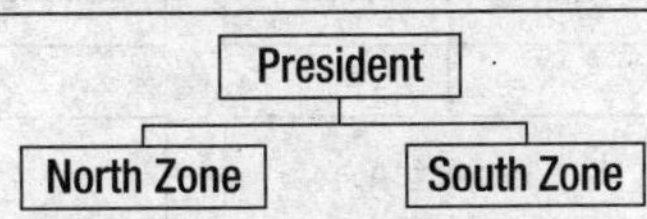
Process	Activities of the same process	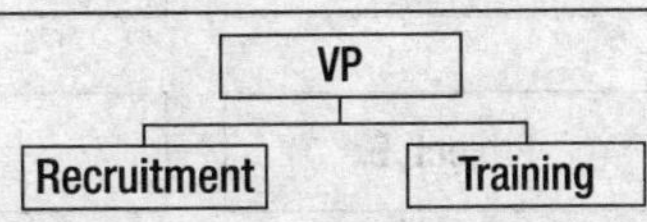

- **Divisional affiliations:** Employees feel more affiliated towards their own divisions and would still lack affiliation to the organization as a whole.
- **Supremacy of divisional goals:** The divisional goals may have priority over the organizational goals.

Matrix Structure

The matrix structure comes into existence when one organizational structure is superimposed on the other. In this structure, an employee is answerable to two immediate supervisors: a functional supervisor and a divisional supervisor. The functional supervisor is in charge of overseeing employees in a functional area, such as marketing or engineering. Divisional supervisor manages specific projects. They absorb employees from various functional areas to complete their project teams. Figure 4.6 depicts the absorption of employees from operations, finance, and marketing for projects A and B. These employees report to both managers at that point of time.

Advantages

- **Flexibility:** Increased flexibility in adding, removing, or changing the activities to meet the changing needs.
- **Motivation:** If it is identified that a particular project is lacking proper motivation, then it is provided to the concerned department.
- **Development of skills:** Since cross-functional teams are formed, it leads to development of skills of the employees.
- **Better service:** There is always a product or project manager answerable to the queries.
- **Improved strategic management:** Top-level managers are relieved from routine tasks to focus on strategic issues.

Disadvantages

- **Power struggle:** Conflicts occur as there is overlapping of responsibility and authority.
- **Slow decisions:** The speed of decision-making retards as there is shared decision-making in the matrix structure.
- **Increased confusion:** As there is dual reporting in the matrix structure, it leads to confusion.

Figure 4.6 Matrix Organizational Structure

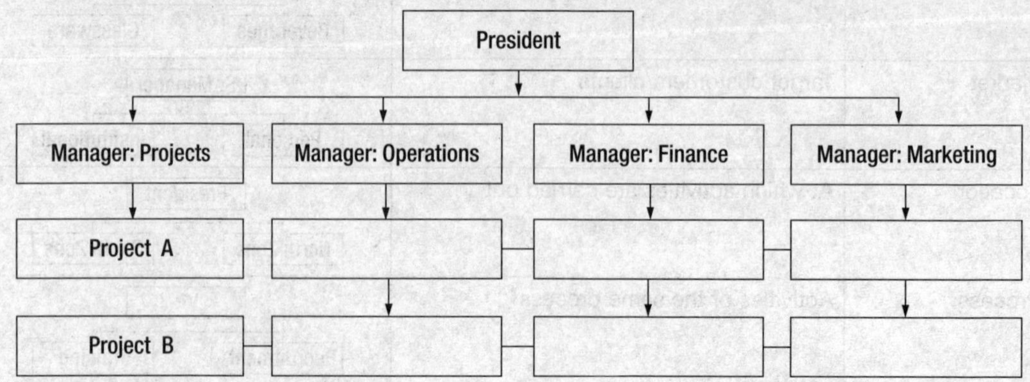

- **Increased administrative and managerial overhead:** Due to duplication of routine activities, the administrative costs increase, and as specialized managers are hired for each project and function, managerial cost also increases.
- **Professional development sidelined:** Professional development is not given priority due to time constraints of the project; therefore, employees forgo opportunities to develop and improve.

Network Structure

A network structure is a cluster of various organizations that coordinate its actions through agreements and contracts instead of hierarchy of authority. Rather than hiring individuals to perform all of its business activities, a company using the network structure depends on outside companies. The organizations using a network structure own only the core or essential components of the business and outsource the rest. It may, for instance, hire an outside advertiser to advertise its products. The network structure reduces costs and brings in flexibility because it utilizes external help as and when required. Creating a network-based company, however, means losing control over whatever processes the company has outsourced (Figure 4.7).

Advantages

- **Flexible:** The most important advantage of network structure is that it can quickly respond to the changing environment. As the business grows, organizations can enter into new partnerships and vice versa.
- **Cost-effective:** As only the essential part of business is owned by the company and the other operations are outsourced, fewer individuals need to be hired, leading to reduction in overheads.
- **Efficiency:** The overall efficiency of the organization increases as the tasks are outsourced to an expert organization.

Disadvantages

- **Coordination problems:** As the business functions are outsourced to different companies, sometimes it would become difficult to coordinate all of these activities.
- **Loss of control:** There is always a fear of losing control over the core activities, which would lead to uncertainties in the relationship.
- **Political pressure:** The change in the political scenario affects the organizations bearing network structure to a large extent.

Figure 4.7 Network Organizational Structure

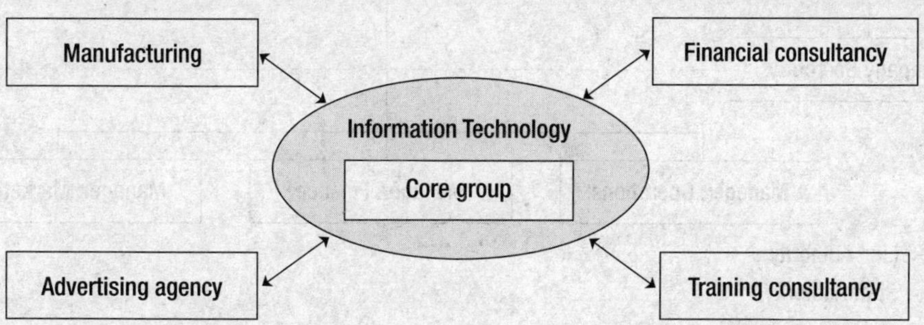

- **Increased pressure:** If there are problems of unemployment in the parent company due to outsourcing, there are likely to be pressures on the government to effect policy changes in this respect.

Line-and-Staff Organization

The oldest and simplest form of organization is line organization. Line functions have direct responsibility of achieving the objective of the venture. In this form of organization, a supervisor exercises direct control over a subordinate, authority flows from top to bottom of the organization. Here the chief executive heads the organization. This type of organization is also called as scalar organization.

The concept of staff organization was developed by F.W. Taylor. The objective of functional organization is to offer specialist services in the organization. Under this plan, specific functions common to all the departments are placed in the hands of an expert of that function.

The line-and-staff organization combines the line organization with staff departments that support and direct line departments. Most medium- and large-sized firms exhibit line-and-staff organizational structures. The distinguishing characteristic between simple line organizations and line-and-staff organizations is the multiple layers of management within line-and-staff organizations (Figure 4.8).

Advantages

- **Top managers relieved from routine work:** In this organization line authorities focus on execution of work and are relieved from thinking function.
- **Expert advice:** Line authorities are not autocrats as they are to take the advice from the experts or staff position.
- **Efficiency:** This results greater efficiency as the line managers spend much of their time on line functions. The line managers function more efficiently as they get support from staff positions.
- **Easy coordination:** This organization ensures co-ordination automatically as the line manager's work along with staff officers.

Disadvantages

- **Confusion:** Line-and-staff organizations are ambiguous in terms of organizational relationships, responsibility, and authority.

Figure 4.8 Line-and-Staff Organization

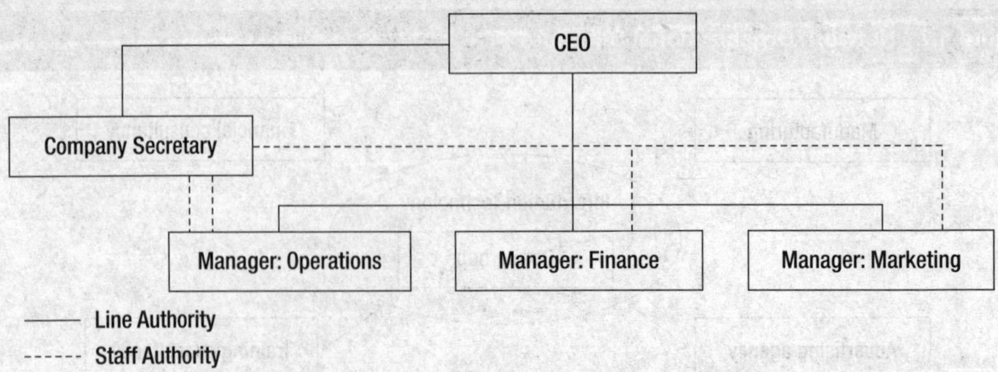

- **Conflict:** Conflicts are common in line-and-staff organizations owing to unclear definition of authority the structure entails.
- **Ineffective and erroneous decision-making:** It is not uncommon for line managers to feel threatened by the advice of staff members. In this case, line managers are liable to make decisions without staff member consultation. Such decisions are not always successful.
- **Slower decision-making:** Decision-making is slower in a line-and-staff organization due to its complexity and layers.
- **Costly:** Most of the line-and-staff executives are experts in their fields and their appointment leads to heavy expenditure.

Virtual Organizations

Virtual organization is a network of independent enterprises, suppliers, and customers linked by information technology. For example, LiveWire Projects is a virtual IT platform that is used by IT companies and professionals to develop their business applications and products on cloud. The virtual organization networks are usually temporary in nature. The significant attributes of virtual organizations are as follows:

- **Technology:** The geographically dispersed partners connect to each other via electronic networks.
- **Flexibility:** It offers flexibility as the partners can link up as and when required. The structure evaporates as soon as the requirement is over.
- **Efficiency:** As each partner brings in his core proficiency, the overall efficiency of the organization is bound to increase.
- **Borderless:** The boundaries that traditionally separate a firm from its customers, competitors, and suppliers are eliminated.

Advantages

- **Boundaryless:** They are appropriate for affinity groups that are geographically dispersed.
- **Suitable for short-term initiatives:** They are suitable and tailored for short-term initiatives with clearly defined objectives.
- **Flexible:** Virtual organizations are highly responsive to changing environment.
- **Cost-effective:** As there is no physical existence, there is little or no organizational overhead.

Disadvantages

- **Dependency on technology:** As the virtual organizations depend on information technology for coordination and interaction, their efficiency may be affected by the limitations and problems inherent to these technologies.
- **Difficult to manage:** Since there is no physical existence, it becomes difficult to manage virtual organizations in some situations.

Tall Organizational Structure

Organizations that require close monitoring of all its business activities opt for tall organizational structure. In such structure, the decision-making authority is the top-level management. This results in a long chain of command similar to military organizations. As the organization expands the operations, the levels of management also increase, which ultimately results in tall organizational structure. In tall organization structure, the span of control is narrow (Figure 4.9).

Figure 4.9 Tall Organizational Structure

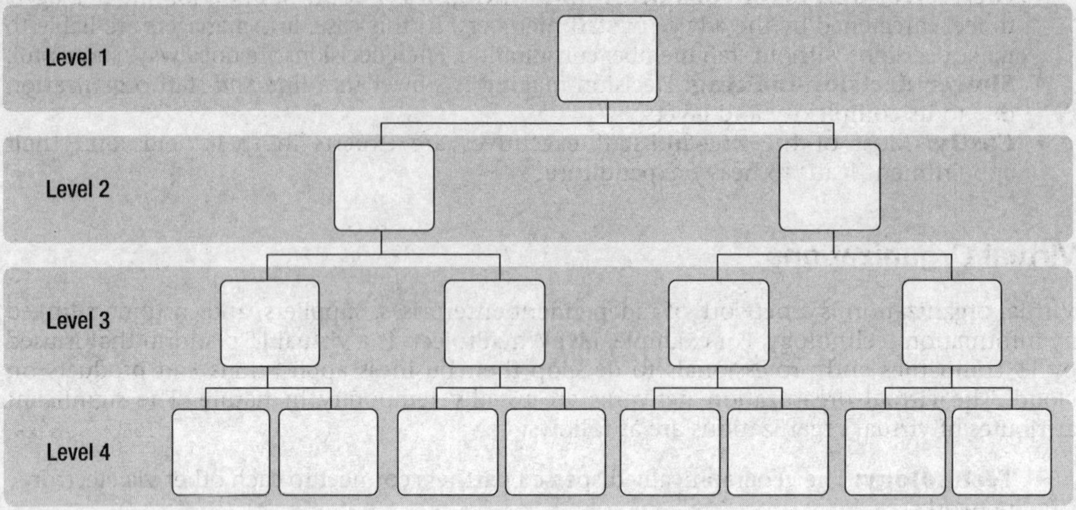

Advantages

- **Improved performance and discipline:** The quality of performance increases as the tall structure facilitates close supervision of activities being carried out. Similarly, discipline in the organization is also maintained.
- **Cordial relations:** As there is a narrow span of control, superiors get time to interact with their subordinates and solve their problems, as a result the superior–subordinate relations improve.
- **Narrow span of control:** The narrow span of control facilitates easy supervision and control.
- **Easy coordination:** The efforts of subordinates can be easily coordinated.
- **Development of staff:** Tall organizations encourage development of the staff. As there is narrow span of control the superior can easily identify the areas in which the subordinate lacks and arranges for training for his/her development.

Disadvantages

- **Delay in decision:** As there are several levels of management, it causes delay in the decision-making process as well as distortion in communication.
- **Cost inefficiency:** As there are increased levels of management, the tall structure adds to the cost of administration.
- **Coordination problems:** As the structure grows taller, it leads to coordination problems.
- **No freedom:** There is strict supervision. Thus, the subordinates have no freedom at all.
- **Dominance:** Managers may become more dominating, leading to loss of loyalty in subordinates.

Flat Organizational Structure

Organizations that require more autonomy and self-control have flat organizational structure. In this structure, there are fewer levels of management. The flat organizational structure is

Figure 4.10 Flat Organizational Structure

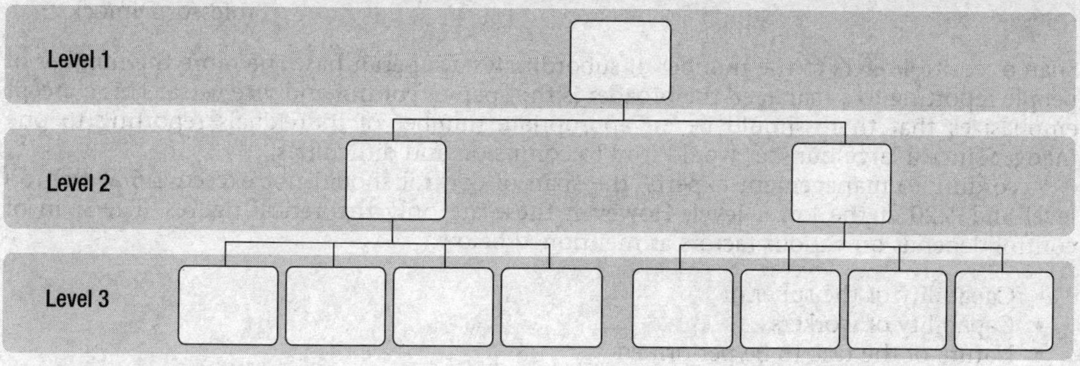

usually adopted by small business firms. Here, the management shows confidence in the decision-making capability of the employees. It focuses on empowering the employees rather than following the chain of command. In this organizational structure, the span of control is wide (Figure 4.10).

Advantages

- **Cost-effective:** This structure proves to be cost-effective as compared with tall structure, since there are fewer managers.
- **Decision-making:** Quick decision-making is possible as there are fewer levels of management.
- **Communication:** The flat structure facilitates easy and fast communication as there are fewer levels.
- **Suitability:** It would be suitable where routine and standardized jobs are performed.
- **Freedom:** Subordinates enjoy some amount of freedom as there is no strict supervision, as seen in the case of tall structure.

Disadvantages

- **Loose control:** As there are a large number of subordinates reporting to a superior, there is loose control. Maintaining discipline also becomes difficult at times.
- **Coordination problems:** It becomes difficult to coordinate the activities of a large number of subordinates.
- **Suitability:** It may not be suitable for organizations having a complex structure.
- **Decreased quality of performance:** As there is no close monitoring, it can lead to decreased performance.

Span of Control

Definitions

Span of control refers to the number of people that a manager can supervise.

Louis Allen

The span of control is the number and range of direct, habitual communication contacts between the Chief Executive of an enterprise and his principal fellow officers.

Professor Dimock

Span of control refers to the number of subordinates a superior has. The more the number of people reporting to a manager, the broader is the span of control and vice versa. This concept emphasizes that there should be an appropriate number of individuals reporting to one manger since a large number would lead to confusion and difficulties.

According to management experts, the span of control should not exceed 1:6 at the top level and 1:20 at the lower level. However, these are only theoretical figures. The span of control depends on various factors as mentioned below:

- Capability of the superior
- Capability of workers
- Nature of the task to be performed
- Geographical dispersion
- Other tasks to be handled

The span of control can be either narrow or broad, each of which has its own pros and cons as given below.

Advantages of Narrow Span of Control

- It facilitates better communication between the boss and the subordinates.
- Supervising fewer number of people requires less managerial skills.
- Subordinates get an opportunity to discuss their problems and provide feedback to their superiors.
- Managers can exercise better control over subordinates.

Disadvantages of Narrow Span of Control

- It tends to increase the levels of management; therefore, it becomes difficult for top-level managers to be in touch with the ground realities.
- It creates problem of coordination.
- It may reduce morale of employees as they operate under a very tight control.
- It leads to distortion of communication when the communication is across various levels of management.

Advantages of Wide Span of Control

- It is cost-effective since fewer managers are appointed.
- There is less confusion.
- Less control and supervision can create more positive attitude among employees.
- It creates a more entrepreneurial culture as workers can take responsibility for jobs.

Disadvantages of Wide Span of Control

- Fewer promotional opportunities can be demotivating.
- Managers with wide span of control may get overloaded with work.
- Loose control over subordinates.

Centralization and Decentralization of Authority

CASE STUDY

Aligning Organizational Structure with Corporate Strategy: A Case Study of Adobe Systems Inc.

Adobe Systems Inc. is a global firm established in 1982 and is an industry leader in digital media and digital marketing business segment offering. The company's vision encapsulates continued growth in these two major areas with a focus on elevating end-user value and establishment of exclusive relationship with past customers and present customers for increased subscriptions. Since it strategized on shifting from continuous licensing to a subscription-based model, this was a very critical step for Adobe Systems Inc.

Centralized and Decentralized Decision Approach in Adobe

In the case of Adobe, it was mandatory to implement a centralized approach in its management of operations to guarantee reliable, universal, end-user know-how with the organization's digital media assets. However, on the sales vertical for selling the cloud solutions, it was required by the company to go for a decentralized mode of execution, to other businesses, who showed an inclination on exercising greater control over asset management and marketing campaigns.

Aligning Organizational Structure to Strategy

The strategy adopted by Adobe to align its corporate strategy with the organization's structure includes setting up performance metrics to be achieved by all members of the organization right from top management to the employee at the lowest level.

Adobe's acquisition of Behance and Neolane to enhance digital media and marketing platforms is evidence in itself that the company is aligning its digital media business solutions with functional and process activities for an increased subscriber base. With 500 new features to its creative cloud service, Adobe is receiving top ranking for offering correct forecasting services for the marketers.

Inference/Lessons Learnt

Adobe's strategy to align its task force with the functional and process aspect of business activities to attain long-term vision has become extremely successful and is aligned to the organization's culture, structure, ethics, values, leadership, and business solutions. Deciding on allocating authority and responsibility to decision makers inside and outside of the organization and matching corporate strategy to structure, Adobe has come out as the finest player in its own domain and competitive advantage gained by it is at its peak.

Definitions

Centralization is systematic and consistent reservation of authority at central points within an organization. Decentralization applies to systematic delegation of authority in an organizational context.

Allen

Everything which goes to increase the importance of subordinate's role is decentralization and everything which goes to reduce is decentralization.

Fayol

Centralization

Centralization is a process where the concentration of decision-making is in a few hands. All the decisions and actions at the lower levels are dependent on approval by the top management. Under centralization, vital and significant decisions are taken by the top management, and the other levels implement the decisions according to the instructions of the top management.

EXAMPLE

Suppose 1, 2, 3, 4, and 5 are subordinates of A and X, Y, and Z are subordinates of 4. Here, X, Y, and Z depend on 4 for the decisions to be made and 4 in turn depend on A. Neither X, Y, and Z nor 1, 2, 3, 4, and 5 can make decisions without consulting A. This is called centralization of authority (Figure 4.11).

Figure 4.11 Centralization of Authority

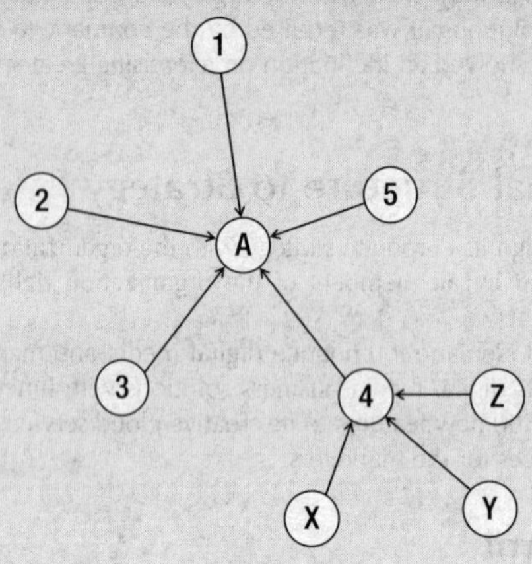

Advantages of Centralization

- **Reduced costs:** Standardized processes and techniques help in considerable reduction of costs incurred. The significant reason for this reduction is specialization of activities to be performed.
- **Flexibility:** In situations of emergency or crisis, standardization of activities requires minimal efforts to revise all the activities at once. This guarantees a greater degree of flexibility in an organization.
- **Avoids replication of work:** Centralized training and standardization of work leaves no possibility for replication of tasks or actions. This eliminates additional expenditure on excessive labour for duplication of work.
- **Better coordination:** Centralization accelerates better coordination among different operations. Direct control and supervision are facilitated, which minimize possibility of conflict of authority and duplication of work.

Disadvantages of Centralization

- **Delay in work:** Centralization results in loss of man-hours and delay in execution of work because of transmission of records from and to the central room. Quick decision is not possible, which also causes delay in execution of work.

- **Dictatorship:** An employee is always expected to work in accordance to what has been dictated to him. No employee at the subordinate level is given the authority to take a decision on any issue in the absence of the lead. This causes psychological reluctance and employee sees no growth or motivation within the organization, which would sometimes result in disloyalty.
- **High level of dependency:** The success of an organization depends totally on the proficiency and decision-making ability of the top management, which might prove to be risky at times.

Decentralization

Decentralization is the systematic delegation of authority at all levels of management. In decentralization, authority is retained by the top management for taking major decisions.

EXAMPLE

Framing policies and procedures considering organization as a whole. The rest of the authority may be delegated to middle- and lower-level management. Large multinational companies follow a decentralized structure because of geographical dispersions and often include redundant executive positions for each region, rather than allowing a single executive team to make decisions across all geographies.

EXAMPLE

Suppose 1, 2, 3, 4, and 5 are subordinates of A and X, Y, and Z are subordinates of 4. Though X, Y, and Z are supervised by 4, they can take decisions on routine matters and depend on decisions to be taken by 4 only in case of important issues. A similar relationship exists between 1, 2, 3, 4, and 5 and A. Here, 1, 2, 3, 4, and 5 and X, Y, and Z also enjoy some part of authority apart from A. This denotes distributed authority. This is called as decentralization of authority (Figure 4.12).

Figure 4.12 Decentralization of Authority

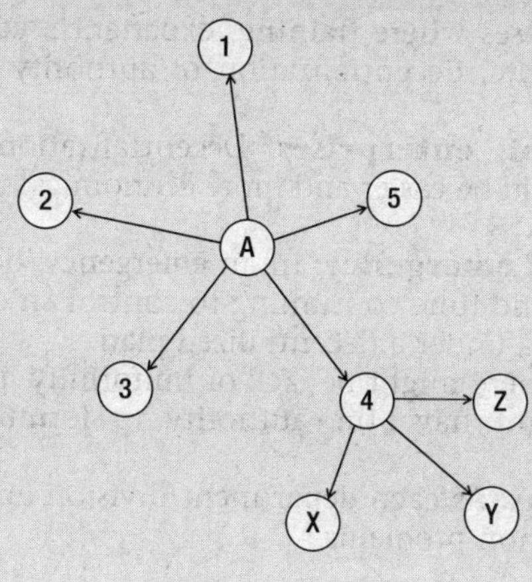

Advantages of Decentralization

- **Reduced burden on top executives:** Decentralization of authority frees top executives from routine work and minor issues so that they can concentrate on more important functions, such as preparing policies and procedures, making strategic decisions, coordination and control, and so on. As the company expands to the level that it goes beyond the reach of the few top-level executives, decentralization becomes indispensable. By delegating authority, the top management can extend its leadership over a giant enterprise.
- **Quick and better decisions:** Decentralization fosters prompt and more accurate decisions because decisions are made by those who are aware of all the realities of the situation. Decisions can be made near the point of action without consulting higher levels and without waiting for approval of top executives over minor matters.
- **Growth and diversification:** Decentralization enables growth and diversification of products and markets. Under decentralization, each area of operation is treated as a different division so that it can respond quickly to changing demands of its market.
- **Better communication:** Decentralization improves the level of efficiency and communication within the organization as there are fewer levels of authority.
- **Development of executives:** Decentralization provides an opportunity to subordinate managers to take initiative and acquire leadership qualities. Executives at lower levels learn to manage by exercising delegated authority. A pool of promotable managers becomes available, which simplifies management successions and support to warrant continuity of management.
- **Motivation and improved morale:** Decentralization increases job satisfaction and morale of subordinates. Providing an occasion to make decisions offers a sense of belonging and satisfies the need of power, prestige, status, and independence. A competitive environment is generated. High motivation and morale help in improving output and working relationships. It also helps make improved utilization of talents at lower levels.
- **Effective supervision and control:** Decentralization results in effective supervision because managers at lower levels have authority to make changes and recommendations. It also promotes effective control through a comparative evaluation of performance and clear-cut accountability for results.
- **Democratic management:** Decentralization leads to democratic management and flexibility of operations. Necessary changes can be accommodated without dislocating the entire structure.

Disadvantages of Decentralization

- **Suitability issues:** In cases where training, experience, education, and so on of the employees is/are inadequate, decentralization of authority would be harmful for the enterprise.
- **Not desirable for small enterprises:** Decentralization is not suitable for small enterprises because it would be easier and more economical to administer the enterprise on a centralized basis.
- **Problematic in case of emergency:** In an emergency, decentralized administration is ineffective. It is costly and time consuming to control an emergency situation, which affects a vital business area under a decentralized plan.
- **Lack of uniformity:** There might be lack of uniformity and inconsistent procedures as each department might have the authority to formulate its own policies and procedures.
- **Coordination problems:** As each department/division enjoys substantial autonomy, it might lead to coordination problems.

Summary

This chapter takes the reader through the types of organization and highlights the perspectives of centralization and decentralization with respect to the authoritative initiative in an organization. It also elaborates on various organizational structures, their advantages and disadvantages, fundamental principles and processes in organizing, how structuring the organization is aligned with strategy formulations, decisions taken by the top and middle management, and the impact these bring to organizations.

Exercise

Objective Questions

1. Organization is viewed as a/an _______ process and a management activity, which is essential for forecasting the utilization of company's resources.
   - Active
   - Passive
   - Intermediary
   - None of the above
2. A sound organization
   - Prevents corruption
   - Enhances creativity
   - None of the above
   - All of the above
3. Which of these is hierarchical concept of subordination of entities that collaborate and contribute to serve a common goal?
   - Formal organization
   - Informal structures
   - Functional structure
   - Divisional structure
4. In which of these an employee is answerable to two immediate supervisors: a functional supervisor and a divisional supervisor?
   - Formal organization
   - Informal structures
   - Functional structure
   - Matrix structure
5. The _______ networks are usually temporary in nature
   - Line-and-staff organization
   - Network organizational
   - Virtual organization
   - Tall organizational
6. Span of control refers to the number of people that a_________ can supervise
   - Manager
   - Leader

- CEO
- All of the above

7. Narrow span of control does not facilitate better communication among the boss and the subordinates.
    - True
    - False
8. Which of these operates on the group psychology?
    - Formal organization
    - Informal structures
    - Functional structure
    - Divisional structure
9. Which of these is a process where the concentration of decision-making is in a few hands
    - Span of control
    - Centralization
    - Decentralization
    - None of the above
10. Decentralization results in effective
    - Supervision
    - Coordination
    - Faster operation
    - None of the above

CASE STUDY

Neliphen Hitech Ltd. is a large-scale private sector manufacturing company running with huge profit for the past 13 years. It has a very good sales force and marketing network all over the country. It has divided its marketing into five regions: east, west, north, south, and central. Abhay Patil is entirely responsible for marking in the eastern region. Abhay, a very dedicated and committed to work, is competent person in the organization. As a marketing manager, he keeps himself engaged with all the problems of the sales and marketing teams. He periodically conducts market research to understand the fluctuating market environment. He also tries to obtain feedback on product quality, price, and design to improve the processes. Abhay is very competent in developing marketing strategies compared with other territory managers. He has been awarded for his efforts. He heads around eight middle-level managers and five junior-level managers. He ensures that he conducts biweekly performance meeting with the managers reporting to him. Because the span of management was manageable to Abhay in the eastern region, he could achieve better sales and profit.

Vineet Mehta, a marketing manager for the southern region, had resigned recently because of a better opportunity. The southern region started running into losses. The situation became critical for the company. To manage this critical situation, the management asked Abhay to take up the dual responsibility by managing the southern region as well. Because the southern region is much bigger than the northern region, the task was challenging for Abhay. Since the management needed one month for the selection of a manager for the northern region, Abhay agreed to the management's call. He started managing two regions. Therefore, all the subordinate managers from both regions started reporting him and took his guidance. He found that he is not able to have regular follow-up meetings with the middle-level and junior-level managers and the sales teams for the regions. Because there was a delay in becoming aware of marketing problems of the new and existing regions, he failed to take strategic decisions for both. The situation later reached up to such a state that he could not control either his region or the new one.

Periodical review of all regions happened, and the top management realized that the regions under Abhay have fallen down drastically within a period of two months. Abhay was called by the top management for explanation for the poor performance. Abhay explained that he took up the additional responsibility of the new division for only one month so that the organization gets sufficient time to recruit a new manager. However, since there was a delay in appointment, both regions became unmanageable for him to handle. Moreover, the span of control was unaffordable to him as a single manager.

Within a week, the organization appointed a new marketing manager for the northern region and relieved Abhay. Abhay was satisfied with the decision because now he could extend functional performance for his own region.

Questions

1. The company could have avoided the loss. Comment.
2. Higher level span of management can lower the communication and flow of information with subordinates. Comment.
3. How does span of control affect managerial control at the operation level?

Critical Thinking Questions

1. Why is decentralization becoming a more popular practice in contemporary organization?
2. From an employee's perspective, state the advantages and disadvantages of the matrix structure.
3. As an employee, in which kind of organizational structure would you prefer to work? Least preferred? Why?
4. Develop a different organizational structure for your company or college. What would be the advantages of the newly suggested structure over the existing organizational structure.

Chapter at a Glance

Organization

Organization is a social unit of people, systematically structured and managed to accomplish a task or to achieve collective goals on a continuous basis.

Organization Viewed in Four Different Senses

- As a framework of relationships
- As a process
- As a system
- As a group of persons

Importance of Organization

- A tool for achieving objectives
- Facilitates administration
- Optimum use of HR
- Enhances creativity
- Prevents corruption
- Fosters growth of enterprise
- Eliminates overlapping of work
- Fosters coordination

(Continued)

(Continued)

Principle of Organizing

It includes principle of objective, specialization, authority, span of control, unity of command, parity of authority and responsibility, supremacy of organizational objectives, and the scalar principle.

Process of Organizing

- Fixing the organizational objectives
- Finding activities which are must for achieving the set objectives
- Grouping similar activities
- Defining responsibilities of each employee
- Delegating authority to employees
- Providing employees the required resources
- Coordinating efforts of all to achieve goals

Formal Structure

This is a hierarchical concept of subordination of entities that collaborate and contribute to serve a common goal.

Informal Structure

Informal organization is any human group interactions that occur spontaneously and naturally over a long period of time.

Types of Organizational Structure

- Functional structure
- Divisional structure
- Matrix structure
- Network structure
- Line-and-staff organization
- Virtual organization
- Tall and flat structures

Span of Control

Span of control refers to the number of people that a manager can supervise.

- Narrow span of control
- Broad span of control

Centralization and Decentralization of Authority

Centralization: Centralization is systematic and consistent reservation of authority at central points within an organization.

Decentralization: Decentralization applies to systematic delegation of authority in an organizational context.

CHAPTER 5

Staffing, Training, and Development

Learning Objectives

- Getting an insight into the staffing concept, the nature of staffing, and process and characteristics of staffing.
- Realizing the benefits of staffing as a function of management.
- Understanding the need of recruitment planning process, recruitment types, and HR planning.
- Understanding the difference between selection and recruitment and types of employee remuneration.
- Being able to have a clear view on training, its types, performance monitoring, and evaluation.

An Opening Vignette

CASE STUDY: RECRUITMENT AT FUTURISTIC

Futuristic is a reputed multinational company with its locations across the globe. The company believes in aligning its recruitment process with other processes of the company to make it more effective.

The company follows the selection process for the middle-level management as follows:

1. **Preliminary interviews:** These are designed to verify the roles and responsibilities undertaken by the professional along with the skills and competencies. The preliminary interview goes on for a few minutes generally taken by the HR Director of the company. If she/he finds the candidate's profile suitable, then the subsequent rounds of interviews are conducted.
2. **Application forms:** Professionals clearing the preliminary interviews are required to fill in the application form to collect data related to the qualification, experience, skills, personal details, and so on about the candidates.
3. **Employment interviews:** These basically involve one-to-one technical sessions between the interviewer and the interviewee. This interview generally is taken by the top-management personnel and continues for an hour or more where the candidate's expertise, approach, and depth are evaluated. Some of the important aspects like salary, duties, and responsibilities are also discussed during these interviews.
4. **Final selection:** The final selection process of Futuristic is quite elaborate with two rounds of interview, one taken by the Board of Management and one final with the Global Head—Asia Pacific. This stage

(Continued)

(Continued)

consists of two aspects—discussion panel and the final interview. All the selectees are given a high-level problem scenario in advance and told to put forth his/her view. The timeframe for the brainstorming session is around 45 minutes followed by an evaluation by the board. The board evaluates the candidates using precision of thought and judgement, eloquence of expression, acceptance of others views, and leadership qualities.

The personal interview which is subsequently conducted by the Global Head is chiefly for salary negotiations, finalizing location preferences, and so on followed by release of the appointment letter.

Questions

1. Comment on the selection process adopted by the company.
2. Why are application forms important?
3. What is the basic objective of the preliminary interview?
4. What should be the size of a group for final selection?
5. What is the significance of final personal interview?

Solutions

1. The selection process adopted by the company is systematic and integrated with standard procedures and unbiased methods of soliciting information about the potential employees.
2. Application forms describe the eligibility of the candidate to the fitment of role, and hence they are important.
3. The basic objective of the preliminary interview is to make certain whether candidate's past experience possesses validity to the current profile he is interviewed for. Preliminary interview is also a filtration technique to remove candidate's profiles which do not match to the current job roles and responsibilities and is a mechanism to optimize on the cost and time of any HR unit of an organization.
4. For the final selection, the size of the group should be limited to about six to seven applications for a senior manager's role.
5. Personal interview is basically a one-on-one with a management professional to round up the final process of appointment by finalizing on the support aspects of the job profile allocated and to ensure his/her readiness for the same.

Meaning

Like planning, organizing, directing, and controlling, staffing is one of the essential managerial functions. Staffing deals with manning the organization structure by selecting efficient individuals and training them to perform the assigned tasks in the best possible ways.

Definitions

Staffing involves the proper and effective selection, appraisal and development of personnel to fulfill the roles designed into a Dale organizational structure keeping the job filled with the right people is the staffing phase of the management job.

Koontz and O'Donnell

Staffing is concerned with the placement, growth, development of all those members of the organization whose function is to get things done through the efforts of other individuals.

Haimann

Staffing is the whole personnel function of bringing in and training the staff and maintaining favorable conditions of work.

Luther Gidick

Nature of Staffing Function

A Significant Managerial Function

Staffing is one of the essential managerial functions. Staffing is a managerial function that provides the required manpower to carry out the other managerial functions like planning, organizing, directing, and controlling.

Pervasive Activity

The staffing function is said to be a pervasive activity since it is carried out by the managers of all the business concerns whether big or small and profitable or non-profitable.

Continuous Activity

Staffing is considered to be an ongoing process as it continues throughout the lifespan of the organization. This is because staffing deals with selection as well as transfers and promotions.

Efficient Management of Human Resources

Staffing consists of procedures like recruitment, selection, orientation and placement, training and development, and remuneration of employees. If all these procedures are managed in a proper manner, it helps in an efficient management of HR.

Right People at the Right Place at the Right Time

Every organization requires people with different qualifications, skills, and competencies to handle different positions in the organization. This can be done by following proper staffing practices so that the organization structure can be filled with right kind of people and at right time.

Process of Staffing

Manpower Requirements

The process of staffing starts with determining the manpower required to run the organization smoothly. Once the requirement is identified, the next step is to match the requirements and supply. It not only deals with the current manpower requirement but also future requirements (Figure 5.1).

Recruitment

After analysing the manpower requirement, the next step is to invite applications for various positions as per the requirement. Based on the requirements, invitations are sent to the prospects whose profile matches the requirement.

Figure 5.1 Process of Staffing

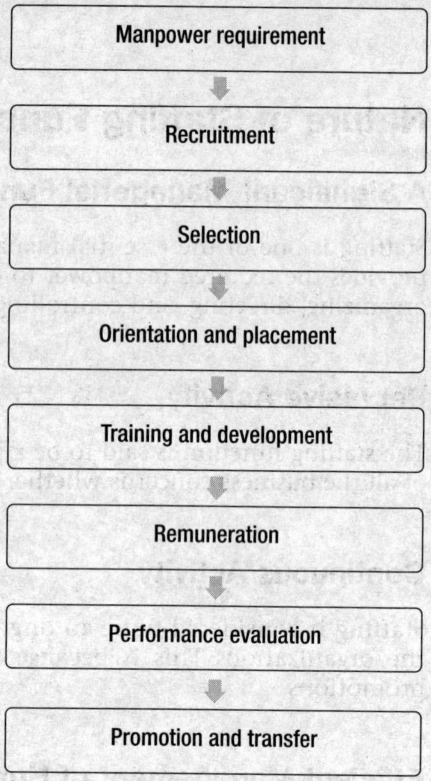

Selection

This is basically the screening phase in the staffing process wherein the solicited applications are screened out and suitable candidates are appointed as per the requirements.

Orientation and Placement

After the selection is done, the candidates are introduced to the various departments and work environment through the orientation programme. According to the suitability, the employees are then placed in the appropriate departments.

Training and Development

Keeping in mind that training the employees helps them perform better as well as motivates the employees, the organization arranges for various training programmes.

Remuneration

It is a kind of compensation provided in terms of money to the employees for the work done. Remuneration to be given is decided on the basis of nature of job, that is, skilled, semi-skilled, or unskilled, physical or intellectual, and so on.

Performance Evaluation

Staffing function also deals with monitoring the performance of the employees so as to keep a track of their dedication and efficiency shown in the assigned jobs. The outputs of performance evaluation play key role in deciding promotions, training needs, and remuneration of employees.

Promotion and Transfer

Promotion is a non-monetary incentive in which the employee moves up in the organizational hierarchy. Transfers deal with moving an employee from one unit or department to another.

CASE STUDY—HR STAFFING

Company Profile

XYZ Incorporation is the largest wholesale distributor of construction and waterproofing materials and grill for doors and windows. Since they started in year 2000, XYX has grown to become a national organization with more than 38 branches across 12 states, ₹20 million in sales, and over 2,000 employees working across the nation.

Business Situation

XYZ's immediate requirement was contractual workforce on an immediate basis to meet their staffing demands for a new project in the subunit of the Ahmedabad branch. These positions included warehouse supervisor, general labourers, clerical staff, purchasing and accounting and material maintenance staff, and some chemical engineers for their dyeing and waterproofing unit. The recruitment of staff had to be done in two weeks, and numbers of resources required were 45 in totality.

Solution

The HR department of XYZ started with analysing the resource requirements in which their main objective was to ensure that while recruiting in bulk, they were not compromising on resource quality. Since there were different job profiles for which resources had to be acquired, they had to carefully lay down a resource-acquisition plan constituting of the time, budget, and process to be carried out for recruiting the resources. So the HR department posted advertisement on prominent Indian job hotspot sites and invited applications from eligible candidates.

They received around 1,700 applications and had to go through a strenuous task of candidate filtration on the basis of resumes. After that process, they set up an interview date, and along with Vice President-HR and Vice President-Sales, the HR team conducted 530 interviews in seven days' time, with each interview spanning 10 minutes on an average using appropriate rating scales.

The day after the interview, the selected 60 candidates were called and scheduled for the job-specific testing, reference and background checks, and medical examination so that offers for a job could be made. Of the 60 candidates, 5 failed medical checks, 10 candidates sent a regret notification, and 8 candidates said that they did not prefer Ahmedabad as their job site. So, to fill the remaining eight positions, the HR department then contacted in-house employees from the database, and used employee referrals, word of mouth, and a walk-in to XYZ, from which they recruited the ones who culturally fit the organization.

The Results

The HR department of XYZ Incorporation within a span was able to recruit a total of 45 employees during this very challenging time. It was not only the count of contractual workforce but also the quality that they were able to deliver with 10% of new inductees working for additional 20 hours per week. The project went on for about a year until the production slowed down, and approximately eight candidates were hired on a permanent role by the company depending on their substantial contribution and performance which was rated with the critical incident method.

HR Planning

HR planning is also called manpower planning. This basically deals with putting right number and right kind of people at the right place and at a right time. HR planning consists of the steps discussed further (Figure 5.2).

Analysing the Existing Manpower Inventory

Prior to making a forecast for future manpower requirements, it is essential for the manager to know the current status of manpower available within the organization. This generally depends on factors like nature of work carried out in the organization, work complexity, size of the organization, number of departments, and so on.

Figure 5.2 Steps in HR Planning

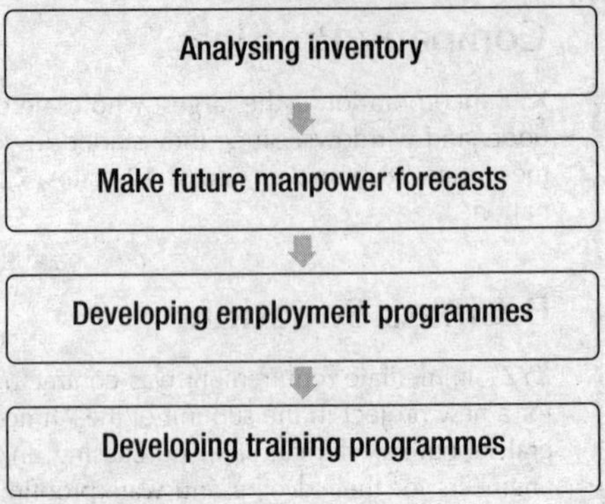

Making Future Manpower Forecasts

Once the current manpower inventory is analysed and the factors affecting requirement are studied, the next step is making future manpower forecasts. Various techniques are used for this purpose like workforce analysis, trend analysis, expert forecasts, work load analysis, and so on.

Developing Employment Programmes

Various employment programmes like recruitment, selection, and placement procedures have to be designed and developed after comparing the current HR inventory and the future requirements.

Developing Training Programmes

After selecting the suitable candidates and placing them in the appropriate departments, the next phase is to develop training so that the employees can carry out their work in more efficient manner.

Recruitment

> *Recruitment is the process of searching the candidates for employment and stimulating them to apply for jobs in the organisation.*
>
> Edwin B. Flippo

Some of the definitions of recruitment are as mentioned below:

- Recruitment is a continuous process whereby the firm attempts to develop a pool of qualified applicants for the future HR needs even though specific vacancies do not exist. Usually, the recruitment process starts when a manger initiates an employee requisition for a specific vacancy or an anticipated vacancy.
- A process of finding and attracting capable applicants for employment. The process begins when new recruits are sought and ends when their applications are submitted. The result is a pool of applications from which new employees are selected.
- Recruitment of candidates is the function preceding the selection, which helps create a pool of prospective employees for the organization so that the management can select the right candidate for the right job from this pool. The main objective of the recruitment process is to expedite the selection process.

- It is the process to discover sources of manpower to meet the requirement of staffing schedule and to employ effective measures for attracting that manpower in adequate numbers to facilitate effective selection of an efficient working force.

Process of Recruitment

The process of recruitment has been shown in Figure 5.3.

Recruitment Planning

The first step is to devise a recruitment plan which consists of drafting the description of the job for open positions and includes the responsibilities to be undertaken, the skills, experience and qualifications needed and the compensation and benefits for that role, the bond/the probation period, location where an individual has to serve, and so on.

Recruitment Strategy Formulation

The strategy for any recruitment to be done can be internal or external to the organization, which means that first the talent pool within the organization can be considered through promotions, retirements, departmental transfers, and so on. If the requirements are not met or are based on very specific terms and conditions, then candidates external to the organization can be hired. The strategy might consist of telephonic interviews, face-to-face interviews with practice managers/heads, HR managers/heads, and so on after advertising for positions through electronic media. Other extensive methods that can be a part of the selection process under recruitment strategy include resume screening, conducting written tests, technical interviews, group discussions, providing letter of intent, getting candidate's acceptance and medical examination, and making a final offer.

Figure 5.3 Process of Recruitment

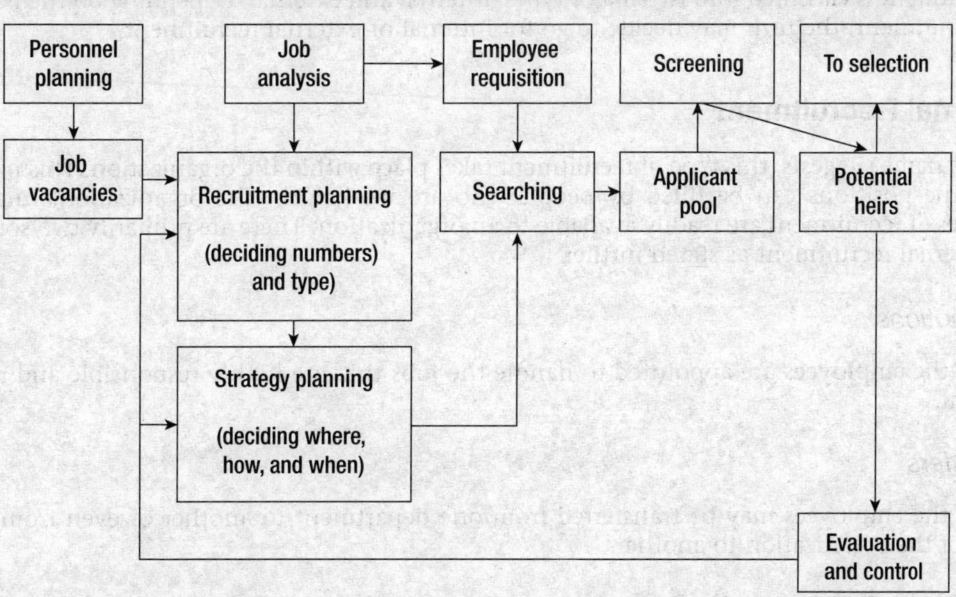

Source Identification

This step involves understanding which source to focus on while looking for the right candidate/candidates. There are basically two sources as stated below:

- Internal sources
- External sources

Candidate Screening

An integral part of the recruitment process is screening of the prospective employee based on qualification, technical, and domain-specific knowledge, years of experience, and so on based on the job specifications. The screening of the prospective employees' resumes is done after the initial process of placing advertisements and inviting resumes from applicants is over.

The techniques used for screening candidates depend on the source of supply and method used for recruiting, which consist of resume filtration, first-level screening of the candidate through deselection test, or interview round.

Recruitment Process Control and Evaluation

Since recruitment process is associated with a cost, its evaluation is mandatory, and the cost of the recruitment process revolves around

- compensation of the recruiters.
- cost in terms of giving advertisements for the job after preparing a job description.
- administrative expenses.
- cost of recruiting personnel through third-party sources.
- cost incurred in improper selection.

Types of Recruitment

Recruitment is classified into two major types: internal and external. Depending on the nature of recruitment, the firm may decide to go for internal or external recruitment.

Internal Recruitment

As the name suggests, this type of recruitment takes place within the organization. This means that the positions can be filled by people who are working in the organization. Internal sources of recruitment are readily available to an organization. There are primarily two sources of internal recruitment as stated further.

Promotions

Here, the employees are appointed to handle the jobs that are highly responsible and more crucial.

Transfers

Here, the employees may be transferred from one department to another or even from one unit of the organization to another.

Internal recruitment proves to be advantageous as it acts as a motivation factor since the employees can get better opportunities within the organization itself. Also, it saves both time and money of the organization. But a drawback of internal recruitment is that it provides a smaller base for selection of suitable candidates.

External Recruitment

External sources of recruitment are those which are external to the organization. This method proves to be beneficial since the organizations can choose suitable candidates from a large base of prospects. But it is time consuming, and organizations have to spend out a lot of money. The external sources of recruitment include advertisements, employment exchanges, employment agencies, educational institutes, labour contractors, recommendations, and so on.

Selection

It is the process of putting right persons on right job. It deals with satisfying the HR requirements of the organization with suitable qualifications and skills of prospects. The success of organization is largely affected by the selection of most suitable candidate for the required job. It may also play a major role in reduction of issues like employee turnover rate and absenteeism. An effective selection procedure helps to identify the potential candidates from the available pool and saves both money and time of the organization (Figure 5.4).

Some of the common steps involved in the selection process are as mentioned below.

Application Forms

Candidates clearing the preliminary interviews are required to fill in the application form. An application form is a document that enables the organization to collect data related to the qualification, experience, skills, personal details, and so on, about the candidates.

Preliminary Interviews

These are designed to verify the eligibility of candidates. The candidates who do not meet the basic eligibility criteria are eliminated after the preliminary interview round. It also includes examining the educational and family background, hobbies and interests, skills, and competencies and checks the candidate's knowledge about the company.

Written Tests

Written tests may or may not be conducted depending on the vacancies being filled. These are generally framed to test the candidate's aptitude, intelligence, reasoning ability, emotional quotient, personality, and so on.

Employment Interviews

These basically involve one-to-one interaction between the interviewer and the potential candidate. During this interview, the candidates undergo a series of questions put forth by the interviewer. These questions test the knowledge, skills, and competencies of the prospects. Some of the important aspects like salary, duties, and responsibilities are also discussed during these interviews.

Figure 5.4 Process of Selection

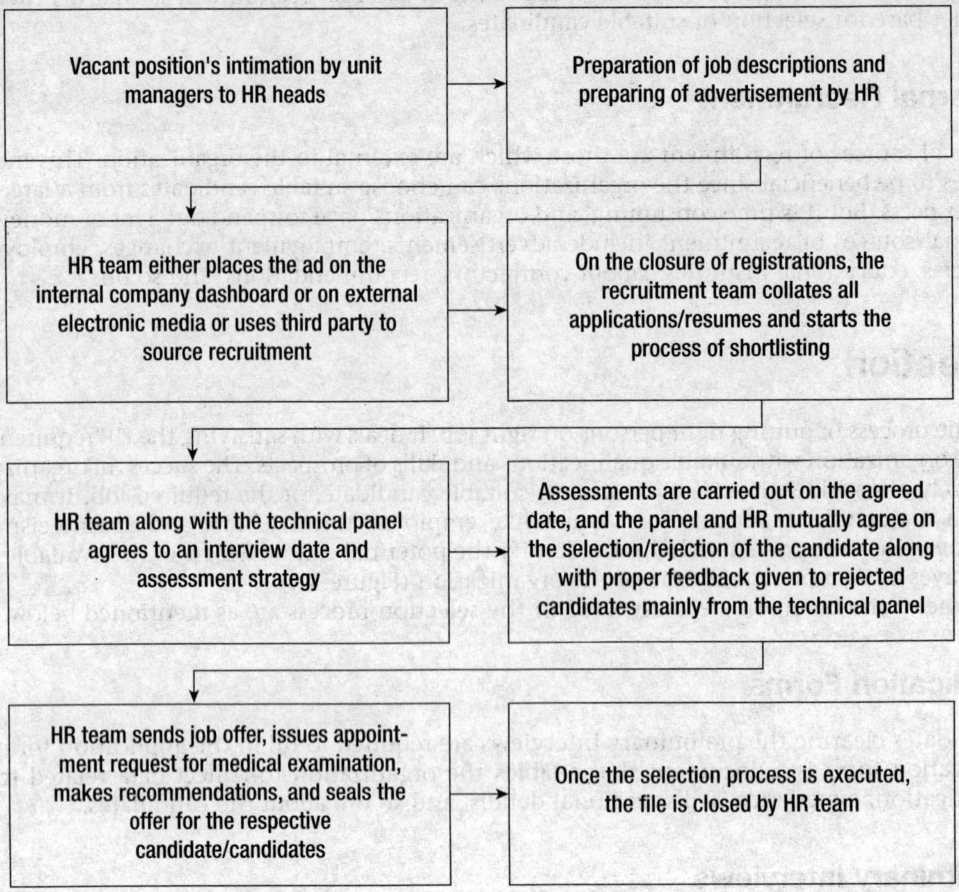

Medical Examination

Since employing unfit people can put the organization in problem, most of the organizations opt for conducting medical examination before actual employment.

Appointment Letter

Final appointment letters are issued to the candidates after making the referral checks. The organization may perform verification on its own or appoint a third party for the same.

Selection Versus Recruitment

The points of differentiation between recruitment and selection are as mentioned below:

- Recruitment aims at searching the candidates for employment and encouraging them to apply against vacancies in the organization. Selection is the process that involves a series of steps through which the candidates are screened so that suitable candidates can be appointed against the vacancies.

- Recruitment is the process that enables creation of the talent pool to facilitate the process of selection of best candidates by motivating more and more prospects to apply for job. Selection involves choosing the right candidates to fill various vacant positions in the organization.
- Recruitment is a simple process, whereas selection is complex.
- Recruitment involves a positive approach, whereas selection involves a negative approach.
- Recruitment is concerned with identifying the sources of HR, and selection is concerned with putting the candidates through various tests and interviews.
- Recruitment involves less time and money as compared to selection.

Orientation and Placement

Once the candidates are selected, the next step is to ensure that the selected candidates have to be fitted in the right positions based on their skills and qualifications. This is called placement. Proper placement of candidates is an essential and tough task, since it can decide the success or failure of the organization in the long run. In other words, if a less-competent person is placed to handle more complex job, he will not be able to perform well, and on the other hand, if a more competent person is placed to handle a less-responsible job, he may feel underemployed and quit the job. In both the situations, the organization would suffer since a less-competent person might not be able to make proper decisions and the organization also might lose out in terms of money, paying heavy salary, and in the second situation, the employee might quit the job and organization would lose out a competent employee. After placing these candidates in the appropriate positions, the next task is to make them aware about the duties they have to perform. This is usually done by arranging an orientation programme for the newly appointed candidates. The general layout of an orientation programme consists of introducing the employees to the following:

- Company's mission
- Company's vision
- Company's goals
- Departmental goals
- Operations of the organization
- Organizational structure
- Rules and regulations
- Code of conduct

An effective orientation programme can facilitate in creating a healthy relation between the newly appointed employees and the organization. It can also facilitate in developing confidence and trust among the new employees so that more productive results can be reaped.

The importance of conducting an orientation programme is well understood, and today, every organization whether big or small conducts an orientation programme that may be in a formal or an informal way.

Training

The organized procedure by which people learn knowledge and skill for a definite purpose.

Dale S. Beach

Training is the act of increasing the knowledge and skill of an employee for doing a particular job.

Edwin B. Flippo

Once the employees are informed about the duties they have to perform, the next step is to train them to do their jobs in the best possible manner. Training is not a one-time process as it goes on throughout the entire employee life cycle. Training is imparted to both the new and experienced employees. Training is the process by which the organization tries to enhance the skills, capabilities, and knowledge of the employees so that the organizational goals can be achieved with ease and efficiency.

Importance of Training

Improved Morale of Employees

Training enables the employees to perform their work in a better manner that leads to higher confidence, job satisfaction, job security, and pay hike, and all these factors lead to improved morale and positive attitude towards the organization.

Increased Productivity

Training increases the skills and knowledge of the employees and facilitates efficient performance leading to higher productivity.

Reduced Employee Turnover and Absenteeism

Training helps the employees to improve their performance and increases the chances of growth within the organization. Acting as a motivating factor, it in turn leads to lower employee turnover and absenteeism.

Less Supervision

If the employees are well trained in the assigned jobs, they can perform efficiently and require very little supervision, saving both time and money.

Lower Accident Rate

A trained employee is aware about the job and safety measures to be taken while performing the particular task, which leads to lesser accidents.

Cost Reduction

A trained employee knows how to perform the task efficiently with least wastage of resources, which helps in reducing operational cost.

Training Types

Trainings imparted in the organization are basically of two types: on-the-job and off-the-job trainings.

On-the-job training comprises coaching, mentoring, or changing job role and responsibility at specific durations, apprenticeship, job instruction technology, or understudy. Off-the-job trainings comprise lectures and tutorials, conferences, simulation studies, T-group and transactional training, and training through prototypes.

On-the-job Training Methods

On-the-job trainings comprise hands-on training under the supervision of peers or managers performing the job and trying to reproduce their way of task execution. These methods are less costly and possess more certainty since the trainee gets a hands-on experience of the similar environment. Some of the commonly used methods are as follows:

Tutoring

Coaching is a training given to an individual in which weaknesses are identified instantly and offers the benefit of practice-based learning. In India, most of the automobile mechanics/ carpenters/masons are coached through this method.

Mentoring

Mentoring is focussed on the development of attitude. It is used for lower and middle-management employees where a senior employee within the organization works as a mentor.

Allocation of Different Job Roles

Allocating different job roles to employees where skill and experience of an employee are aligned to the particular job is a way of imparting training to an employee and also to remove redundancy from delivering.

Job Instructional Technique (JIT)

It is a stepwise sequence of instructional delivery where a trainee has an overview of the job, its purpose, and the targets to be achieved. The trainer then demonstrates the task to the trainee and allows the trainee to show the demonstration back, upon which a feedback is given by the trainer to the trainee. Training material is provided to the trainee, and such types of trainings give a discreet reporting of the trainee's learnability aspect.

Apprenticeship/Internship

Apprenticeship is a method of training which is in vogue in trades, crafts, and technical fields, which requires a long tenure to achieve the desired expertise and supervision of experts. These trainings are expensive, and objective of trainings includes making craftsmen of high calibre.

Understudy

This type of training involves a film director–assistant relationship where the assistant learns through experience and observation by actively participating in the day-to-day schedule of his senior. Later, the assistant assumes the full responsibilities and duties.

Off-the-job Training Methods

Off-the-job training methods include extensive learning and not performing at the shop floor workshop during training. These methods are not practice based. The off-the-job training types are as discussed below.

Lectures and Instructional Delivery

Training mostly in academic institutions is in the form of lectures. The trainers in this case should try to create interest amongst the students. The trainer should possess considerable depth of knowledge in order to effectively train the students through lectures and seminars.

Training Using Prototypes (Vestibules)

In this type of training, trainees are trained on the prototype or simulated version of the product or service, and other working conditions are similar to the actual workshop conditions. An example can be taken of the Second World War, where soldiers/workers were trained in a very small time using this approach, and since trainees work on prototypes, it remains very cost effective because original systems (work condition of cabin crew airliner) are not used.

Mock/Simulation Trainings

Trainings imparted consist of learning through management games, case study sessions, role-plays, and learning through memos, reports, SMS, and so on.

Management Games

This type of training encourages critical thinking; enhances analytical, logical, and reasoning capabilities, time management, and team collaboration; and enriches communication and leadership capabilities and sometimes is very effective for managing stress. They tend to be application based and can also be used for training the top management of an organization.

Case Study Sessions

Case studies depict various problem scenarios and call for handling these scenarios by applying theory to practice using the candidate's logical and analytical abilities.

Through this concept, people are trained to work in groups, communicate, and collaborate to generate ideas.

Role Enactment

The trainings imparted to the trainees through role-plays focus on multiple choices to do a particular task and encourage the trainees to pick up one of the best ways to do them. For example, those who are into people management and administration have multiple ways of motivating their team and keeping them productive but come across situations which require careful handling when they play the role of a manager or an administrator.

The steps involved in role-playing include defining objectives, choosing context and roles, introducing the exercise, trainee preparation/research, the role-play, concluding discussion, and assessment.

In-basket Training

Here, the trainer provides instructional material as whitepapers and reports to trainees to gain knowledge from and for a particular task.

T-group Training

Sensitivity training is also known as laboratory or T-group training. This training increases tolerance level in people for themselves as well as others and also looks at situations from others perspectives by developing employee's social sensitivity and behavioural flexibility.

It reveals information about commonality in behaviour amongst the members of the group and helps him/her to react suitably to a situation. A group's trainer refrains from acting as a

Figure 5.5 Steps in Sensitivity Training

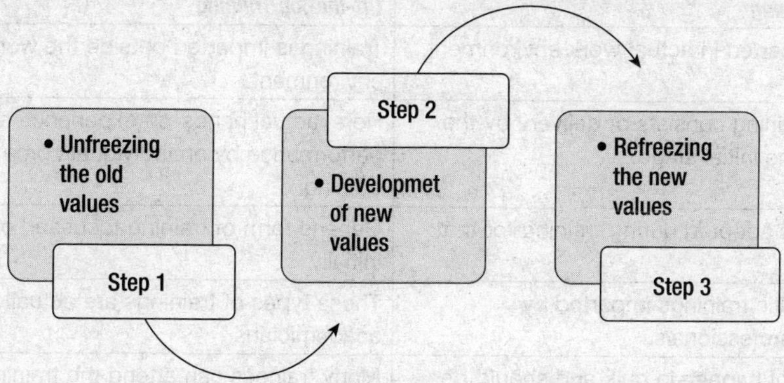

group leader, attempting instead to make precise the group processes using events or situations to clarify general points or provide feedback. For example in Crosby's Organization Development career, he has used T groups in numerous business culture change and performance improvement initiatives, most famously during the Philadelphia Electric Company (PECO) Nuclear turnaround following the shutdown of Peach Bottom Atomic Power Station for human performance issues by the Nuclear Regulatory Commission in 1987.

The sensitivity training programme comprises three steps (see Figure 5.5).

Transactional Analysis

It provides trainees with the guidelines for analysing and understanding the behaviour of other team members. In social dealings, motivation is provided by an entity and received and reacted upon by another which is otherwise known as transaction.

Transactional analysis can be interpreted by considering the ego states of every individual, whether a child, parent, or adult (Figure 5.6).

Figure 5.6 Ego States

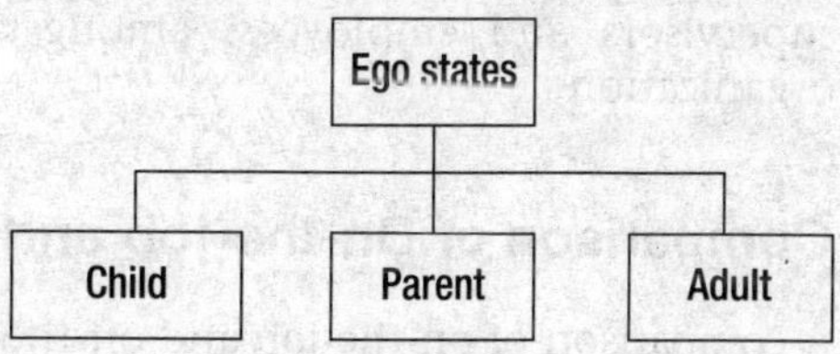

Child

While dealing with transactional analysis, one has to deal with child ego states which consist of behaviour that comes naturally to an individual which evokes spontaneity, intensity, and anxiety. While communicating verbatim, words such as 'I suppose' are more pronounced, nonverbal communications consist of giggling, shyness, seeking attention, and so on.

Parent

It is a collection of recordings in the brain of an individual instilled during their years as a child and emanates the characteristics of overprotectiveness, secluded, constrained, and bossy. Parent ego state comprises verbal clues with the use of words like 'always', 'should', and 'never' and non-verbal clues such as raising eyebrows and so on.

Adult

This ego state comprises more of decision-making, rationality in thought, and testing out the knowledge and concepts already learnt. An individual in this ego state tests the learning derived from the child and parent ego states.

Table 5.1 On-the-job Versus Off-the-job Training

On-the-job Training	*Off-the-job Training*
Training is imparted in actual work environment.	Training is imparted outside the work environment.
On-the-job training consists of delivery by the trainee from the initial stage.	Here, actual hands-on experience and performance by an individual come after the training.
Best practices adopted during training for that specific job.	Generic form of training focussed on learning initially.
Industry-specific trainings imparted by experienced professionals.	These types of trainings are actually imparted by academicians.
Training cannot happen in bulk and should be carefully monitored if anticipated as hazardous.	Many trainees can attend the trainings, and it does not involve risks
These trainings are cost effective since they happen in the real set-up.	Trainings require hiring of set-up, infrastructure, and experts as well.
Imparted mostly in manufacturing and production sectors where trainees are made hands-on experts through job rotations and practice-based learning.	Imparted at training institutions and schools and consists of simulation exercises.

All of us show behaviour from one ego state which is responded to by the other person from any of these three states. During training individuals of both on-the-job and off-the-job modes, the trainer and the trainee exude different ego states during these knowledge exchange programmes. In the workplace, examples of transactional analysis can be between supervisors and employees, amongst team members, and between unit heads of an organization.

Comparison of On-the-job and Off-the-job Training

A comparison of on-the-job and off-the-job trainings has been shown in Table 5.1.

Performance Management and Evaluation

Performance management is an ongoing process of accomplishing organizational goals by the employee, his subordinate as well as his supervisor with supporting activities, such as setting targets, providing feedback, and reviewing results. An effective performance management process is the alignment of employee's efforts to the organizational goals and is achieved by the following:

- Setting performance expectations, thereby resulting in successful completion of the job.
- Eliminating the redundant efforts taken for a particular job through the use of standard procedures and policies.
- Encouraging meetings and discussions which include project or work status reporting, providing reviews and feedback on the work done, and using alternate methods if current strategy does not meet the expectations.

- Ensuring that performance management is an ongoing process rather than being a onetime event and summarizes the output of the entire dialogue and discourse between the team members and managers, which if effective leads to success.

Performance Appraisal Methods

Performance appraisal methods consist of methods specific to organizations based on their working culture, the work they do, the objectives and goals they have set, and so on. The methods comprise broadly of two types:

- Past-oriented methods
- Future-oriented methods

Past-oriented Methods

Rating Scales

They help in rating an individual based on responsibility, ownership, innovative aspect, attitude, attendance, and so on across scale as low as poor to excellent after which summation of the scores helps in understanding the individuals performance. Advantages of this method are the following: it is cost effective, reliable, ease of use, and every type of job and employee can be evaluated using this evaluation scale. The disadvantage of the same method is its human biasness.

Checklist

Performance-based questions are posed for which a yes or no is required and is sent by the manager to the HR, who then does the evaluation of employees' performance. The advantages of this method are that it is standardized, easy to use, and economical. The disadvantages of the same are its human biasness, usage of improper weights and scales, and it disallows an HR to give relative scores.

Forced-choice Method

The sequence of statements for an employee with respect to his performance forces the rater to rate it as true/false, and the HR department does actual evaluation. An Advantage of this method is that it eliminates personal bias because of force, and a disadvantage is that statements can be wrongly framed for employee evaluation. For example, a manager is asked whether an employee comes early, works late, is ready to work in team, and has leadership capabilities.

Forced-distribution Method

In this method, employees are clustered around a high point on a rating scale where the manager is forced to follow normal distribution of performance of all his employees. An advantage of this method is that it is based on a mathematic framework, whereas a disadvantage is that it does not consider the mean error rates.

Critical Incidents Method

The approach identifies the critical behaviour that acts as a differentiator in evaluating a performance of an employee wherein managers record such events and report to the HR team. An advantage of this method is that actual employee behaviour is predicted during job. A disadvantage of the method is that appropriate events specific to jobs might not get reported, and this method might result in very close monitoring of the subordinate by his manager. For example, an employee was badly abused by his senior, causing resignation tendered immediately by the employee

Behaviourally Anchored Rating Scales

These are determined by statements of an effective and ineffective behaviour. The employee performance is accounted for by his behaviour and is to be stated by the evaluator. A positive impact is that it helps in solving rating errors efficiently, and a major drawback is that it suffers from falsifications present in most rating techniques. For example, a rating of four may coax medical practitioners to show sympathy to patients, while a rating of six may require practitioners to show higher levels of sympathy across all dealings with the patient.

Field Assessment Method

This method requires an appraisal done by the HR team. An advantage of this method is chance of less bias, useful for management-level promotions, when there are quite a few employees to be appraised for the same position and where comparative assessment is required, but the disadvantage is rating is done by a personnel or group external to the department where actual observation is not possible.

Performance Assessment through Tests

The tests might be written or verbal and should be apt to rate an employee on the basis of his knowledge and skills. An advantage of the method is that knowledge of an employee is thoroughly tested, but on job performance, testing cannot be done using this scheme.

Personal Records

This performance evaluation technique is used mostly by the government where parameters, such as collaboration, leadership capability, attendance, technical, and analytical and logical abilities, are considered along with attitude and expression for work. The method is highly confidential, and feedback is reported back to the individual in case of some adverse issues. The method though confidential can inculcate highly manipulated ratings as evaluations result in promotions.

Descriptive Method

In this method, the evaluator writes descriptive text constituting of employee's capabilities, strengths, and weaknesses related to his job, the need for mentoring/counselling, and his overall performance. An advantage of this method is that it connects the dots when information on performance shows discontinuity, but the disadvantage is that it is dependent upon the assessors' writing skills.

Return on Investment Method

Here, performance is evaluated from the monetary yields a candidate makes to his organization in comparison to the cost incurred by the company in keeping the individual as their employee.

Comparative Assessment Method

Here, comparison is done with the co-workers, and it consists of the two methods discussed below.

Ranking Methods

A manager ranks his employees from best to worst on the basis of merit. It is relatively easy to implement this method as it does not describe the reason for crediting the employee as best or worst.

Paired Comparison Method

The paired comparison method from Chapter 7 (Decision-making) can be referred to for obtaining a better idea on how performance of an individual can be deduced using this method.

Future-oriented Methods

Management by Objectives

It means that employees' performance should align to the objectives set by the management. MBO process is as follows:

- Establish goals and set performance standards.
- Set expectations from employees based on the above goals.
- Comparison between planned goals and actuals achieved.
- Set new goals or unachieved goals for the next business year.

An advantage of this method is its alignment to managerial position but is not applicable to all jobs. A disadvantage is that employees might fail to view long-term goals if performance is rewarded on the basis of merit pays. For example, the sales head might set the target of increase in sales by 15% over the course of a year. Such goals and objectives adhere to the performance of the organization as well as the individual.

Psychological Appraisals

These appraisals are based on extensive interviews and tests and focus on employees' responsive, rational, motivational, and other personal characteristics affecting his performance. This approach is unhurried and costly and may be useful for talented individuals on whom the psychological tests are performed.

Evaluation Centres

Using this technique first developed in the United States and United Kingdom, assesses are requested to participate in in-basket exercises, work groups, computer simulations, role-playing to measure their performance in relation to their assertiveness, innovativeness, communicating ability, planning and organizational ability, self-confidence, stress handling and enthusiasm level, energy level, decision-making, administrative ability, mental alertness, and so on. An advantage of this is that if assessment centres are rated high, then there is a strong chance that they can provide better forecasts of employees' future performance and can ensure no wrong hiring is done. A disadvantage includes that it is costly and employees might not be comfortable with outside agency assessing them.

360-Degree Feedback

This technique is used by the modern-day industry and is a mechanism where an assessee is evaluated by his peer subordinate, boss, supplier, or customer and is rated on communication, collaboration, customer handling, and so on. An advantage of this is that feedback comes from all ends, but a disadvantage is that feedback from all ends can be at times intimidating when the assessor is not aware of the reporting norms.

Compensation Management

It is a method of providing fiscal and non-fiscal aids to employees, which include payments, such as performance bonus, profit sharing through stock and equity, overtime pay, recognition rewards, and commission. They can also be non-fiscal, such as accommodation and transportation options with an underlying objective of motivating employees.

Benefits of Compensation Management

A good compensation scheme is essential for every business organization as shown below:

- Return on employees' contribution.
- Motivates employees to perform better and achieve standards.
- Retains workforce for a longer time span and keeps them satisfied.
- Helps to achieve realistic standards since compensation encourages employees to perform.
- Less dispute amongst management and employee union as it complies with labour acts.
- Promotes the morale and efficiency of employees and also provides growth opportunities to them.

Types of Compensation

- **Direct compensation:** It comprises salary, pay scales for different roles and responsibilities, and also health benefits. Direct compensation is at par with industry standards, and employer does not have to fear about losing his staff.
- **Indirect compensation:** It includes administering staff development courses to employees, inter-departmental transfers, promotions, preferred location changes, public recognition, flexibility in work schedules such as work-from-home concept and so on.

Components of Compensation

- **Wages and salary:** Wages are hourly rates of pay, and salary is the monthly rate of pay which is annually incremented. Salary has a basic pay component in it.
- **Allowances:** In addition to basic pay, there are following components in the salary:
  - **Dearness allowance:** It is paid as a percentage of basic pay to protect income from inflations.
  - **House rent allowance:** Employers who do not provide living accommodation pay house rent allowance to employees. This allowance is calculated as a percentage of basic pay.
  - **City compensation allowance:** City compensatory allowance is generally a fixed amount per month which differentiates a metro city from a normal city where cost of living is low and sums to 30% of basic pay as per the Indian government rule.
  - **Transport allowance/conveyance allowance:** Industries pay a fixed sum as transport allowance/conveyance allowance to the employees.
- **Incentives:** This is a performance-linked pay to inspire employees to put in more efforts. Bonus, profit sharing, commissions are some examples of incentive compensation which is paid to an individual or to a group.
- **Fringe benefits/perquisites:** These include employee benefits, such as provident fund, gratuity, medical care, hospitalization, accident insurance, health and group insurance, mess facilities, uniform, entertainment, and so on.

Conclusion

In recent years, the compensation systems have gone beyond just money. There has been a considerable increase in the use of performance-linked pay for management professionals, especially for executive management and senior managers. To sustain creativity amongst individuals, rewards and compensations help in a great way by attracting quality workforce, rendering employee satisfaction, ensuring high degree of retention, and motivating employees for higher productivity.

Global Perspectives on Employee Staffing

Many perspectives on staffing have come up in recent times with companies operating across global boundaries and adopting the best practices in staffing. Some of the terminologies and practices adopted by organizations of international stature comprise categorization of employees on an international platform. They are as follows:

Expatriate: He/she is a person working in a foreign country for a company whose headquarter is in the country of which he is a citizen. For example, Ramesh works in Singapore for a company which is head quartered in India of which he is a citizen.

Host country national: Rhenae working in the same company as Ramesh's secretary is a Singapore citizen based in Singapore.

Third country national: Tudor, a citizen of France, is working in the same company in which Ramesh works in Singapore and the company is headquartered in India, then he will be regarded as a third country national.

There are some global staffing norms as well which are as discussed below.

Ethnocentric Staffing

This practice involves staffing the senior-level positions with expatriates who are often believed to look after the offices in foreign shores for better alignment with home headquarters. Ethnocentric staffing reduces communication barrier by reducing language and culture barrier because the positions are held mostly by people of same nationality in the foreign offices.

The disadvantage of this is that the company may lose out on gaining a perspective from the point of view of the locals in the country of operations. There may also be high expenses incurred because expatriates tend to be costly than locals, and also more number of expatriates may create local resentment at foreign subsidiaries.

Polycentric Staffing

In polycentric staffing, a company hires nationals of only developed countries, such as European countries, Canada, Australia, and Japan, where more number of trained resources are available.

The advantages of this are that the company gets a clear view of local market conditions, politics, laws and culture, and the country, and customers get assured of company's commitment to them. Also, relocation expenses and compensation are minimized.

A disadvantage is that chances are that company's broader goals and objectives might get suppressed in front of the local interests.

Regiocentric Staffing

Regiocentric staffing is the staffing practice where company offices and facilities are grouped into regions and work as a single unit with autonomous status from the home headquarters. These regions have their own HR policies, and there is regional transfer for employees.

The advantage is that since they have autonomy, they are free to set their own objectives and goals, and a disadvantage is that being regiocentric does not enable the company to envisage a bigger picture, and many a times, it can so happen that the goals and objectives of the company get shrouded by regiocentric goals and objectives.

Summary

The chapter takes a reader through staffing, its concepts strategies, and benefits, and elaborates on HR plan, the aspects of recruitment and training, the training types, the performance evaluation process, the compensation benefit plan, the employee remuneration process along with the global perspectives on staffing.

Exercise

Objective Questions

1. The staffing function is said to be a ________ activity.
    - Persuasive
    - Continuous
    - None of the above
    - All of the above
2. Which of these is the process of putting right persons on right job?
    - Internal recruitment
    - External recruitment
    - Selection
    - Placement
3. Off-the-job training is imparted outside the work environment.
    - True
    - False
4. Which of these is also called T-group training?
    - Role enactment
    - In-basket training
    - Sensitivity training
    - Simulation trainings
5. Recruitment involves less time and money as compared to selection.
    - True
    - False

6. Mentoring is focused on which of the following?

- Development of attitude
- Tutoring
- JIT
- Understudy

7. Which of these is a method of providing fiscal and non-fiscal aids to employees?

- MBO
- Psychological appraisals
- Compensation management
- None of these

8. Piece rate system is not suitable where the nature of work is repetitive and quantity is emphasized more than quality.

- True
- False

9. Which of these includes employee benefits, such as provident fund, gratuity, medical care, hospitalization, accident insurance, health and group insurance, mess facilities, uniform, entertainment, and so on?

- Wages and salary
- Allowances
- Incentives
- Fringe benefits/perquisites

10. Which of the following is incorrect?

- MBO means that employees' performance should align to the objectives set by the management
- 360-degree feedback is a mechanism where an assessee is evaluated by his peer subordinate, boss, supplier, or customer
- Field assessment method does not require an appraisal done by the HR team
- None of the above

CASE STUDY

Esicizo Technologies manufactures a wide range of hydraulic products. It has a workforce of 2,700, which includes 297 supervisors and executives. Performance appraisal for these supervisors and executives is conducted by their respective superiors yearly. The company has dual rating. Performance appraisal is carried on following factors: goals, collaborative skills, involvement in corporate social responsibility (CSR), team-building skills, dependability on subordinates, sense of responsibility, and potential to take higher positions. All these factors are given an equal weightage.

In the year 2011–2012, some of these supervisors and executives were not given any increment, because they could not match few of the performance appraisal standards like dependability on subordinates and CSR. These supervisors reported their complaint for not getting the increment and claiming that the performance appraisal was faulty. These supervisors were against the CSR activities and dependability on subordinates as part of performance cycle. These factors should not be considered to be a parameter for increments and timely promotions. They had asked for the increment for that year and believed that the system should be more focused in terms of delivering the quality at right time.

(Continued)

(Continued)

Questions

1. As an HR manager, how will you decide the performance appraisal scheme? Would you make changes in the current scheme? If yes, what would be the changes?
2. Should these supervisors and executive be given appraisal?
3. Justify you thought for inclusion of CSR activities and dependability on subordinates as a part of performance appraisal.

Critical Thinking Questions

1. How can you evaluate the effectiveness of training?
2. Comment on whether external sources of recruitment like advertisements, employment exchanges, employment agencies, educational institutes, labour contractors, recommendations, and so on will speed up the recruitment?
3. How will you review your subordinates' performance regularly and provide them feedback about their work?
4. According to you, which is the best among on-the-job and off-the-job trainings?

Chapter at a Glance

Staffing, Training, and Development

Staffing deals with manning the organization structure by selecting efficient individuals and training them to perform the assigned tasks in the best possible ways. Staffing is concerned with the placement, growth, and development of all those members of the organization whose function is to get things done through the efforts of other individuals.

Nature of Staffing Function

A significant managerial function
Pervasive activity
Continuous activity
Efficient management of HR
Right people at the right place at a right time

Process of Staffing

Manpower requirements
Recruitment
Selection
Orientation and placement
Training and development
Remuneration
Performance evaluation
Promotion and transfer

HR Planning

It basically deals with putting right number and right kind of people at the right place and at a right time. It is also called manpower planning. This HR planning consists of the following steps:

Analysing the existing manpower inventory
Making future manpower forecasts
Developing employment programmes
Developing training programmes

Recruitment

Recruitment is the process of searching the candidates for employment and stimulating them to apply for jobs in the organization. It is also defined as a process of finding and attracting capable applicants for employment. The process begins when new recruits are sought and ends when their applications are submitted. The result is a pool of applications from which new employees are selected.

Recruitment Process

Recruitment planning
Recruitment strategy formulation
Source identification
Candidate screening
Recruitment process control and evaluation

Types of Recruitment

Recruitment is classified into two major types: internal and external.

Internal Recruitment: As the name suggests, this type of recruitment takes place within the organization. This means that the positions can be filled by people who are working in the organization. There are primarily two sources of internal recruitment as stated below:

- Promotions
- Transfers

External Recruitment: External sources of recruitment are those which are external to the organization. This method proves to be beneficial since the organizations can choose suitable candidates from a large base of prospects. But it is a time-consuming process, and organizations have to spend out a lot of money. The external sources of recruitment include advertisements, employment exchanges, employment agencies, educational institutes, labour contractors, recommendations, and so on.

Selection

It is the process of putting right persons on right job. It deals with satisfying the HR requirements of the organization with suitable qualifications and skills of prospects.

(Continued)

(Continued)

Effective selection procedure helps to identify the potential candidates from the available pool and saves both money and time of the organization.

Some of the common steps involved in the selection process are as mentioned below:

- Preliminary interviews
- Application forms
- Written tests
- Employment interviews
- Medical examination
- Appointment letter

Selection Versus Recruitment

The points of differentiation between recruitment and selection are as mentioned below:

- Recruitment aims at searching the candidates for employment and encouraging them to apply against vacancies in the organization. Selection is the process that involves a series of steps through which the candidates are screened so that suitable candidates can be appointed against the vacancies.
- Recruitment is the process that enables creation of the talent pool to facilitate the process of selection of best candidates by motivating more and more prospects to apply for job. Selection involves choosing the right candidates to fill various vacant positions in the organization.
- Recruitment is a simple process, whereas selection is complex.
- Recruitment involves a positive approach, whereas selection involves a negative approach.
- Recruitment is concerned with identifying the sources of HR, and selection is concerned with putting the candidates through various tests and interviews.
- Recruitment involves less time and money as compared to selection.

Orientation and Placement

Once the candidates are selected, the next step is to ensure that the selected candidates have to be fitted in the right positions based on their skills and qualifications. This is called placement. The general layout of an orientation programme consists of introducing the employees to the following:

- Company's mission
- Company's vision
- Company's goals
- Departmental goals
- Operations of the organization
- Organizational structure
- Rules and regulations
- Code of conduct

An effective orientation programme can facilitate in creating a healthy relation between the newly appointed employees and the organization. It can also facilitate in developing confidence and trust among the new employees so that more productive results can be reaped.

Training

Training is the act of increasing the knowledge and skill of an employee for doing a particular job. Training is not a one-time process as it goes on throughout the entire employee life cycle. Training is imparted to both the new and experienced employees. Training is the process by which the organization tries to enhance the skills, capabilities, and knowledge of the employees so that the organizational goals can be achieved with ease and efficiency.

Importance of Training

- Improves morale of employees
- Increased productivity
- Reduced employee turnover and absenteeism
- Less supervision
- Lower accident rate
- Cost reduction

Employee Remuneration

Time rate method: Under this method, the remuneration is decided on the basis of time spent by the employee on his job. The amount to be paid to the employee is decided in advance, and it is paid either on hourly, daily, weekly, or monthly basis irrespective of their performance.

Piece rate method: Piece rate system is more suitable where the nature of work is repetitive and quantity is emphasized more than quality. This method of remuneration focuses on the number of units or pieces produced by an employee

Training Types

On-the-job Training Methods

On-the-job training comprises coaching, mentoring, changing job role and responsibility at specific durations, apprenticeship, job instruction technology, or understudy.

The on-the-job training types are as follows:

- Tutoring
- Mentoring
- Allocation of different job roles
- JIT
- Apprenticeship/internship
- Understudy

Off-the-job Training Methods

Off-the-job training methods include extensive learning and not performing in the shop floor or workshop, and it is not practice based.

The off-the-job training types are as follows:

- Lectures and instructional delivery
- Training using prototypes (vestibules)

(Continued)

(Continued)

- Mock/simulation trainings
- Management games
- Case study sessions
- Role enactment
- In-basket training
- T-group training
- Transactional analysis

Performance Management and Evaluation

Performance management is an ongoing process of accomplishing organizational goals by the employee, his subordinate as well as his supervisor with supporting activities, such as setting targets, providing feedback, and reviewing results.

Performance Appraisal Methods

Performance appraisal methods consist of methods specific to organizations based on their working culture, the work they do, the objectives and goals they have set, and so on. The methods are broadly of two types: past-oriented methods and future-oriented methods.

Compensation Management

It is a method of providing fiscal and non-fiscal aids to employees, which include payments, such as performance bonus, profit sharing through stock and equity, overtime pay, recognition rewards, and commission.

Types of Compensations

Direct compensation: It comprises salary, pay scales for different roles and responsibilities, and also health benefits.

Indirect compensation: It includes administering staff development courses to employees, inter-departmental transfers, promotions, preferred location changes, public recognition, flexibility in work schedules such as work-from-home concept and so on.

Components of Compensation

- Wages and salary
- Allowances
- Dearness allowance
- House rent allowance
- City compensation allowance
- Transport allowance/conveyance allowance
- Incentives
- Fringe benefits/perquisites

CHAPTER 6

Directing and Controlling

Learning Objectives

- Knowing the formal concepts on directing and controlling, their characteristics, processes, importance of communication, motivation, supervision, and alignment to organizational goals.
- Understanding why directing and controlling are essential functions of management contributing substantially to growth and productivity of the organization.
- Getting to know the impact of directing and controlling on the HR of the organization and various tradition and modern control techniques used by businesses for increased sustainability in today's world.

An Opening Vignette

Microsoft CEO Satya Nadella's letter to employees which invokes the sense of direction being imparted by the Chief of CEO to his employees. (*TOI Tech*, 26 June 2015)

Direction on Mission, Worldview, Strategy, and Culture

Nadella's belief: Shared mission, clear strategy, and a culture bring the best in employees, individually and collectively.

His direction of shared mission: Mission is to empower every person and every organization on the planet to achieve more. Taking things global and making a difference in lives and organizations in all corners of the planet.

His direction of worldview: Mission should be in synch with the world in which we live and the future we strive to create. Focus on mobile-first, cloud-first world to align ways of doing businesses or transforming the processes centring chiefly around the mobility of experiences that, in turn, are orchestrated by the cloud.

His direction of strategy and ambitions: Strategy is to build best-in-class platforms and productivity services for a mobile-first, cloud-first world which will harmonize the interests of end users, developers, and IT better than any competing ecosystem or platform.

His direction of culture: Perhaps the most important driver of success is culture. A culture is founded in a growth mindset with a belief that everyone can grow and develop.

People need to be always learning and insatiably curious, need to be willing to lean in to uncertainty, to take risks and move quickly after making mistakes, to recognize failure that happens along the way to mastery, and to be open to the ideas of others, where the success of others does not diminish our own.

The final takeaway: Take the opportunity to exercise the growth mindset every day in three distinct areas: Customer-obsessed, diverse, and inclusive—One Microsoft.

Part I: Directing

Introduction

Directing is the function of management in which the managers guide, instruct, and administer the performance of the employees to attain the predetermined objectives. All the planning, organizing, and staffing would be in vain without directing. Thus, directing is said to be a very vital and crucial process of the management. Directing is an incessant process following a top-down approach through organizational hierarchy.

Definitions

Directing consists of process or technique by which instruction can be issued and operations can be carried out as originally planned.

Human

Directing concerns the manner in which a manager influences the actions of his subordinates. It is the final action of a manager in getting others to act after all preparations have been completed.

J.L. Massie

Directing is telling people what to do and seeing that they do it to the best of their ability. It includes making assignments, corresponding procedures, seeing that mistakes are corrected, providing on-the-job instruction and of course issuing orders.

Earnest Dale

Directing is the guidance, the inspiration, the leadership of those men and women that constitute the real core of responsibilities of management.

Urwick and Breach

Directing deals with the steps a manager takes to get subordinates and others to carry out plans.

William Newman and Kirby Warren

Nature of Direction

Function of Management

Direction being an important management function helps in attaining synchronization amongst multiple processes of the company. The purpose of planning, organizing, and staffing is achieved only when there is a certain direction to the plan. Operating with proper procedures and coordinating effectively is a by-product of good managerial directing.

Generality of Direction

Direction is a function that exists at every stage, location, and operation throughout a company. Direction function must be performed by every manager across the levels of the organization. For instance, CEO of an organization delegates authority to the managers across the organization structure and provides direction to achieve the objectives and policies of the organization. The manager then instructs other managers and subordinates beneath him guiding them at every step to attain the goals.

Ongoing Process

Directing is a continuous activity where the manager must incessantly administer the instructions given to the subordinates by him and also motivate his subordinates. A manager has to continue to dedicate substantial time on the direction function. For example, the CEO of a manufacturing company has to direct the top management to continuously adapt to modern manufacturing industry best practices, such as agile and lean manufacturing, ISO 9000 and ISO 14000, process analysis and simulation, supply chain management, statistical process control, and statistical quality control in order to be at par with market competitors.

Need/Importance

Initiates Action

All the planning of the organization goes in vain if efforts are not taken to actualize these plans. The actualization of plans starts when the function of directing begins. It starts with directing the employees to make them understand what they are actually supposed to do in the organization.

Effective Utilization of Resources

Directing helps to make it clear to all the employees their duties and responsibilities. Thus, the scope for duplication and overlapping of work is reduced to a greater extent, leading to effective utilization of all the resources.

Motivation

One of the important elements of directing is motivation. The employee is not only made aware about the tasks to be performed but also motivated for better performance. The managers may use different motivation techniques like monetary (incentive or bonus) and non-monetary (promotion or increase in responsibility) or positive (recognition or appreciation) and negative (warnings or memos).

Helps to Achieve Organizational Objectives

As under the directing function the manager guides, motivates, and supervises the subordinates, it ultimately helps to achieve the organizational goals.

Responding to Change

Every organization is affected by the changes in the environment (both internal and external) in which it operates. It is the human nature to resist a change. In such circumstances, the manager utilizes the element of communication to make the subordinates utilize the benefit of change. This is how the directing function helps respond to a change. For example, in some circumstance, the company might be required to change over from the current technology and adopt a new one to sustain in the market. Here, the employees need to be convinced about the changeover.

Organizational Stability

The four elements of the directing function—leadership, communication, supervision, and motivation—provide stability in the organization and maintain organizational balance. Thus, the organization exists for a long period, and its divisions/departments work in an efficient manner.

Elements of Directing

Elements of directing have been shown in Figure 6.1.

Figure 6.1 Elements of Directing

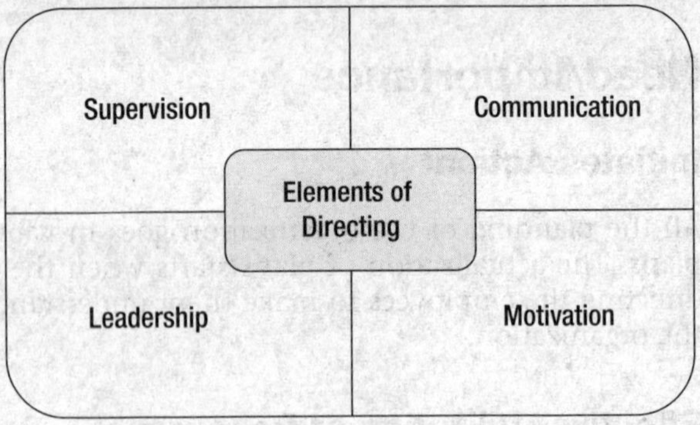

Supervision

Day-to-day relationship between an executive and his immediate assistant and covers training, direction, motivation, coordination, maintenance of discipline, etc.

Newman and Warren

Supervision implies to the process of overseeing the work of subordinates. It is the responsibility of every superior to supervise his subordinates to ensure that they perform their tasks as desired. It is one of the important elements of the directing function. Supervision is significant specifically at the operating level of management. Each organization has some objectives, and this element of the directing function ensures accomplishment of these objectives.

Communication

Communication is the transfer of information from one person to another person. It is a way of reaching others by transmitting ideas, facts, thoughts, feelings and values.

Newstrom and Davis

Communication is an indispensable element for an organization to exist. In simple words, no organization can exist without communication. Communication is the process by which individuals exchange their ideas and information for mutual understanding. The prime responsibility of the manager is to foster two-way communications within the organization to attain better understanding and coordination.

Leadership

Leadership is the ability to awaken in others the desire to follow a common objective.

R.T. Livingston

Leadership is a trait which an individual possesses to influence the behaviour of his/her employees or team mates to work eagerly for accomplishing goals and objectives set by the organization or the team. It is an indispensable constituent for success of an organization. An effective leadership is a major attribute that differentiates a successful organization from an unsuccessful organization.

Motivation

Motivation is the willingness to expand energy to achieve a goal or a reward.

Hodge and Johnson

Motivation means to inspire subordinates to work willingly and more efficiently towards the organizational goals. Motivation is the core of management. Motivation is a complex process that depends on motive and motivating. The manager may choose to motivate his subordinates through various techniques, for example, financial (performance bonus) and non-financial (appreciation emails/letters).

Principles of Directing

Directing is a complex management function since it requires the manager to understand the motives, needs, and attitudes of his subordinates. Different strategies have to be formulated based on the circumstance and individuals. Following are the principles that could prove to be useful for the manager while directing.

Principles Relating to the Purpose of Directing

- **Principle of maximum individual contribution:** The growth and development of an organization depend largely on the efforts of the individual employees working for the organization. Thus, the technique of direction that enables maximum individual contribution should be adapted by the management.
- **Principle of harmony of objectives:** Every organization exists to achieve its predefined objectives. Also, all the employees working in the organization have their own objectives. In such a case, it becomes very important for the management to direct the employees in such a manner so that it would lead to the accomplishment of both the organizational and individual objectives.
- **Principle of efficiency of direction:** The sense of belongingness and commitment of the employees increases when they are given an opportunity to participate in the decision-making. This would also lead to easy implementation of the decisions and increase in efficiency of the subordinates.

Principles Relating to the Process of Directing

- **Principle of comprehension:** It is essential that the employees be communicated about what is to be done and the way in which it should be done. But more important is the extent of understanding by the subordinates. If the subordinates are unable to understand even after informing, the entire directing function goes in vain.
- **Principle of unity of command:** This principle states that a person in the organization should get directions from one superior only. If directions are received from more than one, it creates misunderstanding, clash, and disorder in the organization.
- **Principle of communication:** One of the prime responsibilities of the managers is to communicate the policies, procedures, plans, and responsibilities to the subordinates.

- **Principle of appropriateness of direction technique:** Selecting the directing technique depends on various factors like degree of complexity of the situation, knowledge of the subordinates, and so on. The managers can select from the three available techniques: authorization, participative, or free rein.
- **Principle of follow-through:** Directing is not a one-time activity but an ongoing process. This principle states that only issuing the orders is not sufficient, and the managers should also supervise their subordinates to ensure that the instructions or orders are begin followed and guide them as and when required.
- **Principle of effective leadership:** While guiding the subordinates, superiors should exercise good leadership as it can encourage the subordinates positively without initiating disappointment among them.

EXAMPLE

ABC's CEO has his own style of directing where he directs people of marketing and sales department to contribute maximum to the marketing of the surveillance camera which is an exclusive product of the company and has to be promoted hugely by the team. He also sees to it that his entire team is aligned to the objective of achieving sales growth by 10% in the current financial year, and for this, he has taken up the responsibility of being the one in command for the next two years. He believes that communication is the major key to success and that his team should be updated from time to time with the contract being taken, deals being made, and possible expansion plans of the company; to ensure connectivity and transparency with his employees, he meets with his team once a weak or once a fortnight and uses a participative style of directing technique where he lets employees come up with new product ideas and new strategies to capture the market in the security domain. He also tries to abide by the principle of follow-through for points discussed in the meetings and sees to it that they have been implemented. Recently, the Area Sales Manager of the company proposed that they should not only look at other businesses who would like to install security cameras on high priority but also propose the requirement of cameras to housing societies as well for enhancing the security aspect where control will lie on the security personnel and partly on the machinery, which will not allow any unauthorized person to enter through the gates unless he shows the smart card at the entrance. The CEO having liked the concept adopted the practice of follow-through to understand whether the housing societies are being given free demonstration of the product or not.

Techniques of Directing

- **Autocratic technique:** In this technique, the superior issues orders to his subordinates without prior discussion with his subordinates. Here, the subordinates have no scope to take any initiative or put in their creativity. In simple words, it can be referred as 'do what I say' style.
- **Consultative technique:** This technique implies that the instructions are issued after consulting the subordinates. It does not conclude that the superior is inefficient or incapable. This technique is usually used to identify different alternatives to a problem. Though the superior consults his subordinates, he is free to take his own decision. The success of this technique lies in the co-operation of the subordinates. Increased employee morale is the outcome of this technique.
- **Free-rein technique:** This technique can be used when the subordinates are well qualified and efficient. It emphasizes on encouraging the employees to work independently once the task is assigned.

Characteristics of Directing

- Directing is required at all levels of management. Every superior provides guidance to his subordinate.
- It commands, motivates, communicates, and supervises the employees and controls the organization.
- Directing is not a one-time activity but a continuous process.
- Directing function unearths the complexity in human behaviour mainly the unpredictability, thus increasing its level of significance.
- It facilitates in securing co-operation of the subordinates for achieving goals of the organization.
- Direction function initiates action leading to converting of plans into performance.
- It also provides the necessary leadership in the business.

Part II: Controlling

Introduction

Controlling is another important managerial function which if not exercised properly can drastically impact the organization from every aspect. Each of the organizations strives to achieve the predefined objectives. In order to measure the performance, the management sets some standards against which the actual performance can be measured. It is the controlling process that deals with setting up the standards and taking corrective action whenever the performance is deviated from the stated standards.

Definitions

Control is checking current performance against pre-determined standards contained in the plans, with a view to ensure adequate progress and satisfactory performance.

E.L.F. Breach

Control of an undertaking consists of seeing that everything is being carried out in accordance with the plan which has been adopted, the orders which have been given, and the principles which have been laid down. Its objective is to point out mistakes in order that they may be rectified and prevented from recurring.

Henry Fayol

Controlling is the measurement and correction of performance in order to make sure that enterprise objectives and the plans devised to attain them are accomplished.

Koontz and O'Donnell

Control means to guide something in the direction it is intended to go.

Louis Allen

Controlling is the process of ensuring that actual activities conform to the planned activities.

James Stoner

Need of Controlling

Even the best plans tend to fail if not controlled. This is the prime reason why controlling is required in the organization. The other reasons why control is required in the organization are as follows:

- **Optimum utilization of resources:** Control helps the organization to make optimum utilization of all the available resources. This ultimately results in increased profit.
- **Minimizes deviation:** From the definition of controlling, it is clear that control means to keep a track on the deviations from the set standards and taking corrective actions, resulting in minimal deviations. The Project Manager of IT Company kept a strict control on the deviations in cost and schedule of the project so that they could show a 30% net profit from the project after its successful delivery.
- **Increased efficiency:** Proper utilization of resources and minimal deviations due to the corrective measures bring about efficiency in the organization's processes. Also, as the manager controls the tasks done by the subordinates, the individual performance also increases. Thus, the overall efficiency of the organization rises.
- **Coping with the changes:** There are continuous changes in the social, legal, political, and technological environment in which the business operates. For an organization to survive in the market, it is essential to cope up with these changes. Control is a management function that helps the managers to respond to these changes as and when required.
- **Value addition:** An organization that attempts to survive through competition should be able to add value to products or services so that customers prefer them over those offered by the organization's rivals. In most of the cases, this added value takes the form of above-average quality achieved through demanding quality techniques. For example, students and staff of a particular institution are encouraged to attend courses and workshops which can add value to their existing skill sets and area of expertise. Recently, android, Hadoop, and Python Dzango are the technologies with brighter prospects in the coming years.
- **Facilitates delegation and teamwork:** In modern days, with participative style of management, the nature control process has undergone a prominent change. In initial times, the managers used to set the standards and methods of performance, whereas today, the managers just specify the standards and allow the individual and teams to utilize their own creativity to solve a problem. Thus, the control process assists the manager to monitor his subordinates without impeding their creativity.

Characteristics of Control

- **A function of management:** Management function comprises planning, organizing, staffing, directing, and controlling. Hence, control is an effective function of management.
- **Exercise of control is futuristic:** A manager can take remedial action only for the forthcoming operations. Past is important because on the basis of previous events, it is easy to find the wrong and correct it in future. For example based on the current financial status of an organization, it is possible to formulate a budget for the forthcoming financial year.
- **Control at every level of management:** People at lower middle and uppermost level of management have to exercise control as per their role, responsibility, and authority, and the forms of control exercised would be in strategic (top management), tactical (middle management), and operational control (lower management). For example, at the departmental level, the Unit Heads exercise controls on purchases, sales, and budget.

- **Control is a constant process:** Control has to be continuously exercised, and whatever plans have been devised and standards have to be adhered to need continuous monitoring and so do the activities and events in alignment to changes in the external environment or internal processes and procedures. For example, the Reserve Bank of India is trying constantly to reduce inflation rate and also make housing affordable for everybody in India.
- **Alignment of control to planning:** Planning and controlling are interrelated or very closely related. An organization has its own mission, vision, goals, objectives, policies, and procedures, and control is exerted to understand whether each activity undertaken or task executed is conforming to the said norms of the practices adopted or objectives set. For example, once a plan for the project schedule is made, then control is exercised to let it not deviate majorly.

  Planning can be strongly correlated to a flight simulation activity where the source and the destination are already mapped to the flight path, and the controls in relation to speed, heights, temperature, and cabin pressure are adjusted prior to the take-off, and any alteration/deviation in the above can initiate control and subsequent actions from the Air traffic control department.
- **Exercise of control to achieve goal:** Control is exercised to achieve the long- as well as short-term goals of the organization where individuals work in teams together and expend their effort to achieve the organization goals. Control is exercised on cost, schedule, quality, resources, processes, and quality to achieve organizational productivity.

Steps in the Controlling Process

CASE STUDY ON THE PROCESS OF CONTROLLING

Sohail has business goals for his newly launched company, and for that, Sohail spends substantial time defining company policies, procedures, and standards to measure performance in all aspects, whether services, assets, employees, and so on. His net target turnover (financial objective) for the current financial year was ₹10 million from providing IT-enabled services for total quality management (TQM) to his two new customers.

This could be achieved as per Sohail's understanding by providing excellent services to the existing customer so that they are willing to take up the financial service offering in addition to the TQM services as well from Sohail's Company Bridet India. Enhancing customer satisfaction was also the company's goal for that fiscal year.

With all of the new goals that Sohail set, the next step remains to execute these tasks to achieve each of these goals. Sohail had devised ways to ensure people's productivity and performance. He announced that he would be offering rewards and stock option of 50 shares each of the current 10,000 shares from his company portfolio to the 10 most productive employees of his company if they could achieve the above goals. This was the form of managerial control exercised by Sohail in terms of employee performance and productivity and attainment of organizational goal.

For the IT-enabled financial and TQM service offerings which he could showcase to his customers, he developed a customer satisfaction survey which would help him get ratings for his services from a two-page questionnaire to understand their needs and their honest evaluation for company's offerings. Sohail was hell-bent on controlling quality for fast response and benefits, and for this, he held a meeting with his employees to make them understand the strategic aspect of implementing stringent quality control and performance monitoring norms. Sohail desperately wanted to expand and diversify into other business areas as well, and he could do this only by satisfying his current customers, introducing new service offerings, making employees productive by the clan control approach, and incorporating market research by using feedback from small focus groups. These control strategies were adopted by Sohail to steer his company towards growth and productivity.

The steps involved in the control process are explained in detail with examples as follows (Figure 6.2):

Figure 6.2 Steps in Control Process

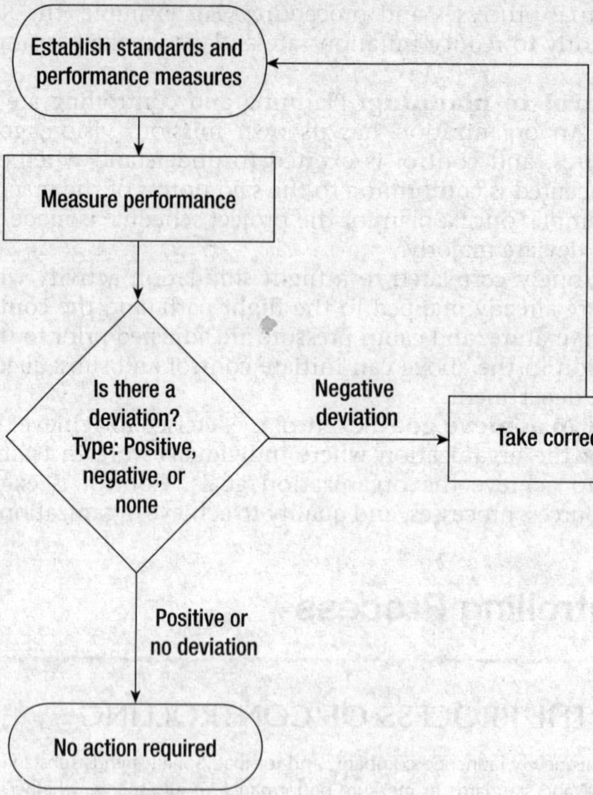

- **Establish standards and performance measures:** A standard is a benchmark against which the actual performance is measured. The standards that can be defined and measured easily are called quantitative standards, for example, number of units manufactured, number of units sold, and so on. And the standards that cannot be defined and measured easily are called qualitative standards, for example, effect of training on the individual's performance and so on. The standards should be such that they can be understood both by the superiors and subordinates. For example, the marketing department has established standard that 1,000 units of product 'A' should be sold in the east region, 2,000 units in the north region, and 1,500 units in the south region per month.
- **Measure performance:** After the establishment of standards, the managers should make sure that the subordinates receive all the required resources to carry out the given task. The next important task of managers is to guide, direct, and motivate his subordinates to perform the job. The next step is to measure the actual performance of the subordinates. For example, after one month, it was observed that 700 units were sold in the east region, 2,200 units were sold in the north region, and 1,500 units were sold in the south region. These are actual performance output of the respective regions.
- **Compare actual performance against established standards:** Here, the actual performance is compared with the standard to identify the deviation, if any, so that necessary action could be taken. For example, Table 6.1 shows the performance comparison between actual and standard.

Table 6.1 Performance Comparison between Actual and Standard

Type of Deviation	*Deviation?*	*Sold (Actual)*	*Target (Number of Units)*	*Region*
Negative	Yes	700	1,000	East
Positive	Yes	2,200	2,000	North
None	No	1,500	1,500	South

Table 6.2 Corrective Action to Be Taken Comparing Actual Performance with Standard

Examples of Corrective Action	*Corrective Action Required?*	*Type of Deviation*	*Region*
More advertising, training the sales executive, or establishing new standards	Yes	Negative	East
No action required	No	Positive	North
No action required	No	None	South

- **Corrective action:** Comparing the actual performance with the established standards makes it clear whether corrective action has to be taken. For example, Table 6.2 shows the corrective action to be taken comparing actual performance with standard.

Resistance to Control

Many people are resistant to the concept of control for the following reasons:

- In today's era, there are organizations whose structures are organic, and these allocate authority to the teams to self-manage their tasks, thus empowering them with authority and decision-making and allowing them to be more receptive and compliant to be in synch with changing environment.
- Some are of the opinion that with change in the nature of the organization, nature of control exercised by the management should also change. In fact according to many, if organization exercises too much of control, then it affects the productivity of employees.
- Some management experts now prefer using the term coordinating instead of controlling since it has a pessimistic undertone, that is, it can sound dominating and heavy.
- Many a times, exercising control leads to reduction in freedom/autonomy, crunching innovativeness, and giving rise to the feeling of insecurity.

Design of Effective Control System

Controlling is one of the most essential ingredients in the success of an organization. An effective control system ensures that the organization is working as per the plan. Thus, designing an effective control system is the most essential and crucial task to be performed by the managers.

- **Objective oriented:** Each organization has some predefined objectives which it strives to achieve. To realize these objectives, various tasks are to be carried out. Also, these tasks need to be monitored at each phase. Thus, a control system should be designed based on these organizational objectives if it is to function as an effective control system.

- **Suitability:** The organization can frame the control system depending on its requirements. In order to design a control system, it is essential to know internal environment, nature of the business, employee requirements, and so on.
- **Flexibility:** The business environment is dynamic and undergoes changes continuously. While designing the control system, this should be kept in mind, and a system capable of accommodating all the changes or failures in plans should be prepared.
- **Quick action:** The management gets the information from various line managers or supervisors about the deviation in standards, and these should be suggested to the planner to take a correct and quick action to avoid future wastage. Actually speaking, the success of control depends entirely on quick action and its implementation.
- **Economical:** The control system must be economical. In simple words, the cost of the control system should not go beyond its benefits.
- **Capability to foresee:** The control system should be designed in such a manner that it helps the managers to keep a control on the operation in advance. If the errors and flaws can be determined in advance, it would reduce the occurrences of deviations, leading to smooth functioning of the organization.
- **Enables feedback:** An effective control system is the one which provides reliable feedback so that the future activities can be planned accordingly.
- **Provides suggestions:** A control system that only identifies the deviations is of no use. It should be capable of suggesting alternative actions.
- **Timely revisions:** With the change in the organizational objective, the control system should also undergo revision to upkeep with the changing requirements.
- **Employee participation:** The benefits of an effective control system can be reaped only when it is implemented in the organization. For this reason, an active participation of employees is a must not only while implementing but also while designing the control system.

Control systems are designed based on the suitability and feedback, and these should be object oriented. For example, a company sets a target for each sales representative to achieve a target of half a million in one financial year, and if 20% of the representatives fail to achieve the target, then they are provided a feedback on their performance by the Director and given an ultimatum to achieve the same in the next quarter, failing which they will have to confront subsequent actions.

Types of Control

Controls can be of numerous kinds. These may be classified on the basis of (a) timing, (b) designing systems, (c) management levels, and (d) responsibility as shown in Figure 6.3.

On the Basis of Time

Controls are classified into three different types depending on the time at which they are brought into action. These types are explained as follows:

- **Feed-forward control:** In an organization, before performing any task, planning is done. An attempt that is made to anticipate the deviations that can occur while realizing the plan is called feed-forward control. Thus, it has a close association with planning. The manager tries to identify problems before the actual operation starts. Also, the alternatives to overcome the anticipated problems are evaluated. For example, some of the sugar industries have an additional manufacturing line apart from those operating

Figure 6.3 Types of Control

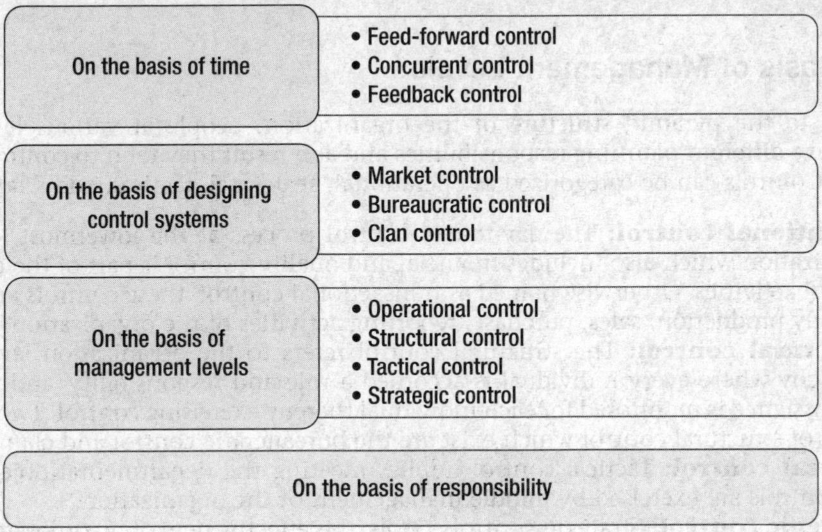

on a daily basis. This extra line is set up so that the production can continue even if any of the line is under maintenance.

- **Concurrent control:** It is an attempt to control the tasks while they are being performed. This type of control ensures that the work is being performed as per the plan, if not, corrective actions are taken. For example, a supervisor at the shop floor in a manufacturing unit monitors continuously that the tasks are being performed as per the predefined methods and standards. If any deviations are noticed, corrective actions are taken by the supervisor.
- **Feedback control:** On completion of a task, a review is made to identify if the anticipated results are accomplished or not. In short, feedback control provides information stating whether the organizational goals are met. It is the basis on which further move of the organization can be decided. For example, if it is observed that the target was not met because some employees were not able to complete the tasks efficiently, then the organization could plan to carry out a training session for these employees.

On the Basis of Designing Control Systems

The three approaches under this category include market control, bureaucratic control, and clan control. However, most organizations do not depend only on just one of them.

- **Market control:** This control is based on establishing a competitive approach in terms of price and market share. Different units are converted into profit-making entities, and their performance is evaluated by revenue, turnover, profit, and the market share. Using market control, managers take decisions in line with the market forces.
- **Bureaucratic control:** Bureaucratic control focuses on power, policies, and procedures, and it has been adopted by most of the Indian public sector undertakings. For example, a hospital cannot issue medicine unless prescribed.
- **Clan control:** It focuses on the organizational culture through shared goals, objectives, norms, policies, and procedures and exercises appropriate control. For example, for

teleworkers, clan control can be used by their managers to exercise control on them for organization benefit. It is suitable for organizations where technology changes very quickly.

On the Basis of Management Levels

In relation to the pyramid structure of the organization, people at various levels of the pyramid have different planning responsibilities and as a result they tend to control whatever they plan. Controls can be categorized as operational, structural, tactical, and strategic:

- **Operational control:** The day-to-day control process at the lowermost level of the organization which also includes financial and quality control is part of the operational control activities. Otherwise named as transactional control, these controls are exercised on daily production, sales, purchase, reporting activities of the organization, and so on.
- **Structural control:** The structural control refers to the organization structure and hierarchy where every individual is accorded a role and responsibility, and progress in tasks assigned is monitored for each individual thereby exercising control. Two important forms of structural control which exist are the bureaucratic control and clan control.
- **Tactical control:** Tactical control implies meeting the departmental objectives, and the controls are exercised by middle management of the organization.
- **Strategic control:** Strategic controls imply the effectiveness of a corporate, business, and functional strategies helpful for organizations to meet its goals. Strategic controls are exercised by top-level management.

On the Basis of Responsibility

Control can be internal or external. Internal means a person is self-motivated to exercise discipline on him/her. The external control means that the control is in the hands of manager, and control is exercised using a formal approach.

Budget

Budget is a financial plan that is used to estimate the revenue and expenses over a specified future period of time. A budget can be made for a person, family, group of people, business, government, country, multinational organization, or just about anything else that makes and spends money. The budgeting process is carried out to identify whether the person/organization can continue to operate with its projected income and expenses. The budget should be objective driven. It means that the expected revenues and expenditures of each department will ultimately be based on the organizational objective.

Budgeting Process

The task of budgeting and monitoring of budgets is an ongoing process. Monitoring involves checking the targets, feedback, and so on. The budgeting process involves the following procedures:

i. Define the Objectives of Organization

First, the management tries to set the organizational objectives. These would include identifying the profits, market share, and other targets to be achieved. The targets should be realistic that are made after studying the potential of the organization and the market situation.

ii. **Set Production, Marketing, and Financial Budget**
   There are three major functional budgets, and each is dependent on the organizational objectives.

   - **Production budget:** It is expressed in quantitative terms only and is geared to the sales budget. It involves costs of raw material, direct labour costs, costs of purchasing components, and so on. This is an expenditure-only budget.
   - **Marketing budget:** It is a combination of both the income and expenses. It involves revenue from sales forecasted and expenses involved in actualizing the marketing strategy.
   - **Financial budget:** The financial budget depicts projected cash flow. it helps to identify if the funds are in a proportion to cover the expenses or not. If not, the management can find alternatives to raise additional funds.

iii. **Fragmentation of Budget**
   Each of the above stated budgets is then broken down, so that there could be different budgets like training budget, sales budget, and so on.

iv. **Budget Monitoring Procedures Must Be Established**
   As per the business objectives and the internal environment of the business, appropriate budget monitoring procedures must be established.

v. **Identify Variances**
   Any variances in the projected budgets must be identified and responded too.

vi. **Feedback**
   The experience and knowledge achieved while setting the budget for one period must be utilized while deciding on the budget for another period.

Advantages of Budgeting

- It helps to monitor and control operations.
- It provides a framework of delegation.
- It creates a sense of responsibility among the managers.
- It can improve communication system within the organization.
- It promotes forward thinking.
- It helps in coordination of different departments and align them towards shared objective.

Limitations of Budgeting

- It can demotivate employees if they do not get an opportunity to participate in the budgeting process.
- It is difficult to estimate all the revenues and expenditure in advance.
- It can result in building perceptions of unfairness.
- If budgets are inflexible, then it fails to reflect the necessary changes.
- Budgeting might result in competition among the departments for resources.

Variance Analysis

Variance analysis is the investigation of the difference between actual and planned behaviour.

For example, if the budgeted sales are worth ₹100 lakhs and actual sales are worth ₹80 lakhs, then variance analysis yields a difference of ₹20 lakhs.

Variance analysis helps to identify the difference between planned and actual results and its effect on the performance of the organization. Variance analysis can help to identify certain types of tasks that regularly overrun their budget, while other tasks may be seen to frequently come under their budget.

The variance can be either favourable (F) or adverse (A) (Figures 6.4 and 6.5).

The variance can be said favourable when

- the expenditure is less than expected or
- the revenue is greater than expected.

The variance can be said adverse when

- the expenditure is greater than expected or
- the revenue is less than expected.

For example, Table 6.3 shows the actual versus budgeted variance.

Figure 6.4 Favourable Variance

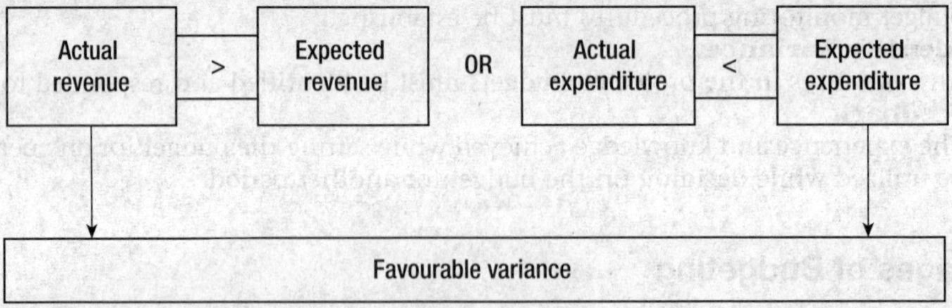

Figure 6.5 Adverse Variance

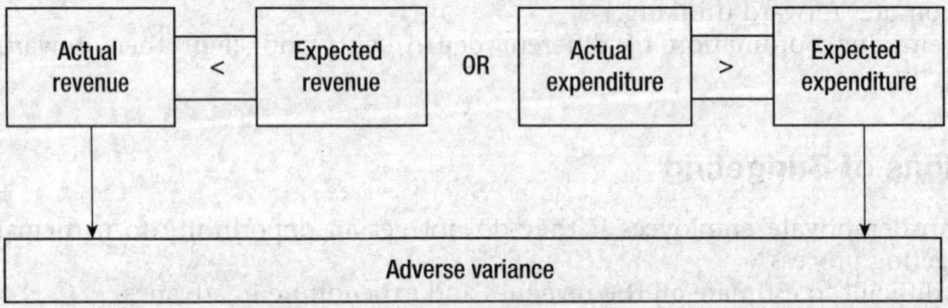

Table 6.3 Actual Versus Budgeted Variance

	Variance (in ₹)	*Actual (in ₹)*	*Budgeted (in ₹)*
Cost of raw materials	1,50,000 (F)	8,50,000	10,00,000
Labour cost	5,000 (A)	5,50,000	5,00,000
Sales revenue	8,00,000 (A)	42,00,000	50,00,000
Total variance		6,55,000 (A)	

Control Techniques

Control techniques are broadly divided into following two categories (Figure 6.6):

- **Non-financial control techniques:** In this technique, there is no requirement of financial data, and it includes rewards or punishments, stringent recruitment and retirement norms, trainings, management by exception, project progress control, production, and inventory and quality control.
- **Financial control techniques:** In this technique, availability of data in terms of profits, costs, turnovers, or revenues is shared so that managers can control costs, sustain liquidity, and maintain a balance between assets and liabilities. This can be possible through elaborate cost plans, budgets, accurate estimates of income and expenditure, detailed break-even analysis, and sound account maintenance and audit.

Financial Controls

Managers of any organization exercise financial controls to monitor performance and calculate growth to achieve financial goals of the organization. Financial goals are achieved using the ways discussed below.

Financial Audits

Financial audits are done in synch with financial policies, procedures, and laws. Audits may be internal, that is, by an auditor of the organization, or external, that is, by chartered accountants and management audit by specialists.

Financial Statements

Financial statements are used by the stakeholders of the company to identify the financial stability of an organization. The stakeholders might include the employees, shareholders, financial institutes, investors, unions, customers, and so on. These statements facilitate

Figure 6.6 Control Techniques

Control Techniques	
Financial Controls	**Non-financial Controls**
• Financial audits • Financial statements • Ratio analysis • Budgetary controls • Break even analysis • Accounting • Return on investment	• Market research • Test marketing • HR control • Production control • Direct supervision and observation • MBO • Self-control • Management audit • MIS • Critical path method and project evaluation review technique

monitoring the liquidity, general financial condition, and profitability of the organization over a given time period. For example, balance sheet, profit and loss account, and so on.

Ratio Analysis

Financial ratio analysis consists of five groups—structural, liquidity, profitability, turnover, and miscellaneous.

Under structural ratio, there exists funded debt to total capitalization, debt to equity, net fixed asset to funded debt, and funded debt to working capital.

Under liquidity, there is current ratio (current assets to liabilities) and acid test ratios.

Under profitability, there is operating ratio, operating profit to sales, net profit to sales, and so on.

Under turnover, there is asset, capital, receivable, and inventory turnover. Each of these has their own mathematical formulas, for example

$$\text{Inventory turnover} = \frac{\text{Cost of goods sold}}{\text{average inventory}}$$

Budgetary Controls

Budgetary control is the formulation of budget, comprising the expenditure forecast across item categories and then comparing actual expenditure with the planned expense. A budget requires to be revised under changed scenarios.

Budgetary control is applicable to all functional areas who take help of budgetary control in order to keep a check on the overall spending.

Budgeting could be categorized as follows: (a) managers prepare the budget and ask their colleagues, (b) budgets are made by the lower management and given to the higher management for approval, (c) zero-based, that is, allotment of funds on the basis of activities or goals, or (d) flexible budget options, that is, depending on the requirements, budget is allotted.

Break-even Analysis

It determines the point at which revenue received equals the costs associated with receiving the revenue. The break-even analysis calculates safety margin, that is, the point above which the revenue is greater than the cost. This is the amount that revenues can fall while still staying above the break-even point

The break-even analysis only analyses the costs of the sales. For example, if it costs ₹50 to make a box of crackers, and this box is sold at ₹200. The fixed cost associated is ₹2,000, then the break-even point would ₹2,000/(200 – 50) = 2,000/150 = 13.5, and if it is sold at ₹300, then it will be

$$₹2{,}000/(300 - 50) = (2{,}000/(250)) = 8.5.$$

This example shows that break-even point comes fast with increased price and decreased demand.

Accounting

Accounting is the measurement, processing, and communication of fiscal data about commercial units.

Accounting can be categorized as follows: financial accounting, management accounting, tax accounting, and auditing. Financial accounting emphasizes on an organization's financial report and information for stockholders, controllers, and dealers, which includes book keeping and consists of financial summaries. Management accounting focuses on the processing, analysis, and reporting of information to be used by top and middle management of the organization. A tax audit happens when the income tax department examines the tax returns and verifies that the income and tax deductions are correct.

Return on Investment

This technique is used generally by the large organizations. Return on investment helps to identify the returns earned on the investments made. The investments include the assets and the capital. Return on investment gives a clear picture about the financial performance of the company and its divisions or departments.

Return on investment (ROI) is calculated using the following formula:

$$\text{ROI} = \frac{\text{Net income}}{\text{Sales}} \times \frac{\text{Sales}}{\text{Total investment}}$$

Non-financial Controls

The controls exercised on the non-financial front have been discussed below.

Market Research

Market research is focused on gathering target customer information. It is a very significant constituent of business plan. Market research aims at gaining competitive edge over competitors. Market research analyses the market need, size, and competition. It can be categorized based on the size, for example, a customer service personnel may ask a group of six to ten people known as focus groups whether they would be interested about a new type of chicken burger combo, and if so, how much they would like the price to be, based on which the companies might narrow down to limited choices of production on the basis of acceptance rate of the customers.

Further, there are phone surveys where a bank may conduct many phone surveys based on the questionnaire designed, which would enable customers to rate the banking services in a scale of 1 to 5 and would use this to make improvements in customer service.

Similarly, Pizza Hut might use five local restaurants as test bed to introduce a special type of chicken pizza and monitor customer's acceptability on the same.

One-on-one interview is about a software tool designed by a company and showcased by a sales and marketing representative to a person to understand his views on the same.

Test Marketing

It is a tool used by companies to project market success of a new product through effective marketing campaign. Test marketing evaluates performance of the product, product acceptance, and product distribution for full launch.

HR Control

Non-financial control attributes to control on HR who are the performing assets of the organization for overall company's productivity. Common controls include performance appraisals and training programmes.

Production Control

To control production in the form of managing schedules, deadlines, quality, inventory, the techniques include inventory control, that is, Economic Order Quantity (EOQ) and JIT, and quality control, that is, inspection and parameter-based quality check. For example, under production control, parameters on which control is exercised are the following:

- Stock error rate
- Late delivery
- Slippage in production schedule
- Out-of-stock situations
- Purchase order errors
- Inventory turnover rate

Direct Supervision and Observation

This is the oldest control technique. In this type, the manager or the superior monitors and controls his subordinates. Thus, the manager is aware about the entire situation. His presence also has an influence on the behaviour of his subordinates. This technique proves to be effective especially in cases where the subordinates are not capable of identifying the issues and controlling them.

MBO

MBO is a technique applied primarily to employee management. It involves goal formulation for individual employees, deciding the time frame during which the goals are to be achieved followed by recording the performance, and then monitoring it.

Self-control

Some of the behavioural scientists state that control is more effective when it is self-directed. This technique is considered to be very effective in the modern era. It increases employee morale since the employees are free to set their own targets and there is no close supervision. Using this technique, the superior can control the entire situation without enforcing any control on his subordinates.

Nowadays, the modern management and control techniques have been implemented by various organizations across the nations for effective governance of the organizations.

Management Audit

Management audits are becoming popular in the recent times since they deal with controlling the overall performance of the organization. It is an effective tool that can be used to examine the efficiency and effectiveness of the various organizational processes. It is an internal audit wherein an expert team reviews quality of management. The management audit is intended to serve the interest of the organization as a whole. For example, though it is said that management audit is intended to serve the purpose of the organization, even top management can also commit fraud if they are under the pressure to meet expectations of market analysts, debt covenants requirements, and/or to comply with tightly performance-based compensation program. In that case, they do so by falsifying journal entries and recording transactions at the wrong time, overstating revenues, profits, and assets, and understating expenses, losses, and liabilities. So, there are auditors who do a total financial audit with regard to the number of facilities, the number of customer accounts, the number of employees and their turnover, and the number of products. This example appropriates the fact that there exists control over the top management as well.

Management Information System

For the process of planning and decision-making, it is important that the information available must be reliable so that the performance or output can be evaluated. To provide such information readily and speedily, available MIS is installed in the organizations. This would in turn help the managers to take decisions without a waste of time.

Critical Path Method and Project Evaluation Review Technique

The critical path method (CPM) and project evaluation review technique (PERT) are techniques used to plan, schedule, and control many tasks associated with projects.

There are six steps common to both PERT and CPM. The procedure is as follows:

- Identify the tasks and activities of a new or an existing project.
- Sequence the tasks such that there is a start time and an end time to complete each and every task and also the project.
- Draw the network connecting all of the activities or tasks as per the predecessor and successor sequence.
- Allocate time and/or cost to each activity or task.
- Compute the longest path through the network, that is, the maximum time a project will take to come to closure; the path is called the critical path.
- Use the network diagram to help schedule, observe, and manage the project.

EXAMPLE

Given the following information regarding a project as activities and estimates of the optimistic, most likely, and pessimistic times in days for completion of various activities

- Draw the PERT network diagram.
- Identify the critical path.
- Find the expected duration and variance for each activity. What is the expected project length?
- What is the probability that the project will be completed in 40 days?

Activity → time ↓ estimates (days)	*1–2*	*1–3*	*2–4*	*2–5*	*3–7*	*4–6*	*5–6*	*6–8*	*7–8*
Optimistic (t_o)	4	1	6	2	3	5	3	1	4
Most likely (t_m)	7	5	12	5	9	11	6	4	19
Pessimistic (t_p)	16	15	30	8	27	17	15	7	28

Solution: Using the given data, we calculate the expected time and the variance for activity.

	Time estimates (in days)			*Expected time* $t_e = \frac{t_o + 4t_m + t_p}{6}$	*Variance* $\sigma^2 = \left(\frac{t_p - t_o}{6}\right)^2$
Activity	*Optimistic* t_o	*Most Likely* t_m	*Pessimistic* t_p		
1–2	4	7	16	8	4
1–3	1	5	15	6	49/9
2–4	6	12	30	14	16
2–5	2	5	8	5	1

(Continued)

(Continued)

Activity	Time estimates (in days)			Expected time $t_e = \frac{t_o + 4t_m + t_p}{6}$	Variance $\sigma^2 = \left(\frac{t_p - t_o}{6}\right)^2$
	Optimistic t_o	Most Likely t_m	Pessimistic t_p		
3–7	3	9	27	11	16
4–6	5	11	17	11	4
5–6	3	6	15	7	4
6–8	1	4	7	4	1
7–8	4	19	28	18	16

- The project network is shown below:

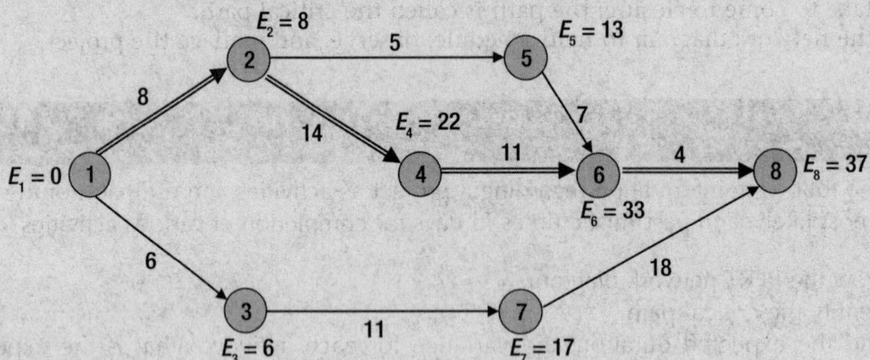

- The critical activities are 1 → 2, 2 → 4, 4 → 6, and 6 → 8. Hence, the critical path is 1 → 2 → 4 → 6 → 8.
- The expected duration of the project is 37 days.
  The variance of the project length is the sum of the variances of the critical activities.
  $\therefore \sigma_e^2 = 4 + 16 + 4 + 1 = 25$
  ∴ Variance of the project length = 25 days
  $\therefore \sigma_e = \sqrt{25} = 5$
- Probability that the project will be completed in 40 days is given by
  The standard normal deviate is given by

$$z = \frac{\text{Due date} - \text{Expected date of completion}}{\sqrt{\text{Variance}}}$$

$$\therefore z = \frac{40-37}{\sqrt{25}} = \frac{3}{5} = 0.6$$

$\therefore P(z \le 0.6) = 0.5 + \Phi(0.6)$
$= 0.5 + 0.2257$
$= 0.7257$
Hence, the probability that the project will be completed in 40 days is 0.7257.

Summary

This chapter summarizes on directing and controlling the essential functions of management and deals with both the functions separately, justifies the necessity of both the functions exclusively using examples and scenarios, and gives a deep insight into the various traditional and modern control techniques that businesses use in today's era.

Exercise

Objective Questions

1. The purpose of planning, organizing, and staffing is achieved only when there is a certain ____________ to the plan.
   - Actions
   - Directions
   - Control
   - None of the above
2. Directing is a complex management function since it requires the manager to understand the motives, needs, and attitudes of his subordinates.
   - True
   - False
3. Which of the principle of directing states that all the employees working in the organization have their own objectives?
   - Principle of maximum individual contribution
   - Principle of efficiency of direction
   - Principle of harmony of objectives
   - Principle of comprehension
4. ________ if not exercised properly can drastically impact the organization from every aspect.
   - Actions
   - Directions
   - Control
   - None of the above
5. Which of these statements is incorrect?
   - Control is at every level of management
   - Control is exercised to achieve only the long-term goals
   - Control is a constant process
   - Exercise of control is futuristic
6. When an attempt is made to anticipate the deviations that can occur while realizing the plan is called feed-forward control.
   - True
   - False

7. Which of these controls focuses on organizational culture through shared goals, objectives, norms, policies, and procedures and exercises appropriate control?
   - Market control
   - Clan control
   - Concurrent control
   - Bureaucratic control

9. Which of these promotes forward thinking?
   - Controlling
   - Directing
   - Budgeting
   - None of these

10. To take other's opinions and finally taking his/her own decision are a part of which technique?
    - Autocratic style
    - Consultative style
    - Free rein
    - None of the above

11. Variance analysis helps to identify the difference between planned and actual results and its effect on the performance of the organization.
    - True
    - False

CASE STUDY

Koudran Engineering Company is a multinational company which manufactures automotive and hydraulic parts. It has its manufacturing locations in Nasik, Nagar, Pondicherry, and Hyderabad. The company gives more importance to production expenses. The budget is allocated to every manufacturing operation on the analysis done on production facilities and operation. The manufacturing locations at Nasik, Nagar, and Pondicherry are working properly and are on the right track of budget. However, the Hyderabad location was not able to maintain their budget target.

Mr Anderson was transferred from the Nagar location to Hyderabad as plant manager. Mr Anderson did preliminary investigation for the Hyderabad plant and made some changes in the plant working. He instructed all the departments to strictly follow the budget allocated and adhere to it, so that profits can be achieved. He monitored the operations in the plant after implementing the changes. There were few supervisor terminations during this time for not adhering to the budget targets.

With all the efforts, the Hyderabad location was back on track. Within next six months, he found that the budget targets are met by 7.2% and profit was then increased by 10%. On setting the Hyderabad plant right, the management decided to call Mr Anderson back to the Nagar location. However, shortly after Mr Anderson left, the productivity of the Hyderabad location fell below the earlier level and the budget was again in trouble.

Questions

1. Analyse the organizational climate created by Mr Anderson at the Hyderabad plant.
2. Why was there a drop in budget level after Mr Anderson left?
3. Did Mr Anderson have an autocratic style of directing?

Critical Thinking Questions

1. Comment on whether understanding of human behaviour helps in directing.
2. You are the chief financial officer for a restaurant, how will you use the current year's financial statement to set the budget for the next operating year?
3. Can an organization function without controlling. Comment.

Chapter at a Glance

Directing and Controlling

Directing deals with the steps a manager takes to get subordinates and others to carry out plans.

Need of Directing

- To initiate action
- To utilize resources
- To motivate people
- To help organization to achieve objective
- To bring organizational stability
- To continuously managing change

Elements of Directing

- Supervise
- Communicate
- Motivate
- Lead

Principles of Directing

The principles of directing are basically dealt from the aspect of purpose and process. Under the purpose concept, the focus is chiefly on individual contribution, harmony of organizational objectives, and efficiency in direction.

From process perspective, it would centre on principle of comprehension, unity of command, communication, and appropriateness in direction, follow-through, and leadership.

Techniques of Directing

- Autocratic style: 'Do as I say'.
- Consultative style: To take other's opinions and finally taking his/her own decision.
- Free rein: Giving independence to experienced employees.

Characteristics of Directing

- It is a continuous process.
- It gets significance because of complexity in human behavioural traits.

(Continued)

(Continued)

- It facilitates in securing co-operation of the subordinates.
- It helps to transform plans into performances.
- It provides leadership in business.

Controlling is the process of ensuring that actual activities conform to the planned activities.

Need of Controlling

- Optimum utilization of resources
- Minimized deviation
- Increased efficiency
- Coping with the changes
- Value addition
- Facilitates delegation and teamwork

Control Process Steps

- Establish standards and performance measures.
- Measure performance.
- Compare the actual versus the planned measures.
- Take the corrective action.

Design of Effective Control Systems

The control system should be flexible, suitable, action oriented, economical, have feature ability to forecast, enable feedback, timely revisions, and, for its total effectiveness, should actually call for active participation of employees.

Types of Control

- **Feed-forward control:** It is an attempt that is made to anticipate the deviations that can occur while realizing the plan.
- **Concurrent control:** This type of control ensures that the work is being performed as per the plan, if not, corrective actions are taken.
- **Feedback control:** Feedback control provides information stating whether the organizational goals are met. It is the basis on which further move of the organization can be decided.

Budget

Budget is a financial plan that is used to estimate the revenue and expenses over a specified future period of time.

Budgeting Process

- Define organizational objectives.
- Set production, marketing, and financial budget.

- Fragmentation of budget.
- Processes should be established for monitoring budget.
- Variance identification.
- Provide feedback.

Advantages of Budgeting

- It helps to monitor and control operations.
- It provides a framework of delegation.
- It creates a sense of responsibility among the managers.
- It can improve communication system within the organization.
- It promotes forward thinking.
- It helps in coordination of different departments and aligns them towards shared objective.

Limitations of Budgeting

- It can demotivate employees if they do not get an opportunity to participate in the budgeting process.
- It is difficult to estimate all the revenues and expenditure in advance.
- It can result in building perceptions of unfairness.
- If budgets are inflexible, then it fails to reflect the necessary changes.
- Budgeting might result in competition among the departments for resources.

Variance Analysis

Variance analysis helps to identify the difference between planned and actual results and its effect on the performance of the organization.

Control Techniques

These are categorized as *financial control* and *non-financial control* techniques. Financial control comprises following:

- Financial audits
- Financial statement
- Ratio analysis
- Budgetary control
- Break-even analysis
- Accounting

Non-financial control comprises following:

- Market research
- HR control
- Production control
- Direct supervision and observation
- MBO
- Management audit
- MIS
- PERT/CPM

CHAPTER 7

Decision-making

Learning Objectives

- Understanding the concept of decision-making and its relevance to managerial traits and management study.
- Obtaining an understanding of decision types and decision models.
- Getting insight into decision-making for organizational effectiveness, which enables the reader to gain understanding of the importance of decision-making in context of organization's growth, diversification, and opportunity utilization.
- Getting an insight into the quantitative techniques of decision-making essentially based on mathematical models.

An Opening Vignette

Let us take the case of Aditya Birla Group of companies led by Kumar Mangalam Birla. After Kumar Mangalam Birla stepped in, several changes to organizational reporting structures, retirement policies, and recruitment strategies happened as a result of his decision-making. He also implemented following policies for organizational effectiveness:

- Implementation of 'economic value added model' focusing on profitability, asset productivity, and growth.
- Establishment of Aditya Birla Management Corporation Limited, for ensuring the best practices across the group companies.
- Reduction of group's dependence on fibre-based business and shift to non-ferrous metals as there was less competition in the market then.
- Introduction of a 360-degree feedback programme with expectation list from employees.
- Promoting excellence amongst student's community to cultivate the leaders of tomorrow with organization culture centring on people, performance, energy, and enthusiasm.
- Implementation of employee satisfaction index for increased retention of talent pool.
- Instituted a performance appraisal system and implemented performance management systems, to bring meritocracy.
- Implementing changes to reporting structure, thereby increasing accountability and autonomy.

Outcome

- The turnover of Aditya Birla Group of Companies increased from $2 billion in 1995 to $45 billion today due to the incorporation of value-added models.
- The company's expansion has skyrocketed because of organization restructuring and changes in reporting structures done by K.M. Birla, and now it operates across 41 countries with employee potential of 120,000 with increased meritocracy.
- The company has made 31 acquisitions in 20 years, a never-before-seen growth by an Indian multinational, and this was due to incorporation of modern management approaches.

Summing up the case in context of decision-making, it is said that an incorrect decision can ruin an organization or make an organization fail, whereas correct decisions across all levels might enrich the organization in terms of growth, profit, and opportunities as can be seen from the Aditya Birla Group of Companies. In the succeeding section, we now explore the concepts associated with decision-making.

Part I: Organizational Decision-making

Decision-making Concepts

The managers of any organization are allocated the responsibility of taking decisions related to various aspects of the organization. The decisions can be operational decisions like sanctioning leave to any employee, tactical decisions like formulating the budget for their unit, or strategic decisions like mergers and acquisitions or organization diversifying into other business areas. For such decisions, the chief elements of decision-making comprise alternatives, states of nature, and pay-offs where alternatives are courses of action, states of nature are possible future conditions, and pay-offs are profit or loss earned from each combination of alternative and future state. According to Henry Sisk and Clifton Williams, a decision is the selection of a course of action from two or more alternatives, and decision-making is a sequence of steps leading to the selection of that alternative.

Herbert Simon's model for decision-making states that there are three stages to decision-making—intelligence, design, and choice phase accompanied by a feedback phase. In the intelligence phase, the problem is identified for which the decision has to be made, followed by a design phase where alternatives are constructed, and then in the choice phase, the most feasible alternative is chosen and implemented as a decision. To make aspects of decision-making clear to the reader, let us take an example. A decision has to be taken about buying a house by Meera. The steps to be followed while making a decision are depicted in Table 7.1.

As observed by Peter Drucker, an alternative is evaluated based on the following:

- Risk associated with each alternative
- Cost, time, and effort which have to be spent for each alternative
- Limitations of financial, human, and material resources

Generally, a decision maker (manager) while taking a decision chooses an alternative based on experience, experimentation, research, and analysis.

Table 7.1 Scenario Representing Decision-making

Identification of the problem	***To buy a house***
Decision conditions based on collection and analysis of relevant information	Price, size, layout, location, accessibility, amenities, house conditions, repair options, available home loan options, legal aspects, and so on
Allocating weights to decision conditions	10, 9, 8, 7, 6, 5, 4, 3, 2, and 1
Generating alternatives	**Option 1:** Moderately priced, good size two-bedroom resale apartment in Kalyaninagar with accessibility to railway station, airport, and bus terminus with minor repairs to be done, and attractive home loan options from a nationalized bank with clear legal documents. **Option 2:** A spacious new property less priced downtown.
Analysing alternatives	Option 1 has been rated higher by Meera
Choosing an alternative	Meera chose option 1
Implementing the alternative	Meera bought the two-bedroom apartment in Kalyaninagar.

Decision-making Environment

The decisions made by managers are sometimes taken under certainty where outcome is known and sometimes the decisions are taken under uncertainty and the outcome is not known. When decisions are taken under risk, there can be several outcomes with probability that each outcome might occur. For example, let us consider a situation when decision is taken under certainty.

Decision-making under Certainty

- The consequence of every alternative is known as shown in Table 7.2.
- Usually there is only one outcome for each alternative.

The solution to such problems can be found out using Linear Programming Problem (LPP, a method to achieve the best outcome, such as maximum profit or lowest cost), assignment models, sequencing models, and so on. From Table 7.2, it is seen that the decision to invest in policy II is the most optimal solution.

Table 7.2 Decision-making under Certainty

Alternative	***Outcome***
Invest in policy I	200,000
Invest in policy II	250,000
Invest in policy III	225,000

Decision-making under Uncertainty

- All the possible states of nature or outcomes are known as shown in Table 7.3.
- Probabilities of the possible outcomes are not known.

When decision is made under uncertainty, some criterion is followed. The first is the maximax criterion which has an optimistic approach. It depicts the maximum value of the maximum outcome for each row. Table 7.3 portrays decision-making using optimistic approach.

Table 7.3 Decision-making Using Maximax Approach

	States of Nature Market Acceptability			
Alternatives	***Poor***	***Good***	***Excellent***	***Row Maximum***
Shampoo I	8,000	10,000	12,000	12,000
Shampoo II	5,000	10,000	15,000	15,000
Shampoo III	2,000	7,000	10,000	10,000

Decision is to choose option II using the maximax criterion. Under uncertainty, decision-making is also done using a pessimistic approach which is known as the maximin criterion. Table 7.4 clearly illustrates decision-making using the pessimistic approach. This approach uses maximum value of the minimum outcome for each row.

Table 7.4 Decision-making Using Maximin Approach

	States of Nature Market Acceptability			
Alternatives	***Poor***	***Good***	***Excellent***	***Row Minimum***
Shampoo I	8,000	10,000	12,000	8,000
Shampoo II	5,000	10,000	15,000	5,000
Shampoo III	–2,000	7,000	10,000	–2,000

When a decision is taken by narrowing on alternatives whose pay-offs are equally likely, then the approach followed is known as the Laplace approach. So, the approach in Table 7.5 depicts alternative I or the alternative II as the most feasible alternative.

Table 7.5 Decision-making Using Laplace Approach

	States of Nature Market Acceptability			Expected Pay-off = Sum of the Pay-offs Number of Future States
Alternatives	***Poor***	***Good***	***Excellent***	
Shampoo I	8,000	10,000	12,000	10,000
Shampoo II	5,000	10,000	15,000	10,000
Shampoo III	–2,000	7,000	10,000	5,000

Hurwicz criterion: This criterion is a compromise between optimistic and a pessimistic decision and is also known as the criterion of realism. The coefficient of realism α if close to 1 allows the decision maker to be optimistic, and if it is close to 0, it allows him to be pessimistic. Using the above criterion, one has to find out the maximum and minimum pay-off for every alternative. The expected pay-off is calculated as

Expected pay-off = α × (maximum pay-off) + (1 – α) × (minimum pay-off)
Here, α = 0.8; 1 – α = 0.2, expected pay-off is calculated as
Expected pay-off = α × (maximum pay-off) + (1 – α) × (minimum pay-off)
(Shampoo I) 0.8 × 12,000 + 0.2 × 80,000 = 11,200
(Shampoo II) 0.8 × 15,000 + 0.2 × 5,000 = 13,000
(Shampoo III) 0.8 × 10,000 + 0.2 × –2,000 = 7,600

So using the Hurwicz criterion, the best option is to choose the second alternative (shown in Table 7.6).

Table 7.6 Decision-making Using Hurwicz Approach

	Market Acceptability					
Alternatives	***Poor***	***Good***	***Excellent***	***Row Maximum***	***Row Minimum***	***Expected Pay-off***
Shampoo I	8,000	10,000	12,000	12,000	8,000	11,200
Shampoo II	5,000	10,000	15,000	15,000	5,000	13,000
Shampoo III	–2,000	7,000	10,000	10,000	–2,000	7,600

Minimax regret criterion: The minimax regret approach requires the construction of a regret table. For each state of nature, the difference between each pay-off and the largest pay-off for that state of nature is calculated. The maximum regret for each possible decision is listed. The decision chosen is the one corresponding to the minimum of the maximum regrets. The regret matrix shows shampoo I or shampoo II as the alternative.

The Pay-off Matrix: See Table 7.7.

Table 7.7 Decision-making Using Minimax Regret Criterion

	Market Acceptability (States of Nature)		
Alternatives	***Poor***	***Good***	***Excellent***
Shampoo I	8,000	10,000	12,000
Shampoo II	5,000	10,000	15,000
Shampoo III	–2,000	7,000	10,000

The Regret Matrix: See Table 7.8.

Table 7.8 Regret Matrix

	Market Acceptability (States of Nature)			
Alternatives	***Poor***	***Good***	***Excellent***	***Row Maximum***
Shampoo I	0	0	3,000	3,000
Shampoo II	3,000	0	0	3,000
Shampoo III	10,000	3,000	5,000	10,000

Decision-making under Risk

- All the possible states of nature or outcomes are known.
- Probabilities of the possible outcomes are known.

The decision-making criterion used for decision-making under risk is the Expected Monetary Value (EMV). This is the best expected value among alternatives to determine the expected pay-off of each alternative, and choose the alternative with the best expected pay-off.

EMV (for *i*th alternative) = (pay-off of 1st state of nature) × (probability of 1st state of nature) + (pay-off of 2nd state of nature) × (probability of 2nd state of nature) + ··· + (pay-off of last state of nature) × (probability of last state of nature). Hence, the decision was to choose the second option as shown in Table 7.9.

Table 7.9 Decision-making under Risk

Probabilities ***Alternatives***	***Poor 0.2***	***Good 0.3***	***Excellent 0.5***	***Expected EMV***
Shampoo I	8,000	10,000	12,000	10,600
Shampoo II	5,000	10,000	15,000	11,500
Shampoo III	–2,000	7,000	10,000	6,700

Expected profit with perfect information (EPPI): The decisions taken by managers are more accurate when proper information is available. Also, the information should be available on time, be accurate, relevant, and understandable. Perfect information would tell us with certainty which outcome is going to occur. Having perfect information before making a decision would allow choosing the best pay-off for the outcome. If proper information is available, an individual would be able to select the best pay-off for every state of nature. The EPPI is given as follows:

EPPI = (Best pay-off of 1st state of nature) × (probability of 1st state of nature)
+ (best pay-off of 2nd state of nature) × (probability of 2nd state of nature)
+ (best pay-off of 3rd state of nature) × (probability of 3rd state of nature).

EPPI = 8,000 × 0.2 + 10,000 × 0.3 + 15,000 × 0.5 = 12,100.

Table 7.10 Decision-making Using EPPI

	Market Acceptability (States of Nature)		
Probabilities Alternatives	***Poor 0.2***	***Good 0.3***	***Excellent 0.5***
Shampoo I	8,000	10,000	12,000
Shampoo II	5,000	10,000	15,000
Shampoo III	–2,000	7,000	10,000

Expected value of perfect information (EVPI): It is the increase in the expected profit that would result if one knew with certainty that if the alternative was chosen, it would give the highest pay-off.

EVPI = EPPI – EMV_{max}, where EPPI = expected profit with perfect information EMV_{max} = maximum EMV. For this example, we have EVPI = 12,100 – 11,500 = 600.

Types of Decisions

Programmed Decisions

When managers take decisions for simple and straightforward problems (structured problems), the decisions are known as routine or programmed decisions. The programmed decisions adopt solutions from the past. Some of the routine decisions which come under programmed decisions are resulting in increase in pay to the employees or performance rewards and sanctioning leave requests made by employees.

Non-programmed Decision

When managers have to take decisions which are not routine but unique in nature for unstructured problems and are not supported by proper information and bear certain risks, such types of decisions are known as non-programmed decisions. These decisions are generally customized for specific type of situations. The senior management mainly takes such type of decisions involving choice of strategies and objectives in situations of uncertainty. For example, after the Satyam fiasco, the strategy of Tech Mahindra to go for a Mahindra Satyam merger is an example of non-programmed decision. Here, the solution timeframe is relatively long.

Strategic Decisions

The decisions taken by the top-level management to fulfil organizational goals and objectives are said to be strategic decisions. It involves expansion of business or diversifying into other business areas. Strategic decisions are generally non-programmed decisions.

Tactical Decisions

Tactical decisions are taken by the middle-level management and constitute allocation of roles and responsibilities to employees and formulating the budget for the department. These are generally programmed in nature.

Major and Minor Decisions

Some examples of major decision include acquisitions of organizations or mergers or diversifying into other business area, and minor decisions might range from granting leave to an employee to preparing monthly budget for the unit's expenditure.

Individual and Group Decisions

Group decision-making generally outperforms individuals who make decisions in isolation, but in some instances, individual decision-making can work wonders in an organization when group fails to arrive at a consensus.

Decision-making Models

There are decision-making models which stress on the approach of decision-making, and these models have specific assumptions. For example, the classical model of decision-making assumes that managers are logical and they will work for the best interest of the organization. This scenario in business organizations is really infrequent, so the next-generic model which gained popularity was the rational decision-making model.

- **Classical model:** The classical model states that managers have access to all possible types of information to reach a decision. If there is more than one alternative, the manager ranks the alternatives. He implements the best alternative, and it is assumed that the manager knows what is best for the organization. In reality, it is that most of the time the manager does not have all the information he or she requires. This model is otherwise known as the rational model.
- **Rational model:** This model assumes that there exists a problem, for which a decision has to be taken by first understanding the problem, identifying alternatives constrained by legal and ethical norms, and technology, resource, and budget constraints. An evaluation of these alternatives is done by considering the feasibility, satisfaction, and affordability parameters and the consequences of implementing the alternative. The steps in rational decision-making are as follows:
    - Identify the problem.
    - Find out the criteria for the decision.
    - Attach weights to the criteria.
    - Generate alternatives.
    - Rate each alternative on each criterion.
    - Compute the optimal decision.
    - Implement the decision.
    - Evaluate the outcome.

All these steps have been already explained by taking an appropriate example under the section 'Decision-making Concepts.'

- **Administrative model:** This model states why classical model is not used by managers while making the decisions. The reason being that most of the times, a decision taken is accompanied by risk and uncertainty mainly due to incomplete or ambiguous information. On the other hand, information at times may be costly and not available on time or managers may not have time to explore all possible alternatives. For each problem, there are so many solution alternatives that it is not possible for the manager to consider all. Further decisions are limited by people's cognitive limitations and are known as bounded rationality, which means that leaders tend to take decisions based on choosing solutions that meet minimum requirements and are good enough.
- **Political model:** According to the political model, an individual seeks to take decisions with an aim to satisfy their own or organization's interest or goals such as the stakeholders of the company. The tilt in the outcome of the decision is always in their favour. Collation of data and searching for relevant information happen with a perspective to obtain individual paybacks in commercial dealings.

Herbert Simon's Model of Decision-making

Herbert Simon states that decision-making consists of intelligence, design, and choice phase.

According to Herbert A. Simon, the decision-making process is basically divided into three branches:

- Intelligence
- Design
- Choice

Intelligence Phase

The first step in decision-making is the intelligence phase or otherwise known as primary quantitative process. In the intelligence phase, raw data are collected and processed to generate information, which, in turn, is analysed to generate intelligence.

General intelligence consists of proper analysis of problem. Analysis consists of identification of problems, types of problems, proper understanding of problem, and pattern of problem.

Analysis is done on the basis of data or the facts that are present. It also depends upon the available information related to problem. But only analysis is not helpful in problem solving. With proper analysis, knowledge to solve a problem is equally important. Also, consideration of situation, priorities, goals, and alternatives is necessary.

- **Problem identification:** It depends on managerial scenes and abilities to produce ideas (brainstorming). Problem identification also depends upon visualization, structuring, and clarification of ideas.
- **Problem definition:** In this step, managers have to create the correct business case for any problem scenario.
- **Problem classification:** Here, managers classify the problem based on the degree of complexity and on the analysis performed on it.
- **Structural modelling:** Structural modelling encompasses objective functions, such as profit maximization/cost minimization, explicit and implicit constraints, outcomes, and conditions of invariance, all of which can be portrayed using a model. The example includes a small segment of organization producing a product for the same customer segment for the same demographic zone. The model assumes profit maximization, production, and quality assurance functions and the demands they face. Also, the amount of information they have of each other and their focus on different variables like price, quantity, or quality can be represented using the structural model to denote the scenario.

Design Phase

This is the next step after the analysis phase. After proper understanding and analysis, effective steps are designed to solve the problems. The action on problem solving is present in the design phase. The model of decision-making is constructed, tested, and validated.

Modelling contains abstraction of problems and their relationship among variables and also an alternative course of action. In designing, decision-making variables like situation, time, people, and schedule are considered. The decision models designed at this phase clearly depict managerial situation and decision variables, and identify performance measure that reflects the objectives of decision-making.

Choice Phase

It is a direct act of decision-making process and correlated with finding optimal solution to the problem with decision modelling. Actual action is performed in this phase. The decision is taken in this phase only. If the person has some choice to solve some problems, it means that person is making decision to move in one direction. Choice makes direction of decision. And it depends upon the previous understanding of problem or perceptions.

Common Difficulties in Decision-making

Decision-making becomes difficult due to the following reasons:

- When the information is inadequate or incomplete.
- When there is a lack of information on political, social, and economic variables.

- To arrive at a rational decision, it is mandatory for a decision maker to be an expert in the respective domain, should be highly intelligent, and have farsightedness for future situations, which generally is a rare occurrence.
- Decisions should be impartial and closely align to organization's goals and objectives. Individual preferences and attitudes often come in the way of decision-making.
- Decisions taken by managers are always accompanied by compromise and adjustments, for example, a compromise on the cost of a service delivered can directly bring in a compromise on the benefits obtained from that service so that decisions are balanced.

Decision-making for Organizational Effectiveness

Decision-making needs to be done for organizational effectiveness because effect of too poor and slow decision-making can generate negative ripples throughout the organization. Hence, decision-making needs to be defined and refined at frequent intervals. Decision-making is closely related to control and is used for managing trading issues that require organizational decision-making. Decision-making encompasses cataloguing critical decisions that must be made, identifying appropriate authority of who has the relevant information that will help them make these decisions, and keeping evidence of who will be ultimately accountable for decisions made. Effective decision-making empowers individuals to make the right decisions at the right time.

Decision-making Styles

Autocratic

The leader takes up the entire responsibility of making the decisions and will be held responsible for the outcome being good or bad. Generally, managers who imbibe autocratic style do not take suggestions from others. An autocratic style results in quick decision-making, which is an advantage, but the disadvantage is that it solely depends on the decision-making ability of that individual who weighs the pros and cons of each and every alternative and finally implements the same. If the outcome is negative, then the leader loses his image as the team or people from that team feel that they could have come out with a better solution.

Participative

In the participative style, the leader involves the members of his team to take the decision, though the total control resides with him. He makes the teams feel of actually taking ownership for finding solution to the problem. If the leader is a good listener and open minded, then he can with the information collected take better decision, but the disadvantage of the participative style is that it is a slow and time-consuming process and is somewhat less secured.

Consultative

Consultative decision-making is when a leader gives up total control of the decision to his team. Now if the entire team agrees to the decision, then the decision is said to be taken on consensus, but if some members have agreed to the decision and some have not, then the style becomes democratic. The advantage of this is that if the group consensus is 100%, everyone has a stake if the outcome is successful. Also, the decision is more accurate because the skill and the brain of every individual are best utilized. This style is strenuous because a lot of effort is put in getting the employees to collaborate and work together.

Democratic

In this style of decision-making, a leader allows his team to vote for a decision. The alternative which gets the majority of the votes is taken as the final alternative. The decision-making is faster in this case, though responsibility is not accorded to any individual for the outcome of implementing the alternative for that decision.

Part II: Quantitative Techniques for Decision-making

Business managers depend on their knowledge and intuition to make robust decisions. They show substantial interest towards analytics from interpretation of the data. In this age of big data, quantitative techniques used by analysts provide strong proof to show management decisions on production, distribution, marketing, and personnel management. These methods also help managers to project future business conditions, enabling them to adjust their strategies as needed. The first technique which is useful for managers to take decisions on levels of inventories or optimizing inventory carrying cost for big manufacturing organizations is explained below. This model which is deterministic in nature is known as the EOQ model. There also exist some probabilistic models.

Inventory refers to idle goods or raw materials that are kept by any organization for future use, and consists of components, subassemblies, work in process, finished goods, and so on. Thus, inventory acts like buffer when the demand level varies at customer's end or at an organization's end. The cost associated with inventory can run into the millions of dollars. To optimize on the cost, following two crucial questions need to be answered:

- Order level of goods for replenishing.
- Time interval when order has to be replenished.

The purpose of this topic is to show how quantitative models can assist in making these above decisions and to understand that one has to have a brief idea about the following models:

- Deterministic or EOQ model (rate of demand is constant) for satisfying consistent demand.
- Probabilistic model (rate of demand is fluctuated) for satisfying variations in demand.
- Material requirements planning model for managing inventories.
- Just-in-time model for managing waste.

We will limit our study with respect to the first model since the sole intention is to make the readers understand how the inventory model works and how the decision-making by the managers is aided with the help of this model. There are other models which are probabilistic in nature, and the just in time models are the material requirements planning model.

Deterministic or EOQ Model

Let us consider the situation faced by the Red Herring, a cosmetic company. Red Herring is the distributor of lipsticks, nail polishes, deodorants, and perfumes. From a central location in Basel in Germany, Red Herring supplies nearly 1,000 retail stores with cosmetic items. The total inventory for the cosmetic company for perfumes averages approximately 50,000 units with an average of \$10 per unit. The total inventory carrying cost estimates to \$500,000. Since the carrying cost is an exceptionally large amount, the Head of Inventory decided to do a detailed study of the inventory costs associated, with the purpose to arrive at how-much-to-order and when-to-order decisions that will result in deriving the lowest possible total cost. So he started collecting demand figure from the inventory manager. Let the average demand per week is 412 units of shampoo. Based on the model, the prediction for the demand is seen to be a constant, an impossible situation under business conditions. Now, to compute the number of units to be ordered, the manager has to take decisions to do the following:

- Keep small inventories and order frequently (high ordering costs).
- Keep large inventories and order at long intervals (high inventory costs).

So to find an optimal compromise between the two, the total cost is taken into account, which constitutes the ordering cost and the holding cost.

Holding costs include the cost associated for maintaining or carrying a given level of inventory (small/large); these costs depend on the size of the inventory and are usually calculated on a percentage basis. There are a number of other holding costs, such as insurance, taxes, breakage, pilferage, and unit's overhead that also depends on the value of the inventory. The total holding cost as calculated by Red Herring amounted to 20% of each unit's (shampoo) cost, that is, \$2.

Ordering costs which are fixed cover the preparation of the voucher and the processing of the order, including payment, postage, telephone, transportation, invoice verification, receiving, and so on. It has been seen that Red Herring spends on an average \$20 per unit of shampoo irrespective of the quantity ordered. For the usage of the EOQ model to answer questions such as how much and when to order, we have now three values in hand and we need to find the value of *Q*, that is, how much to order.

The inventory level for Red Herring will have a maximum value of *Q* units when an order of size *Q* is received from the supplier and will come to 0 units in a week's time, and then the next lot will arrive. On an average, Red Herring will have *Q*/2 inventory level across the months as shown in Figure 7.1 for a constant demand situation.

Figure 7.1 Inventory Pattern

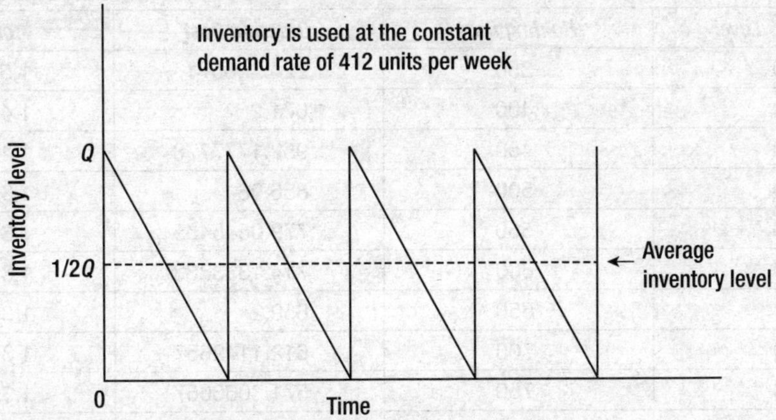

Inventory pattern for EOQ inventory model

Now, the holding and ordering costs have to be calculated annually to get the yearly predictions of how much to and when to order for the correct inventory level.

Let I = annual holding cost rate,
C = unit cost of the inventory item, and
C_h = annual cost of holding one unit in inventory.
The annual cost of holding one unit in inventory is $C_h = I_C$.

Then for the $Q/2$ inventory level, the total annual holding cost is as follows:

$$\text{Annual holding cost} = (\text{Average inventory}) \times (\text{Annual holding cost for one unit})$$
$$C_{AH} = (Q/2)C_h$$
$$\text{Annual Ordering Cost} = (\text{Number of orders per year}) \times (\text{Unit order cost})$$
$$= (D/Q)C$$

Let D be annual demand and Q units are ordered every time, and number of orders per year equates to D/Q. Let cost per order be C. So, total ordering cost = $(D/Q)C$. Thus, the total annual cost, denoted by TC, can be expressed as follows:

$$\text{Total annual cost} = \text{Annual holding cost} + \text{annual ordering cost}$$
$$= (Q/2) \times C_{AH} + (D/Q) \times C$$
$$= (Q/2)\$2 + ((412 \times 52)/Q) \times C = Q + 428{,}480/Q.$$

The weekly demand is 446 as calculated previously, and for 52 weeks, C being \$20, the total cost of the inventory becomes $Q + 428{,}480/Q$.

Above is the general total-cost equation for inventory situations in which the assumptions of the EOQ model are valid.

The Decision—How Many Units

In order to minimize the total inventory cost, different values of Q have to be put in the equation and the cost has to be found. It is seen that cost becomes minimum for the inventory level of 650 units using a trial-and-error approach for different values of Q (Table 7.11 and Figure 7.2).

Table 7.11 Inventory Data

Inventory Level	*Holding Cost*	*Ordering Cost*	*Total Cost*
350	350	1,224.228571	1,574.229
400	400	1,071.2	1,471.2
450	450	952.1777778	1,402.178
500	500	856.96	1,356.96
550	550	779.0545455	1,329.055
600	600	714.1333333	1,314.133
650	650	659.2	1,309.2
700	700	612.1142857	1,312.114
750	750	571.3066667	1,321.307
800	800	535.6	1,335.6
850	850	504.0941176	1,354.094

Inventory Level	Holding Cost	Ordering Cost	Total Cost
900	900	476.0888889	1,376.089
950	950	451.0315789	1,401.032
1,000	1,000	428.48	1,428.48
1,050	1,050	408.0761905	1,458.076
1,100	1,100	389.5272727	1,489.527

Figure 7.2 Graph Showing Optimized Inventory Cost

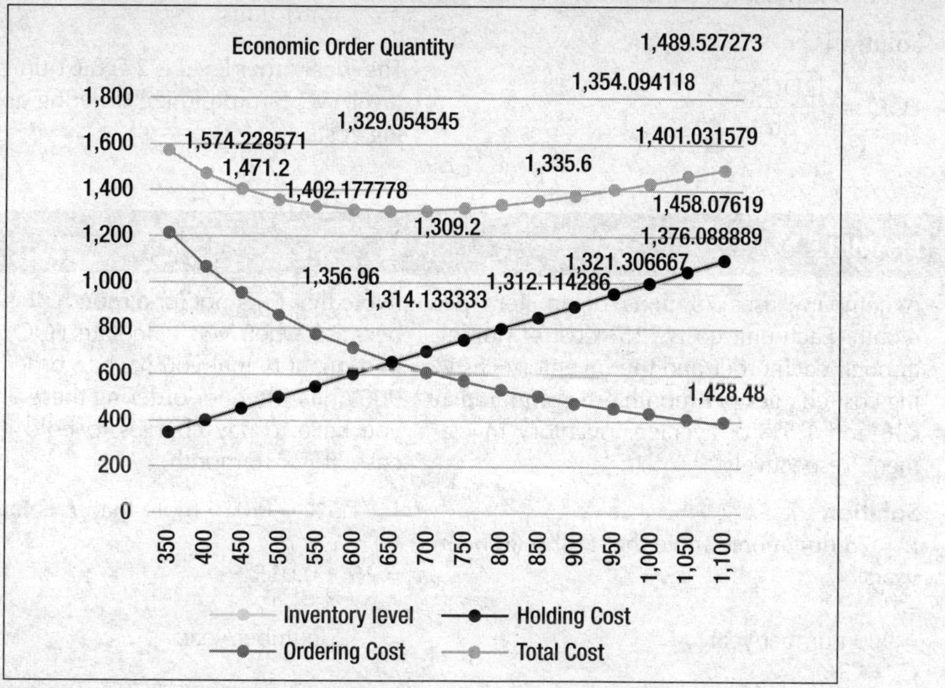

The disadvantage of the trial-and-error scheme is that it does not provide the exact minimum-cost order quantity. So, a more appropriate formula can be obtained using differential calculus, so that the value of Q^* that minimizes the total annual cost is given by the formula

$$Q^* = \sqrt{\frac{2DC_0}{C_h}}, \text{ that is, } \sqrt{2(412 \times 52 \times 20)/2} = 654.58 \text{ units}$$

The When-to-order Decision

Total demand placed in one year or 52 weeks = 412 × 52 = 21,424.

Inventory level considered is 654.58 units.

So, total number of orders considered is (21,424/655) = 32 orders.

Suppose the company has 6 working days per week, so cycle time for the order will be $(52 \times 6)/32 = 9.75$ days (considering only Sunday as holiday). But if the company is operational 300 days per year, only then cycle time is given by $300/32 = 9.3$ days a year.

The when-to-order decision is taken as number of operational days of the company/D/Q^*.

So the manager has to order for the inventory after every 9 days to optimize on the cost.

Two other simple examples have been also given for easy read and understanding by the reader in context of the decision-making to be done by the manager.

EXAMPLE

Demand for a commodity is 15,000 units/year. Holding cost per year/unit is ₹1.20, and the cost of one procurement is ₹300. Find EOQ.

Solution

$$EOQ = \sqrt{\frac{2DCo}{Ch}}$$

$$= \sqrt{\frac{2 \times 15{,}000 \times 300}{1.20}}$$

$= 2738.61$ units

The ideal order level is 2738.61 units. At this level, we can minimize ordering and carrying costs.

EXAMPLE

A company uses 75 units of an item per month. Each unit costs ₹25. Cost of putting through each order and the inventory carrying cost charges per month are computed at ₹36 and 1.5% of average inventory investment, respectively.

Solution

$D = 75$ unit/month (note that D should be in years)

$= 75 \times 12$

$= 900$ number/year

$C_o = ₹36$

(Note that C_o is not for a month. It is per unit because when you calculate EOQ, you get best quantity that you have to order, say it is 900 units. Then for ordering these 900 units, you have to pay charges to hold it. In this case, it is ₹36/month)

$I = 1.5\% = 0.015$ (note that 'I' is Inventory)

$C_h = C \times I$

$= 25 \times 0.015$

$= 0.375 \times 12$

$=$ ₹4.5/number/year.

Just-in-time Manufacturing

It is also known as 'lean manufacturing', which refers to manufacturing of products which are ordered and paid for companies that have successfully implemented just-in-time manufacturing, which include companies such as Toyota and Dell. The objective behind implementing the just-in-time concept is to control unnecessary wastage as listed below:

- Avoid
- Reduce
- Reuse
- Recycle
- Recover
- Treat
- Dispose

Let us consider the case of Toyota in context of the just-in-time production strategy. Toyota production strategy is highlighted by the fact that raw materials are brought to the production floor only when an order is received and this product is ready to be built. Neither the raw material nor subparts are ordered until a requisition is received. This philosophy has allowed Toyota to keep a minimum amount of inventory, thus reducing the inventory capital. This also means that Toyota can adapt quickly to changes in demand without having to worry about disposing of expensive inventory.

- Small amounts of raw material inventory are kept at each node in production for use.
- Precision of forecasting is important for implementation of the just in time concept, and Toyota has acquired the desired precision.

There is again the case of Dell which has also leveraged the just-in-time concept to make its manufacturing process a success. Dell's approach to just-in-time concept is to delegate responsibility to its suppliers to implement just-in-time concept, resulting in short lead times on components so that products can be assembled by Dell quickly and then shipped to the customer. The model on which Dell operates has become successful due to a strong supplier support, seamless demand projection of material, or semi-finished products by Dell to its suppliers.

Material Requirements Planning

Material requirements planning, a computer-based inventory requirement planning, is used to manage manufacturing processes.

Objectives of Material Requirements Planning

- Ensures material availability for production to avoid shortages.
- Reduces waste by maintaining lowest possible products levels in stock.
- Helps manufacturing company in planning, scheduling, and controlling inventory for raw materials and products.

Benefits of Material Requirements Planning

- Helps to identify what is required, when it is required, and quantity of raw materials.
- Helps to reduction purchasing cost, freight cost, manufacturing cost, and so on.
- Helps to reduce lead time.
- Helps in reducing inventory levels.
- Helps in enhancing customer service.
- Improves productivity.

Disadvantages of Material Requirement Planning

- Dependency on forecasts.
- Costly implementation.
- Time consuming.

Decision-making Tools

It is said that organizational effectiveness comes with effectiveness in decision-making, which is a trait to be compulsorily possessed by the managers taking strategic, tactical, and operation decisions within the organizations. To take the decisions, these managers use various decision-making tools, some of which are explained using examples for better understanding and also to get a practical insight into how a decision is arrived at.

Cost–Benefit Analysis

This is a technique in which the values of the benefits of a course of action are added, and the costs associated with it are subtracted to determine the net result.

The senior management of a small organization is deciding whether or not to invest in a new computerized customer service (CSS) system. Realizing the potential of the CSS which can reach a large number of customers and provide more efficient customer services, the management implemented the CSS. The senior management carried out the cost–benefit analysis, and it was inferred that the system would pay for itself within the second year of operation (Table 7.12).

Table 7.12 Decision-making Using Cost–Benefit Analysis Tool

Costs					*Benefits Per Annum*	
Category	***Item***	***Quantity***	***Price (₹)***	***Total (₹)***	***Category***	***Total (₹)***
Material resources	Workstation	5	20,000	100,000	Electronic advertisement	120,000
	CSS Software	5 licences	150,000	150,000	Lead conversion	85,000
	Server	1	80,000	80,000	Customer retention and enhancing customer base	60,000
	LAN infrastructure	1	50,000	50,000	Data accuracy	25,000
					Process improvement	40,000
Training	CSS Software	5	30,000	150,000		
Maintenance (yearly)	Updations and support		40,000	40,000		
Others	Sales lost during transition and hiring people for technical support		60,000	60,000		
Total				630,000		330,000

In this example, we see that the costs incurred sum to an amount of ₹630,000. This is a one-time cost excepting the maintenance cost which is to be incurred by the company year on year. The benefits to be incurred every year would sum up to ₹330,000, which makes the fact evident that in subsequent years, the company would incur profit if the system is implemented.

Force Field Analysis

This is a technique for looking at all the forces for and against a decision. It differs from the pros and cons method by identifying ways to strengthen the forces that support the decision and reduce the impacts of the opposing decision on it. The earlier example can again be considered. Since total forces for change (value 13) is less than forces against change (value 14), the senior management should not go ahead with the decision of buying the CSS Solutions. This is actually what happens when we use the pros and cons technique. But using force field, we can think of certain forces which can act against the final result. For example, if management decides to buy two licences of the software instead of five, trains two people instead of five, and also uses in-house staff, having done some technical support job in the past, then the cost–benefit analysis would incline more towards benefit with the costing going down. So the purchasing and training cost would get a low score, and acquiring people for technical support would also score less, thus bringing down the total score for forces against change (Figure 7.3).

Grid Analysis Method

It is a technique for doing analysis for each of the options based on the factors used to arrive at a decision. The grid analysis table (Table 7.13) lists options as rows of a table and the factors as columns of the table. Weights are allocated to show the factors, and these are multiplied by the ratings to each of the options. Then, the highest scoring option is taken.

For example, a student of a certain Institute of Pune got three offers from three Pune-based Companies. He used the grid analysis method to decide which company to join after getting an offer.

The immediate inference is that the student should take up the offer of Persistent from the three.

Figure 7.3 Decision-making Using Force Field Analysis Tool

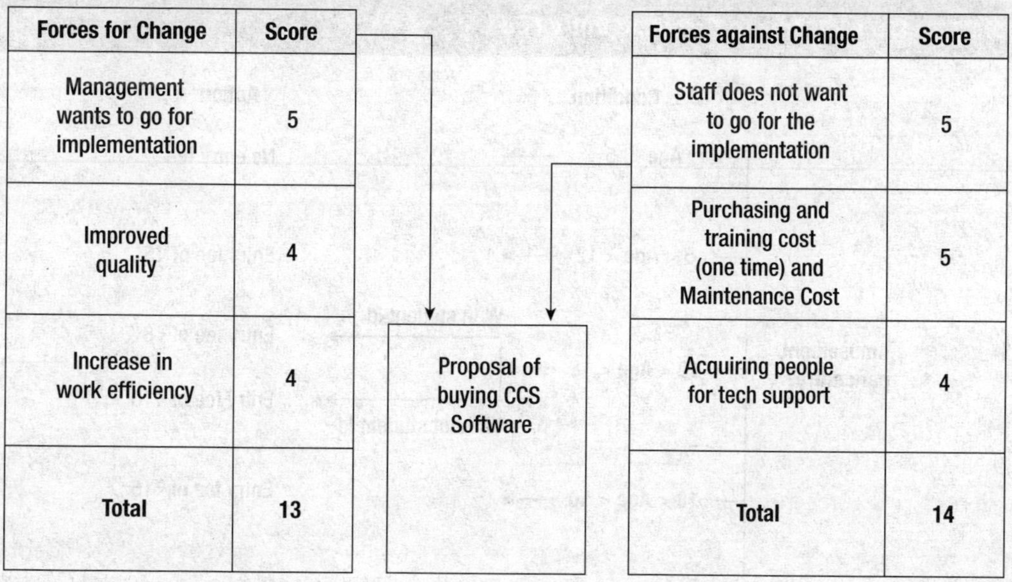

Table 7.13 Decision-making Using Grid Analysis Method

Factors	Role and Responsibility	Salary Structure	Company Profile	Location Category	Other Benefits
Weights	4	5	3	2	2
First insight	3	3	2	4	2
Bitwise	4	3	3	4	3
Persistent	4	4	4	4	4

Factors	Role and Responsibility	Salary Structure	Company Profile	Location Category	Other Benefits	Total
Weights	4	5	3	2	2	
First insight	12	15	6	8	4	45
Bitwise	16	15	9	8	6	54
Persistent	16	20	12	8	8	64

Decision Trees

A decision tree is a way of representing various decisions and its combinations for specific situations and mainly aims at representing action sequences. The decisions taken are based on the conditions, and then actions are executed. To understand or draw a decision tree, follow or draw the 'branches' of the tree, the 'branches' being the lines that connect the process to the conditions and actions. Figure 7.4 shows a decision tree used to calculate the entry fee for amusement park is as follows:

Figure 7.4 Decision Tree to Calculate Entry Fee

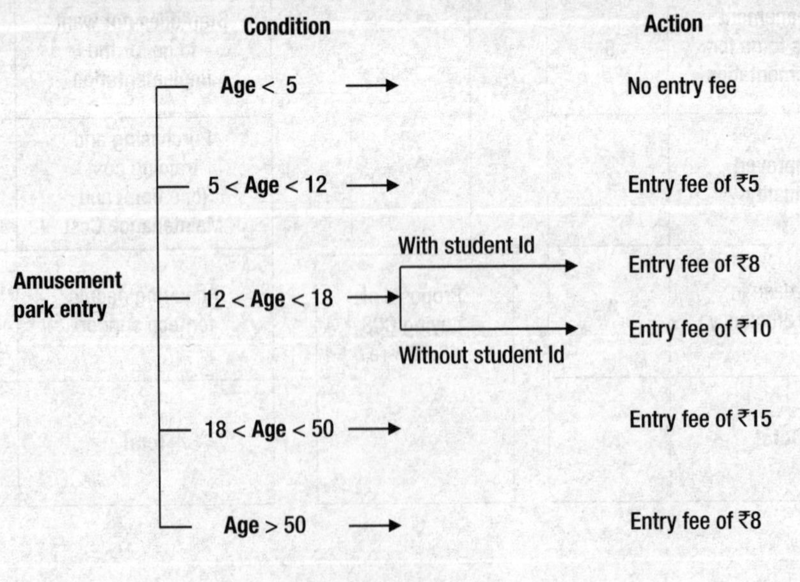

Figure 7.5 Decision Tree to Generate Feedback Percentage Given by Students (Aggre_per, Aggregate Percentage)

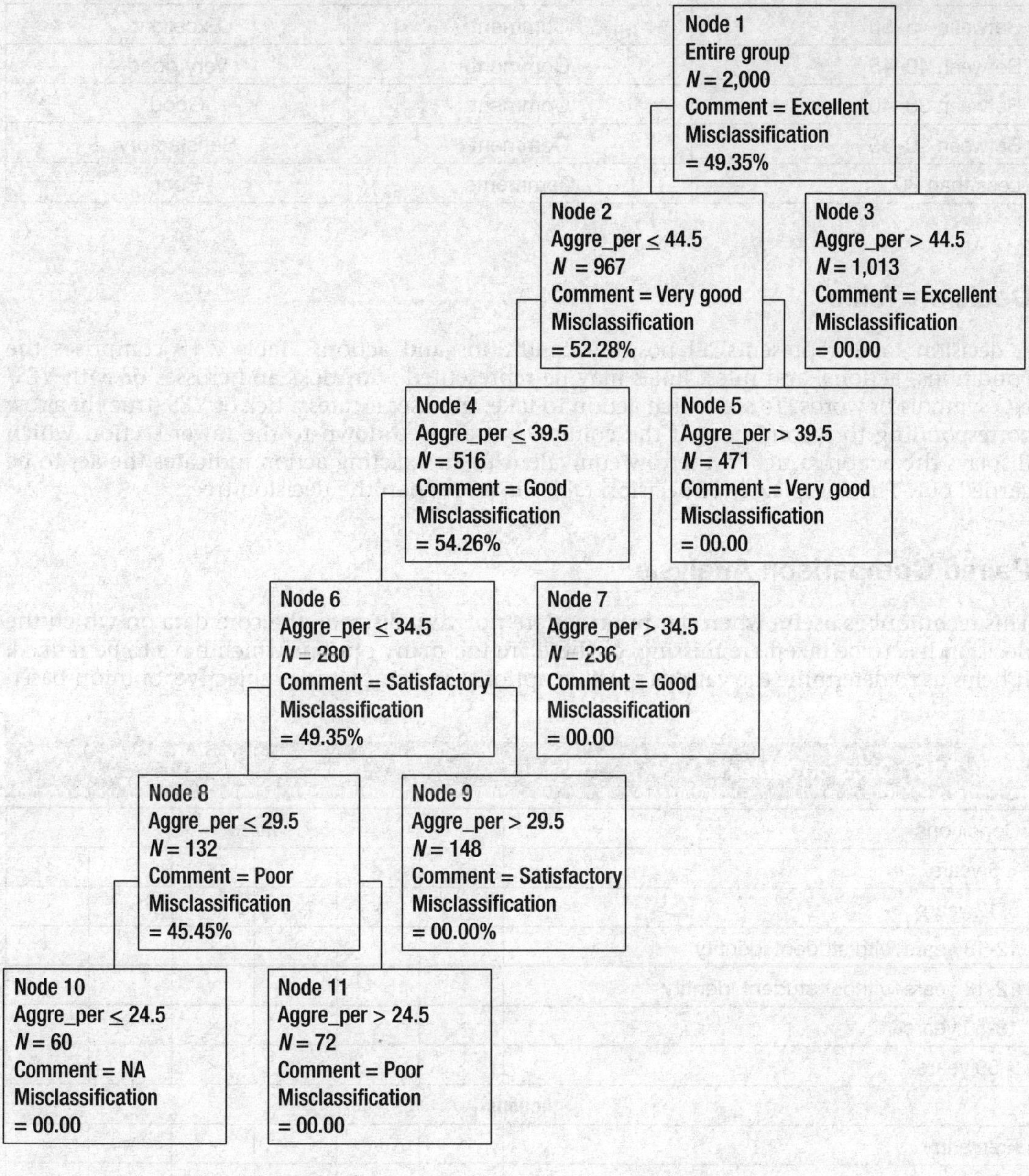

In the example, children under 5 years of age are to be admitted free of charge, children 5 years and over but under 12 years are charged ₹5, children between 12 and 18 years are charged ₹8 (carrying a student identity) and ₹10 (without identity), respectively, and children over 18 but under 50 years of age are charged ₹15. Senior citizens over 50 years are charged only ₹8. The next (Figure 7.5) is another example of a decision tree generated using a tool.

This decision tree shows that out of a sample of 2,000 students, how many gave feedback categorized as excellent, very good, good, satisfactory, and poor based on the rules as shown in Table 7.14.

Table 7.14 Tabular Representation of the Feedback

	Cumulative Feedback	
Between 45–50	Comment	Excellent
Between 40–45	Comment	Very good
Between 35–40	Comment	Good
Between 30–35	Comment	Satisfactory
Less than 30	Comments	Poor

Decision Table

A decision table represents all possible conditions and actions. Table 7.15 comprises the conditions, actions, and rules. Rules may be represented with ticks and crosses or with YES/NO symbols or words. To see which action to take, the user locates a tick or YES (true) in a row corresponding to a condition. If the column is traversed down to the lower section which displays the action, a tick in the row equivalent to an exacting action indicates the act to be carried out. The complexity of decision tables is more than the decision trees.

Paired Comparison Analysis

This technique is useful when our priorities are not very discrete, the core data on which the decision has to be taken are missing, or there are too many options which have to be ranked. It helps us to determine the various possible options, and since it is a subjective, opinion-based

Table 7.15 Decision Table

Conditions	***Rules***					
< 5 years	√	×	×	×	×	×
5-12 years	×	√	×	×	×	×
12-18 years with student identity	×	×	√	×	×	×
12-18 years without student identity	×	×	×	√	×	×
18-50 years	×	×	×	×	√	×
> 50 years	×	×	×	×	×	√
Actions						
Free entry	√	×	×	×	×	×
Entry fee of ₹5	×	√	×	×	×	×
Entry fee of ₹8	×	×	√	×	×	×
Entry fee of ₹10	×	×	×	√	×	×
Entry fee of ₹15	×	×	×	×	√	×
Entry fee of ₹8	×	×	×	×	×	√

Table 7.16 Paired Comparison Analysis I

Options	*Pramod*	*Richa*	*Manpreet*	*Makrand*	*Arpit*	*Abhinav*
Pramod		R,2	Man,2	Mak,2	A,1	P,1
Richa			R,1	R,1	R,2	R,2
Manpreet				Man,1	Man,2	Man,2
Makrand					Mak,1	Mak,1
Arpit						Ab,1
Abhinav						

Table 7.17 Paired Comparison Analysis II

Candidate	*Preference Value*	*Difference Value*	*Percentage of Totalled Difference*	*Rank*
Pramod	1	1	4.5	4
Richa	5	8	36	1
Manpreet	4	7	32	2
Makrand	3	4	18	3
Arpit	1	1	4.5	4
Abhinav	1	1	4.5	4
Total		22		

technique, it is useful in situations where precise cause and effect relationships are difficult to measure. Let us understand it with the help of a specific example.

To choose from among a group of students who can be nominated for anchoring a specific event. The nominations stood as follows: Pramod, Richa, Manpreet, Priyanka, Makrand, Arpit, and Abhinav (Table 7.16).

First row compares Pramod with everyone else. So, Richa exceeds Pramod by 2 points, Manpreet by 2 points, Makrand by 2 points, Arpit by 1 point, and Pramod scores over Abhinav by 1 point.

Similar operations are performed for 2nd till 6th row. Next, using mathematical framework, we evaluate the total scores of each (Table 7.17).

Inference: Richa has scored the highest followed by Manpreet and Makrand in second and third places, respectively.

Pros and Cons Method with Benefits

This technique allows one to check on whether or not a course of action will actually improve the situation and is worth taking. So along with pros and cons to a particular decision, there are benefits aligned with the decision. An example (shown in Table 7.18) will make the scenario clearer.

A student wants to opt for a Master of Computer Applications (MCA) course. The option should be to pursue MCA course by the student.

Table 7.18 Pros and Cons Method Decision Style

Pros	*Cons*	*Benefits/Loss*
Professional course (+4)	Three-year PG Degree course (–2)	Skill sets will include proficiency in programming languages (+2)
Job opportunities are moderate (+3)	Graduate engineers and MCAs are considered at par (–3)	Salary of fresh recruits is 0.3 million per annum (+3)
Course approved by AICTE and Universities across India (+4)	Investment for the course is 0.45 million per annum (–4)	Considered to be at a second grade in comparison to engineering courses (–3)
+11	–9	2

Pareto's Analysis

Pareto's analysis is a tool to find out all the root causes of the problem and also finding the ones that have the greatest frequency. Pareto analysis also states that 80% of the problems originate from 20% of the causes. Pareto was an economist and sociologist of the 19th century whose analysis was used to identify problems for different business situations. Steps conducted to identify the problems and the causes are defined in Figure 7.6.

This sequence of steps can be clearly depicted using an example about customer satisfaction for a Web-deployed application used by 250 customers (Table 7.19 and Figure 7.7).

Figure 7.6 Pareto's Analysis of Causal Effect

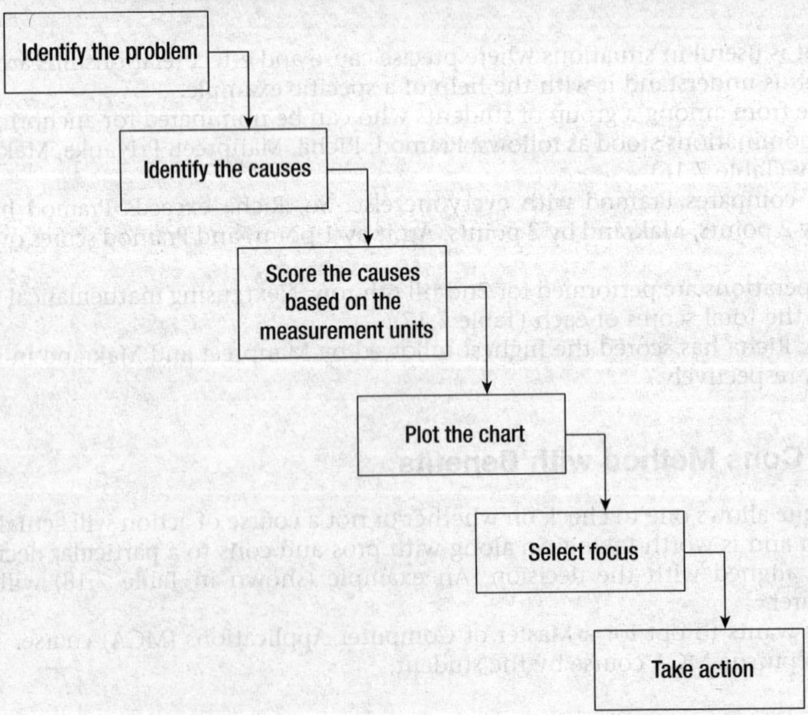

Table 7.19 Decision-making Using Pareto's Analysis

Problem	***Cause***	***Score***	***Cumulative***
Not so user friendly	Graphic user interface was made by people with less experience	98	98
Website was slow	Dedicated server was not used	57	155
Add to Cart was not working for multiple items	Functionality still on the make	29	184
Saving data into the database was not happening through front-end application for some number of forms	Due to slow website	14	198

Figure 7.7 Graphical Representation Showing the Problem-centric Area

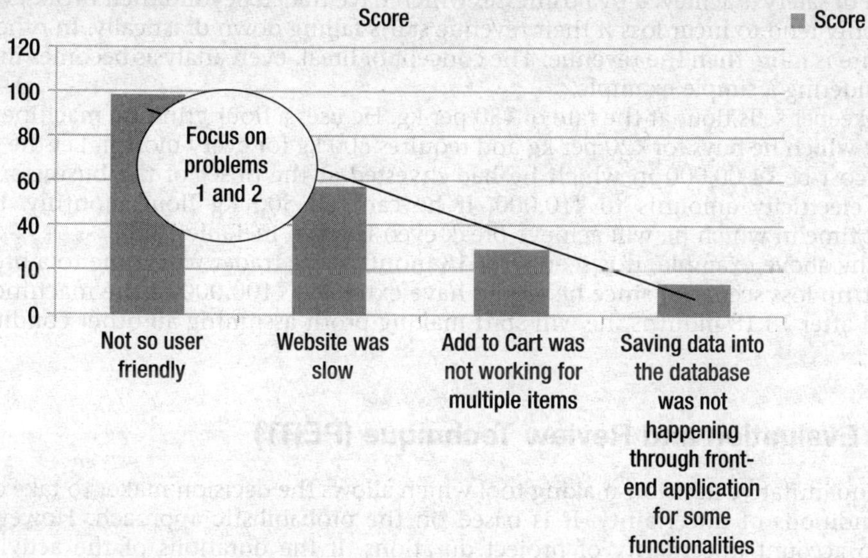

Break-even Analysis

The break-even analysis helps business managers to take decisions related to goal setting, achieving targets in terms of revenue, production, sales, and cost optimization, and so on.

A break-even analysis is the analysis of total cost versus the total revenue of a business. If the total cost equates to the total revenue, then the business has achieved its break-even point.

The calculation can be applied to the business entity as whole, or to the sales, product, or business unit.

For a new business, the break-even point refers to sustaining its own expenses and paying from its own pockets instead of taking loans from other entities. Therefore, from a business planning perspective, cash reserves of the business should be proper to stay buoyant till the break-even point is exceeded.

Business costs can be categorized as fixed or variable. The total costs will vary based on the expenses incurred and also will depend on factors, such as seasonal demands, the market scenario, and so on.

Table 7.20 Break-even Analysis

Fixed cost	Machinery cost (₹)	1,00,000
	Electricity cost per month (₹)	5,000
	Transport cost per month (₹)	2,000
	Packaging cost per month (₹)	2,500
Variable cost	Price of 500 kg wheat at ₹20 per month (₹)	10,000
Sales	500 kg flour at ₹50 per month (₹)	25,000
Profit/loss statement	Per month profit (₹)	5,500
Number of months required to extract the machine cost from the profit earned		100,000/5,500 = 18.18 months

Margin of safety is achieved by businesses which have traded beyond their break-even point and will only tend to incur loss if their revenue starts falling down drastically. In other words, expenditure is more than the revenue. The concept of break-even analysis becomes more clear after considering a simple example.

A shopkeeper sells flour at the rate of ₹50 per kg. He uses a flour grinding machine to grind the wheat which he buys for ₹20 per kg and requires 500 kg for every month. Let the grinding machine cost be ₹1,00,000 in which he had invested at the onset of the business, and the monthly electricity amounts to ₹10,000. If he can sell 500 Kg flour monthly, then the estimated time in which he will achieve break-even is given in Table 7.20.

From the above example, it is seen after 18 months, the trader will come to a break-even (no profit/no loss scenario) since he would have extracted ₹100,000 of the machine cost by then, and after 18.18 months, he will start making profit assuming all other conditions are stable.

Project Evaluation and Review Technique (PERT)

PERT is a quantitative decision-making tool which allows the decision maker to take decisions under conditions of uncertainty. It is based on the probabilistic approach. However, CPM takes into account uncertainty of project durations. If the durations of the activities in a project are uncertain, then the scheduling is done using the expected values of the durations. In other words, under the conditions of uncertainty, the estimated time for each activity for the PERT network is represented by a probability distribution. This probability distribution of activity time is based upon three different time estimates made for each activity. These are as follows:

t_o = the optimistic time, it is the shortest possible time to complete the activity if all goes well.

t_p = the pessimistic time, it is the longest time that an activity could take if everything goes wrong.

t_m = the most likely time, it is the estimate of the normal time an activity would take. If only one time was available, this would be it. Otherwise, it is the mode of the probability distribution.

The t_o, t_m, and t_p are combined statistically to calculate the expected time t_e of an activity. The fundamental assumption in PERT is that the three time estimates form the end points and mode of Beta distribution.

Figure 7.8 Time Estimates

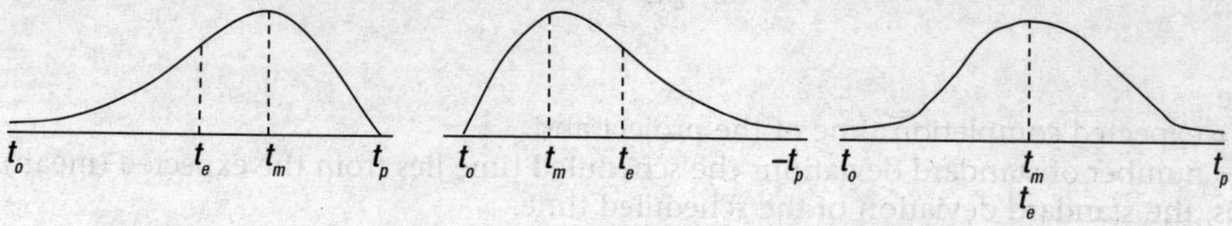

The range specified by the optimistic time (t_o) and pessimistic time (t_p) estimates supposedly must enclose every possible estimate of the duration of the activity. The most likely time (t_m) estimate may not coincide with the midpoint $(t_o + t_p)/2$ and may occur to its left or to its right as shown in Figure 7.8.

It may be justified to assume that the duration of each activity may follow Beta (β) distribution with its unimodal point occurring at t_m and its end points t_o and t_p.

In Beta distribution, the mid-point $(t_o + t_p)/2$ is assumed to weigh half as much as the most likely point (t_m). Thus, the expected value of the activity duration can be approximated as the arithmetic mean of $(t_o + t_p)/2$ and $2t_m$. Thus, we have

$$t_e = \frac{1}{3}\left[2t_m + \left(t_o + t_p\right)/2\right]$$

$$\therefore \quad t_e = \frac{t_o + 4t_m + t_p}{6}$$

Since almost (99%) all values of random variables fall within ±3 standard deviation from the mean or fall within the range of approximately 6 standard deviation in length, the interval (t_o and t_p) is assumed to enclose about 6 standard deviation of a symmetric distribution. Thus, if *s* denotes the standard deviation, then

$$6\sigma = t_p - t_o$$

$$\therefore \sigma = (t_p - t_o)/6$$

The variance, therefore, is

$$\sigma^2 = [(t_p - t_o)/6\,]^2$$

Remark: In the PERT analysis, a Beta distribution is assumed because it is unimodal, has non-negative end points, and is approximately symmetric.

Probability of Meeting the Schedule Time

PERT enables to determine the probability of completing a contract on schedule. The scheduled dates are expressed as a number of time units from the present time. Initially they may be the Latest times (Li) for each event but after a project is started we shall know how far it has progressed at any given date, and the scheduled time will be the latest time if the project is to be completed on its original schedule.

The probability distribution of times for completing an event can be approximated by the normal distribution due to the central limit theorem. Thus, the probability of completing the project by scheduled time (T_s) is given by

$$\text{Prob}\left(z < \frac{T_s - T_e}{\sigma_e}\right)$$

The standard normal variate is given by

$$Z = \frac{T_s - T_e}{\sigma_e}$$

where

T_e = expected completion time of the project and

σ_e = number of standard deviations the scheduled time lies from the expected (mean) time, that is, the standard deviation of the scheduled time.

Using the cumulative normal distribution tables, the corresponding value of the standard normal variate is read off. This will give the required probability of completing the project on scheduled time.

EXAMPLE: PERT

Given the following information regarding a project as activities and estimates of the optimistic, most likely, and pessimistic times in days for completion of various activities.

Activity → Time Estimates ↓ (Days)	1–2	1–3	2–4	3–4	3–5	4–5
Optimistic (t_o)	2	9	5	2	6	8
Most likely (t_m)	5	12	14	5	9	17
Pessimistic (t_p)	14	15	17	8	12	20

- Draw the network diagram.
- Determine the critical path.
- Determine the expected project completion time and its variance.
- What is the probability that the project will be completed in 30 days?

Solution: Using the given data, we calculate the expected time and the variance for each activity.

Activity	***Time Estimates (Days)***			***Expected Time***	***Variance***
	Optimistic t_o	***Most Likely*** t_m	***Pessimistic*** t_p	$t_e = \frac{t_o + 4t_m + t_p}{6}$	$\sigma^2 = \left(\frac{t_p - t_o}{6}\right)^2$
1–2	2	5	14	6	4
1–3	9	12	15	12	1
2–4	5	14	17	13	4
3–4	2	5	8	5	1
3–5	6	9	12	9	1
4–5	8	17	20	16	4

The project network is as follows (refer to the figure below):

- The critical activities are 1 → 2, 2 → 4, and 4 → 5.
- Hence, the critical path is 1 → 2 → 4 → 5.
- The expected duration of the project is 35 days.

The variance of the project length is the sum of the variances of the critical activities.

$\therefore \sigma_e^2 = 4 + 4 + 4$

$= 12$

$\therefore$ Variance of the project length = 12 days

$\therefore \sigma_e = \sqrt{12} = 3.464$

Probability that the project will be completed in 30 days is given by the standard normal deviate, that is,

$$z = \frac{\text{Due date} - \text{Expected date of completion}}{\sqrt{\text{Variance}}}$$

$$\therefore z = \frac{30-35}{\sqrt{12}} = \frac{-5}{3.464} = -1.44$$

$\therefore P(z \leq -1.44) \quad = 0.5 - \Phi(1.44)$

$= 0.5 - 0.4251$

$= 0.0749$ (From Normal Table)

Hence, the probability that the project will be completed in 30 days is 0.0749.

Figure 7.9 Network Diagram

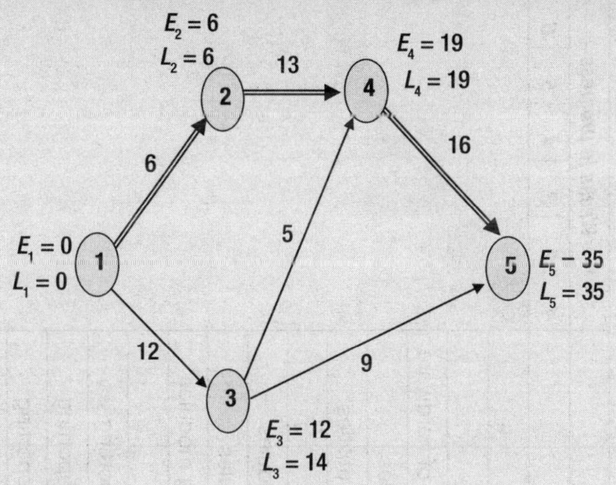

Gantt Charts

A Gantt chart is a matrix or an essential production control tool which helps in planning, tracking, and controlling specific project tasks. The chart lists on the *y*-axis all the tasks to be performed. Each row contains a single task and the work breakdown structure consisting of a number and name. The horizontal axis indicates estimated task duration or skill level needed to perform the task and the name of the person assigned to the task followed by one column for each period in the project's duration. Each period may be expressed in hours, days, weeks, months, and other time units.

The Gantt chart consists of a horizontal bar for each task connecting the start and end of a time period. A set of indicators are used to indicate estimated and actual start and end of a time period. The name of each person is assigned to the task on a separate line. This becomes

Table 7.21 Gantt Chart

		Weeks in progress →																	
WBS	**Task Name**	**1**	**2**	**3**	**4**	**5**	**6**	**7**	**8**	**9**	**10**	**11**	**12**	**13**	**14**	**15**	**16**	**17**	**18**
1	High-level analysis																		
2	Selection of hardware platform																		
3	Installation and commissioning of hardware																		
4	Detailed analysis of core modules																		
5	Detailed analysis of supporting utilities																		
6	Programming of core modules																		
7	Programming of supporting modules																		
8	Quality assurance of core modules																		
9	Quality assurance of supporting modules																		
10	Core module training																		
11	Development of accounting reporting																		
12	Development of management reporting																		
13	Development of management reporting																		
14	Detailed training																		
15	Documentation																		

possible using blank rows between tasks. When the project is progressing, this row is used to indicate the progress, indicated by a second bar which starts in the column where actual start date of the task is specified and continues until the task is actually completed. Comparison between estimated start and end and actual start and end should indicate project status on a task-by-task basis. A simple type of Gantt Chart represented for a typical software project on specific h/w platform shown in Table 7.21.

Summary

This chapter summarizes on the concepts of decision-making and provides an exemplary approach on the usage of various decision-making tools and stresses on the needs of decision-making, a core function of management.

Exercise

Objective Questions

1. Which of the following is a programmed decision?
    - Buying your favourite toothpaste or shampoo at the supermarket.
    - Acquire another organization.
    - Formulating the budget for the department.
    - Toyota launching new car.
2. Which one of them is not a decision-making tool?
    - Force field analysis.
    - Grid analysis method.
    - Pros and cons method with benefits.
    - Carrot and stick approach.
3. In which of the following when is decision-making easy?
    - You have complete information.
    - You are new to a domain.
    - You are expert in a domain.
    - Market is fluctuating.
4. Which of the following is the decision style where a leader gives up the total control of decision to his team?
    - Autocratic.
    - Participative.
    - Consultative.
    - Democratic.
5. Which decision-making style is useful when our priorities are not very discrete?
    - Force field analysis.
    - Paired comparison analysis.
    - Pros and cons method with benefits.
    - Decision trees.

6. In which model an individual seeks to take decisions with an aim to satisfy their own or organization's interest or goals?
    - Administrative model.
    - Political model.
    - Statistical model.
    - Classical model.
7. Is grid analysis method a technique for doing analysis for each of the options based on the factors used to arrive at a decision?
    - True
    - False
8. Which decision-making tool allows one to check on whether or not a course of action will actually improve the situation and is worth taking?
    - Force field analysis.
    - Grid analysis method.
    - Pros and cons method with benefits.
    - Carrot and stick approach.
9. Which among the following is the correct order for Herbert Simon's model of decision?
    - Intelligence, design, choice phase.
    - Design, intelligence, choice phase.
    - Choice, design, intelligence phase.
    - None of the above.
10. In which decision-making environment, consequence of every alternative is known?
    - Decision-making under risk.
    - Decision-making under uncertainty.
    - Decision-making under certainty.
    - None of the above.

Make a Choice

1. You promised your grandparents to spend coming weekend with them for the whole day, but in the meanwhile, your office team outing is planned. What will you do?
2. Pretend that you are playing cricket in your society and you break a window of a nearby house. The owner of the house hears the window break and comes running to see. What will you do?
3. You have one test question left to be answered and time is about to finish. You know the answer, but you just could not recall at that time. What would you do? Would you ask your neighbour to show the answer or would you leave it unanswered?

CASE STUDIES

Case 1

Sanjana is taking violin lessons since she was 8. Now a teenager, she misses other fun activities because of hectic schedule as she has to practice violin lessons every day after her school. She wants to quit violin lessons, but her parents do not allow her to do so.

What are the options that Sanjana would take to handle this scenario? Would she make a compromise?

Case 2

There are already huge websites available to resell used goods likes furniture, home appliances, machinery, and many more. You decide to start with a similar kind of website.

What decisions would you take to get more traffic on your website?

Case 3

The Foodpanda group is a worldwide mobile food delivery marketplace headquartered in Berlin, Germany. It was launched in March 2012. It allows to select from local restaurants and place orders via the mobile application as well as the website. Customers order food by entering their postcodes on the site and browsing for food from a list of restaurants. Customers create meals by browsing restaurant menus and select items they want to order before entering an address and proceeding to the payment. Restaurants receive these orders and then deliver to customers. Foodpanda sends an SMS to confirm orders and to inform them about estimated delivery time.

Foodpanda is growing by acquisitions. It acquired Room Service in Malaysia and Singapore, City Delivery in Philippines, EatOye in Pakistan, Koziness in Hong Kong, and TastyKhana and Just Eat in India.

Just three months after acquiring Pune-based competitor TastyKhana, global online food delivery marketplace, Foodpanda has bought one of its biggest rivals in India Just Eat.

Just Eat was first launched as Hungry Bangalore, but was changed to Just Eat in 2011 when it was acquired by the international brand which competes with Foodpanda worldwide. Just Eat has now received a minority holding in Foodpanda as a part of the deal, and the management will be kept on as it is. In Bengaluru, Just Eat has over 800 partner restaurants, and the business has already achieved success. Chains like Pizza Corner, Kati Zone, and VasudevAdigas and restaurants like Birinz are the top clients of Just Eat in Bangalore.

According to the Managing Director of Food Panda, Mr Chadda, the two companies will continue to operate independently, that is, Just Eat brand will continue to exist separately. The acquisition has made Foodpanda the largest player in the food ordering market in India.

Questions

1. Discuss about Foodpanda increasing its business through acquisition.
2. The decision of keeping Just Eat as a separate brand name is reasonable. If yes, justify.

Survey-Based Questions

Determine by circling the number that you think applies to you.

1. Strongly disagree
2. Disagree
3. Neither agree nor disagree
4. Agree
5. Strongly agree

1.	Do you consider your team's welfare while making decision?	1	2	3	4	5
2.	Do your team members work in collaborative style?	1	2	3	4	5
3.	Do you consult others, if required?	1	2	3	4	5
4.	Do you feel communication between members is open enough when they arrive at a particular decision?	1	2	3	4	5
5.	Do you remain calm when you have to make decision quickly?	1	2	3	4	5
6.	Do you make decisions considering all the pros and cons of it?	1	2	3	4	5

(Continued)

(Continued)

7.	Do you prefer to avoid making decisions, if you can?	1	2	3	4	5
8.	Do you plan well ahead?	1	2	3	4	5
9.	Do you carry on looking for something better even if you have found a course of action that is just about ok?	1	2	3	4	5
10.	Do you find it difficult to think clearly when you have to decide something in a hurry?	1	2	3	4	5

Critical Thinking Questions

1. Tell about any past critical situation in which you had to make an immediate decision.
2. What process do you follow for making decisions for these different circumstances and were you satisfied with the results?
3. What would happen if you do not decide on the issue immediately?
4. Whom will this decision affect mostly?
5. What are the positive and negative consequences of this decision?

Chapter at a Glance

Decision-making

A decision is the selection of a course of action from two or more alternatives, and decision-making is a sequence of steps leading to the selection of that alternative. There are three stages to decision-making—intelligence, design, and choice phase accompanied by a feedback phase. In the intelligence phase, the problem is identified for which the decision has to be made, followed by a design phase where alternatives are constructed, and then in the choice phase, the most feasible alternative is chosen and implemented as a decision.

Decision-making Environment

Decision-making under Certainty

- The consequence of every alternative is known.
- Usually, there is only one outcome for each alternative.

Decision-making under Uncertainty

- All the possible states of nature or outcomes are known.
- Probabilities of the possible outcomes are not known.

Decision-making under Risk

- All the possible states of nature or outcomes are known.
- Probabilities of the possible outcomes are known.

Types of Decisions

- Structured decision
- Unstructured decision
- Programmed decisions
- Non-programmed decision
- Strategic decisions
- Tactical decisions

Decision-making Models

- Classical model
- Administrative model
- Political model

Decision-making Styles

- Autocratic
- Participative
- Consultative
- Democratic.

Decision-making Tools

- **Cost–Benefit analysis:** This is a technique in which the values of the benefits of a course of action are added, and the costs associated with it are subtracted to determine the net result.
- **Force field analysis:** This is a technique for looking at all the forces for and against a decision.
- **Grid analysis method:** It is a technique for doing analysis for each of the options based on the factors used to arrive at a decision.
- **Decision trees:** A decision tree is a way of representing various decisions and its combinations for specific situations and mainly aims at representing action sequences. The decisions taken are based on the conditions and then actions are executed.
- **Decision table:** A decision table represents all possible conditions and actions. The table comprises the conditions, actions, and rules.
- **Paired comparison analysis:** This technique is useful when our priorities are not very discrete, the core data on which the decision has to be taken are missing, or there are too many options which have to be ranked.
- **Pros and cons Method with benefits:** This technique allows one to check on whether or not a course of action will actually improve the situation and is worth taking.

Herbert Simon's Model of Decision-making

According to Herbert A. Simon, the decision-making process is basically divided into three branches.

(Continued)

(Continued)

- Intelligence
- Design
- Choice

Steps in Rational Decision-making

- Identify the problem.
- Find out the criteria for the decision.
- Attach weights to the criteria.
- Generate alternatives.
- Rate each alternative on each criterion.
- Compute the optimal decision.
- Implement the decision.
- Evaluate the decision.

Common Difficulties in Decision-making

- When the information is inadequate or incomplete.
- When there is a lack of information on political, social, and economic variables.
- A decision maker should be an expert in the respective domain and highly intelligent and have farsightedness to arrive at a rational decision.
- Individual preferences and attitudes often come in the way of decision-making.
- Decisions taken by managers are always accompanied by compromise and adjustments.

CHAPTER 8

Organizational Behaviour

Learning Objectives

- Thorough understanding of organizational behaviour and its impact on organizations.
- Gaining insight into the contributing disciplines of organizational behaviour.
- Deeper awareness of how effective organizational behaviour has positive impact on organizational performance.
- Understanding the impact of people, structure, technology, and environment on key elements of organization behaviour.
- The reader gets to know about the various models of organizational behaviour and the modern trends and implementation of models.
- Gaining insight into the emergence of e-organizations, giving rise to new ways of doing business.

An Opening Vignette

Selena was running a manufacturing company which made televisions lamps and bulbs. The company was headquartered in Noida and a supplier to local TV manufacturers. Selena wanted to expand across China, Japan, Korea; for this, she had to enthuse her employees to work aggressively across all sectors, including marketing, sales, production, delivery, and logistics. To date, her approach was custodial, which means that she used to pay her employees well, and make employees to feel more secured, she used to reward them in the form of bonus and additional perk, health insurance benefits, and accommodation allowances. Employees were happy and worked hard to improve organizational productivity. However, with aggressive growth plans to seize the deals from international TV manufacturers, she set out to follow a mix of autocratic and supportive model, a hybrid of authoritative as well as supportive for new ideas, innovations, and opinions from the employees. From the day she had set her goals, Selena started working rigorously. She told the marketing head to come up with new strategies to advertise and market the product, and instructed the quality head to attain a defect-free scenario for the lamps and bulbs, making them more durable and, at the same time, consuming less power when in active state.

She also requested the production head to crack down on employees and eliminate all idle time, thereby eliminating delays and ramping up production by 5%. For the sales head, she gave him the freedom to choose his sales strategy as she knew that he would come up with dazzling sales figures.

In a few months, because of a carefully laid down production and marketing plan, Selena observed that she had received an order of 1 million TV lamps from the biggest player of Asia. She was too excited and announced that she would soon float an initial public offering (IPO) wherein every company person would be allotted a percentage of shareholding based on his/her performance. The employees became self-motivated and started their own in-house mentoring and training programmes with the managers in the lead role, working after office hours to arrive at the designated milestones, and carrying out effective supplier engagement for the raw material arrival. All in all, it was a wave of motivation in the internal environment of the company.

Introduction

The study of organizational behaviour is both interesting and challenging. It relates to individuals or a group of people working together in the organization to achieve a common goal. With the situational factors interacting with each other, the study tends to become more complex. Organizational behaviour is a branch of study which has special focus on behaviour within an organization pertaining to individuals, groups, and structure. This knowledge is used for making organizations work more effectively. Organizational behaviour aims at increasing group/individual productivity, reducing attrition and absenteeism, and increasing job satisfaction. Organizational behaviour draws inputs from behavioural science psychology, sociology, and cultural anthropology. The areas on which organizational behaviour focuses are individuals who will often be working within groups, the interrelationships and how these individuals within the organization function with each other to get the job done. Organizational behaviour encompasses mostly human behavioural traits, such as personality, attitudes, motivation, interpersonal behaviour, team and group dynamics, leadership traits, organizational structure and design, decision-making, conflict, and stress management.

Definitions

Organizational behavior is a field of study that investigates the impact that individuals, groups and structure have on behavior within organization for the purpose of applying such knowledge toward improving an organization's effectiveness.

Stephen P. Robbins

Organizational behavior is the study and application at knowledge about the how people --- as individuals and a groups --- act within organization. It strives to identify ways in which people can act more effectively.

Keith Davis

Organizational behavior can be defined as the understanding; prediction and management of the human behavior affect the performance of the organizations.

Luthans

The study of application of knowledge about human behavior related to other elements of an organization such as structure, technology and social systems.

L.M. Prasad

A field that seeks knowledge of behavior in organizational settings by systematically studying individual, group and organizational processes.

Baron and Greenberg

Levels of Analysis

Organizational behaviour involves the study of organizations' behaviour across levels (Figure 8.1) as follows:

- Micro-organizational behaviour refers to an individual's behaviour or group behaviour.
- Macro-behavioural theory studies organizations as a whole, their adaptability, and the policies, structures, and possibilities that guide them.
- Meso-scale organizational structures involve control, culture, and people network, and the analysis of people's interaction within the organization.

Organizational behaviour, whose focus area is majorly people's behaviour and interaction amongst them, can play a significant role in organizational development, enhancing organizational performance and enhancing performance of the individual or group as well as their level of contentment and dedication.

Organizational Behaviour and Its Contributing Disciplines

Organizational behaviour is an applied field of behavioural study and evolved from the following fields discussed further (Figure 8.2).

Psychology

It is the study of behaviour and mental process of a human being that are affected by the physical, mental, and environmental conditions, which can impede the work performance of an individual because of fatigue, boredom, stress, and unfavourable working conditions. Other factors included within modern psychology with respect to human behavioural traits in professional environment include learning, attitude, insight, personality, sentiments, guidance, leadership abilities, motivation, job satisfaction, decision-making, performance appraisals, recruitments, and so on.

Figure 8.1 Levels of Analysis

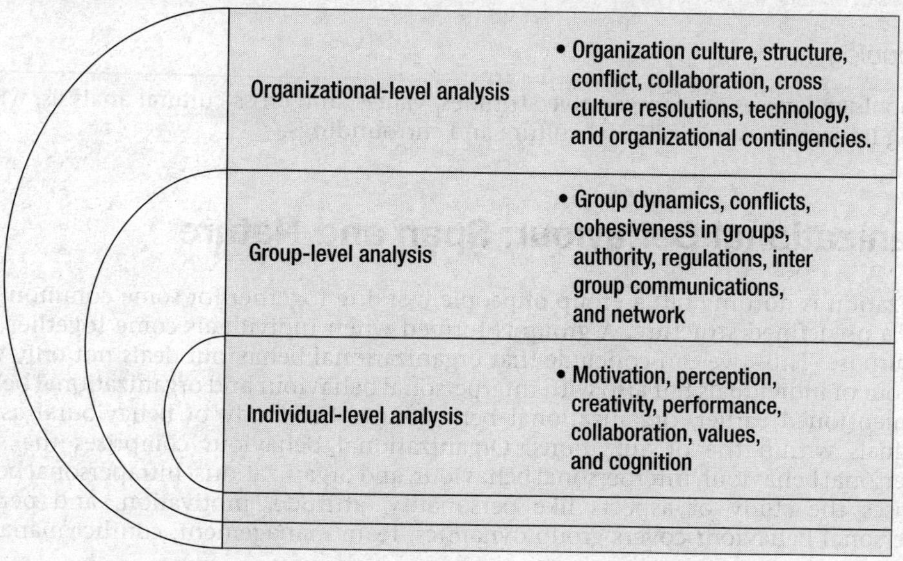

Figure 8.2 Contributing Disciplines of Organizational Behaviour

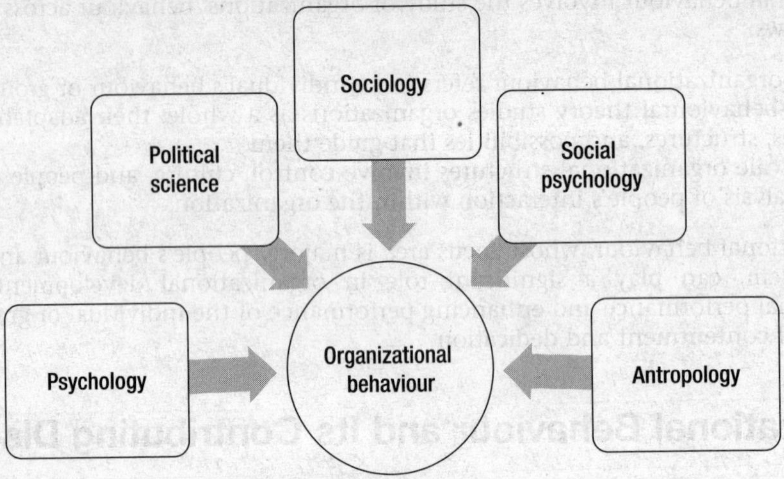

Political Science

Political science is the study of behavioural sciences in political environment and focuses on disputes within the group and intra-organizational politics and authority issues.

Sociology

This discipline contributes significantly through the study of group behaviour in complex and recognized organizations.

Social Psychology

Social psychology integrates sociology and psychology and discusses the barriers and acceptances across groups or individuals within and across the organizations.

Anthropology

Anthropology focuses on comparative attitudes, values, and cross-cultural analysis, which has a lasting impact on organizational culture and surroundings.

Organizational Behaviour: Span and Nature

Organization is nothing but a group of people working together for some common purpose within a predefined structure. A group is formed when individuals come together to work for a purpose. Thus, we can conclude that organizational behaviour deals not only with the behaviour of individuals but also with interpersonal behaviour and organizational behaviour.

As mentioned earlier, organizational behaviour is the study of behavioural aspects of individuals within the organizations. Organizational behaviour comprises the study of intrapersonal behaviour, interpersonal behaviour, and organizations. Intrapersonal behaviour comprises the study of aspects like personality, attitude, motivation, and perception. Interpersonal behaviour covers group dynamics, team management, conflict management,

Figure 8.3 Major Components in Study of Organizational Behaviour

Organizational environment	• External forces such as legal, political, technological, and economic constraints or development changes. • Societal requirement and customer demands. • Management's reaction to the above situations.
Individual's performance directly impacting organizational performance	• Key influencers are individual's nature comprising of attitude, personality, learning, foresight, and values • Individual's motivation. • Rewards/punishments—to encourage productive behaviour and control misbehaviour. • Stress which impacts individual's performance in a negative way.
Group and intergroup behaviour	• Group and interpersonal behaviour affect organizational performance whether the group is formal or informal. • Conflicts between groups may distort the functioning of the organization, but cooperation between groups can impact the organization positively. • Authority and politics in groups, between groups can have a substantial impact.
Organizational structure behavioural process and design	• The various subunits within the organization and how these subunits interact with each other and work towards a common goal. • The behavioural process encompasses leadership capabilities that are important for obtaining individual or group performance, effective communication to link various units and also link the organization with the external environment, sound decision-making techniques, and planned approach to implement change and incorporate innovation.

and so on. In addition, the study of an organization covers aspects like its structure and formation, interaction sequences between the various organizational entities while focusing on the organizational goals. The study of organizational behaviour is summarized as follows (Figure 8.3):

- Organizational behaviour is not based on only theoretical framework and guidelines and hence cannot be considered only as a discipline.
- It is an interdisciplinary approach since it has evolved from various disciplines and knowledge from them has been integrated in a form well suited for the study of human behaviour in the professional environment.
- This field of study comes under the applied sciences, where human behavioural sciences are researched to solve problems at the organizational level.
- Organizational behaviour is prescriptive in form according to research findings and analyses, and implementing better methods on the same can be used to increase the productivity of organizations.
- Organizational behaviour deals with inner thoughts and feelings of resources and states that the common human approach is to be creative, independent, and productive, and given favourable work conditions they put in their utmost effort towards organizational growth.

Goals of Organizational Behaviour

Organizational behaviour, which is a scientific field of study, focuses on the following points (Figure 8.4):

- Applying leadership skills and knowledge to understand people's behaviour, demarcating those which are not conducive to the organization and appreciating rudiments of behaviour which positively impact the organization. Aspects of good behaviour can also be set as norms or standards to be followed by other employees within the organization.
- Goals of organizational behaviour strongly accentuate the responsibility of a leader in relation to behavioural aspects and a proper reporting structure of the organization. An organization has three elements:
  - People
  - Structure
  - Technology

For managing these elements, an appropriate organizational structure is extremely important, together with incorporation of management principles, such as principle of unity of command, delegation of power and responsibility, formulation of objectives to achieve contentment, since people's value and faith builds an organization. In addition, leaders should be equipped with handling people within the organization and should have the following skills.

- They should be able to describe people's behaviour, attitude, and nature and identify team members' reaction so that appropriate measures can be taken for productive workers (concept of rewards and so on.) and punitive measures for disruptive workers.
- They should be able to carefully identify an employee's behaviour, which will help the leader to channelize employees' actions to higher productivity level. Other responsibilities include exercising control in the form of
  - upgrading team's skill sets through training for improved performance,

Figure 8.4 Organizational Behaviour Goals

- aligning unit's/individual's objective to organizational objective, and
- promoting conducive environment in the unit and organization, which should be appropriately aligned to the external environment for effective handling of contingencies.

Managing the Elements of Organizational Behaviour

The four vital elements of an organization are people, infrastructure, technology, and environment, in which the organization operates. There is a continuous interaction among three elements—people, structure, and technology. It is technology and structure that facilitate individuals to come together and work towards a common goal. Also, the environment in which the organization operates plays a significant role since it has impact on the other three elements (Figure 8.5).

Figure 8.5 Elements of Organizational Behaviour

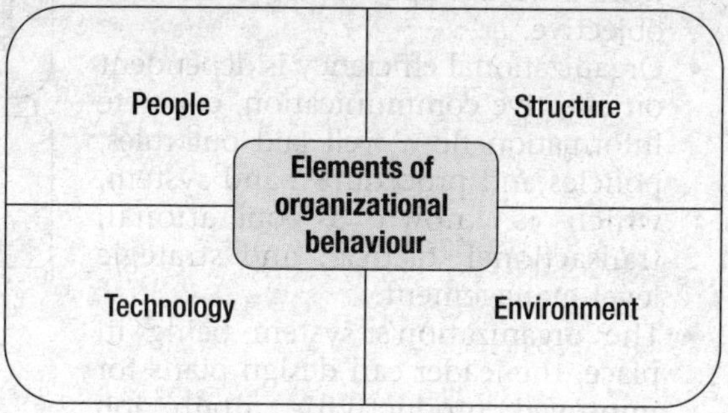

People

- Groups may be small, large, formal, or informal and work together to achieve organizational objectives.
- Characterized by their personal goals and aligning personal to professional goals and group goals.
- Effective collaboration with team members and healthy relationships with superiors and subordinates to accomplish long- and short-term goals.
- Interest of various stakeholders constituting the people element of organizational behaviour who play a dominant role in the society and are important from the perspective of business (Figure 8.6).

Figure 8.6 The People Element of Organizational Behaviour

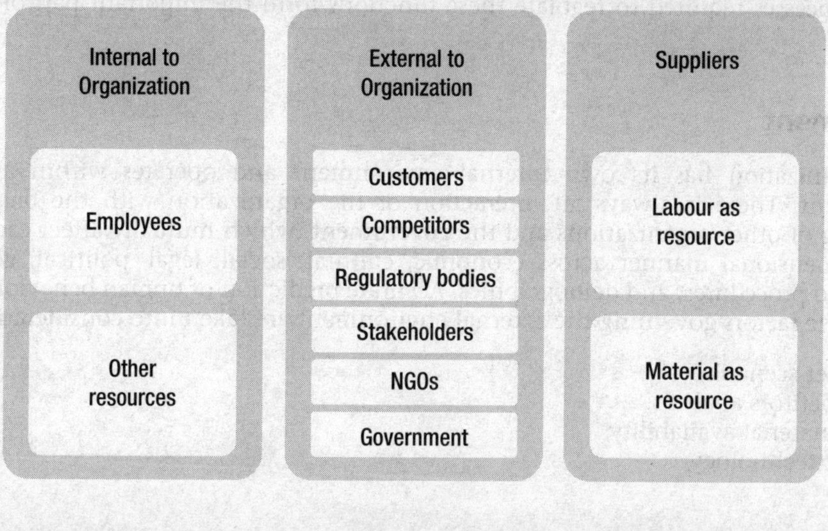

Structure

There are two types of organizations: formal and informal. Attributes of formal organizations are as follows (Figure 8.7):

- Objectives are concrete.
- Organization is hierarchical or flat in nature.
- At each level of organization, people work towards a specific organizational objective.
- Organizational efficiency is dependent on effective communication, concrete information flow, well laid out rules, policies and procedures, and system, which is known as operational, transactional, tactical, and strategic level management.
- The organization's system being in place, the leader can design plans for improved productivity, attain job satisfaction, and ensure that his employees are content.

Figure 8.7 The Structure Element of Organizational Behaviour

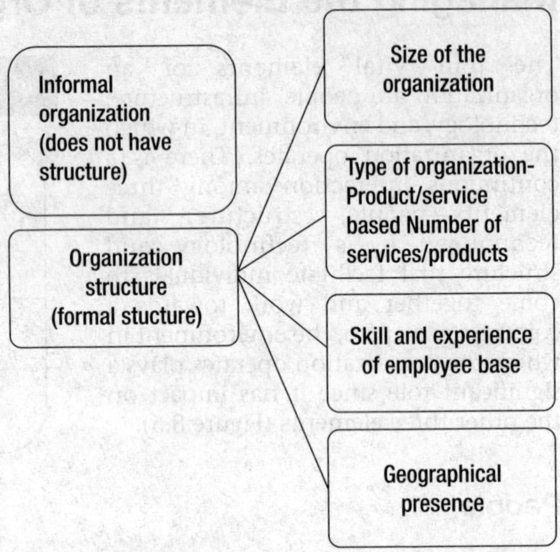

Technology

Technologies, such as machineries, equipment, and work procedures, are the resources with which people work and these also affect the tasks that they perform. The technology used has a substantial impact on working relationships. It enables people to do increased amount of work, that too in an effective manner. Procuring the latest technology, installing, operating, and maintaining it is very crucial for organizational effectiveness. The technology and the system in place should be compatible to one another. Job design and HR requirements are based on technology. Adequate attention should be paid to the service industry. For example, in an institute, a web-enabled student and staff information system will constitute student attendance, admission, examination, accounting records as well as staff workload record, leave record, research record, and so on for quick retrieval, update, search, reporting, and analytics. Various processes required to regulate these functions form the important part of education industry.

Environment

Every organization has its own internal environment and operates within an external environment. There is always an interaction of the organization with the bigger system comprising of other organizations and the government, which mutually affect each other in a multidimensional manner across economic, cultural, social, legal, political, government policies and procedures, and demographics. Accurate prediction of human behaviour happens when all the factors governing the external environment are taken into consideration such as

- market scenario,
- competitors analysis,
- raw material availability,
- latest technology,

- availability of skilled resources, and
- cultural climate.

Having considered the above parameters, the manager realizes the impact of these factors on the individuals and their reaction towards the same, some of which can be very productive for the organization. Also, a realistic approach ensured by the manager will help his team to prepare for contingencies like changing political climate and government rules (Figure 8.8).

Figure 8.8 The Environment Element of Organizational Behaviour

Environment	
Internal • Employee relations • Organizational culture • Team collaboration • Managerial decision-making • Leadership capabilities • Employee satisfaction • Productivity and growth	**External** • Political • Social • Economic • Legal • Cultural • Demographics

Importance of Organizational Behaviour

Organizational behaviour provides guidelines to the management about the way in which human element should be emphasized in order to achieve organizational objectives. Organizational behaviour provides an outlook to the management to analyse behaviour of individuals and suggests an effective direction.

It not only analyses the behaviour of individuals at different levels, such as intrapersonal, interpersonal, intergroup, and inter-group levels but also answers to the questions like why and how human beings behave in a particular manner, which in turn helps in building cordial relations in the organization.

Organizational behaviour gives an insight to the managers to understand the behaviour of their subordinates and select the most effective method to guide and control them so that the organizational goals can be achieved with little or no resistance.

It also helps managers to select the most effective style of leadership depending on the behaviour of individuals within the organization. It also helps in effective conflict management, better decision-making, commitment to ideas, teamwork, and so on.

Approaches to Organizational Behaviour

The four major approaches to organizational behaviour are as discussed further.

HR Approach

This approach recognizes the fact that human resources are the greatest assets of any organization and is concerned with the growth and development of people towards higher levels of competency, certainty, and fulfilment. This enables employees to perform in a better way. The HR approach is also called the supportive approach.

Contingency Approach

According to this approach, the methods or behaviour that work in one situation will not necessarily work in all situations. Therefore, the identification of the variables that are effective and efficient is necessary.

Systems Approach

This approach considers the organization as a system that consists of various interrelated parts. Any activity performed by any of the interconnected parts affects the whole system. Hence, it is necessary to make sure that every part of the system is working in coordination.

Productivity Approach

Productivity is the ratio of the unit of output to the unit of input. Generally, it is calculated in economic terms. The higher the value of the ratio, the higher will be efficiency.

Models of Organizational Behaviour

Models of organizational behaviour have been shown in Figure 8.9.

Autocratic Model

The traits of the autocratic model are as follows:

- The control of the organization lies with the management, which can direct and exude authority over the employees of the organization.
- Key decisions lie with the top management of the organization.
- Lower level employees have little expertise/control over the work function.
- The top management of the organization has substantial expertise and the middle- and lower-level management are fully guided by the top management.
- This model was used in factories during the Industrial Revolution.

Figure 8.9 Model of Organizational Behaviour

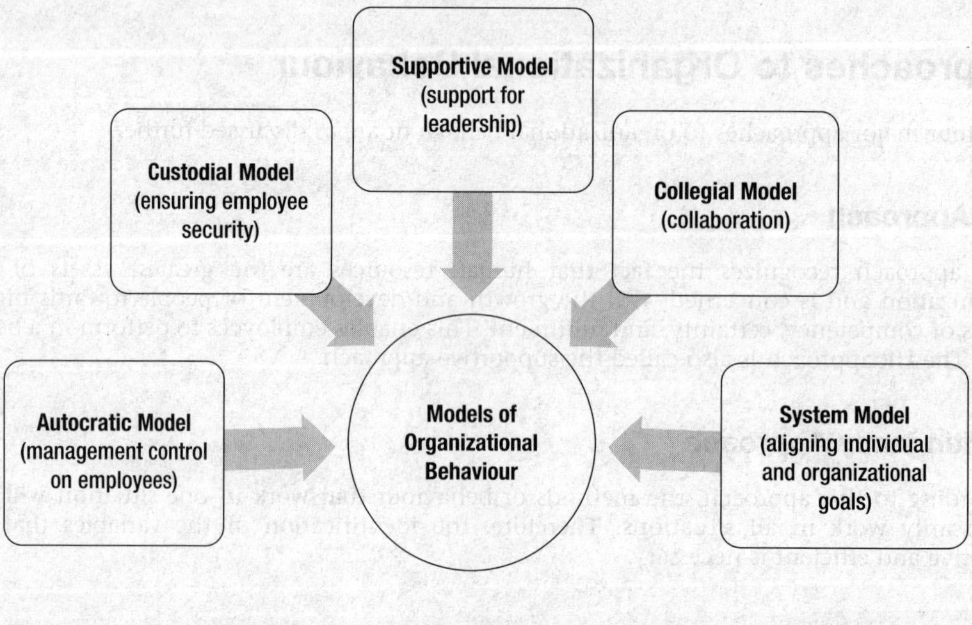

Disadvantages

- Management has to give adequate time to handle minor issues as decision-making does not rest with the employee base.
- This model is highly disadvantageous in today's era because there are potential resources at each level of the organization which have required skill set or decision-making power.
- Employees do not acquire job satisfaction and do not feel valued, which results in their performance degradation.

Custodial Model

- This model promotes financial security for the employees by incorporating a rewards and benefits programme for keeping the employee motivation high.
- Other benefit programmes include health insurance benefits, accommodation allowances, company vehicles, stock options, and so on to retain worthy staff.
- Using this model, organizations want to keep intact skilled resources with good knowledge and expertise.

Disadvantage

- This model revolves around allocating wages and benefits to employees and employees who do not perform well are also facilitated.
- Also, every organization is constrained by its own work culture and the services it provides or the products it designs; therefore, a potential resource might remain tied up with the organization for the benefits received and will not explore opportunities to exploit his own potential.

Supportive Model

- This model is focused on promoting leadership traits amongst individuals.
- It works in opposition to the autocratic model, as it enforces that employees are self-motivated, have sufficient knowledge and decision-making power, and, apart from being in an operational role, can create, innovate, and implement ideas.

Collaborative Model

- It is a collaborative model where every employee is a colleague of the other.
- It does not consider status and designation of the employees, though hierarchy is maintained and every individual is encouraged to contribute to build a better organization.
- Role of the manager is to encourage teamwork, create a positive work environment, and make all the members of the team perform well.
- This is very advantageous for organizations that have to work constantly on innovation, creation and find new approaches, that is research and development, designing new services, and so on.

System Model

- This model ensures alignment of an individual's goal to an organization's goal, and every individual's partners with the organization or team and works towards common goal.
- It considers that individuals have varied potential, skills, and talent.

- Positive factors of this model which impact the individuals are good remuneration, job security, positive work culture, where the organization provides value-added services to its customers.

Current Trends in Challenges and Opportunities of Organizational Behaviour

Upgrading Employees' Skills

The skills can be broadly categorized as under:

- **Technical skills:** These include technology-based skill sets and are acquired by people at the operational and transactional levels and training programmes are arranged to refine the skills.
- **Managerial skills:** These include planning, organizing, motivating, leadership, and decision-making skills, which can be refined and updated by conducting series of training programmes and workshops.

Today, because technological and environmental changes are happening at a quick pace for various businesses, there is a strong need to equip the employees with the required skill sets so that organizational goals can be achieved. Designing an appropriate performance appraisal system with embedded training programmes will align managers appropriately with the ever-changing business scenarios. As for technical skills, the operational and transactional staff are required to be trained on technology and domain as per the requirements of the organization.

Enhancing Value and Output

Enhancing value or, in other words, quality is to achieve a minimal defect or defect-free situation and attain a stage where customers' needs and expectations are surpassed in relation to product or service quality or value. For example, a customer who wants to purchase a mobile might look for features such as fast response time, good sound and picture quality, faster download, and so on. If his expectations are met, then the customer perceives that the product is of good quality and if not he will perceive the quality of the mobile phone as poor. Deming defined quality as a predictable degree of uniformity and dependability, at low cost and suited to the market. The parameters of quality are as follows:

- Performance
- Features
- Conformance
- Reliability
- Robustness
- Maintenance
- Aesthetics
- Reputation

Nowadays managers are working towards total quality management (TQM) in order to improve quality, which also require extensive employee participation.

Total Quality Management

It aims at continuous customer satisfaction through incessant enhancement of all organizational processes and quality, measurements with precision, and empowerment of employees. For example, TQM was implemented in Ford Motor Company in the 1990s to provide increased customer satisfaction, stable work environment for the employees, and profitability for the company. For this, it joined hands with ChemFil, a PGP group of Industries, for quality paint designs since that was foremost in their TQM approach. Ford, along with ChemFil, structured the entire production process based on surveys from the customers.

Business Process Reengineering

Business process reengineering employees a methodology that reduces work process to their core optimum and dramatically improves performance. Both functional and cross-functional processes are assessed through workflow investigation and event-based pricing. With advent of new technology and industries, best practices will process and attain maturity through reengineering. Its implications on the managers or the management are as follows:

- Continuously strive for quality
- Managements intervention at all levels
- Extensive training programmes imparted to all employees
- Effective communication across all levels

For example, Ford's account payable process was slow and inefficient, now they have a faster and more efficient accounts payable system.

Managing Workforce Diversity

Employee mix can be across multiple traits, and to manage a heterogeneous collection of employees is a challenge for managers and must be done very efficiently by addressing their needs, views, and work styles for greater employee retention and productivity. The heterogeneity in employee base is found across various parameters, such as

- gender,
- region,
- religion,
- background,
- age,
- community,
- disabled, and so on.

Organizations have a dire need to induct employees from across regions and countries in order to tap the best of the talent and potential, promote innovation, improve decision-making, and maintain a synergy between diverse groups of employees. Mismanagement of workforce diversity might lead to high turnover and interpersonal conflicts.

Impact of Globalization

Today's business is not constrained to a specific region or locality and spans across the globe, where it finds a greater market potential (Figure 8.10). This has been possible because the product and the service providers have got a platform of greater connect and reachability through mobile marketing, electronic marketing (Internet) to spread their existence, and researching on the customers requirement of that zone. Many new businesses and business models have come into existence along with intra- and inter-industry partnership venture. Low cost and competitive pricing has tremendously encouraged businesses to spread across the globe. For example, a French wine seller can sell wine online at a lower price and to a greater audience. Similarly, more German, Japanese, and Korean car companies sell various car models across the globe, and this has become easier because of high visibility, flexible EXIM strategies, and faster modes of transport.

Figure 8.10 Trends in Global Business Strategies

Source: Korea Herald (http://www.koreaherald.com/view.php?ud=20130618000630)

Empowering People

The main issue is delegating more power and responsibility to the lower level cadre of employees and assigning more freedom to make choices about their schedules, operations, procedures, and the method of solving their work-related problems. Encouraging the employees to participate in work-related decisions will sizably enhance their commitment at work. Empowerment is defined as putting employees in charge of what they do by eliciting some sort of ownership in them. Managers are going considerably further by allowing employees full control of their work. An increasing number of organizations are using self-managed teams where workers operate largely without boss. Due to implementation of empowerment concepts across all the levels, the relationship between managers and the employees is reshaped. Managers will act as coaches, advisors, sponsors, and facilitators and help their subordinates to do their task with minimal guidance.

The concept of empowerment is all about reshaping the relationship between the manager and the employees in an organization.

A manager must encourage employees to participate in work-related decisions, which may also enhance the commitment of the employees to work.

Implementation of the empowerment concept has resulted in a positive change in the relationship between managers and employees, where managers act as coaches, advisors, sponsors, and facilitators and help their subordinates to perform their task with minimal guidance.

Coping with Temporariness

In the recent years, one thing that everyone in the organization faces permanently is temporariness. Whether it is the manager or employees of the organization, everyone must learn to cope up with the constant changes happening by developing their skills and continually updating their knowledge. The concept of continuous improvement implies constant change.

Stimulating Innovation and Change

In today's world, to be successful, the organization must come up with various innovative ideas. To survive in the competitive market, the organization must maintain flexibility and improve their quality of products and services. Managers need to stimulate employees' creativity and tolerance for change.

Emergence of E-organization

E-commerce

Electronic commerce (e-commerce) is the electronic exchange of information pertaining to various businesses using electronic data interchange (EDI) and associated technologies. The other way to visualize e-commerce is that it facilitates digitally enabled commercial transactions between and among organizations and individuals. Students who are familiar with electronic mail (email), computer bulletin boards, online funds transfer (OFT), and electronic payments (e-payment) will have a better understanding of e-commerce and associated activities. E-commerce systems have replaced manual and paper-based business transactions with faster, cheaper, more efficient, and more robust communications between machines. EDI commerce is the most recent e-commerce technology. E-commerce is the smartest way to do business. It puts more work on customers, right from viewing the product details, filling in the order form online, checking the order and delivery status, so that huge cost in terms of money and time can be saved and, at the same time, customers are happy.

E-commerce Versus E-business

Electronic business (e-business) is one stride ahead of e-commerce. E-commerce is all about using information and communications technology (ICT) for various types of transactions, whether between organizations or business-to-consumer transactions focusing mainly on

- marketing and selling of products and
- buying of products and services over the Internet.

In e-business, ICT is used to enhance one's business performance with a vision towards improving service and reducing costs. The processes enhanced using ICT are as follows:

- **Production processes:** These include material procurement, ordering, and replenishment of stocks (that is, inventory control), processing of e-payments, and online association with suppliers and vendors.
- **Marketing and selling processes:** These include promotional and marketing strategies for making a sale of the product over the Internet, processing of customers' purchase orders and payments, and customer support.
- **Internal organizational processes:** These include employee services, training, internal information sharing, video-conferencing, recruiting sales people, and training them to improve productivity.

Growth of E-business

The concept of e-business has become prominent in the last 10 or 15 years and has been growing at a rapid pace with 40% of the total worldwide Internet users buying and selling goods using the Internet. This concept facilitates

- reduction in operating, administrative, inventory, and procurement costs.
- increase in customer satisfaction.
- improved and efficient interaction with employees, vendors, customers, and strategic partners.
- productivity, competitiveness, and growth.
- reduction in business environment barriers.
- reduction in poverty.

E-business can be accelerated by implementing the following changes:

- Continued reforms in ICT infrastructure, trust and security regulations, and policy reforms.
- Government-to-business ventures to reduce transaction costs and expand growth.
- Training programmes to enrich knowledge on e-business.
- Inclusion of micro-business firms for doing better business by reaching out to low-income groups.

EXAMPLE

For example, Tortas Peru, an organization in Peru, is doing e-business in the segment of bakery products. This organization is reaching out to groups of women in Peru who have proficiency in cake baking and dessert making and establishing a bigger chain of suppliers. It now caters to eight provinces in Peru and the products are mainly consumed by Peruvian emigrants.

The e-business functions carried out by this team are as follows:

- Web-based marketing
- Online bakery store with item display
- Online ordering
- Online payment

Business Growth

- Fifty orders per day, now with a client base of 500 customers.

Employment

- Fourteen female employees.

Wages and Profitability

- Twice the minimum wages with a profit margin of 30%.

Intangible Benefits

- Technological advancement for women groups
- Exposure to global processes
- Financial independence

E-organizations/E-governance: The Government in Focus

E-organization/e-governance is the arranging of state governance based on electronic tools for collecting, processing, and dissemination of information and providing of government services to all groups of population and businesses by electronic tools. For this purpose, the

Figure 8.11 E-governance

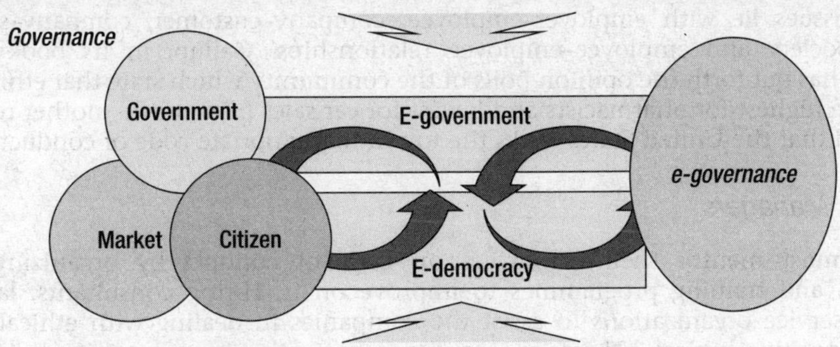

e-governance model provides a road for guaranteeing governmental organizations to accomplish their endeavour in providing centralized, accessible, on-time, total, and accurate information to personnel, business organizations, and people. E-governments offer government services through the Internet, phone, fax, public access centres, wireless devices, and other communication facilities. Implementation of e-governance is a complex organizational, economical, social, and technological process which requires substantial financial and administrative efforts (Figure 8.11).

Impact on Managers

Managers should be open to accept ever-changing technology and to refine their skills and knowledge with the technological changes, ensuring that the team also complies with adopting and learning technology innovations. The paradigm of e-governance is to make it citizen centric, hence the manager and his team, in charge of development and implementation, are exposed to a large base of customers, much larger than private customers or clients. Therefore, to make such government projects successful, the management has to carefully steer their team through all phases of the project.

Citizen-centric Governance

Amongst the successful implementations of the e-government practices, one of the most successful attempts has been the implementation of eSeva in Andhra Pradesh that has become a success story because of deft handling of change management issues.

Some other examples where e-government solutions have become successful are municipalities like the Ahmadabad Municipal Corporation where appropriate e-governance solutions have been used to increase revenue generation by a phenomenal 125%. The Kalyan Dombivli Municipal Corporation (KDMC) has used e-governance to create a highly successful online citizen service with the objective of making each citizen's interaction with KDMC easy, simple, and efficient, while ensuring accountability and transparency.

Code of Ethics

Employees should follow code of ethics while executing their tasks. For example, should the chemical company employees report to appropriate authorities that discharging its untreated sewages into the river is contaminating its water resources? Are managers biased about some subordinates they like and evaluate their performance accordingly? Following unethical practices have become common, for example, people who use insider information for personal financial gain as the case of the American, Indian, and companies who are involved in massive cover-ups of defective products such as the Volkswagen emission rigging scandal.

Ethical issues lie with employer–employee, company–customer, company–shareholder, company–society and employee–employee relationships. Gallup, in its book on ethical behaviour, has put forth the opinion polls of the community which state that ethical codes of conduct are highest for pharmacists and lowest for car sales persons. In another report, it has been found that the United States ranks the top in inappropriate code of conduct.

Impact on Managers

Managers must mentor their employees on code of conduct by organizing seminars, workshops, and training programmes to improve on it. Hiring consultants, lawyers, and voluntary service organizations to assist the companies in dealing with ethical issues will guarantee positive ethical behaviour, keeping organization's productivity flying and not incurring controversial reputation for any unethical deed.

CASE STUDY: OVERCOMING ABSENTEEISM AT SANDHAR AUTOMOTIVES, DHUMASPUR

Sandhar Automotive (mirror division) is a manufacturing unit belonging to the Sandhar group of companies located at Dhumaspur, Gurgaon, Haryana. This company was started by Mr Jayant Davar, an engineer. The company has its technical collaboration with Honda Lock manufacturing company, Japan division. Its rear-view mirror manufacturing division started operations in 1993, initially only for two-wheelers, manufactured by Hero Honda and TVS–Suzuki. The current unit at Dhumaspur was established in 1999 with a manpower of 160 employees, supplying mirror assembly consignments only for a single customer, Hero Honda Motors Ltd.

New business opportunities were explored, and in 2004, fresh orders from four-wheeler segments were placed, for example, Tata Motors Ltd, Eicher Motors Ltd, Ashok Leyland, and so on. Despite the above-mentioned growth, high rate of customer returns and in-house rejections were some of the never-ending problems. After a thorough analysis of facts, the company found poor commitment levels amongst employees and workers and lack of ownership over activities, machines, and processes in general as reasons for these problems. Lack of motivation among employees resulted in high rates of absenteeism, thereby affecting aspects like quality and productivity.

In the beginning of 2007, Sandhar Automotive received an invitation from UNIDO and ACMA to join their business partnership programme, and also received technical support in implementing a company-wide process of continuous improvement based on lean manufacturing principles and total employee involvement tools.

Accepting the invitation, they entered in the programme, but their concern was less involvement of employees in improvement activities, high absenteeism rates, and quality issues.

To minimize these hurdles, a methodology was developed under the guidance of a counsellor and the following steps were taken:

- Increase in the number of technical and behavioural training programmes for employees across all levels.
- Alignment of individual roles and responsibilities with respect to the company's goal.
- Frequent meetings with top- and middle-management employees to address issues and concerns of the employees.
- Performance-based awards to employees and announcement of various beneficial schemes for employees by the CEO.

The main objective was to make it interesting and simple. Employees started realizing their self-worth and importance of working as a team for a common goal. Things started making sense to them, such as transparent communication, ownership of tasks/processes/machines, public appreciation, and family gatherings. Apart from methodology, the following initiatives were taken:

- Creating a conducive atmosphere within the company and organizing Friday dinner for informal interaction and communication amongst the employees.

- Sending birthday greetings via mail to employees and celebrating the occasion with company-sponsored snacks.
- Covering employees and their medical expenses through various schemes.
- Organizing company-sponsored yearly meet with employees and their families to promote social acceptance and relation.
- Team-building activities with certain management games for stronger collaboration.

In addition, employees were briefed on emergency control procedures in the wake of fire, accident, scrap dissolution, and quality control procedures such as targeting zero-defect situations for the products in specific.

Key Results

- Employee participation increased significantly.
- Trainings happened frequently, though cost of training increased but so did profitability.
- Employee attendance turnover became low.
- Inventory costs went down and so did customer returns and internal rejections.

Summary

This chapter focuses on organizational behaviour, its nature, scope, benefits, and approaches with a special focus on models of organizational behaviour and their case-specific industry-level implementations. The chapter also revolves around modern trends in organizational behaviour with emphasis on TQM, business process reengineering, managing employee mix, and impact of globalization on organizational behaviour, which will enable the reader to get an extensive idea of the current behavioural trends of modern-day organizations.

Exercise

Objective Questions

1. The four vital elements of organization are
   - People, structure, technology, and environment
   - People, infrastructure, technology, and resources
   - People, property, technology, and resources
   - None of the above
2. Anthropology does not focus on comparative attitudes, values, cross-cultural analysis.
   - True
   - False
3. According to which approach, methods or behaviours which work in one situation will not necessarily work in all situations?
   - HR approach
   - Contingency approach
   - Systems approach
   - Productivity approach

4. Which approach is also called the supportive approach?
    - Systems approach
    - Contingency approach
    - HR approach
    - Productivity approach
5. Custodial model promotes financial security for the employees by incorporating rewards and benefits programme for keeping the employee motivation high.
    - True
    - False
6. Which model is focused on promoting leadership traits amongst individuals?
    - Autocratic model
    - Custodial model
    - Supportive model
    - System model
7. Which of these is a methodology that reduces work process to their core optimum and dramatically improves performance?
    - TQM
    - Business process reengineering
    - Managing employee mix
    - Globalization
8. Which of these aims at continuous customer satisfaction through incessant enhancement of all organizational processes and quality?
    - TQM
    - Business process reengineering
    - Managing employee mix
    - Globalization
9. Which of these is the electronic exchange of information pertaining to various businesses using EDI and associated technologies?
    - E-business
    - E-organizations
    - E-commerce

CASE STUDIES

Case 1

Mr Mandar was appointed general manager in Krishna Manufacturing Center. He had joined the company around three years back. Prior to joining this company, he had served other company for two years. He did his MBA at IIM, Bangalore. He considered himself as a major contributor to drive the results. After being promoted as general manager three departments—raw material, warehouse, and sales—started reporting to him. Each of these departments had a manager.

As Mr Mandar was promoted at a very young age, these four managers and their team considered him as a junior executive.

The new general manager made some changes in the existing operations. He started weekly meetings with all four managers. However, these managers hardly responded in any of the meetings. At a later stage, Mr Mandar started receiving quality complaints, so he decided to visit these departments. He found that the raw material being used for manufacturing was not of defined quality standards. He also had a word with raw material supervisor. When the four managers knew that Mr Mandar had visited the departments and queried a few employees, they called up a meeting. On discussion, they concluded that the general manager did not have confidence in them. This manager could not even discuss about this with top-level management as he was hired by them. So, they all decided they will continue the current work the way they were doing and start looking for the other opportunity, and the meeting ended.

Questions

1. Discuss the problems on this case.
2. Explain the reason for behaviour of managers.
3. What action should have being taken to prevent the problems?
4. Propose a solution so that managers continue with their jobs in the organization.

Case 2

Vishwajeet Vas left for Delhi for official work on 4th September, by 3:50 pm train. On 5th September in Delhi, he received a call from his colleague saying that his family had met with an accident. He immediately called his home to know about his family. He flew back to Bombay the same evening.

Vishwajeet stays in a house provided by his office. The day before he left to Delhi, he had asked the office car to pick his family from the station.

The driver picked up Vishwajeet's family at 7:54 pm and half the way the car met with an accident. A truck hit and damaged the car. The driver and Vishwajeet's mother received minor injuries, while Vishwajeet's sons and wife were badly injured. A nearby RTO officer took the driver and Vishwajeet's family to the police station. From there, Vishwajeet's son told one of his uncles about the accident, who then took them to the hospital for treatment.

The next day, on 5th September, Vishwajeet's brother called the company's administrative department to inform about the accident and to ask where Vishwajeet could be contacted, but there was no proper response. After reaching office, Vishwajeet complained about the lack of concern by administrative office for the accident. The administrative officer had not taken any actions on the driver. He also gave more details about the accident.

The chief executive took this issue to the employees association of the company on 6th September. On the same day, he received a memorandum from the association about the inaction of the administrative officer concerning the accident.

Questions

1. What kind of behavioural change is required on part of different levels involved?
2. Was the problem to be deal in more formal way?

Chapter at a Glance

Organizational Behaviour

Organizational behaviour can be defined as the understanding, prediction, and management of the human behaviour that affect the performance of organizations.

Levels of Analysis

- Individual-level analysis
- Group-level analysis
- Organizational-level analysis

(Continued)

(Continued)

Disciplines of Organizational Behaviour

- Psychology
- Political science
- Sociology
- Social psychology
- Anthropology

Elements of Organizational Behaviour

The four vital elements of organization are

- People
- Structure
- Technology
- Environment

Nature and Scope of Organizational Behaviour

- Organizational behaviour is the study of behavioural aspects of individuals within the organizations.
- Organizational behaviour comprises the study of intrapersonal and interpersonal behaviour and organizations.
- Intrapersonal behaviour comprises the study of aspects like personality, attitude, motivation, and perception.
- Intrapersonal behaviour covers group dynamics, team management, conflict management, and so on.
- The study of organization covers aspects like its structure and formation.

Importance of Organizational Behaviour

- Provides guidelines to the management about the way in which human element should be emphasized.
- Provides an outlook to management to analyse behaviour of individuals and suggests an effective direction.
- Answers to the questions like why and how human beings behave in a particular manner, which in turn helps in building cordial relations in the organization.
- Gives an insight to the managers to understand the behaviour of their subordinates.
- Helps the managers to select the most effective style of leadership.
- Helps in effective conflict management, better decision-making, commitment to ideas, teamwork, and so on.

Approaches to Organizational Behaviour

- HR approach
- Contingency approach
- Systems approach
- Productivity approach

Models of Organizational Behaviour

- **Autocratic model:** In this model, key decisions lie with the top management of the organization.
- **Custodial model:** It promotes financial security for the employees by incorporating rewards and benefits programme.
- **Supportive model:** This is focused on promoting leadership traits amongst individuals.
- **Collaborative model:** This model states that every employee is a colleague of the other.

Current Trends in Organizational Behaviour

- Upgrading employee skills
- Enhancing value and output
- TQM
- Business process reengineering
- Managing employee mix
- Globalization
- Empowering people
- Coping with temporariness
- Stimulating innovation and change

E-commerce

E-commerce is the electronic exchange of information pertaining to various businesses using EDI and associated technologies.

E-business

In e-business, ICT is used to enhance one's business performance with a vision towards improving service and reducing costs.E-organizations/E-governance

E-organization/e-governance is the arranging of state governance based on electronic tools for collecting, processing, and dissemination of information and providing of government services to all groups of population and businesses by electronic tools.

CHAPTER 9

Understanding and Managing Individual Behaviour

Learning Objectives

- Getting a detailed idea on the attitude, its aspects and components, and impact of workplace attitudes on organizational productivity.
- Understanding the detailed aspect of learning and behaviour with learning theories, human perception, and decision-making.
- Getting an insight into the personality traits and factors influencing those traits and their impact from the perspectives of the organization.

An Opening Vignette

The ABC group of hotels, which focuses on outlook to promote retention, has maintained its trends on retaining staff and high quality of service provisioning for customers by keeping in focus personnel recruitment with correct attitude and code of conduct.

The ABC group operates three types of hotels, namely the budget, comfort, and the luxury hotel, catering to different customer segments and wants to take its customer service to the next level. For this, it implemented a performance management system for the organization as well as the employee with a motive to promote organizational productivity, because of the fact that for hotel industries, maintaining high customer service levels is considered vital.

According to the chief managing director of the company, the rationale was that success of the hotel industry depended a lot on etiquettes and behaviour of the employees.

With the new behavioural and goal-oriented performance management system in place, the self and managers' online feedback are taken once in every quarter via a scoring system that rates an individual a performer if he has scored above 75 in a 100-point scale and poor performer if below 50%.

Individuals discuss and match the results with their managers, and in case of any discrepancy, well-documented reasons act as the guidelines to take appropriate actions. This activity makes it easier for the group to compare the performance of employees across the hotel chain.

Since the performance system was implemented, the non-performers have also become aware of their performance projections being exposed to the senior management and have started working with passion, dedication, and attitude.

The main challenge was to educate and train the employees on the new evaluation system not all of whom were Internet savvy by encouraging them to use it.

Another breakthrough which the ABC group achieved using this performance management system was that they were able to conduct an online test for the new hires and a scenario was given to the prospective recruits to provide solutions based on which decision to hire was taken based on the behavioural analysis of the candidate. So even if the candidate did not possess the right set of skills, the hotel group hired him or her if he/she had the right attitude because people are better equipped and more willing to go the extra mile for customers and have high probability to be with the company for an extended time period, which is a major problem faced by the hotel industry.

Meaning of Attitude

Attitude can be described as a trend to react positively or negatively to a person or situation. Thus, attitude comprises of inclination and direction of inclination and has been defined as a mental state of readiness. The encyclopaedia of social sciences described attitude as a comparatively enduring organization of interrelated beliefs which describe and evaluate the action with respect to an object or a situation, with each belief having cognitive effect and behavioural components. Each of these beliefs is a predisposition that results in some preferential response towards the object or the situation. The concept of attitude originated in the United States.

Definition of Attitude

An attitude is mental state of readiness, learned and organized through experience, exerting a specific influence on person's response to people, object and situation with which it is related.

Ivancevich

Attitudes are learned predispositions towards aspects of our environment. They may be positively or negatively directed towards certain people, services or institutions.

Anonymous

A relatively enduring organization of beliefs, feelings, and behavioral tendencies towards socially significant objects, groups, events or symbols.

Hogg and Vaughan

Types of Attitude

Attitude can be referred to as a combination of emotions and thought processing. It represents the degree to which an individual likes or dislikes a person, place, job, thing, or an event. Attitude are of two types positive and negative. If someone has a positive approach about something, for example, towards his/her job, or an individual, then it is positive attitude, else it would be considered as negative attitude.

- **Positive attitude:** An inclination that brings out a desired output for persons and organizations can be referred to as positive attitude. Individuals with positive attitude generally believe that there is some good opportunity in every situation. In other words, these people are optimistic. In order to encourage such kind of attitude among individuals, positive attitude is often rewarded.
- **Negative attitude:** The inclination of a person that leads to an undesirable result for individuals and organizations can be described as negative attitude. People with negative attitude are pessimists who feel that they are often surrounded by problems and difficulties and also view all the individuals and situations as unfavourable. Negative attitudes are punished in order to discourage the same action in the future.
- **Neutral attitude:** People with a neutral attitude do not feel like giving suggestions with respect to an event or feel that there is a need to change.

Components of Attitude

Every attitude has three components that are represented in what is called the ABC model of attitudes: A for affective, B for behavioural, and C for cognitive. Although every attitude has these three components, any particular attitude can be based on one component more than another.

In other words, each component can also be the answer to the question: Where does an attitude come from? There are affectively based attitudes, behaviourally based attitudes, and cognitively based attitudes.

The ABC model of attitude represents the three basic components of attitude, where 'A' stands for affective, 'B' stands for behavioural, and 'C' stands for cognitive (Figure 9.1).

Figure 9.1 Components of Attitude

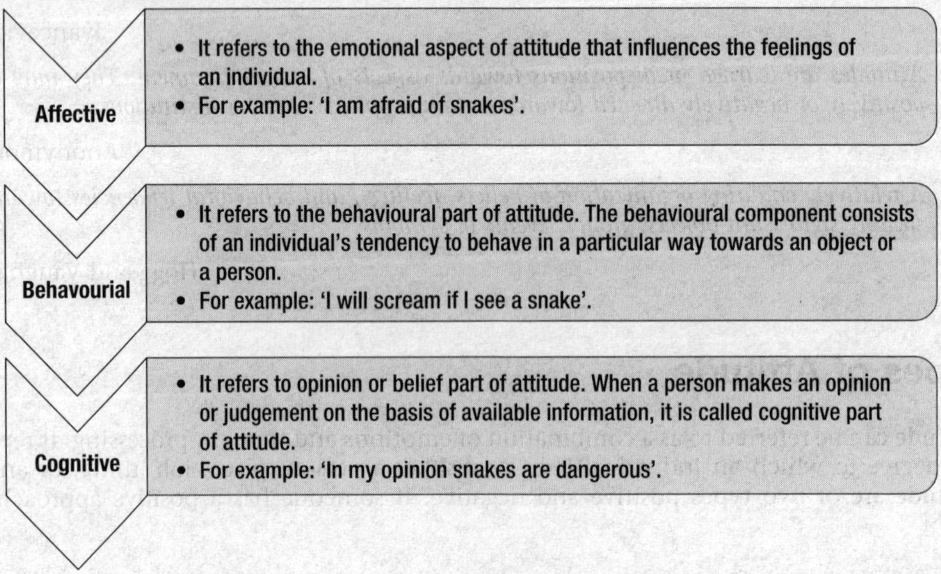

Attitudes and Behaviour

Individual Attitudes and Behaviours

Attitudes and behaviours correlate to a considerable extent. A person possessing positive attitude spreads positivity in the environment for his colleagues. These people are always active as well as productive and perform better. Similarly a person with negative attitude may affect the environment in a negative manner and shows less efficiency and productivity.

Organizational Attitudes and Behaviours

Attitudes can have significant impact on the behaviour of individuals and those around them. Organizations must therefore create a conducive work environment, job satisfaction, some type of reward or bonus, and code of conduct amongst the employees in an organization. An individual's behaviour can be changed by keeping organizational attitudes consistent for which everyone in the organization needs to be committed. Some employees might be affected by the change while others might not. So management might devise certain strategies to change the behaviour across the organization and also take into consideration the diversity inherent in any group.

Classification of Attitudes

Attitudes of people are said to have implications on the individual's behaviour and govern them accordingly. Daniel Katz classified attitudes into four different groups based on their functions:

- **Utilitarian:** This refers to the attitude of an individual which has been created through self- or community interest and a classic example can be hike in pay, which exudes positive reaction and attitude from an employee, which in turn impacts the environment positively.
- **Rationale and Knowledge:** Understanding the rationale behind why a task is being allotted to a particular individual or a group or why the organization has devised a specific type of strategy is another means by which people form attitudes, which are positive dispositions of the form and are better for the organizations' environment.
- **Ego-defensive:** Usage of attitude to protect the ego results in negative attitude. For example, a manager's criticism of an employees' work without offering suggestions for improvement can evoke a negative response from the individual. So it is mandatory for the managers to offer guidance along with identifying the problem or the issues in the work of the employee.
- **Value-expressive:** People develop central values over time and it is the responsibility of managers to understand the importance of values from employee perspective. The managers then can align to organizational vision with individual values, thereby creating enthusiasm amongst the task force.

Impact of Attitudes on Workplace

Workplace attitudes have an impact on every person in the organization, right from the lowest level staff to the highest level stakeholder. Workplace attitudes aim at developing employee confidence, efficiency, and team-building abilities. Understanding the impact of positive and negative workplace attitudes aims at creating a harmonious environment in the organization. Following can be the impacts of workplace attitudes:

- **Validation:** The workplace attitude contributes substantially to the events that happen within the organization. For example, if there is a sales drop in a particular product for an organization, then an organization with a negative attitude will try to be defensive about the same while the one with a positive attitude will immediately find out the causes behind the sales drop. The sense of optimism amongst the workforce sometimes works wonders for the organization.
- **Competition:** Attitudes in general boost the competitive environment at the workplace. A negative attitude is responsible for creating mistrust among employees whereas in a workplace with a positive attitude, inducing competitiveness is taken positively, which inspires employees to perform better.
- **Inventiveness:** Innovation has always remained an important aspect for business of any kind and a positive workplace attitude encourages inventiveness because employees feel that their ideas will contribute towards achievement of organizational goals. A negative attitude restricts inventiveness as employees do not feel obliged to contribute to company growth.
- **Withholding:** Employee retention is impacted by the attitude in the workplace. An organization with positive attitudinal environment makes the employees feel that they have a big role in the contribution towards organizational success. A negative attitude leads to loss of experienced employees, which degrades the company's growth.

Changing Attitudes in the Workplace

Negative attitudes within the workplace impact customer satisfaction and decrease employee morale, leading to lack of productivity and efficiency. It is extremely crucial to exhibit positive attitudes at the workplace so that they lead to a healthy business environment.

- **Set example:** The mindset, thought process, and the communication by the manager often sets the tone of the unit or the office and to display positive attitude is the initial responsibility of the manager or the company stakeholder. While it is not possible for every individual to be positive most of the time, but one can directly try to implement the same most of the time keeping a note of the fact that positive attitude is essential for improved productivity of the organization.
- **Identify motivators:** There are people in the organization who are motivated by either goals or rewards. The management should identify them and find out what works the best for each individual so that the workforce remains positive and motivated.
- **Eliminate troublemakers:** An employee with a bad attitude can ruin the atmosphere of the organization and inject negativity amongst the people and their attitudes. It is highly recommended that these employees should be encouraged to participate in attitude-building workshops, and if they respond negatively to such strategies then it is better to eliminate them from organizations.
- **Proper ambience:** Neat and clean office surroundings contribute in building positive attitudes amongst employees in the organization. Also, the office décor contributes a lot to the building of attitude through the use of wall colour, artwork, and having modern furniture or equipment.
- **Recognition:** Employees should be praised and encouraged for good attitude and also rewarded for promoting enthusiasm amongst others, and such groups should be steered to work towards the company's goals and objectives and their deeds should be well acknowledged by the company and its managers. Employees should have a feeling that they are appreciated by the top management.

- **Support:** Offer support for employees going through difficult periods. When employees bearing positive attitude exhibit negative behaviour, there should be a mechanism and communication channel where they can discuss their problems with the managers of the organization. Many companies set up an employee counselling service to help employees going through troubled times.

Definition of Learning

Any process through which experience at one time can alter an individual's behavior at a future time.

Peter Gray

Learning associated with changes in a person's behavior to something situation caused by repeated experiences in that situation, where changes in behavior cannot be explained or basic innate response tendencies, maturation.

Hilhard Bower

A relatively settled change in behaviour that occur as a result of training or experience.

Morgan

Learning is a change in personality self-described as a new pattern of reactions in the form of skills, attitudes, habits, intelligence or an understanding.

Wetherington

Learning Theories

Classical Conditioning

This theory of learning was developed by Ivan Pavlov, a Russian physiologist. He performed an experiment in which he tried to relate the dog's salivation and the ringing of a bell. He made efforts to teach dogs to salivate in response to the ringing bell. He used a simple surgical procedure while conducting his experiment.

The dog started to salivate as soon as Pavlov gave it a piece of meat. But when he rang the bell the dog did not salivate. Pavlov then tried to relate the meat and the ringing of bell before presenting meat. He noticed that after a few days the dog started to salivate as soon as the bell rang, even though no food was offered.

Through this experiment it was evident that the dog had learned to respond (to salivate) on the ringing of bell.

This theory includes four concepts as follows:

- **Unconditioned stimuli:** The meat being offered to the dog was unconditioned stimuli that forced the dog to act in a specific manner.
- **Unconditioned response:** The response to unconditioned stimuli is referred to as unconditioned response. In this experiment, the unconditioned response was increase in salvation.
- **Conditioned stimuli:** Ringing of the bell was a conditioned stimulus.
- **Conditioned response:** The response of the dog in reaction of ringing the bell alone is known as conditioned response.

Operant Conditioning Theory

This theory was developed by B.F. Skinner. It is also known as instrumental conditioning. This theory states that behaviour is a function of its consequences. According to operant conditioning, behaviour is expected to be repeated if consequences are favourable and vice versa. Therefore, the connection linking actions (behaviour) and consequences is the core of operant conditioning theory.

The word 'operant' means an organism that helps generate a consequence. According to B. F. Skinner, individuals learn to behave in a particular manner in order to achieve or avoid something.

Operant behaviour refers to learned behaviour. Skinner states that creating of favourable consequences can help to bring about the desired behaviour pattern or to increase the repetition of a particular behavioural pattern. This should be done because a desired behaviour will lead to reward. For example, even in our daily lives we tend to repeat the past behaviour if it leads to a favourable outcome and try to avoid the behaviour that leads to an unfavourable one.

Operant conditioning theory of learning is used in educational research, control of alcoholism, and control deviant children in a classroom.

Reinforcement

The meaning of the word 'reinforce' is to strengthen. This term has been used in operant conditioning to refer to any stimulus that helps strengthen or increases the possibility of a particular response. For example, if you want a monkey to perform somersault on demand, you may give it a treat every time it does so. The monkey will ultimately realize that performing a somersault on order will result in a reward (treat). This reward (treat) is reinforcing as the monkey likes it and will tend to perform somersault as and when instructed in the future.

This theory is applicable to our day-to-day lives, a few examples of which are stated below:

- A child may tend to study harder for the next time if he/she realizes that the teacher appreciates good marks.
- An employee tends to refrain from doing a particular action if he has been punished for doing so in the past.

Reinforcers may be either primary or secondary.

- **Primary reinforcers:** It is any reinforcer that does not need to be learnt. It occurs naturally. A few examples of primary reinforcers include air, food, water, and so on.
- **Secondary reinforcers:** These are also known as conditioned reinforcers. It is a learned reinforcer. For example, hike in salary for good performance.

Reinforcements are of four types: positive, negative, punishment, and extinction (Figure 9.2).

Learning and Behaviour

As we get to know things, we change our ways of perceiving our environment, the way of interpreting the incoming stimuli, thereby resulting in the way we behave or react to a situation. This process, which leads to a relatively permanent behavioural change or potential behavioural change, can be termed learning. John B. Watson (1878–1958) first studied the

Figure 9.2 Types of Reinforcements

Positive reinforcement	• Involves the addition of something to increase a response. Praise and rewards are most common form of positive reinforcement. • For example, appreciating a child for scoring good grades in examination.
Negative reinforcement	• Involves removing something in order to increase a response. • For example, a student sharing hostel room tries to clean the mess in order to avoid getting into fight with the roommate.
Punishment	• Punishment refers to adding something aversive in order to decrease behaviour. • For example, warning an employee for misconduct.
Extinction	• When you remove something in order to decrease behaviour, this is called extinction. • For example, parent stops giving the child chocolate when he throws tantrums.

effects of learning process on our behaviour and established the psychological school of behaviourism. Behaviourism basically focuses only on an individual's observable behaviour, which is worthy of research. Unlike behaviour, the other abstractions such as a person's mood or thoughts are too subjective. This belief was dominant in psychological research in the United Stated for a good 50 years. One of the most well-known behaviourist, B.F. Skinner (1904–1990) very much followed Watson's research and findings. His belief that the internal states could influence behaviour just as external stimuli resulted in him being considered as a radical behaviourist. However, these days it is very much believed that both internal and external stimuli influence our behaviour.

Behavioural psychology aims at finding behaviour results from the stimuli both in the environment and within an individual. They go to the minute detail of the behaviour exhibited while controlling as many other variables as possible, and this has helped understand the behaviour of human beings, what effects the environment has on the behaviour of humans, and what motivates the individuals to change their behaviour or show consistency in the behaviour.

Perception

Perception can be defined as a process by which individuals select, organize, and interpret their sensory impressions, so as to give meaning to their environment. Perception is a multifaceted cognitive process and varies from one individual to another.

Perception is the process in which individuals receive a wide range of information about their surroundings through all the five senses, assimilate them, and then interpret them. The same information can be perceived differently by different people. Perception plays a vital role in identifying how an individual behaves in the organization.

Perceptual Process

The perceptual process consists of six phases that have been explained in detail in Figure 9.3:

- **Receiving:** The process of perception begins with the reception of stimuli from the environment. These stimuli may be received from different sensory organs. The sensory organs receive data regarding both physical and non-physical objects.
- **Selection:** It deals with separating the significant and insignificant data so that the relevant data can be processed further. The selection phase is influenced by external and internal factors.
  - **External factors:** These include size, intensity, motion, repetition, location, familiarity, and so on.
  - **Internal factors:** These include age, personality, motivation, learning, and so on.
- **Organizing:** Once data are selected, these are organized systematically to make these meaningful. There are three magnitudes of perceptual organizing as mentioned below:
  - **Figure background:** This principle states that the correlation of an object to its background influences perception. According to this principle, the object stands out separately from their background.
  - **Perceptual grouping:** The principle of grouping includes the following:
    - **Similarity:** The greater the similarity of stimuli, the greater would be the tendency to consider it as a group.
    - **Proximity:** It refers to considering the factors that are close to each other as a group.
    - **Closure:** It means to perceive the whole part when nothing exists.
    - **Continuity:** It refers to individual's ability to perceive continuous lines or patterns. It refers to an individual's capability to perceive some features of an object as remaining constant, regardless of variations in the stimuli.

Figure 9.3 Perceptual Process

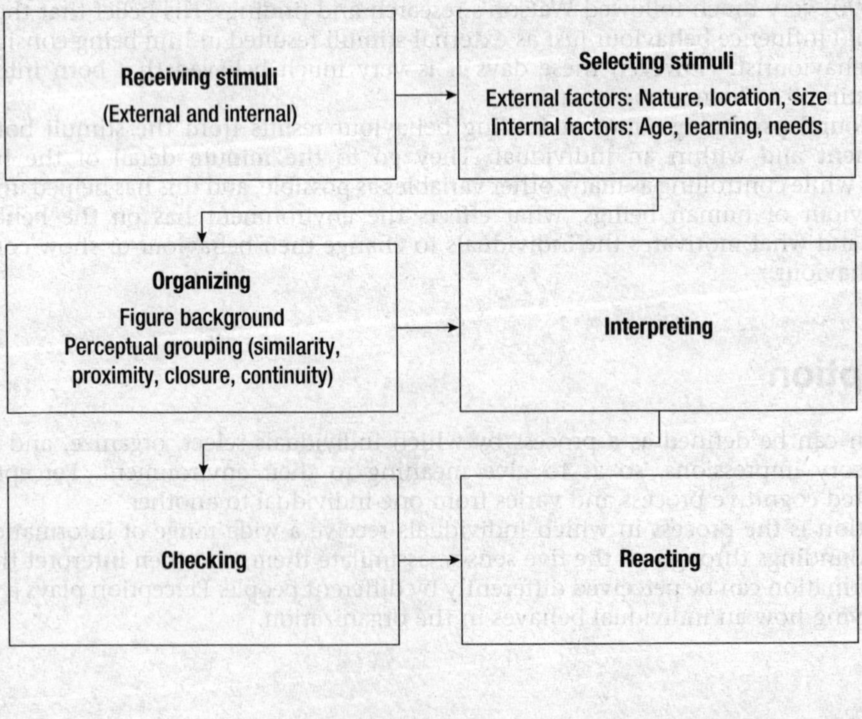

- **Interpreting:** Once data are received and organized, the perceiver then interprets the information. In other words, this is the phase in which the perceiver assigns meaning to the information. There are three major factors that affect the process of interpretation. These include the perceiver, the perceived, and the situation.
- **Checking:** The next phase checks whether the interpretations made are right or wrong. To check the consistency of the interpretation, an individual can put up a series of questions to himself or others and try to get answers for these questions to verify if the interpretation was correct.
- **Reacting:** The last phase of the perceptual process is reacting. In this phase, the perceiver takes an action in response to the perception. The action taken is influenced by the perception made. It means that the action will be positive if the perception is favourable and negative if the perception is unfavourable.

Factors Influencing Perception

Perception is an individual's experience of the surrounding. This includes receiving and responding to the environmental stimuli. Through the perceptual process, we get to know about the properties and elements of the environment that are critical to our survival.

There are three major factors that tend to shape or distort perception, explained as follows (Figure 9.4):

- **The Perceiver:** The personal characteristics of the perceiver play a crucial role in the process of interpretation. Some of the personal characteristics of the perceiver that influence the process of perception include the perceiver's personality, attitude, values, beliefs, habits, and so on. The interpretation of any target of an individual is heavily influenced by the personal characteristics of the individual perceiver. For example, if one expects military personnel to be strict, teenagers to be rude, or individuals holding office to be corrupt, he/she may peeve them as such, regardless of their cultural traits.

Figure 9.4 Factors Influencing Perception

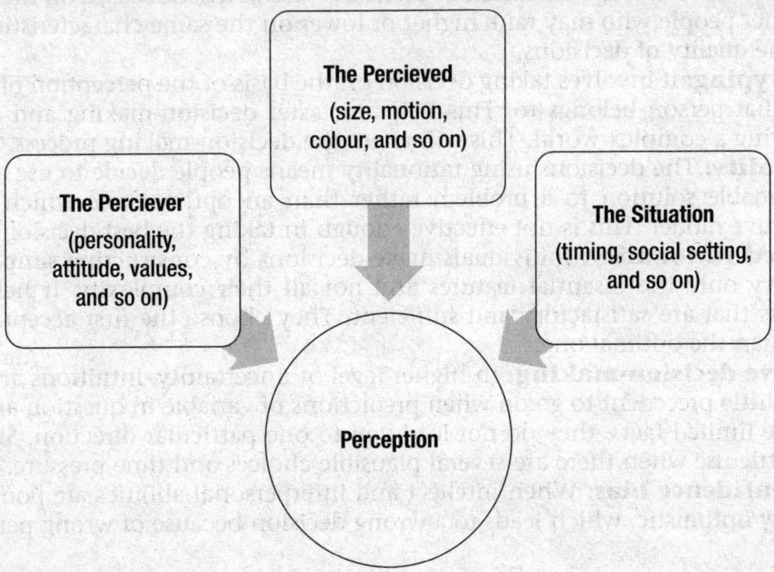

- **The perceived (object):** Characteristics of the object or target being observed also influence a person's perception. No object is perceived in isolation. Since every object has a relationship with its background, it is one factor that plays an important role in perception. The targets are not looked at in isolation; the relationship of a target to its background also influences perception and also tendency to group close and similar things together. Characteristics of the target being observed affect what is perceived. People who are vocal are more likely to be noticed in a group than quiet ones, as are extremely attractive or unattractive individuals. For example, generally people working in the same department are seen as a group. If two people working in the marketing department resign at around more or less the same time, people tend to assume a link between these resignations, although they might not be related at all.
- **The situation:** The physical, societal, and organizational setting of the situation also dominate a person's perception. The situation in which the interaction between the perceiver and the target takes place has an influence on the perceiver's impression of the target. For example, there would be a difference in your approach towards the same sales executive of the furniture showroom who talks to you about the space-saving furniture when you had attended the party and when you had actually been to the showroom.

Perception and Decision-making

The behaviour of a person is based on his or her perception of what reality is, which may actually not be the reality itself as it is not necessary that when two persons see the same thing, they interpret the same way.

Based on the above, the following are some factors that affect perception and the process of decision-making:

- **Selective perception:** People interpret what they see only on the basis of their interest, background, experience, and attitudes, which does not allow them to draw an accurate picture. This may lead to people's decision impaired by wrong perception.
- **Halo (horns) effect:** People draw a general impression about the individual based on a single characteristic and not considering others factors, which may lead to wrong decisions.
- **Contrast effects:** It is evaluations of a person's characteristics based on the comparisons with other people who may rank higher or lower on the same characteristics which also affect the quality of decisions.
- **Stereotyping:** It involves taking decision on the basis of the perception of the group to which that person belongs to. This helps in faster decision-making and also helps in simplifying a complex world. This will affect the decision-making process.
- **Rationality:** The decisions using rationality means people decide to use an acceptable or reasonable solution to a problem rather than an optimal one which is a defined prescriptive model. This is not effective enough in taking the best decision.
- **Bounded rationality:** Individuals make decisions by constructing simplified models that carry only the essential features and not all their complexity. It helps in taking decisions that are satisfactory and sufficient. They choose the first acceptable solution rather than the optimal one.
- **Intuitive decision-making:** In higher level of uncertainty, intuitions are often used; there is little precedent to go on when predictions of variable in question are less. When there are limited facts, they do not lead you to one particular direction. Similarly, data are of little use when there are several plausible choices and time pressure.
- **Overconfidence bias:** When intellect and interpersonal abilities are poor, we tend to be overly optimistic, which leads to a wrong decision because of wrong perception.

- **Anchoring bias:** At times our mind appears to place a disproportionate amount of emphasis on the first information it receives, which leads us to focus on the initial information only, which in turn does not help in taking an optimal decision.
- **Confirmation bias:** When we avoid the information that contradicts our past decisions, it leads to the uncertainty that it is the optimal solution.
- **Availability bias:** This means the tendency of people to take decisions on the basis of the information readily available to them without doing further research on it.
- **Representative bias:** The inclination to evaluate the probability of an event happening by drawing similarities and speculating about similar situations will lead to weak decision-making.
- **Escalation of commitment:** An increased commitment to a previous decision even after getting negative information also leads to wrong decisions.
- **Randomness error:** Taking decisions based on the random events happened is not an effective way to get optimal solution.
- **Hindsight bias:** After that outcome is actually known, we tend to believe falsely that we would have accurately predicted the outcome of an event.
- **Personality:** Many special characters like thoroughness and self-respect may affect insight and hence affect the decision-making process.
- **Gender:** The fact that women tend to analyse decisions more than men will lead to more accuracy in making decisions as well as much time consumed for taking a decision by women.
- **Cultural differences:** There are differences in focusing on the problem areas, analytical depth, importance of judgement and reasonableness, and penchant for individual versus group decision-making.

EXAMPLES

Job Interviews

Interviewers' perceptual judgement in selecting the candidate might result in wrongful hiring.

Performance Appraisals

The performance evaluation of an individual is done based on the standard parameters set by the organization. But the process and decisions taken are largely affected by the perceptions of both the appraiser and the appraisee. In order to eliminate this pre-defined conception of the appraiser and the appraisee and to increase the accuracy of the performance appraisal, organizations conduct trainings for both the concerned parties.

CASE: PERCEPTION OF EMPLOYEE TOWARDS AUTOMATION

A furniture company used to function with the help of labour and only a few machines. But due to the increasing opportunities in the market, the company decided to go for automation of several activities that were done manually. According to the management, automation would increase the production rate as well as precision with which work was done. The company had decided to train its employees on the new technology that was going to be installed.

Hearing about company's decision, two groups of employees were formed in the company; one perceived the change to be positive (Group A) and the other negative (Group B). Group A perceived automation as an opportunity of self-development, since they would learn new technology, whereas group B perceived it as a threat to their job.

(Continued)

(Continued)

Question: How would you manage to change the perception among the employees of group B?

- Make a quick survey of the category of employees showing positive attitude towards this change and those who exude negativity.
- Communicate continuously with the employees in face-to-face mode, joint sessions, and open conversations to understand their fear.
- Make the peers interact with the group and convince them that they will be adequately trained prior to using the computerized systems and that managers will actively support them by providing continuous help without retaliation.
- Conduct a formal workshop in association with other companies where these companies also bring in their employees and discuss the benefits of automation across various levels of employees, which can induce a competitive spirit amongst the employees of the furniture company and also make them well convinced of the benefits when they hear from employees at the same level in other organizations.

Personality: Definitions

A stable set of characteristics and tendencies that determine those commonalities and differences in the psychological behavior and that may not be easily understood as the sole result of the social and biological pressures of the moment.

Maddi

Personality is the set of psychological traits and mechanisms within the individual that are organized and relatively enduring and that influence his or her interactions with, and adaptations to, the intrapsychic, physical, and social environments.

Larsen and Buss

Personality refers to individuals' characteristic patterns of thought, emotion, and behavior, together with the psychological mechanisms — hidden or not — behind those patterns. This definition means that among their colleagues in other subfields of psychology, those psychologists who study personality have a unique mandate: to explain whole persons.

Funder

Personality is that which permits a prediction of what a person will do in the given situation.

Cattell

Factors Influencing Personality

The factors influencing personality are as mentioned below:

- **Biological factors:** Biological factors are primary determinants of personality. These include heredity, physique, and physical stature, nervous system, and so on. According to the psychologists and geneticists, hereditary is one of the most crucial factors that shape the individuals personality. The physical stature and make-up of nervous system also plays a major part in influencing an individual's personality.
- **Family and societal factors:** Family and societal factors are also responsible to a great extent in formation of individual's personality. The size of family and relations among the members of the family may be a major factor in deciding the personality of a person. Apart from the family background, society leaves a mark on the personality of an individual.

- **Situational factors:** A person's personality is also influenced by situational factors. The effect of surroundings on personality is fairly strong. Mostly the actions of a person are influenced by situation, rather than his behaviour. Therefore, the situation may potentially have a very big impact on the actions and expressions.

Big Five Personality Traits

- **Extraversion and introversion:** These terms were popularized by Carl Jung. People who are talkative and like to be surrounded by people are referred to as extroverts. People who prefer being alone and not interested what is going on around him/her is referred to as introvert. People scoring high on extraversion like to party and be a part of social gathering and vice versa. The extraversion trait includes characteristics such as talkativeness, assertiveness, and so on, whereas the introversion trait includes characteristics such as shyness, reserved, nervousness, and so on.
- **Agreeableness:** This trait refers to a person's ability to adjust in all the situations and non-reluctance to change. They accept the changes whole heartedly and try to overcome problems and help others. Individuals scoring high on this trait are friendly and accommodating than those scoring low on this trait. This trait includes characteristics such as faith, selflessness, sympathy, friendliness, and so on.
- **Conscientiousness:** Individuals with this trait think in detail before coming to any decision or acting. These people are extremely cautious and follow their conscience. Common characteristics of this trait include attention to detail, proactive, disciplined, goal oriented, and so on. Individuals scoring high on this trait are more methodological and thoughtful and strive to accomplish their goals within set time frame.
- **Neuroticism:** People high on this parameter have a pessimistic view about life. They tend to see only the negative things in life and often suffer from depression. People with this trait are likely to experience anxiety, emotional instability, and misery, and so on.
- **Openness:** People with this trait have a liking for creativity and are active. These people prove to be good at learning due to their readiness to learn and experience new things. People scoring more on this parameter are broad-minded as compared to those who score low on the same parameter. Some of the characteristics of this trait include imagination, creativeness, insight, and so on.

Myers–Briggs Type Indicator (MBTI)

The MBTI is used to identify a person's personality type, fortes, and preferences. Isabel Myers and her mother, Katherine Briggs, designed the questionnaire based on their work with Carl Jung's theory of personality types.

Based on the answers to the questionnaire, the personality of the people can be correlated to one of the 16 personality types. The goal of the MBTI is to allow respondents to explore further down the levels, their own personalities, including their likes, dislikes, strengths, weaknesses, career choices, and compatibility with other people.

The MBTI tool does not portray any dysfunctionality in the personality of an individual, rather it helps to learn more about oneself.

The questionnaire is made up of four different scales:

- **Extraversion (E)–Introversion (I):** The extraversion–introversion dichotomy was first explored by Jung describing how people respond and interact with the environment around them. Extraverts are types who display action in an outward fashion, enjoy more recurrent social collaboration, and feel energized and motivated after communicating and collaborating with people. Introverts, on the other hand, are speculative, tend to be thought-oriented, enjoy deep and meaningful exchange of communication, and feel motivated after spending time alone. Human beings possess one of the traits over the other.

- **Sensing (S)–Intuition (N):** This is a scale which acknowledges how people gather information. According to the MBTI, people who prefer sensing pay substantial attention to reality, and learn from their senses. They tend to focus on facts and details and enjoy getting hands-on experience. People who are intuitive pay considerable attention to patterns and impressions. Their thinking revolves around possibilities, and they think on the levels of abstraction.
- **Thinking (T)–Feeling (F):** This scale elaborates on people's decisions making based on the information gathered from sensing or intuition and emphasize on facts and objective data. They tend to be consistent, logical, and impersonal when taking and weighing a decision. Those who prefer feeling, consider people and the emotions when coming to a conclusion.
- **Judging (J)–Perceiving (P):** The final scale involves how people are dealing with the external world and those who lean towards judging prefer structure and stable decisions. People who lean towards perceiving are more open, flexible, and adaptable. These two scales interact with the other scales, and the judging–perceiving scale helps describe whether an individual extraverts when he/she is sensing and intuiting or making decisions. Each type is then listed by its four-letter code. For example, ISTJ, ISTP, INTJ, ESTJ, and so on.

According to the Myers & Briggs Foundation, all the four measures are equally important and that every type has value. When working in groups in college, for example, recognizing one's own strengths and understanding the strengths of others can be very helpful. When working towards completing a project with other members of a group, one might realize that certain members of the group are accomplished and gifted at performing certain tasks. By recognizing these traits, the manager can better assign tasks to the group members and work together on achieving their professional and personal goals.

Values

Values offer a vital basis for understanding the personality, attitudes, and perception of an individual. Values contain judgemental element as to what is right or wrong, good or bad, favourable or unfavourable, and desirable or undesirable.

Values consist of two attributes: content attributes and intensity attributes. The content attribute refers to what is important and the intensity attribute refers to the degree of importance. An individual's value system can be recognized when the values are ranked based on intensity. Each individual has a hierarchy of values that forms his/her value system. The value systems are unique to each individual.

Value system is a major influencer of a person's personality, attitude, behaviour, and perception. Thus, study of values can be very useful in identifying appropriate motivation techniques, leadership styles, and managing conflicts.

Definition of Values

An enduring belief that a specific mode of conduct or end-stated of existence is personally or socially preferable to an opposite or converse mode of conduct are end-state of existence.

Milton Rokeach

Concept of the desirable, an internalized criterion or standard of evaluation a person possesses. Such concepts and standards are relatively few and determine or guide an individual's evaluations of the many objects encountered in everyday life.

Ronald D. White and David A. Bednar

The constellation of likes, dislikes, viewpoints, should, inner inclinations, rational and irrational judgments, prejudices, and association patters that determine a person's view of the world.

Edward Stranger

Types of Values

Six different types of values identified by G.W. Allport and his associates are as follows:

- **Economic:** The emphasis is on usefulness and practicality.
- **Theoretical:** It has high significance for discovery of truth through crucial and rational approach.
- **Aesthetic:** The highest value is on form and harmony.
- **Political:** The emphasis is on attainment of authority and influence.
- **Social:** The highest value is to the love of people.
- **Religious:** It is concerned with the unity of experience and understanding of the universe as a whole.

Values at Workplace

The formation of an individual's value system is based on several internal as well as external factors like family, society, customs, culture, traditions, and so on. The values that a person possesses play a vital role at their workplace. It would be highly impossible for an organization to employ or continue the employment of any individuals whose values are against the norms of the society.

An organization should try to encourage positive values and discourage negative values so that it leads to creation of a healthy work environment. If an individual has a set of moral values then these will decide the way in which he/she behaves with others and conducts himself/herself. There would be reflection of unethical behaviour when the person does not have such basic moral values and this can put the organization in problem. In order to maintain a cordial work environment, every organization has to strive to understand the value system of each of its employees. Although this is a very difficult task, the outcome would be of huge help. Depending on the outcome, the organization can frame various strategies to handle the employees.

Summary

The chapter presents various aspects of attitudes and its organizational impact. It also emphasizes on how individual's positive attitude in collation can work wonders for the organization, various personality traits of an individual and collectively of a group can actually help in promoting the productivity, efficiency, and growth of the organization. The chapter also throws adequate light on the assessment tool to assess the characteristics that a person possesses and whether his traits will help the company achieve the desired performance.

Exercise

Objective Questions

1. _______ can be referred to as a combination of emotions and thought processing.
    - Attitude
    - Learning
    - Behaviour
    - Values
2. _________refers to the attitude of an individual which has been created through self or community interest
    - Rationale and knowledge
    - Ego-defensive
    - Value-expressive
    - Utilitarian
3. Proximity does not refer to considering the factors that are close to each other as a group.
    - True
    - False
4. A negative attitude is not responsible for creating mistrust among employees whereas, in a workplace with a positive attitude, inducing competitiveness is taken positively which inspires employees to perform better.
    - True
    - False
5. Operant conditioning theory of learning is used in educational research, control of alcoholism and control deviant children in a classroom.
    - True
    - False
6. __________ can be defined as a process by which individuals select, organize, and interpret their sensory impressions, so as to give meaning to their environment.
    - Attitude
    - Learning
    - Behaviour
    - Perception
7. Perceptual process consists of six phases:
    - Receiving, selection, organizing, interpreting, checking, reacting
    - Receiving, organizing, interpreting, selection, checking, reacting
    - Receiving, interpreting, checking, selection, organizing, reacting
    - Receiving, selection, organizing, checking, interpreting, reacting
8. Overconfidence bias will lead to wrong decisions.
    - True
    - False
9. Characteristics such as talkativeness, assertiveness, and so on belong to
    - Agreeableness
    - Introversion

- Extraversion
- Conscientiousness

10. Social values emphasize on attainment of authority and influence.
    - True
    - False

CASE STUDY

Firoz, a 28-year-old woman, works in a mental hospital as a technician for the last three years. At the beginning, she found the job interesting and value added. As the time passed, the environment began to affect Firoz in a negative manner. As a medical technician, she was not given opportunity to utilize her skills and knowledge which she possessed as she had experience in social service for four years. At the start, Firoz was allowed to chart on the patients and to engage in conversation with the patients. These interactions helped Firoz to make her believe that she is making a difference to somebody. After one year, a new policy was implemented where only the licensed staff can prepare the charts. There was also a change in the job of a technician; they were now only supposed to visit patients and keep track every 15 minutes. Firoz was most affected as was underutilized and needed to use her experience and skill. Even after she completed her bachelors' degree, the hospital did not increase her pay. Also, the yearly hikes were very low and all the employees in the hospital were told that they all were lucky to have the job during slack. In contrast, the hospital continued to make improvements in its infrastructure. The mentor was difficult to deal with, as he was unpredictable and maintained distance believing that the staff have minimal skills.

Firoz noticed that her attitude towards work had become negative. She gets up in the morning, goes to work, and never smiles while she is in office. She was affected by work and was often feeling boredom. She followed the hospital policies and found that her stress level and negative attitude towards job has started affecting her personal life.

About two months ago, a job offer for a counsellor training was there in a nearby clinic. Firoz did not want to go for job change at that time. Still, she went for the interview and was selected. After getting the new job, her stress level decreased and she started feeling good and regained positive attitude. She again started working at her best at the work.

Firoz was now able to have one-on-one sessions with patients and felt that her skills were being fully utilized. This was extreme satisfying and her pay was much better than that of the previous job. As the supervisor was cooperative and kind, Firoz was very comfortable and could really begin to build her career in the new job.

Questions

1. Does individual behaviour always follow from attitude? Explain.
2. What are the negative and positive attitudes being observed in Firoz?
3. What are the personality traits you see in Firoz?

Critical Thinking Questions

1. Does behaviour always follow from attitude?
2. Explain that factors that influence an individual's perception.
3. How does workplace play a role in an individual's behaviour?

Chapter at a Glance

Meaning of Attitude

Attitude can be described as a trend to react positively or negatively to a person or situation.

(Continued)

(Continued)

Types of Attitude

Attitudes are of two types positive and negative.

- **Positive attitude:** An inclination that brings out a desired output for persons and organizations can be referred to as positive attitude.
- **Negative attitude:** The inclination of a person that leads to an undesirable result for individuals and organizations can be described as negative attitude.
- **Neutral attitude:** People with a neutral attitude do not feel like giving suggestions with respect to an event or feel that there is a need to change.

Components of Attitude

Every attitude has three components that are represented in what is called the ABC model of attitudes:

- A for affective
- B for behavioural
- C for cognitive
- **Affective:** It refers to the emotional aspect of attitude that influences the feelings of an individual. For example: 'I am afraid of snakes'.
- **Behavioural:** It refers to the behavioural part of attitude. The behavioural component consists of an individual's tendency to behave in a particular way towards an object or a person. For example: 'I will scream if I see a snake'.
- **Cognitive:** It refers to opinion or belief part of attitude. When a person makes an opinion or judgement on the basis of available information it is called cognitive part of attitude. For example: 'In my opinion snakes are dangerous'.

Attitudes and Behaviour

- **Individual attitudes and behaviours:** Attitudes and behaviours correlate to a considerable extent. A person possessing positive attitude spreads positivity in the environment for his colleagues. These people are always active as well as productive and perform better.
- **Organizational attitudes and behaviours:** Attitudes can have significant impact on the behaviour of individuals and those around them. Organizations must therefore create a conducive work environment, job satisfaction, some type of reward or bonus, and code of conduct amongst the employees in an organization.

Classification of Attitudes

Attitudes of people are classified into four different groups based on their functions:

- **Utilitarian:** This refers to the attitude of an individual which has been created through self or community interest.
- **Rationale and knowledge:** Understanding the rationale behind why a task is being allotted to a particular individual or a group or why the organization has devised a specific type of strategy is another means by which people form attitudes which are positive dispositions of the form and is better for the organizations' environment.

- **Ego-defensive:** Usage of attitude to protect the ego results in negative attitude. For example a manager criticizes employees' work without offering suggestions for improvement can evoke a negative response from an individual.
- **Value-expressive:** People develop central values over time and it is the responsibility of the managers to understand the importance of values from employee perspective.

Impact of Attitudes on Workplace

Workplace attitudes have an impact on every person in the organization. Workplace attitudes aim at developing employee confidence, efficiency, and team-building abilities.

- **Validation:** The workplace attitude contributes substantially to the events that happen within the organization. For example, if there is a sales drop in a particular product for an organization, then an organization with a negative attitude will try to be defensive about the same while the one with a positive attitude will immediately find out the causes behind the sales drop.
- **Competition:** Attitudes in general boost the competitive environment at the workplace. A negative attitude is responsible for creating mistrust among employees whereas in a workplace with a positive attitude, inducing competitiveness is taken positively which inspires employees to perform better.
- **Inventiveness:** Employees feel that their ideas will contribute towards achievement of organizational goals. A negative attitude restricts inventiveness as employees do not feel obliged to contribute to company growth.
- **Withholding:** Employee retention is impacted by the attitude in the workplace. An organization with positive attitudinal environment makes the employees feel that they have a big role in the contribution towards organizational success. A negative attitude leads to loss of experienced employees, which degrades the company's growth.

Changing Attitudes in the Workplace

Negative attitudes within the workplace impact customer satisfaction, decrease employee morale, leading to lack of productivity and efficiency. It is extremely crucial to exhibit positive attitudes at the workplace so that they lead to a healthy business environment.

- **Setting example:** The mind-set, thought process and the communication by the manager often sets the tone of the unit or the office and to display positive attitude is the initial responsibility of the manager or the company stakeholder.
- **Identify motivators:** There are people in the organization who are motivated either by goals or rewards. The management of the company should identify them and find out what works the best for each individual so that the workforce remains positive and motivated.
- **Eliminate troublemakers:** An employee with a bad attitude can ruin the atmosphere of the organization and inject negativity amongst the people and their attitudes. It is highly recommended that these employed should be encouraged to participate in the attitude building workshops and if they respond negatively to such strategies then it is better to eliminate them from the organizations.
- **Proper ambience:** Neat and clean office surroundings contribute in building positive attitudes amongst employees in the organization. Also the office décor contributes a lot to the building of attitude.

(Continued)

(Continued)

- **Recognition:** Employees should be praised and encouraged for good attitudes and also rewarded for promoting enthusiasm amongst others and such groups should be steered to work towards the company's goals and objectives.
- **Support:** Offer support for employees going through difficult periods wherein employees bearing positive attitude, if they exhibit negative behaviour, then there should be mechanism and communication channel where they can discuss their problems with the managers of the organization.
- **Learning:** Learning is a change in personality self-described as a new pattern of reactions in the form of skills, attitudes, habits, intelligence or an understanding.

Learning Theories

- **Classical conditioning:** This theory includes four concepts as mentioned below:
  - Unconditioned stimuli
  - Unconditioned response
  - Conditioned stimuli
  - Conditioned response
- **Operant conditioning theory**
  - According to operant conditioning, behaviour is expected to be repeated if consequences are favourable and vice versa. Therefore, the connection linking actions (behaviour) and consequences is the core of operant conditioning theory.
  - Operant behaviour refers to learned behaviour. Operant conditioning theory of learning is used in educational research, control of alcoholism and control deviant children in a classroom.
- **Reinforcement**
  - Reinforce is to strengthen. This is used in operant conditioning to refer to any stimulus that helps strengthen or increases the possibility of a particular response.
  - This is applicable in our day-to-day lives. A few examples of which are stated below:
    - A child may tend to study harder for the next time if he/she realizes that the teacher appreciates good marks.
    - An employee tends to refrain from doing a particular action if he has been punished for doing so in the past.
- Reinforcers may be either primary or secondary.
  - **Primary reinforcers:** It is any reinforcer that does not need to be learnt. It occurs naturally. A few examples of primary reinforcers include air, food, water, and so on.
  - **Secondary reinforcers:** These are also known as conditioned reinforcers. It is a learned reinforcer. For example, hike in salary for good performance.
- Reinforcements are of four types:
  - **Positive Reinforcement:** Involves the addition of something to increase a response.
  - **Negative Reinforcement:** Involves removing something in order to increase a response.
  - **Punishment:** Punishment refers to adding something aversive in order to decrease behaviour.
  - **Extinction:** When you remove something in order to decrease behaviour, this is called extinction.

Learning and Behaviour

As we get to know things, we change our ways of perceiving our environment, the way of interpreting the incoming stimuli, thereby resulting in the way we behave or react to a situation. This process, which leads to a relatively permanent behavioural change or potential behavioural change, can be termed learning. Behavioural psychology aims at finding behaviour results from the stimuli both in the environment and within an individual.

Perception

Perception can be defined as a process by which individuals select, organize, and interpret their sensory impressions, so as to give meaning to their environment.

Perceptual Process

- **Receiving:** The process of perception begins with the reception of stimuli from the environment. These stimuli may be received from different sensory organs. The sensory organs receive data regarding both physical as well as non-physical objects.
- **Selection:** It deals with separating the significant and insignificant data so that the relevant data can be processed further. The selection phase is influenced by external and internal factors.
  - **External factors:** The external factors influencing the selection of data include size, intensity, motion, repetition, location, familiarity etc.
  - **Internal factors:** The internal factors influencing selection of data include age, personality, motivation, learning, and so on.
- **Organizing:** Once the data is selected it needs to be organized systematically so that it becomes meaningful. Following are the magnitudes of perceptual organizing as mentioned below:
  - **Figure background:** This principle states that the correlation of an object to its background influences perception. According to this principle, the object stands out separately from their background.
  - **Perceptual grouping:** The principle of grouping includes the following:
    - **Similarity:** Greater the similarity of stimuli, greater would be the tendency to consider it as a group
    - **Proximity:** It refers to considering the factors that are close to each other as a group.
    - **Closure:** It means to perceive the whole part when nothing exists
    - **Continuity:** It refers to individual's ability to perceive continuous lines or patterns. It refers to an individual's capability to perceive some features of an object as remaining constant, regardless of variations in the stimuli.
- **Interpreting:** In this phase, the perceiver assigns meaning to the information. There are three major factors that affect the process of interpretation. These include; the perceiver, the perceived and the situation.
- **Checking:** The next phase checks whether the interpretations made are right or wrong.
- **Reacting:** The last phase of perceptual process is reacting. In this phase the perceiver takes an action in response to the perception. The action taken is influenced by the perception made. It means the action will be positive if the perception is favourable and negative if the perception is unfavourable.

(Continued)

(Continued)

Factors influencing Perception

- **The perceiver:** The personal characteristics of the perceiver play a crucial role in the process of interpretation. Some of the personal characteristics of the perceiver that influence the process of perception include the perceiver's personality, attitude, values, beliefs, habits, and so on.
- **The perceived (object):** Characteristics of the object or target being observed also influence a person's perception. No object is perceived in isolation. Since every object has a relationship with its background, it is one factor that plays an important role in perception.
- **The situation:** The physical, societal, and organizational setting of the situation also dominates a person's perception. The time at which an object or event can influence attention are light, heat, location, or any number of situational factors.

Perception and Decision-making

Because people's behaviour is based on their perception of what reality is, not on reality itself, it is possible that two persons can see the same thing and interpret it differently. Based on the above, the following are some factors that affect perception and hence it affects the decision-making process:

- **Selective perception:** People selectively interpret what they see on the basis of their interest, background, experience, and attitudes. This factor allows people to speed-read others but not without the risk of drawing an inaccurate picture. Hence, people's decision will be impaired by wrong perception.
- **Halo (Horns) effect:** People are drawing a general impression about an individual on the basis of a single characteristic. This will negatively affect their decisions.
- **Contrast effects:** It is evaluations of a person's characteristics that are affected by comparisons with other people recently encountered, who rank higher or lower on the same characteristics. This factor also affects decisions quality.
- **Stereotyping:** It is judging someone on the basis of one's perception of the group to which that person belongs. This will affect decision-making process.
- **Rationality:** People are usually content to find an acceptable or reasonable solution to a problem rather than an optimal one.
- **Bounded rationality:** Individuals make decisions by constructing simplified models that extract the essential features from problems without capturing all their complexity. This may not ensure the best decisions.
- **Intuitive decision-making:** Intuition is often used when there is a high level of uncertainty. It may be used in decision-making process when all given factors are ambiguous.
- **Overconfidence bias:** We tend to be overly optimistic especially when our intellect and interpersonal abilities are low. This wrong perception will lead to wrong decisions.
- **Anchoring bias:** It is the tendency to focus on initial information as a starting point. This occurs because our mind appears to give a disproportionate amount of emphasis to the first information it receives. This results in not to take the optimal decisions.
- **Confirmation bias:** We tend to selectively seek out information that reaffirms our past choices and we discount information that contradicts our past judgements. This could happen even if we are not sure that this is the optimal choice.
- **Availability bias:** The tendency of people to base their judgements on information readily available to them irrespective of whether this information is enough to make the best decisions or not.

- **Representative bias:** The tendency to assess the likelihood of an occurrence by drawing analogies and seeing identical situations in which they do not exist. This will lead to make the decisions on a very weak base.
- **Escalation of commitment:** An increased commitment to a previous decision in spite of negative information which often creeps into decision-making process.
- **Randomness error:** We tend to create meaning out of random events which is not enough to ensure the optimal decision-making process.
- **Hindsight bias:** We tend to believe falsely that we would have accurately predicted the outcome of an event, after that outcome is actually known. This will confirm the situation even if we believe that it was a wrong decision.
- **Personality:** Many personal characters like conscientiousness and self-esteem may affect perception and hence, affect decision-making process.
- **Gender:** Women tend to analyse a decision prior to and after the fact. This difference in length of thinking in problems will lead to more accuracy in making decisions as well as much time consumed for taking a decision by women.
- **Cultural differences:** There are differences in what problems to focus on, the depth of analysis, importance of logic and rationality, and preference for individual versus group decision-making.

Personality: Definition

Personality is the set of psychological traits and mechanisms within the individual that are organized and relatively enduring and that influence his or her interactions with, and adaptations to the intrapsychic, physical, and social environments.

Factors Influencing Personality

The factors influencing personality are as follows:

- **Biological factors:** Biological factors are primary determinants of personality. These include heredity, physique and physical stature, nervous system, etc.
- **Family and societal factors:** Family and societal factors are also responsible to a great extent in formation of individual's personality. The size of family and relations among the members of the family may be a major factor in deciding the personality of a person. Society leaves a mark on the personality of an individual.
- **Situational factors:** A person's personality is also influenced by situational factors. The effect of surroundings on personality is fairly strong. Mostly the actions of a person are influenced by situation, rather than his behaviour.

Big Five Personality Traits

- **Extraversion and introversion:** People who are talkative and like to be surrounded by people are referred to as extroverts. People who prefer being alone and not interested what is going on around them is referred to as introvert.
- **Agreeableness:** This trait refers to a person's ability to adjust in all the situations and non-reluctance to change. They accept the changes whole heartedly and try to overcome problems and help others. Individuals scoring high on this trait are friendly and accommodating than those scoring low on this trait. This trait includes characteristics such as faith, selflessness, sympathy, friendliness, and so on.
- **Conscientiousness:** Individuals with this trait think in detail before coming to any decision or acting.

(Continued)

(Continued)

- **Neuroticism:** People high on this parameter have a pessimistic view about life. They tend to see only the negative things in life and often suffer from depression.
- **Openness:** People with this trait have a liking for creativity and are active. These people prove to be good at learning due to their readiness to learn and experience new things.

MBTI

The MBTI is a self-inventory designed to identify a person's personality type, strengths, and preferences.

The questionnaire itself is made up of four different scales:

- **Extraversion (E)–Introversion (I):** Extraverts are 'outward-turning' and tend to be action-oriented, enjoy more frequent social interaction, and feel energized after spending time with other people. Introverts are 'inward-turning' and tend to be thought-oriented, enjoy deep and meaningful social interactions, and feel recharged after spending time alone.
- **Sensing (S)–Intuition (N):** People who prefer sensing tend to pay a great deal of attention to reality, particularly to what they can learn from their own senses. They tend to focus on facts and details and enjoy getting hands-on experience. Those who prefer intuition pay more attention to things like patterns and impressions. They enjoy thinking about possibilities, imagining the future and abstract theories.
- **Thinking (T)–Feeling (F):** People who prefer thinking place a greater emphasis on facts and objective data. They tend to be consistent, logical and impersonal when weighing a decision. Those to prefer feeling are more likely to consider people and emotions when arriving at a conclusion.
- **Judging (J)–Perceiving (P):** The judging–perceiving scale helps describe whether you extravert when you are taking in new information (sensing and intuiting) or when you are making decisions (thinking and feeling).

Values

Values offer a vital basis for understanding the personality, attitudes and perception of an individual. Values contain judgemental element as to what is right or wrong, good or bad, favourable or unfavourable, or desirable and undesirable.

Values consist of two attributes:

- content attributes and
- intensity attributes

Types of Values

There are six different types of values, as stated below:

- **Economic:** The emphasis is on usefulness and practicality.
- **Theoretical:** There is high significance for discovery of truth through crucial and rational approach.
- **Aesthetic:** The highest value is on form and harmony.
- **Political:** The emphasis is on attainment of authority and influence.
- **Social:** The highest value is to the love of people.
- **Religious:** It is concerned with the unity of experience and understanding of the universe as a whole.

CHAPTER 10

Group and Group Dynamics

Learning Objectives

- Understanding the significance of forming groups supported by the characteristics and classifications they possess.
- Understanding the essence of group dynamics and what role it plays in the survival of the group in the context of the organization.
- Explaining the significance of unity, roles, and rules in regard to the behaviour of group members.
- Identifying the six stages of group development.
- Identifying the impact of the environmental factors affecting the group behaviour within an organization.

An Opening Vignette

The opening vignette is about the concept of forming a formal group within an organization with proper reporting structures and assigning tasks to the group based on their skill sets to attain high productivity and keeping an open work culture and high level of group cohesiveness. Once two men, who were supposedly friends, thought of starting an organization on advisory services and giving a formal structure to it. By mutual consent, one took up the leadership role and the other took up the position and the role next to him. In their organization, they desperately wanted to implement the buddy model, and accordingly started reaching out to their mates from yesteryears to join their organization.

The idea was to induct people by offering salaries at par with their present salaries and later when the business would pick they would do the profit sharing with reference to employees' contribution and effort. The people who were inducted at the senior management level had considerable years of experience and were focused on achieving organization's growth. Each of them formed their own group to head projects across continental Europe.

The formal groups so formed comprised of satisfied employees because of flexible work culture, transparent inter- and intra-group communication and tremendous support from the organization's top management in terms of implementation of a group member's idea for increasing productivity to working for very big clients such as Lufthansa and Turkish Airlines. Since the group size was small, every member was given a chance to face the clients, which boosted members' confidence. Also, the company ensured that employees had a yearly gathering at some picturesque location to give them a feel-good factor, and this benefit was also extended to the family members. So the project groups constituting the top management, the senior members, and the team were very closely united and a consensus decision-making style was adopted in which every individual could feel that he was important for the group and that his ideas were valued motivating him to contribute further. With strong employee support and excellent business strategies, the organization's turnover in a span of two years reached to $400 million.

Introduction

Group dynamics are the dominant deeds, methods, and transformation that take place within and between groups. Groups come in all forms and their objectives are several and of a wide range, but their impact is widespread. The affinity to bond with colleagues in groups is often the solitary and the crucial trait of individuals and the practices that open up within this crowd make a permanent impression on their associates and on the public. To recognize populace, one should recognize group and the dynamics of that group.

Definitions

A group is defined as a number of individuals who join together to achieve a goal. People join groups to achieve a goal that cannot be achieved by them alone.

Johnson and Johnson

A group consists of any number of people who:

- *interact with each other*
- *are psychologically aware of one another*
- *perceive themselves to be a group*

Schein

Group dynamics is referred to as the field of inquiry dedicated to advancing knowledge about the nature of groups.

Cartwright and Zander

Meaning of Group

A group is defined as a minimum of two or more than two people who in collaboration undertake tasks to achieve certain goals. These individuals come together either via an organization or through some societal bodies. The groups can be categorized into formal and informal groups and have common ideas, principles, and goals. In a group, these individuals can be given a collective identity. The group sizes can be in dyads or triads. The members in a group react to any situation differently than they would do it on an individual basis. For example, various religious groups can be considered a plausible example.

Group Characteristics

The characteristics of a group are as follows:

- Assembly of a minumum of two people with no upper limit
- Group identity: Ascertains the identity of the group, which becomes the identity of member
- Collaboration and comminucation: Sharing ideas and opinion through a certain communication medium
- Common goal: The members work towards a common objective

Classification of Groups

A group can be classified into two types:

Classification of Groups	
Formal • Team groups • Work groups • Technology groups • Committees • Status groups • Command groups	**Informal groups** • Friendship groups • Interest groups • Reference groups • Membership groups • Cliques

Formal Groups

These groups evolve from the organization's structure and work towards a common goal. A committee formed by the organization can be considered a formal group; for example, research and development group, or placement group, and so on. These groups have to abide by certain rules and regulations of the organization specific to the task allocated. The contributions of the formal group towards an organization are as follows:

- They can complete a task by working together, which otherwise is impossible to be accomplished individually.
- Formal groups can solve problems effectively and can analyse the problem from different perspectives to generate solutions.

- Inventing new ideas and finding innovative ways and methods have remained the forte of formal groups.
- Implementing the new ideas or putting the devised plans into action.
- Imparting guidance and training to the new recruits.

Formal groups include permanent and temporary groups, where permanent groups can be any departmental unit and temporary groups are formed to perform a specific task such as event management group. Under formal group, the command group constitutes a boss and his immediate subordinates and the chain of command is defined by the power and accountability accorded to the individual as per his role. The leader plays an important role and sets the objective for the group. The military groups are the command group. Formal groups include the following:

- **Team group:** The members within the team group have interchangeable roles and work in a specific project in a team.
- **Task group:** Here, the group is formed and members are allocated a specific task, and nobody is in command of the group. Employees are not constrained to report to their immediate superior and often to seek approvals and bring the task to completion. Command relationships are crossed. These employees work together to complete the task and the groups may be temporary and open ended.
- **Technological group:** The team has to work as per the laid down goals, roles, and responsibilities.
- **Status group:** Members of a particular group/status enjoy special privileges, such as members of an elite club and so on.
- **Committees:** A group of people who are allocated a particular task or function. The committees are generally formed to address issues such as grievance redressal committee and investigate the issue and provide solutions for the same. Committees consist of members at the consultant, administrator, and other levels. Recommendations of possible solutions are sent to the designated persons for implementation.
- **Command group:** This group consists of a manager and his team of members. The members of the group work on a project, and progress is monitored by the manager from time to time. Membership of each employee in the group is directly correlated to his/her designation.

Informal Groups

An organization's informal groups are the groups that evolve to meet social or affiliation needs by bringing people together on the basis of shared interests or friendship. Thus, informal groups are alliances that are neither formally structured nor organizationally determined. These groups are natural formations in the work environment that appear in response to the need for social contact. Many factors explain why people are attracted to one another. One explanation is simply proximity; when people work near one another every day, they are likely to form friendship. That likelihood is even greater when people also share similar attitudes, personalities, or economic status. The most obvious example is the friends group.

- **Friendship groups:** Groups often develop because the members within the groups are compatible to one another with similar opinions, thought process, common interest, and wavelengths and are known as social alliances. We call these formations 'friendship groups'.
- **Interest groups:** Groups that work for a specific objective or for a common cause is said to be having common interests.
- **Reference groups:** Comparing and analysing and then taking decisions or forming opinions keeping in view a specific group, such groups are termed as reference groups. These groups are internal or external to the organization and for many one obvious

example is the reference group. Other groups include religious groups, or social groups, or group of colleagues. While referencing such groups, the comparison need not be done positively always. It can be against negative scenarios as well.

- **Membership groups:** They are members of formal and informal groups. Members of this group are allocated roles and responsibilities and they enjoy benefits from the groups achieving a particular goal.
- **Cliques:** These are groups which have people from different professions and are permanent in nature and informal in type. Here employees develop opinions about, exercise some form of control, and establish norms regarding productivity and relationship with superior, peer, and subordinate. The members of this group do not allow any external entity to intervene or join the existing group.

Formal Groups Versus Informal Groups

Parameters	*Formal Group*	*Informal Group*
Source/evolution	• It possesses a structure and works for the organization. • Members of the group report to the manager and are dependent on one another due to operational aspect.	• Voluntary formation • Formation of such groups happens in formal organization. • Groups are formed from informal interaction between people of different units and work locations where they share and exchange sentiments and views, which gives them social satisfaction not cared for by the organizations.
Authority	• Authority is allocated to a member as per organizational hierarchy. • Top management delegates authority to the individual.	Authority is allocated to the person based on his seniority, age, and capability.
Communication	Communication happens in a top-down or a bottom-up approach, but strictly through the designated authority.	There is no organizational hierarchy where communication is concerned, though people are connected with one another informally and information flows from every person to every other person.
Behavioural trends	Employees' behaviour is controlled by organizational rules and regulations to attain productivity and efficiency. In case of any violation of the rule, the group member is subjected to punitive actions.	For an informal group, it is the moral value of any member to prevent himself/herself from breaking the norms. If the member still continues breaking the norms, then he/she is forced to exit the group.
Size	They are groups of large size.	They are smaller and close-ended groups.
Stability	These groups are stable for longer time frames.	These groups are unstable due to high level of emotions and sentiments attached.

(Continued)

(Continued)

Parameters	***Formal Group***	***Informal Group***
Performance rewards	May be financial or non-financial.	Non-financial rewards in terms of status and prestige.
Group dissolution	As per group dissolution directive from the management.	Group dissolution might lead to disintegration into different groups.
Number of groups	Organization is divided into smaller units or spread across locations, and these units or locations can be treated as formal groups.	In case of informal groups they can be within or outside organizations and members can belong to various groups as well.

Why Do People Join Groups?

People join groups for the following reasons:

- People get a sense of 'security' when they are in a group. They develop confidence while in a group and can face obstacles comfortably. Basically, the novices in an organization turn towards the others for support and guidance, whereas employees working for long in the organization already belong to some formal group or the other.
- People join groups basically to have more interaction, work closely with one another, exchange information, and share knowledge.
- The identity of an individual is well established if he/she joins a group and a group helps the individual to understand his/her own potential.
- When people are in a group and if the group is considered important by outsiders, then people in that group enjoy the social status also.
- When people join groups for achieving certain objectives, they realize their self-importance and worth, which give them a very good feeling.
- It is said that there is power in numbers, so group thinking and group decision are more effective than being done on an individual basis.
- Goal achievement becomes easier while in a group, because certain tasks or activities may be easily performed while in a group.
- Groups can easily get adopted or associated with regulatory bodies, enjoy regular interaction, and fulfil social needs.

Models of Group Development

CASE STUDY: MODEL OF GROUP DEVELOPMENT

DeLaso caters to various IT and IT-enabled services, and a group has been formed from various locations of this organization to work on the process improvement project for supporting the huge clientele base. The project management group comprises of both senior people and junior members.

Stage 1: Project Group Formation or Forming Stage

- Group lead Jennifer with 16+ years of experience in managing process quality.
- Madeline with 10 years of experience as a project manager for quality assurance in banking domain.

- Timothy with seven years of experience and a strong application and database development background.
- Anderson with eight years of experience in working on various project management roles and serving as a business analyst also.
- Donna with two years of experience as a team member in the process improvement project.
- Agni with three years of experience as a team member in the process improvement project.
- Rohit with five years of experience as a technical architect.

Since the group members were new to one another, Jennifer decided that they should have an informal introductory meeting to put everybody at ease so that they could work comfortably on the virtual platform with one another.

The initial meeting consisted of introduction of members followed by a small agenda consisting of

- allocation of roles and responsibilities,
- creating awareness of the project they are going to handle,
- team-building exercises,
- team communication norms and procedural workflow,
- introduction on how to use the SharePoint site that will be used for this project to share ideas, brainstorm, store project documentation, and so on.

The group members met one another on a positive note, and roles and responsibilities were allocated with some opposition from their side, since everybody wanted a key role.

The architecture of the project and design of the database were handed over to Rohit, but there was opposition from Rohit since he thought that he required at least Donna with him to complete the assigned task.

Since Timothy was assigned the application development part, it was decided that he would help Rohit at intervals to validate the database design. Agni was put in Timothy's team.

It was then decided that Anderson would look after the analysis and reporting and Madeline the quality. Project execution guidelines were discussed so that every member was on the same platform.

Stage 2: Project Kick-off or Initiation (Storming)

Project service-level agreement was signed by Jennifer, and the schedule and milestones for the project were put up by Madeline after discussion with Anderson. Here again, there was opposition from Timothy for unrealistic delivery deadlines. Jennifer sorted out this issue by looking up at the company's archive of previous projects and finding out the most pessimistic schedule for that project milestone.

Stage 3: Project Execution or Norming Stage

With moderate modifications in the project plan consisting of development and quality plan, the team has now been working together and supporting one another with project major and minor issues. Only the project updates were not happening as per schedules on SharePoint, which Jennifer had to resolve so that the project group could be brought onto a common platform. Weekly meetings happened and project progress was up to date. Within the group, some acted as mentors while others were on the receiving side. Members expert in their own domains cross-trained one another as and when they found the opportunity.

Stage 4: Project Delivery or Performing Stage

The development and testing of the components of the project have reached their deadlines, and customer acceptance phase was to be initiated prior to implementation on-site. Regular remote demonstrations through TeamViewer were being given by Madeline and Jennifer and the delivery and deployment team of two members (Timothy and Donna) were getting ready to work at client's side for successful implementation.

Stage 5: Project Closure or Adjourning Stage

The project closure was initiated after a period of seven months by handing over the deliverables to the customer's project head and resources were released by Jennifer formally after the team met to discuss the strengths and weaknesses of the project, the learning they got from this project, the documenting the best

(Continued)

(Continued)

practices which they were not fully able to implement, and also the tingling issues of squabbles and differences they had in the past seven months. Since the project was a big success with 14% profit margin, the project sponsor and some executives from the top management hosted a dinner to celebrate the successful completion of the project.

Summary

The success of the project can be attributed to efficient project group formation, effective role and responsibility allocation, sound ownership of responsibilities allocated, excellent group collaboration and communication, and proper execution of team and project guidelines.

Five-stage Model

The five-stage model of group development was proposed by Bruce Tuckman in 1965 and the stages of group development are as follows:

- **Forming:** In the first stage, the members of the group try to acclimatize with one another and start learning new techniques and methods to work and interact with the teams. Since the team is newly formed, there is very little difference in opinion amongst the members. During the initial stage of group formation, the group needs to set up their goal, develop group rules and practices, allocate roles and responsibilities to the members within the group, and build rapport and belief. In the forming stage, the contribution of the leader is quite significant in group formation.
- **Storming:** In the second stage, disagreements and differences within the group members arise as they try to showcase the validity of their opinions and objectives. At this stage, identification of roles and proper allocation of responsibilities to the individual members within the group are allotted. The group gets a necessary structure and builds consensus by revisiting and refining the purpose. Conflict resolution is the forte of this stage.
- **Norming:** This stage is characterized by incorporating problem-solving strategies and concepts and resolution of conflict. At the norming stage, the team learns to make decisions and implement course of actions. Responsibilities taken up by the team members are more and leaders become less directive, team members feel empowered, and multiple leaders emerge.
- **Performing:** The teams are engaged in identifying their strengths and weaknesses while accomplishing the objectives. Teams become flexible in terms of taking up roles and responsibilities and the team is able to evaluate its effectiveness. Based on the age of the team, expectations are set high, for which the team uses smaller groups for decision-making and task completion. Also, the team is aware of the degree of alignment each member has towards the stated goal. In this stage, there is frequent sharing of roles.
- **Adjourning:** A well-integrated group disintegrates after the task is accomplished to reform task-oriented groups once again. These groups are given schedules and deadlines to perform the tasks. It is said that the stages attained by the group are not sequential, rather some stages can go on in parallel or sometimes a group goes back to its previous stage and ignores organizational context. For example, the cabin crew of Air India, who were strangers at the very first instance on a flight to Paris from Delhi, in a few minutes, had become a high-performing group. The organizational framework provides the rules, task descriptions, data, and resources required for the group to execute efficiently.

Punctuated Equilibrium Model

This type of group model is for transitory groups with deadlines, and the formation of the group does not follow the five-stage process. They go through transitions, that is, for some duration they are active and then they switch to inactive modes. Mostly during the mid of their tenure they experience rise in productivity levels. A good example of punctuated equilibrium can be found in our own evolution. Homo erectus originated in Africa and migrated to places as far as China and Java, but persisted largely unchanged for nearly 2 million years, before becoming extinct shortly after modern humans migrated out of Africa about 60,000 years ago. Homo sapiens, in turn, originated in Africa about 150,000 years ago. There are certainly some changes in modern humans, since some of us migrated out of Africa, but these changes are minor, and are certainly part of the 'stasis' part of punctuated equilibrium. Currently, with relation to group development models, there are two phases attributed to this punctuated model.

Phase 1

The group's direction is set first. Then they are in the inactive mode locked in fixed course of action until a transition takes place when they have reached the midway. The midpoint then becomes an indicator which urges the group to act fast and implement changes if need be in short bursts with replacement old arrangements, and implementation of new viewpoints. The course of action goes in for revision and transits to phase 2.

Phase 2

This period again starts with inactivity and the group executes plans created during the transition period. The group's last meeting is characterized by many activities. The model attributed to temporary groups with deadlines follows the sequence as prescribed below:

- First meeting assigns group's direction.
- Then there is a transition to phase 2.

Figure 10.1 Punctuated Equilibrium Model

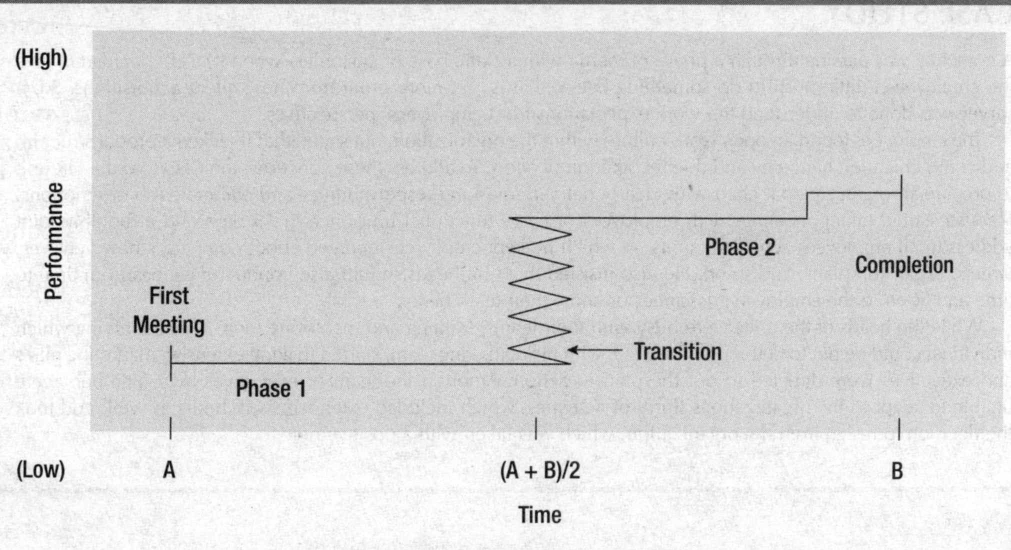

- Before onset of phase 2 half of the time is used up.
- A transition takes place which initiates a major changes in the second phase.
- Last meeting of the group is characterized by activities taking place at quick pace.

Summarizing, the punctuated equilibrium model is characterized by long periods of inactivity, with massive changes during transition with constraints of fixed schedules and deadlines (Figure 10.1).

Meaning of Group Dynamics

Group dynamics basically relates to a group's formation, structure, interaction between people of the group, the processes followed by the group, and so on. The processes followed by the group can be task-centric—where individuals concentrate on collating information, summarizing it, drawing up an analysis for the same—or can focus on societal aspects, including bringing harmony between different groups of society, or entertaining masses, or encouraging groups, and so on. When we deal with formal groups, the processes include allocation of roles, responsibilities, and authority to the people, building up synergy between members of the group, work on the level of effectiveness of the group, resolve various conflicting issues amongst the members, and so on. When the group is an informal group, then the group dynamics does not encompass any definite structure.

The *Oxford Dictionary* states group dynamics to be an interaction of complex intra- and interpersonal forces operating in a group which determines its character, development, and long-term survival. Stating it in another way, it is a field of study concerned with determination of laws underlying the group behaviour.

A formal definition of group dynamics is that it is a branch of social psychology which explores or unearths difficulties regarding formation of a group, the psychology of people who have joined the group, the change in conduct or mindset of the people after interacting with the group or while in a group, analyse the performance of the group, and the effect of authority and deeds on the group processes.

CASE STUDY

A company was passing through a phase of inertia with a static base of customers when its CEO decided to give the employees a little push to do something better, that is, get more profit from new client acquisitions. So, a survey was done to understand the work expectations from employees' perspectives.

The employees found an open work culture within the organization, but stated that it lacked a proper structure and communication hierarchy and due recognition of effort. To address these concerns, the CEO told the HR unit to prepare an organizational chart with clearly defined roles and responsibilities and elaborate job descriptions. He also started taking meetings with employees of every functional unit once in 15 days and a monthly joint address to all employees across the units, in which he kept employees updated about company's new ventures, targets, expansion plans, and so on. He also insisted that unit heads should also conduct meetings from time to time and listen to the employee grievances or know their team better.

While the heads of the units were busy with their teams, training and mentoring them and identifying which individual could be put to better use, the CEO, with his marketing team, started making extensive marketing plans and executives were directed to put the plan in action. Amongst the team of executives, two members were unable to adapt to the organizations flurry of activities, which included extended work hours as well, and took the decision to resign from the organization, which was taken with a positive note.

> The customer unit head thought it was at this juncture he would make proper arrangement to conduct customer service trainings for the entire helpdesk for consecutive seven days, which ramped up sales substantially and bottom-line profitability.
>
> Because of added consultation, training, and coaching, the CEO reported the following improvements during the board meeting:
>
> - Satisfaction level of the staff increased because of additional investments in terms of training and staff development programs.
> - Employees allocated tasks as per their skills and work styles.
> - Customer service training increased employees' ability to recommend appropriate products and services to the customers.
> - They have a process in place to add and keep new customers.
>
> Overall, there was a change in the business model, and business practices were up to date and profitability increased, thereby facilitating employees to enjoy monetary benefits and perks as well.

Group Behaviour

Group Size

- Small groups, varying from 2 to 10 people, are very effective, because every member of the group can actively participate and perform the tasks.
- Large groups do not allow every member to participate and their turn comes in sequence and a lot of time is wasted in structuring out processes. A member's satisfaction is of lesser importance in large groups because they do not get the opportunity to show their own skills very often and experience unity with others.
- Based on the size of the group, the behaviour of the group also changes in terms of frequency of conflicts, group norms, unity, and decision-making.

Group Rules

These are rules or code of conduct which are established by the group members and the members have to follow them religiously. Group norms are standard guidelines which enable the member to know how to behave once they are in a group. These norms can be formal and informal.

For example, colleagues in a group going out for lunch together make the norm that they would sponsor lunch on a rotational basis and that they would have such type of informal meetings over lunch once a month.

Rules or norms are of two types: one which is essential and the other which is applicable. The essential norms have to be followed by every member, while the applicable norms require to be confirmed by the members. Small deviation from the set of rules is acceptable, but significant deviation results in punishment. For example, if a company is perceived as a group of people serving, then adherence to certain norms such as non-disclosure agreements signed by the employees of that company, if violated, is an offence which is punishable by law.

The rule formulated by the group possesses certain characteristics:

- Rules of a group reflect the group's personality, behaviour, and purpose.
- Rules impose behavioural constraints on every member of the group.
- Rules are applicable to every member within the group.

Group Role

The role of an employee within the organization entails the responsibility the candidate is entrusted with along with the position title. Similarly, group roles are entrusted to the formal groups within the organization. These roles are prescribed by the organization in an attempt to distribute workload amongst the various members of the group. In informal groups, the workload is not uniformly distributed.

Types of Group Roles

In practice, three important group roles can be described:

- **Work roles:** These roles are assigned to accomplish a specific task. For the said tasks, strategies are devised, tasks are assigned, and progress is evaluated. For example, during the semester staff members are assigned the role of academic coordinator whose responsibility is to monitor the conduction of lectures in a smooth manner.
- **Maintenance role:** These roles help maintain participation and obligation to group by the group members on an emotional level. Examples of these roles may be encouraging other fellow members to participate, fawning and recompensing other members for their excellent contribution, and the like.
- **Blocking roles:** These roles are harmful for the group and tend to disrupt the group. The traits of a group assigned such roles are being dominant, aggressive, disruptive, and distracting other group members.

Role Identity

The milestones of a role are attitudes and actual behaviours, which gives its identity to a particular role, the role identity. Clearly defined roles form a clearly visible role identity. On the other hand, the opposite makes it clouded.

Fast and unstable change in roles is human nature, and it occurs when there is a need of change detected in surroundings. For example, if an employee is currently being promoted to a managerial position, his attitude will be changed from pro-worker to pro-manager may be in a month.

Role Ambiguity

Role ambiguity can be defined as a difference between the defined role and perceived role. This can be the confusing results, obtained from assigning job responsibilities. This happens when sometimes undefined jobs assigned to employees and situations, other than job descriptions, arise and employees are asked to do something, which leads them to a confusing state. Role ambiguity is a very harmful parasite for manpower in a company. Consequences can be listed as frustration, job dissatisfaction, stress, and tension. However, role ambiguity, if extreme, can result in absenteeism and affect turnover.

Role Conflict

Human life is filled with different types of roles at a time. While serving as an employee in an office, the same person plays the role of a father or a husband and many more when he is at home or within the society he lives in. The natural roles are compatible with each other, whereas others may create a conflict. When a person faces a situation where playing one role becomes an obstacle for another, because of the diversity of its nature, it creates conflict, which is called 'role conflict'. In some cases, two or more roles turn out to be mutually contradicting or conflicting. For example, a role conflict can occur where an individual has to be a father and coach to his child at the same time.

Role Expectations

Role expectations are predefined behaviour guidelines, of a particular role, in the eye of surroundings. How one should behave in a given situation at that point of time is determined internally, otherwise, by the defined role in the surroundings, he is behaving or acting in. For example, a teacher plays the role of a humble guide, being sincere and always seen as a guardian, whereas a manager will be expected to be strategic, controller, and inspirational for his employees.

Group Cohesiveness

Group cohesiveness refers to the extent to which members interact with one another in the group, are influenced by the thought process of the members within the group, the extent to which they have faith and belief in the group, and are enthused to remain part of the group and work towards a specified set of objectives.

Group cohesiveness is affected by the following factors:

- The extent of interaction amongst the members of the group.
- External threats, which enhance unity amongst the members.
- Level of intrusion, which means a person who is interested to join the group faces resistance from the group if the group is highly cohesive.
- Leadership traits in a person, which can increase or decrease the group cohesiveness.
- The goals and objectives laid down by the group and the degree to which members are aligned to the goals and objectives of the group.
- The attitude and value of the group, that is, with the set of right attitude and values, the cohesiveness within the group increases.
- Size of the group: The bigger the group, the lesser is the interaction amongst the people, the less is degree of alignment of people towards goals and objectives, and there is increase in workload distribution, which imposes restriction on within the group communication.

A typical example of group cohesiveness: Meera joined a gym to stay fit. When Meera and other group members started sharing their fitness schemes and discussed their diet plan together with instructor, Meera started feeling close to the other members and was happy with her decision to join the group.

Advantages and Disadvantages of Group Cohesiveness

A highly cohesive group has the following advantages: more of teamwork and less difference in opinion, which result in less conflict and improved dialogue with team members. Generally, a cohesive group is more productive because every member gives his/her acceptance to work for the common cause with fewer obstacles in matters related to work. As a result, the productivity of a cohesive group is high compared with that of non-cohesive groups.

The above benefits accrue to by the members of a cohesive group, but whether a cohesive group is beneficial from organizational perspectives depends on performance norms. If performance norms are slightly towards the positive side, then a highly cohesive group is not very beneficial and it is harmful for the organization to nurture such groups. Also, group cohesiveness can promote the aspect of groupthink in not such a productive manner, because many a time the ultimate goal is set aside due to the fear of members' separation from the group.

In sum, we can state that high performance and high cohesiveness result in high productivity, whereas high performance and low cohesiveness result in moderate productivity. Low performance and high cohesiveness give low productivity and when both factors are low, the productivity is low.

For a cohesive group to be working towards organizational goals, the leader or the group manager should do the following:

- Emphasize on accomplishment of their tasks.
- Increase the commitment level of the members within the group by encouraging increased. Participate to achieve organizational goals.
- Increase the competitive spirit within the members of the group for sooner and better task accomplishment.
- The manager should dissolve the group once the tasks are accomplished and send the members to other departments or projects and again start with a new group for diversifying experience and control.

Group Decision-making Process

It is a circumstance featuring individuals to jointly form an alternative from the set of options. The alternative chosen is not the responsibility of a single individual but a group of individuals who contribute directly or indirectly to it. Decisions made by groups vary from those made by individuals. Group decisions are more extreme than individual decisions as the decisions have the support of a majority of the group. Group decision-making process is similar to a normal decision-making process comprising of the following steps:

- Problem identification
- Information retrieval
- Evaluation of alternatives
- Selection of an alternative
- Implementation of the alternative
- Result concluded from implementation

For example, the production team at ABC Steel received a huge assignment for hot rolled steel bar. They need to come up with this new version for launch into the market in three months. The production team is working on its design and discussing it with all the members of the group, which is group decision-making.

Benefits of Group Decision-making Process

- With a group formulating the decision chances that the decisions are stoic and bold and has a high probability of considering criteria, effect, and alternative. Overall integrity of the group also remains intact.
- Group decision-making also promotes tapping into a large information base where people providing such information are experts in their own domain.
- Group decision-making can enhance the complexity of the entire decision-making process because there are too many alternatives and ideas made available by the people.
- If a decision is taken by a group there is greater acceptance by the relevant authority, and implementation of such decisions is much faster.
- People hold themselves more responsible and accountable in their own arena and of the decisions they have taken.

- The participants and the implementers of decision-making are the same, so the commitment to see the implementation to success is also high.

Disadvantages of Group Decision-making

- With too many opinions and absence of a consensus, group decision-making might lose its effectiveness.
- In group decision-making, time required to take the decision is more, which can indirectly affect the productivity of the group.
- Incorrect groupthink might make group decision-making less effective.
- Responsibility taken up by the members of a group may not be equally distributed within the group.
- Conflicts may arise within the group refraining it from being productive.
- Decisions can have high degree of polarization leading to problems.
- Group decision-making enhances cost in terms of money, time, and resources.
- Competition can arise within the group members.
- Groups without a leader lack focus and the decisions taken by that group are vague.

Group Decision-making Strategies

Group decisions can be autocratic, democratic, or can be made by consensus. Three forms of decision-making are elaborated as follows:

- **Autocratic** form of group decision-making implies that decisions are taken solely by the leader of the group and the success or failure of implementing that decision lies with the leader himself. Decision-making is fast and less time consuming. When autocratic form of decision-making is used, it is imperative that the leader has the entire information base and is very clear about which decision works the best. For example, Leona Helmsley of Helmsley Hotel Chain used autocratic style, which made the hotel chain popular, but employees were bogged down due to her demand for perfection.
- **Democratic style** of group decision-making is a strategy in which a leader allows his team to vote for a decision. The alternative which gets the majority of the votes is taken as the final alternative. Decision-making is faster in this case, though responsibility is not accorded to any individual for the outcome of implementing the alternative for that decision. In this approach, the leader may not have the critical information to him. For example, Steve Jobs followed a democratic style of leadership wherein he actively involved the top management group to make key decisions with regard to product designs and manufacturing.
- In **consensus style** of group decision-making strategy, a decision is reached only after a group consensus. Though this is time consuming, it is highly effective, since the decision is a blend of many ideas and information. Here, consultation might be one to one or with the group itself.

Whether it is an individual's decision or a group's decision, the goal should be kept foremost in the mind, and discussion should be pushed to higher levels of generality as generalization of ideas unites people of the group. Also, resolution of an issue should be done efficiently and the group should collect ideas and establish decision-making criteria. If there is no consensus within the group, then the approach is to give thinking time to individual candidate and pen down their issues and concerns to be dealt separately in a fresh discussion later. In some cases, the strategy is to organize small groups, bring them to a consensus, and finally make the decision with the largest group. Sometimes, it is the strategy of the leader to create a contradictory statement to refocus the discussion and identify real concerns or choose another facilitator for decision-making. For example, in small business partnerships, if the decision of one partner to induct people from his previous organization where he worked is not accepted by another partner, a consensus process could help both arrive at a decision, and feel supported, respected, and trusted by each other.

Impact of Group on Individual's Behaviour

Individual behaviour is influenced by the group where he belongs to. For example, religious fanatic groups actually mould an individual's mind from a negative aspect. On the other hand, an individual belonging to the groups that provide services to people impacts him in a positive way. The key phenomena of group influence are as follows:

- **Groupthink:** It is basically a group decision-making process where smooth and quick decision-making is the key without focusing on more result-oriented options. In groupthink, individuals are forced to think like a group rather than voicing their own ideas. Sometimes the performance of the group deteriorates due to groupthink behaviour. The factors responsible for groupthink behaviour are as follows:
  - Isolation from external environment
  - Extreme loyalty to the group, forbidding individuals to raise controversies
  - Loss of innovation or creativity
  - Achievement of unrealistic levels of certainty
  - Leader has bias
- **Groupshift:** This is a phenomenon where a person loses his sanctity and identity and acts in accordance with the group. In this, all the control and constraints are lost, and a racist person with group support will act in a more racist manner or a liberal individual will be more liberal without judging the consequences. People in groups evaluate risks differently than when they are alone and hence tend to take more risks.
- **Deindividuation:** It is the loss of a person's individuality and tends to undertake activities dictated by the mob or the group. Some experts are of the opinion that deindividuation can have positive or negative consequences and chances are high that the individual maintains anonymity while carrying out activities from negative aspects. A larger group has a greater percentage of members showing the traits of deindividuation. Hogg and Vaughan (2008) define deindividuation as 'a process whereby people lose their sense of socialized identity and engage in unsocialised, often antisocial behaviors'. The Halloween experiment was one of the most interesting experiments which brought out the concept of deindividuation very strongly amongst group members, where the children took to extra Halloween candy in response to situations such as group activity and anonymity.

Impact of External Factors on Group Behaviour

Various external factors impacting group behaviour within the organization are summarized as follows (Figure 10.2):

- Organizations' strategy will actually evaluate the authority of task groups, which will enable the management to decide the allocation of resources to the task group to perform the desired tasks.
- Organizations use proper reporting structures, which shows who reports to whom and who all are empowered with the authority of decision-making.

Figure 10.2 External Factors Impacting Organizational Behaviour

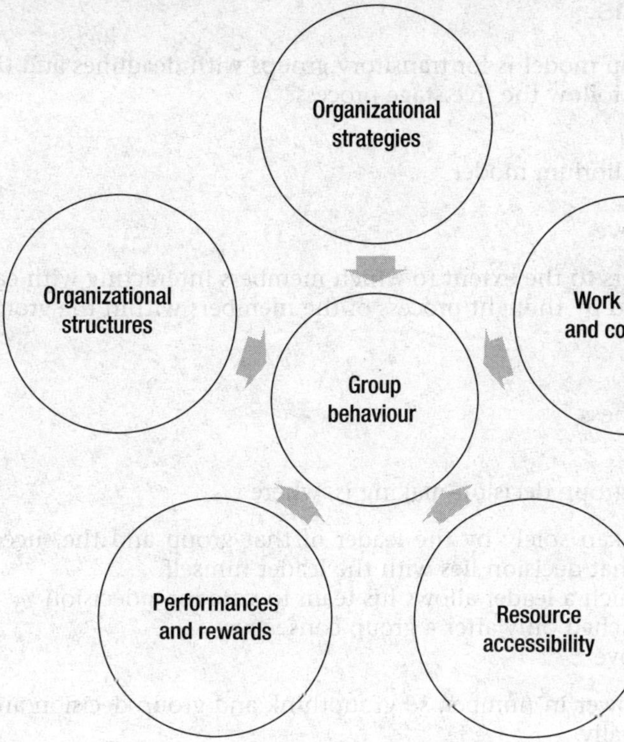

- Organizations formulate rules and regulations, policies and procedures, job roles, responsibilities, and descriptions to standardize employee behaviour.
- Availability and allocation of schedules, deadlines, material resources, and machineries also dictate the behaviour of the group within the organization.
- The behaviour of the group is also attributed to rewards and benefits accorded by the organization to employees.
- Organizational culture defines standards of acceptable and unacceptable behaviour for employees, who have to align themselves to the organization's culture.
- Physical infrastructure in the organization provides barriers and opportunities for task group interaction.

Summary

This chapter takes you through the concept of group, its characteristics, types, and its contribution to organizational growth, the fundamentals of groupthink, and its impact on individual behaviour. The chapter also elaborates on various models of group development and their implementation in organizations and the perceived outcome, group behaviour, cohesiveness within a group and its impact, and advantages and weaknesses of group decision-making. The chapter summarizes every aspect of group and group dynamics from the organizational context.

Exercise

Objective Questions

1. Which type of group model is for transitory groups with deadlines and the formation of the group does not follow the five-stage process?
   - Five-stage model
   - Punctuated equilibrium model
   - Star model
   - None of the above
2. Which of these refers to the extent to which members interacting with each other in the group are influenced by thought process of the members within the group?
   - Role ambiguity
   - Role conflict
   - Group cohesiveness
   - Role identity
3. Autocratic form of group decision-making is, where
   - Decisions are taken solely by the leader of that group and the success or failure of implementing that decision lies with the leader himself
   - A strategy in which a leader allows his team to vote for a decision
   - A decision is reached only after a group consensus
   - None of the above
4. It is said there is power in number, so groupthink and group decision are more effective than done individually.
   - True
   - False
5. Group dynamics does not relate to a group's formation, structure, interaction between people of the group, the processes followed by the group, and so on.
   - True
   - False
6. Which of these roles helps maintain participation and obligation to group by the group members on an emotional level?
   - Work roles
   - Maintenance role
   - Blocking role
   - None of the above
7. Leadership traits in a person can increase or decrease the group cohesiveness.
   - True
   - False
8. Which of these is the loss of a person's individuality and tends to undertake activities as dictated by the mob or the group?
   - Group size
   - Groupthink

- Groupshift
- Deindividuation

9. Which is the correct order for the five-stage model?
   - Forming, storming, norming, performing, adjourning
   - Forming, norming, storming, performing, adjourning
   - Forming, performing, storming, norming, adjourning
   - None of the above
10. When a person faces a situation where playing one role becomes obstacle for another, because of the diversity in its nature, is called
    - Group size
    - Groupthink
    - Role conflict
    - Role expectations

CASE STUDY

Mr Anderson is the CEO of a consultancy firm in Aguascalientes, Mexico. The annual turnover of the company for the last year was ₹1.32 crore. Anderson is dedicated and finds ideas to get more projects for the company.

The company was expanding to a new location in Denmark. He had a handful of young and talented professionals. As the company was growing, he believed that more workforce is required and it should get more business. A meeting was scheduled with all senior leadership members, where all the alternatives for how the working of the new location would carry were discussed. It was decided that as the team in Aguascalientes would get more projects, a new team should be formed for Denmark. All the pros and cons of these alternatives were discussed and a separate team was formed that would work dedicatedly on getting business. A plan was put into action and the team started understanding the environmental factors, possibility of markets from where they could get business. At the time of the financial review, Denmark location was found to have made considerable profits in its first working year.

Questions

1. If you were in the CEO's position, would you take a similar step of group decision-making or would you be using a different method?
2. What could be the pros and cons of group decision-making in the above case?
3. Can you think of other alternatives than those mentioned above?

Critical Thinking Questions

1. Can group decisions result into low efficiency?
2. Does group decision-making influence individual behaviour?
3. When a group decision is taken, do you think group roles are being followed completely?
4. How does goal achievement become easier when activities are performed in a group rather than by an individual?

Chapter at a Glance

Introduction

A group consists of any number of people who:

- *interact with each other*
- *are psychologically aware of one another*
- *perceive themselves to be a group*

—Schein

Group dynamics is referred as the field of inquiry dedicated to advancing knowledge about the nature of groups.

Cartwright and Zander

Group Characteristics

- Assembly of minimum two people with no upper limit
- Group identity: Ascertains the identity of the group becomes the identity of member
- Collaboration and communication: Sharing ideas and opinions through a certain communication medium
- Common goal: Members work towards a common objective

Classification of Groups

Formal Group

- Team group
- Work group
- Technology group
- Committees
- Authority group
- Segment

Informal Group

- Group of friends
- Group having common interest
- Groups that are referenced (family and colleagues) positively or negatively
- Institutional members
- Cliques

Why Do People Join Groups?

- Sense of security
- More interaction, work closely with one another, exchange information, and share knowledge
- Helps the individual to understand his/her own potential

- Social status
- Self-importance and worth
- Groupthink and group decision
- Goal achievement
- Associated with regulatory bodies

Models of Group Development

Five-stage Model

- Forming
- Storming
- Norming
- Performing
- Adjourning

Punctuated Equilibrium Model

- Phase 1: A structure of behavioural patterns and assumptions emerges.
- Phase 2: The group executes plans created during the transition period.

Group Role

A role means a set of expected behaviour pattern attached to a position or post in a social unit.

Types of Group Roles

- Work roles
- Maintenance role
- Blocking roles

Role Identity

People shift roles rapidly when there is a change in situation, and demand for change is also recognized. For example, when union leaders were promoted to foremen positions, their attitude changed from pro-workers to pro-management within a month of their promotion.

Role Ambiguity

Role ambiguity refers to the discrepancy between the defined role and perceived role.

Role Conflict

A person is confronted by divergent role expectations; this is called 'role conflict'. For example, one performs the role of the servant; but when the same person is off the job, he performs roles like a husband, a father, a brother, and so on.

(Continued)

(Continued)

Role Expectations

Role expectations are what other people believe one should behave in a given situation.

Group Cohesiveness

Group cohesiveness refers to the extent to which members interact with one another in the group, are influenced by the thought process of the members within the group, the extent to which they have faith and belief in the group, are enthused to remain the part of the group and work towards a specified set of objectives.

Advantages of Group Cohesiveness

- More of teamwork
- Less difference of opinion
- Improved dialogue with team members
- Productivity of a cohesive group is high compared with non-cohesive groups

Disadvantages of Group Cohesiveness

The ultimate goal is set aside because of the fear of separation of members from the group.

Group Decision-making Process

- Problem identification
- Information retrieval
- Evaluation of alternatives
- Selection of an alternative
- Implementation of the alternative
- Result concluded from implementation

Benefits of Group Decision-making Process

- Decisions are stoic and bold and have a high probability considering criteria, effect, and alternative.
- Promotes tapping into a large information base.
- Enhances complexity of the entire decision process.
- Greater acceptance by the relevant authority and implementation of such decisions is much faster.
- People are more responsible and accountable.

Disadvantages of Group Decision-making

- Decision-making might lose its effectiveness.
- More time is required to take the decision.
- Incorrect group makes decision less effective.

- Responsibility of members of a group may not be equally distributed.
- Conflicts may arise within the group.
- Decisions can have a high degree of polarization leading to problems.
- Group decision-making enhances cost in terms of money time and resources.
- Competitions can arise within the group members.
- Groups without a leader lack focus and the decisions taken by that group are vague.

Group Decision-making Strategies

- Autocratic style: decisions are taken solely by the leader of that group.
- Democratic style: leader allows his team to vote for a decision.
- Consensus style: decision is reached only after a group consensus.

Impact of Group on Individual's Behaviour

- **Groupthink:** It is a group decision-making process where smooth and quick decision-making is the key without focusing on more result-oriented options.
- **Groupshift:** It is a phenomenon when a person loses his sanctity and identity and acts in accordance with the group.
- **Deindividuation:** Here, a person loses his individuality and tends to undertake activities dictated by the mob or the group.

CHAPTER 11

Team and Teamwork

Learning Objectives

- Getting a detailed view on teams, their characteristics, nature, and benefits from the perspective of the organization and individuals.
- Entrusting the reader with the knowledge of the processes of teamwork, and how the team evolves and operates within its framework and boundaries.
- Understanding the evaluation factors which rate a team on its performance and the essence of very productive teamwork, which has brought many organizations to limelight.
- Getting a realistic conclusion on the significance and importance of teamwork and healthy team dynamics through an excerpt from Jack Welch, the CEO of GE Electric, who talks about his high-performance teams, the reader

An Opening Vignette

Many a time, a colony of ants has been seen to work together as a team for finding food and shelter. These ants operate with a high degree of collaboration and cooperation and strategic directions from the leader. This is story of a group of ants carrying an insect much bigger in size on their backs, to their shelter, for the entire group to feed upon. This large insect was carried by the ants by forming a parallel chain beneath it. The way they carried the insect is a portrayal of effective teamwork with strong focus on achieving the goal. The situation they were operating in was not conducive since the big insect was quite heavy, but with every member's contribution and effort in carrying the insect, the complex task became quite achievable with effective load distribution.

Every team should have a leader to guide, mentor, and show the team the right direction. Among the ant species, a leader performs the above tasks. Also, the famous story of the grasshopper and ants talks about how the ants had worked to silage and stored food during the summer and autumn and had fed on the stored food in winter, and also helped a lazy grasshopper to eat their food as well. The story also gives an evidence of how good planners the ants can be, perceiving the risks of the winters, how they could strategize on storage and optimum consumption of food throughout the winter days. Correlating the above situation to the management concept provides us evidence of planning, envisaging risk of contingencies, devising, and executing plans with focus on optimum utilization of resources with high degree of collaboration from the team.

Introduction

With the changing business scenario and increasing project complexities, the concept of teams is gaining more and more importance. Organizations these days assume and believe that teams can bring in more innovative and creative ideas and help achieve the organizational goals more effectively and efficiently. The stages of team development include forming, storming, norming, and performing. Some tasks always require people participation, where they discuss and work together a common goal. The individuals who form a team are aligned to common goals and interests. The members within the teams are entrusted to contribute to the maximum and do the task in stipulated time slot, and the member owns up the responsibility to perform the task. Whenever there is a requirement by any of the team members, it is the norm of the other members to provide him the required help. Whenever a team is involved, the performance of the team directly correlates to the sum of individuals.

The team characteristics suggest that every member is not equally capable and does not show the same performance. Also, every member is not compatible with every other member, and within groups there might be subgroups as well. If a team member is not productive or fails to perform, then his/her performance directly impacts the team's performance. Team management events consist of putting the team on the same platform and work towards a common objective.

Nature of Teams

Teams consist of a small number of people with complementary skills working towards a common goal or objective and hold a mutual accountability.

It is now clear that a team consists of a small number of people. The communication among the team members and the impact they have on each other plays a vital role in the success of the team. Thus, it is essential that the team does not have a large number of members as it would make the process of communication and influencing more difficult.

Teams include individuals having different skills. All the members may not have common skills, but when put together, these diverse skills would help accomplish the desired output. However, along with the growth, development, and maturity of the team the members of the team would acquire additional required skills.

All the members of a teamwork towards the achievement of a common goal and hold mutual accountability unlike in groups.

Team Characteristics

Various organizations across the industry verticals are increasingly forming team-based structures and creating a strong linkage between organizational and team goals. Around 80% of the companies who are listed under Fortune 500 category carry out operations through the team-based structures, hence it is very much necessary to understand the characteristics of the teams so that the protocol of operating in collaboration with the other members is followed by every member who is a part of that team.

Various facets play a role in creating effective teams. Although the list of what constitutes towards making an effective team is too long, a few are as discussed below.

Clarity of Goals and Objectives

Teams generally have goals and objectives, which are essential as these will help the team members to have better clarity about the vision and purpose of the team. It is necessary that team members are aware about the direction of team. Team members who were involved in establishing the goals will also work towards accomplishment.

Communication

Communication is a critical element in any situation. Communication among the team members plays a crucial role in the success of the team. No problem can be solved unless it is discussed considering different viewpoints.

Clarity of Roles

One of the important characteristics of team is clarity of roles. Each member has a clear understanding of the role to be played and tasks to be carried out by him/her.

Suitable and Situational Leadership

Every team has a formal leader. However, the unique characteristic of the team is that the role of a leader can be performed by any other team member if the circumstance so demands. In such cases, the formal leader monitors appropriate behaviour and facilitates in creating positive norms.

Participation

Opinions are valued and taken from the members whenever required. The leader specifies what kind of participation he expects from the members. Leaders help to create a climate of participation.

Open Discussion and Conflict (Functional Conflict)

In a team, members express their viewpoints and opinions on the ways of operation as well as the various functions of the team without any hesitation. There may be some hidden agendas as well. During this process, there can be disagreement among the team members. Such disagreements are taken positively by the team; thus, the conflict turns out to be a functional conflict.

Consensus Decisions

For important decisions, the goal is substantial but it is not necessarily a unanimous agreement through open discussion of everyone's ideas, avoidance of formal voting, or easy compromises.

Valued Diversity

Each member of the team may have different skills or talent. Also, they might have diverse ideas, thought processes, and problem-solving skills. These diversities are valued in a team.

Continuous Self-assessment

While performing assigned tasks, the team stops in between to assess how well it is performing. Also, the team tries to identify roadblocks that interfere with its effectiveness.

Teams Versus Groups

Generally, terms groups and teams are used as synonyms. However, it is not so; there is a difference between groups and teams. The points of difference are as shown in Table 11.1.

Table 11.1 Teams Versus Groups

No.	Teams	Groups
1	Performance depends on individual as well as collective efforts.	Performance depends on individual members.
2	There exists both individual and mutual accountability.	Members of a group are accountable only for their individual work.
3	There is a focus on team goals.	Each member focuses on his own goals.
4	Teams are self-managed.	Goals are set by the management.
5	Members of the team possess complimentary skills.	Members of the groups possess diverse skills.
6	Team members are aware of the contributions made by other members of the team and they all contribute to achieve the result.	Group members are unaware of the accountability possessed by other members.
7	Team members bond with each other and resolve the conflict mutually and bring the manager into picture only when it is needed.	During conflict, members are quick to bring out what other members default at and allocate responsibility to the manager to solve the disputes.
8	Communication is open and benefits from different perspectives are appreciated in finding solutions to the problems.	Communication is closed in case of groups and level of trust is not so high as with that in the teams.
9	Effective management of teams encompasses idea generation and implementation and control by the manager as well as members of the group to achieve the objective.	In groups, management is done only by the manager and others are instructed to perform a task, reducing them to a position where they can only take instructions.
10	Members of the team are trained in professional and technical aspects and team dynamics.	Developing the group members' skills required to execute the task.
11	Good performance is celebrated by all the members of the team.	Feedback is given when a member has committed a mistake and success is claimed by the manager only.
12	Teamwork is often a vital part of the business and a collaborative effort has always helped in the growth of the company.	For groups, it is only a short-term goal achievement.

Teamwork

Teamwork is the process of working in collaboration with a group of people in order to achieve a business goal. Here, people cooperate using their individual skills and provide combined effort, despite any personal grievances against any person or authority. From small- and medium-scale enterprises to large multinationals, teamwork is a vital aspect of contributing to organizational goals. From creating or exploring new opportunities, idea for a product or service, to delivering to customers, employees work together to accomplish day-to-day tasks. Teamwork helps employees build trust amongst them to reduce burnout and help the company in attainment of goals.

Benefits of Teamwork

Working in teams provides several benefits, some of which are mentioned below:

- **Effective utilization of resources:** Duplication of work is avoided when people work in teams. This leads to effective utilization of organizational resources.
- **Better decisions:** When individuals work in teams, each of them gets an opportunity to share their ideas. Thus, before arriving at a decision on any of the issues, most feasible and effective ideas can be selected from an array of ideas.
- **Motivation:** The motivation level is higher when people work together as a team to accomplish any goal, rather than when they try to achieve it individually.
- **Self-development and growth:** A team consists of people with different skills. Thus, while working as a team, members get an opportunity to upgrade and acquire skills that would lead to self-development and growth.
- **Organizational enhancement:** Teams help the management through organizational enhancement that comprises of flexibility, increased innovation, and creativity.

Benefits of Teamwork from Organizational Perspective

- Higher productivity from a collaborative approach results in quality output.
- Consensus-based decision-making always leads to better decisions.
- A consortium of ideas is generated when a team is there.
- Different perspectives expose team members to the broader concepts.
- Group discussions help team members to clarify issues and provide optimal solutions.
- In a team, problem solving becomes an easy task.
- Team members focus on the team's goals for longer periods of time.
- Seamless knowledge transfer between members and collaboration of skills result in formulation of innovative concepts which benefit the business.
- Team effort enables projects to get completed within deadlines and schedules.
- Implementation of a project plan, which includes allocation of team members to the project, allocating tasks to the team members, checking their project progress, and milestones, definitely helps the manager to execute the project in a structured manner and makes it more achievable.

Benefits of Teamwork from the Perspective of an Individual

- Teamwork provides a rich work experience because of the exposure to diverse skill sets of others and is a source of motivation for every individual.
- Team members help in providing mutual support, which enables an individual to attain goals, and the support can be in the form of work assistance or encouragement.

- A greater sense of accomplishment is perceived when there is an outcome from the collective effort expended for a task which was unachievable for a single individual.
- Greater and broader set of business benefits can be achieved through effective teamwork.

Disadvantages of Teamwork

- Some people do not enjoy working in a team.
- Equal level of job satisfaction might not be there for members working in a team.
- There might arise conflicts amongst the team members.
- Decision-making though is a team effort may be time consuming because every individual's approval is sought.
- Groupthink can dwarf a team's creativity and decision-making capability.
- Every member's performance is the team's performance, which suggests that if somebody is underperforming, then he gets a free ride to success if the team is successful.
- In case of personnel replacement or transfer from a team, to get another member into the team becomes awkward if the team has stayed in the project for a long time.

Processes of Teamwork

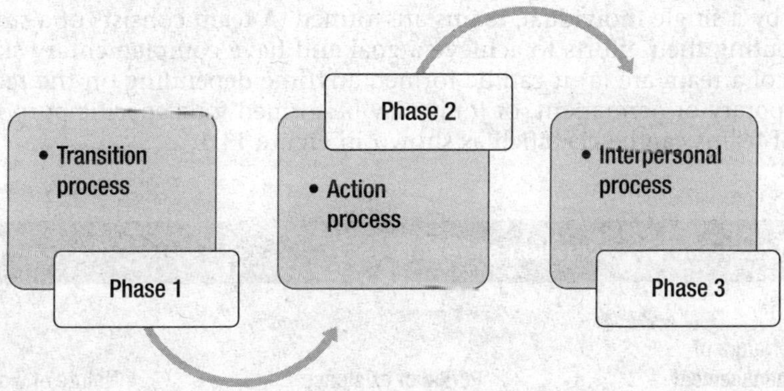

Transition Process

The transition process deals with formation of the team, mission, vision goals, and strategies the team is devising.

- Mission of a team is basically laying down the objectives of the team. If the team is an organization of people, then it will be the objective of the organization.
- Goal specification is the identification of tasks and prioritizing them to achieve the objective.
- Strategy formulation is developing a sequence of deeds to attain the goals and accomplish the mission.

Action Process

Action process is the phase when the team performs its task or, in other words, executes the project it is allocated. The action process includes the following:

- Tracking project progress toward completion of tasks and activities.
- Tracking and monitoring the use of technological, human, and informing resources.

- Coordinating the workflow and information flow between the various tasks and activities.
- Mentoring of the team members by providing extensive coaching and feedback on their performance.

Interpersonal Process

Interpersonal processes include activities that occur during the transition and action processes. These include the following:

- Issue or conflict management to manage difference of opinions and avoid disagreements amongst the members.
- Motivate the team to work towards the common goal or achieve the organizational objective.
- Control of emotions by the various members of the team while working together.

Types of Teams

In an organization, when the tasks to be performed are complicated and cannot be accomplished by a single individual, teams are formed. A team consists of a small number of people contributing their efforts to achieve a goal and have complementary skills. The main characteristics of a team are (a) it can be formed anytime depending on the requirement, (b) it may be temporary or permanent, or (c) it may be formed for a specific purpose.

The types of teams can be classified as shown in Figure 11.1.

Figure 11.1 Types and Classification of Teams

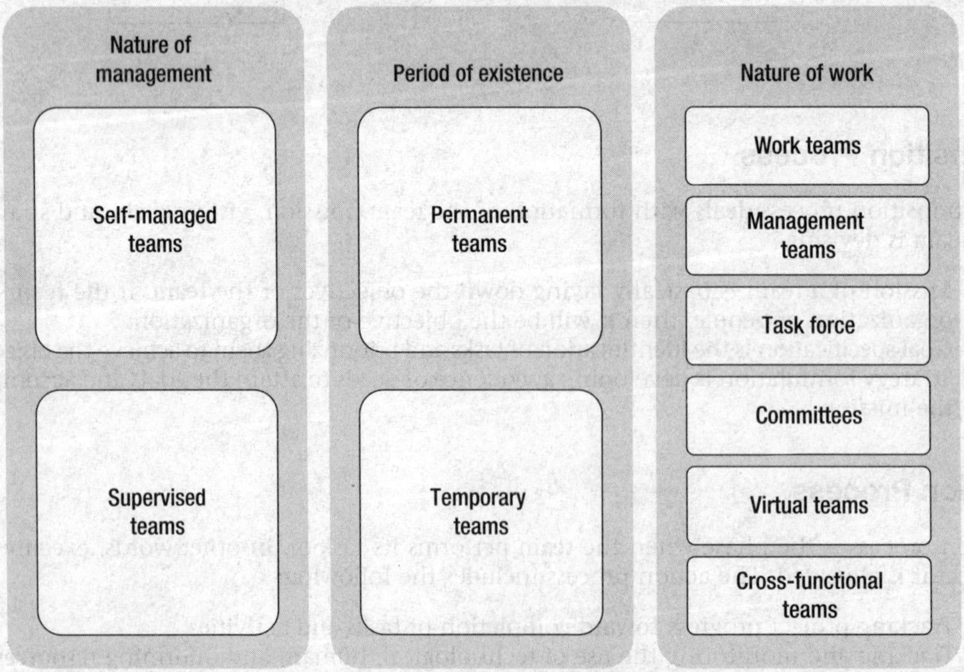

Classification of Teams Based on Nature of Management

Self-managed Teams

These teams include a group of employees assigned to accomplish a particular task for the organization. A self-managed teamworks towards the achievement of self-defined goals. Although these teams are independent, the members are interdependent. These teams are self-regulated and self-operated. These teams do not have any supervisor or leader. Every member is responsible for his performance.

Self-managed or self-directed team organizations have given improved team performance over the years. A self-managed team is the one where the responsibility of operating lies on the team itself to achieve the target. The members of self-managed teams have considerable amount of autonomy and respect, the boundaries in which they are scheduled to operate as are decided by the management. Decisions taken by the self-managed team are the independent decisions with very less interference from the management. An organization in itself is a self-managed team.

Supervised Teams

Unlike the self-managed teams, supervised teams are managed by a leader or a supervisor. The leader/supervisor sets the goals to be achieved and monitors the performance of all the team members. The leader is responsible for the overall performance of the team. Such teams enjoy less autonomy, and boundaries are not defined by the leader or the management as the objectives are attained under the supervision of the leader or the management.

Classification of Teams Based on the Period of Existence

Permanent Teams

Functional departments like HR, finance, operations in an organization are best examples of permanent teams. These teams are not dissolved when one purpose is over. For example, Ronita and Janet were a part of a branding team with a leading company, and their task was to promote their brand and increase the brand value along with coming up with innovative marketing strategies for increased sales and turnover. They were extremely focused, ambitious, and managed to achieve their yearly targets, along with keeping their team spirit high and motivating the members at frequent intervals. In addition, they mentored the members well, and for the last 10 years, the team was not dissolved at any point of time. Such teams are called permanent teams. Generally, the production, marketing and sales, HR, audit and accounting, and purchase teams are never dissolved.

Temporary Teams

Temporary teams are generally formed to assist the permanent teams. These teams exist for a short period of time and are dissolved once the task is over. Such teams are usually formed for a shorter duration either to assist the permanent team or work when the members of the permanent team are busy in some other projects. When organizations have excess work, they generally form temporary teams, which work in association with the members of the permanent team for the accomplishment of the task within the stipulated time. For example, during natural calamities such as earthquake or floods or tsunami, many temporary teams evolve that look after the provision of food, shelter, clothing, and security of the people living in these affected areas. Another example is the formation of temporary teams by an assessment provider conducting high-stake examination across cities in India, where the teams created are responsible for the execution of the examinations at the allotted centres.

Classification of Teams Based on the Nature of Work Performed

Work Teams

The work teams are predominantly concerned with the work done by organizations like manufacturing products, providing services, developing new products and services, and so on. The prime function of these teams is effective utilization of the organizational resources. Have you ever heard the phrase 'two heads are better than one'? This implies that there are additional benefits to combining the thoughts, perspectives, opinions, and experiences of two individuals as opposed to those of a single person. If this notion is true, just imagine the advantage of combining three, four, five, or even more individuals. Typically, these small groups have complementary skills that they use to work towards a common goal for which they are mutually accountable. Many organizations recognize the benefit of having multiple people working together in a collaborative and cooperative environment to develop and deliver their products. For this reason, the use of work teams has become a routine way of managing organizations. This lesson identifies the different types of work teams, commonly found in contemporary organizations, including functional, cross-functional, and self-directed teams. For example, functional teams handle specific functions such as production, finance, and so on, and cross-functional teams having members from finance, production, marketing, and so on put forth the perspective for a common problem from various angles. For example, Northwestern Mutual, a life insurance company, in the early 1950s brought in people from the financial, investment, and wealth management sectors to understand the role of information technology and information systems on the business world and went on to create an Information Systems (IS) repository that gave the organization a large competitive advantage over its peers.

Management Teams

These teams consist of individuals of managerial positions. These teams are permanent in nature since the purpose of these teams does not end with the completion of a specific project or problem. The two major responsibilities of these teams include:

- providing guidance and counselling to other teams and
- coordinating the work of interdependent teams.

Employees who are on the board of management of any company comprise the management team of the organization.

Task Force

The organizations may sometimes form special teams in order to deal with a particular situation or to solve a specific problem, such teams are called task force or problem-solving teams. These teams are temporary in nature and are dissolved once the purpose is served. For example, the Bangalore Metropolitan Task Force was entrusted with the responsibility of better protection of government property and lakes, rivers, and tanks given to the forest department.

Committees

Committees are formed to take care of a particular task or project. These may be either temporary or permanent in nature. Individual members of the team usually possess common interests and background. For example, cultural committee, sports committee, and so on.

Virtual Teams

The teams that do not meet physically in a meeting room but are connected via a network are called as virtual teams. For example, a manager in Australia can communicate to a manager in India and the United States at the same time via the Internet. Virtual teams have now evolved in today's world of the Internet, email, videoconferencing, teleconferencing, and so on. In the traditional approach to team meetings, members were either physically present or absent. Virtual teams, on the other hand, can meet any time of the day from any part of the globe and from any organization. So virtual teams are location-distributed task force which operate the business from different geographies and have strong information base and skill levels. The main drawback of virtual teams is that are not able to meet face to face to build more accountability and trust.

Cross-functional Teams

A cross-functional team comprises individuals with different functional proficiency working towards a common goal. The members of this team may be working in different functional departments like marketing, operations, finance, and so on. Cross-functional teams might include people from different managerial levels. Also, the members may be internal or external to the organization. A task force can be called temporary cross-functional team with people from diverse functional units of an organization to solve a particular problem. Bringing the cross-functional team on a common platform takes a lot of time because of difference in team members' views, ideas, and perspectives, and it takes substantial time to build accountability and trust amongst the members. Even big IT project teams have people from various functions; for example, for a banking system there are domain experts building domain knowledge, business analyst analysing customer requirements, developer group writing the business case-specific functionalities, testing unit developing test cases, and quality assurance unit ascertaining the minimal defect scenario.

Reasons for Team Failure

Unclear Roles

Roles for each individual should always be clearly defined when assigning tasks. Unclear and vague roles can create confusion amongst the individuals, and the team might end up failing in its objectives. Roles, in terms of leadership, have also to be defined so that the leader can do effective task distribution and members can put forth the problems they come across.

Absence of Team Dynamics

Team dynamics ensures that each member is respectful of the other member and that the communication process is extremely transparent across members in the group. Lack of trust or too much of interference amongst the members might lead to nonattainment of results. Useful interaction, knowledge transfer and exchange of ideas, and using the right code of conduct and transparent communication are key to strong dynamics.

Inconsistent Vision and Goals

Every team has to have some goals set in the form of short- and long-term goals, and each goal has to be interpreted and understood by the team in the correct manner. If the goals are not realized properly, then the entire environment becomes chaotic and confusing with the muddle up of the vision set for the organization. This problem can be resolved by discussing the vision from time to time and enduring its continuing validity. If the goal needs to be refined, then it has to be done by taking the consensus from all, so that everybody is in sync with respect to vision refinement.

Time Management

Effective time management incorporates designing a detailed time plan, allocating resources, schedules, and deadlines, and the milestones, so that they work with the fullest commitment and always remain focussed to achieve the goal. If there are multiple projects running, then time management becomes a challenge for the project manager as well as team members. Apart from doing project work, managers at the middle and senior levels are engaged in other tasks as well, so allotting needful work hours becomes extremely mandatory for the management, which can happen through effective time management. Interference or interruptions need to be minimized during project period.

Impact of Changing Market Scenario

With the change in the market conditions or business situations, teams have to equip themselves with the ability to do correct analysis based on current market trends and changing scenarios keeping in vision the long-term impact of the decision undertaken, otherwise there are chances that the project might fail, leading to chances of team failures.

Creating Effective Teams

Building an effective team involves more than just gathering a group of skilled individuals. The most important aspect of building an effective team is to motivate all the members to work towards a common goal. Some of the steps involved in creating effective teams are as follows:

- It is of prime importance to define the purpose of the team. Setting a clear vision leads to successful functioning of the team and makes it easier to guide and direct the team members.
- The members of the team should be selected in a manner such that they possess complementary skills and can suggest a wide range of standpoints and ideas. It is necessary to ensure that the team has a balance of personality types so that it can function smoothly and can contest each other when required.
- After assembling the team the next step is to identify the tasks that help in achieving the desired output. Each task has to be assigned a deadline, and each member should be assigned a responsibility. In order to enable the team members to complete their responsibilities effectively and within the specified time, timely and adequate supply of resources to the team must be ensured.
- Operating standards and the expected output should also be clearly specified. This enables the team members to understand what they have to do and how it is to be done.
- Regular meetings should be conducted, and the performance should be monitored to make sure that the work is on track and according to the set standards. If there is any deviation, corrective actions need to be taken.
- One vital aspect in creating effective teams is to recognize and reward both individual and team performance. Recognition and rewarding foster the morale of team members and motivate them to perform better.
- Creating an effective team is not a one-time task, it requires continuous efforts and monitoring, but the result is much more rewarding.

Discussion and Case Study

Discussion: Teamwork at its Peak

The success of a business is accredited to the teamwork of the talent pool. Jack Welch, CEO of General Electric, stated that 'We've developed an incredibly talented team of people running our major businesses, and, perhaps more important, there's a healthy sense of collegiality, mutual trust, and respect for performance that pervades this organization'. Jack Welch not only created a team of high performing executives who later went on to hold leading positions in various Fortune 500 companies. In Welch's 20-year tenure, GE's revenue increased nearly seven-fold, such is the achievement of strong and capable teams.

It has been further seen that poor leadership teams bring in politics and rebuff, whereas strong teams bring in coherence and focus.

According to a Mckinsey report, the most effective teams using a three-step technique to implement an idea and make it a success. As stated, the teams focus on working together in the first phase so that they achieve the desired result in the second phase and finally do a review of the lessons learnt in the final phase. Workshops on team building can be helpful sometimes, but actually do not contribute much to the building of the teams, and it is good teams that first address business issues, which are central to their growth, and later focus on behavioural issues after the event.

According to Mckinsey, three performance dimensions mastered by teams to achieve their objective are as shown in Figure 11.2.

Three Performance Dimensions

According to experts at McKinsey, it is not a single person, preferably the CEO at the topmost position of the organization, who can lead the organization towards its growth, rather it is team dynamics which contributes to the growth of a unit or the organization. The prime areas of scrutiny are that the teams should have high degree of fruitful interactions, be adaptable to changes, and work towards a common goal where every individual in the team is aligned to the goal.

Figure 11.2 Performance Dimensions

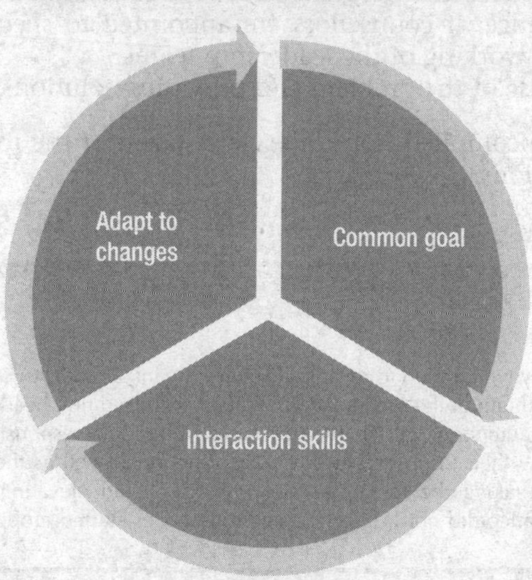

The actual problems, as per McKinsey's report, of the underperforming teams are as follows:

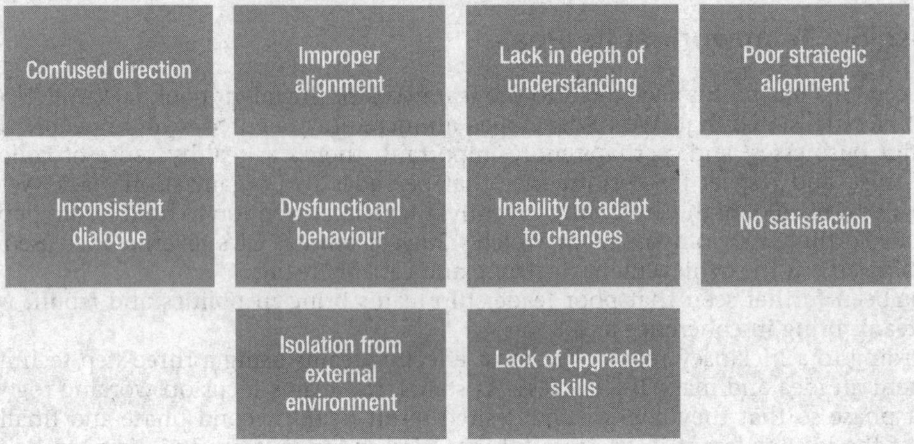

The issues on underperformance are determined by taking a survey of the prominent organizations by interviewing employees at the leadership positions and drawing conclusions from their holistic inputs.

McKinsey's Takeaway on Underperformance of Teams

Mckinsey's report states that any artificial programme, event, or workshop does not actually enable the teams to perform well. The team performance comes from the actual execution of tasks by teams in a collaborative fashion and replication of how senior teams work together. The report states, that for making teams perform well, the following points should be taken into consideration:

- **Address issues simultaneously:** For example, stakeholder management, managing organization's performance, and reviewing of top talent.
- **Proper channelization of team's discontentment:** By bringing in comparisons with competitors, focusing on threats, and analysing alignment to industry best practices.
- **Minimization of external interference:** Theoretical do's and don'ts do not affect the team's performance. If counsellors are appointed to speculate performance, then they need to see the working of the leadership teams.
- Finding the root cause of the problem and providing solutions.

The above findings are compiled from interviews taken of the top leadership teams from very prominent organizations.

CASE STUDY

This is the case of a company which tried to revamp its entire organizational structure and allocate controlled autonomy to every functional unit of the organization, which comprised unit heads and their small teams. The idea was that granting little autonomy will enable the teams to be more responsible for their functional unit and encourage them to grow their unit. Initially, the units functioned well as their efforts and contributions surfaced within the units, making the members more confident and elevating their sense of ownership. However, the good performance did not last long, since differences started cropping up between unit heads and the top-level team of the organization because of a lack of flexibility and resistance to the change shown by the middle management with the change in market scenarios.

The top management of the organization wanted the business unit heads to show considerable involvement in the expansion of business overseas and they wanted each unit head to plan the overseas operations by replicating the processes, but the middle management was reluctant to welcome the change as it was operating in their own comfort zone with the stipulated autonomy.

Also, on taking feedback from the other team members of every unit, it was found that the middle management was stuck with its old methods and needed the change to be implemented fast, thereby preventing the decline in growth of the organization. Therefore, changes were prioritized and the middle management was put into action to align its priorities and formulate a common strategy for the expansion of the business, right from unit-level expansion plans to organizational-level expansion plans. Prior to that, management sessions were conducted for all unit heads where they were put on role plays of top management and were taken through reflective working sessions.

The teams conducted fortnightly meetings to discuss talent, strategy, performance, and growth keeping in loop the top management and considering their ideas as well, which opened new opportunities for the company. In between the meetings, a few members worked on issues for the members of every unit to resolve keeping in mind the global expansion plans.

Soon there was an improvement in the performance dimensions:

- A common goal which enabled members to reach a consensus on performance, strategy to be used to attain performance of individuals unit, which would collate with organizational performance, and with relation to people responsible for progress of units and employees' productivity within the unit. At each instance, the top management was kept in the loop for its inputs and implementations of new ideas, as was required.
- Interaction amongst team members was healthy, and the level of trust loses due to open and honest communication accompanied with constructive debates on issues and ideas.
- Even external information relayed by the top management to the middle level with relation to market trends and competitors' analysis as well as location-specific strategy to be adopted for expansion of business was taken positively along with inputs from new recruits at the senior- and middle-management positions. These recruits shared strategies adopted by their past organizations in global business expansions.

Gradually, flexibility, adaptability, and openness amongst employees of middle management grew, leading to a conducive environment for Increased productivity.

Summary

This chapter summarizes the concepts on team and team dynamics, focusing on realistic views on team formation through evolution, transition, and action approach. It also encompasses the benefits of teamwork from organizational and individual contexts and, using a case-based approach, enforces the effectiveness and efficiency of strong teams, and how these teams can support an organization on its roadmap to success, that is, increased productivity and sustainability.

Exercise

Objective Questions

1. Teams include individuals having different skills.
    - True
    - False

2. Group performance does not depend on individual and collective efforts.
    - True
    - False
3. Which of these is the correct order for processes of teamwork?
    - transition process, interpersonal processes, action processes
    - transition process, action processes, interpersonal processes
    - interpersonal processes, transition process, action processes
    - None of the above
4. Which of these helps motivate the team to work towards the common goal or achieve the organizational objective?
    - Interpersonal processes
    - Transition process
    - Action processes
    - None of the above
5. Which of these is/are not type/s of team/s?
    - Management teams
    - Task force
    - Committees
    - All of the above
6. Which of these teams is temporary in nature?
    - Task force
    - Committees
    - Both of the above
    - None of the above
7. Which of these teams is formed to assist the permanent teams?
    - Supervised teams
    - Work teams
    - Temporary teams
    - Management teams
8. A cross-functional team comprises individuals with different functional proficiency.
    - True
    - False
9. Operations department in an organization is an example of
    - permanent teams
    - work teams
    - temporary teams
    - committees
10. Which of these includes benefits of teamwork?
    - Organizational enhancement
    - Self-development and growth
    - Helps in providing mutual support
    - All of the above

CASE STUDY

Impetus Solutions manufactures automotive and vehicle parts in Cleveland. To increase the core functioning of manufacturing operations, it has decided to implement SAP in its IT operations. Its IT operations are carried out in India. The top management decided how this team should come into existence. Discussions were carried out. Few suggestions that came up were of outsourcing the SAP operations to another IT company, separate dedicated team in the organization. Pros and cons of these ideas were evaluated and the result was a separate team.

As the company is now entering into its SAP operations, it requires good quality of SAP HR, so that a separate work team is put into place. It has hired a few SAP resources of have around four to five years of experience across the locations. It also appointed a separate leader to manage all the SAP resources. A few members of the manufacturing team should also be involved into it, so that proper business knowledge is there among the team members. A virtual team and cross-functional team were put into existence by hiring distributed workforce. The top management decided to start with the functioning of the SAP team. Coordination was carried over the teleconferences over the AT&T. The team started functioning, and all the activities and discussions were carried out virtually.

A mid-year progress check (MYPC) was conducted, which found that the team was performing its operations well.

Questions

1. Do you think going the idea of virtual teams was correct? Justify.
2. What other alternatives could you suggest to implement SAP operations in the company?
3. Discuss the complexities of a virtual team.

Critical Thinking Questions

1. What are your expectations when you join a new team?
2. Do you think the team members to work out on their interpersonal difficulties by their own?
3. How does the teamwork affect the organization's day-to-day operations?

Chapter at a Glance

Team and Teamwork consist of a small number of people with complementary skills working towards a common goal or objective and hold a mutual accountability.

Team Characteristics

- Collaboration and cooperation
- Follow comprehensive approach
- Maintain cordial relations
- Focus on team and individual development

Benefits of Teamwork

- Effective utilization of resources
- Better decisions

(Continued)

(Continued)

- Motivation
- Self-development and growth
- Organizational enhancement

Processes of Teamwork

- **Transition process:** It deals with formation of the team and formulation of the mission, vision goals and strategies the team is devising.
- **Action process:** In this phase the team performs its task or, in other words, executes the assigned project.
- **Interpersonal process:** It includes activities that occur during the transition and action processes.

Types of Teams

- **Self-managed teams:** These teams include a group of employees assigned to accomplish a particular task for the organization.
- **Supervised teams:** These teams are managed by a leader or a supervisor, and the leader is responsible for the overall performance of the team.
- **Permanent teams:** These teams are not dissolved when their task is over.
- **Temporary teams:** Temporary teams are generally formed to assist the permanent teams.
- **Work teams:** These teams are predominantly concerned with the work done by the organization, and their prime focus is on effective utilization of the organizational resources.
- **Management teams:** These teams consist of individuals of managerial positions and the purpose of these teams does not end with the completion of a specific project or problem.
- **Task force:** These teams help the organizations to deal with a particular situation or solve a specific problem.
- **Committees:** Committees are formed to take care of a particular task or project.
- **Virtual teams:** The teams that do not meet physically in a meeting room but are connected via networks are called as virtual teams.
- **Cross-functional teams:** A cross-functional team comprises individuals with different functional proficiency working towards a common goal.

Reasons for Team Failure

- Unclear roles
- Absence of team dynamics
- Inconsistent vision and goals
- Time management

CHAPTER 12

Leadership

Learning Objectives

- Getting knowledge of the importance of leadership from organizational perspectives and of the different styles of leadership and their usage across organizations and by history.
- Getting an elaborate know-how on the leadership models, theories, and the alignment of right leadership style for the right leader.
- Understanding the traits of a good leader and theories on the leadership traits and its implications.
- getting a detailed insight into the behavioural and contingency theories of leadership.

An Opening Vignette

LEADERSHIP CASE STUDY

This case study is about the leadership styles of two people in succession of a company. In the first case, Peter, the vice chairman, used to exhibit the autocratic style of leadership and in the second case Ronald, who was assigned the role of vice chairman, was a more amicable person and chose democratic style to lead the department.

Peter went into the details of crafting out rules, regulations, and policies and ensured that people followed them. In his reign, people were more disciplined, but less innovative. But the team never felt his pressure and thought him to be an interfering sort. Their enthusiasm and morale remained high during his tenure. The productivity of the team remained consistent and targets were achieved.

After retirement of Peter, Sam, who was handling a division in the company and a firm believer of delegating tasks to people in order to show his trust on them, was promoted to the post of vice chairman. So he allocated the task of scheduling milestones to Dick, formulated the quarterly budget and expenditure for the unit to Harry and stock auditing to Delma. His was more a democratic style of leadership. For the others he thought that they would discharge the duties as they had been doing till date.

Departmental meetings during Peter's tenure were frequent, with members forced to attend regularly, while Sam speculated that it was faculties' own responsibility to attend them and never monitored their absence and presence.

(Continued)

(Continued)

The freedom given to the team by Sam did not work rightly and soon the members started complaining the absence of guidance from the leader and failure in achieving the departmental goals.

Question

Having read this small case, identify the problem area and write assumptions and recommendations to the style adopted by Peter and Sam.

Model Answer

Problem Area

Change in leadership style by the management resulting in change in the work culture of the unit.

Assumptions and Analysis

Low morale and enthusiasm amongst team members resulting in low productivity and irregular attendance in team meetings showcase dissatisfied behavioural attitudes amongst the employees.

Also, it is stated very aptly that the common tendency of a human being is to show resistance to change. Under Peter's leadership employees were comfortable in being nurtured in his lap and they were far from taking up any form of ownership.

Peter was keener on attaining the targets and had less concern about his team's dynamics. He only wanted the tasks to be done efficiently and took vow from his team that they should perform to the minutest detail. The team had envisaged paternal instincts in him and had felt relaxed that during his reign he would not let any untoward situation arise in the unit which would disturb them.

When Sam was appointed the chairperson, he did not continue this tradition, which the team felt was the norm. This may have led to some of the initial distrust of Sam when he did not follow the conventional way of Peter. It is said that a leader tries to create leaders within an organization which Peter never did. Sam, in this democratic style, tried the same, but it had the opposite effect on people and later on the management, because, as per the case study, he never had rich communication with his subordinates or the upper management of the organization and nobody was aware of his initiatives to build leaders. Also, the team was not ready for such initiatives.

Recommendations Suggested

The leadership style followed by Sam should have been based on employees' readiness to accept the responsibility and ownership of the newly allocated task, and the leader's role of slowly easing himself out of the responsibility once the employee's readiness is affirmed. This would have been possible only by mechanisms of directing, delegating, supporting, and coaching as per the comfort of the followers. Henry and Blanchard had categorized the follower's attitude as able and unable, with willingness and confidence as their behavioural trait or showcasing unwillingness and insecurity to take up the ownership of the task. Sam should have researched employees' behaviour before allocating them new responsibilities and strongly remained aligned to their day-to-day progress with regular coaching, supporting, and directing them as and when required.

Introduction

The success or failure of an organization is, to a large extent, influenced by the leadership available within the organization. A strong leadership within the organization can contribute to its sustainability and growth, whereas a lack of effective leadership can ruin the entire organization. Many organizations today have understood the importance of effective leadership within the organization and hence are trying to develop leadership skills within their employees. Effective leadership can foster organizations in several ways, like coming up with innovative strategies, helping reduce resistance to change, finding creative ways of doing things, and so on.

Definitions

Leadership is the activity of influencing people to strive willingly for mutual objectives.

—George Terry

Leadership is a means of direction. It is the ability of management to induce subordinates to work towards group ideals with confidence and keenness.

Robert Appleby

Leadership is the ability of a manager to induce subordinates (followers) to work with confidence and zeal.

Koontz and O'Donnell

Leadership is the lifting of man's vision to higher sights, the raising of man's performance to higher standards, and building the man's personality beyond its normal limitations.

Peter Drucker

Leadership is the ability to awaken in others the desire to follow a common objective.

R.T. Livingston

Importance of Leadership

The growth rate of Infosys, one of the leading IT companies, started declining in the year 2013. According to a few experts and core team members, the reason for this decline was lack of focused leadership within the organization. Then, it was decided that Mr Narayana Murthy, the cofounder of the company, who had retired from the company, would rejoin the company to guide and mentor the potential leaders who could then take the company ahead.

It is evident from this example that effective leadership plays a crucial role in the success of an organization.

Whether big or small, profit making or non-profit making, every organization requires an effective leadership. Effective leadership can benefit the business in the following ways:

Clarity and Communication

Effective leadership ensures that there is clarity in the vision of the organization. At the same time, it also sees that the vision of the organization is communicated to all the employees so that they can clearly understand the purpose and work accordingly.

Motivation

An effective leadership plays a key role in motivating the employees. A leader may use different types of motivation techniques depending on the individual to be motivated. A motivated individual in turn puts in more efforts and performs better, thus helping in achieving the organizational goals in an effective manner.

Change Management

Several changes occur in the internal as well as external environment of an organization. The organization can sustain only when it takes necessary actions to adjust to these changes. However, bringing a change is not an easy task; it will, in most of the cases, have resistance from employees. In such cases, effective leadership has a significant role to play, as it has the capability and power to make the people realize the need and importance of change. In other words, effective leadership helps in change management by reducing or eliminating the resistance to change among the employees within the organization.

Planning

Without effective planning, all the other efforts would go in vain. A leader has clear vision about the organizational goals and objective and thus helps in effective planning.

Employee Relations

A leader helps in building cordial relations among his team members, which in turn helps in easy coordination.

Crisis Management

Good corporate leadership can assist a team stay focused in times of crises, reminding the team members about their accomplishments and inspiring them to set and achieve goals.

Leadership Traits

- **Sympathy:** Chances of sharing vision with the leader becomes a common phenomenon if the team is well aware of the leader's sympathetic edge for the team.
- **Steadiness:** A steady leader will gain reverence and trust, which is very crucial to get group support, and the team also orients itself towards these virtues.
- **Uprightness:** Honesty or uprightness about issues or concerns makes it highly probable that they will be addressed at proper time because such traits pave the way for better valuation and growth.
- **Direction:** Setting proper direction and taking in current and futuristic conditions are the prime characteristics of a good leader and carving out a road to that desired goal can bring in a major change.
- **Communication:** Transparent communication across team, keeping with the norms of communication in terms of achieving goals, setting expectations, and resolution of issues will motivate the staff work towards the goals.
- **Flexibility:** Open-mindedness of a leader will increase the possibility of finding the most optimal solution by letting the teamwork on the ideas and formulate strategies from the same.
- **Faith and belief:** The leader who believes or has faith in the mission and works to achieve the same will be an embodiment of inspiration to his followers.
- **Complexity resolution:** Resolution of issues and managing complexities are traits of a good leader, who can decide and implement courses of action under fast-changing situations.
- **Strategic action:** Incorporating global and forward-thinking approach to capture emerging opportunities is very important characteristic of leaders with strategic bent of mind.

- **Innovation:** To have a competitive edge over others, the leaders should continuously manoeuvre different courses of action for increased sustainability and emphasize on innovation to take the business to the next level.

Leadership Styles

Leadership style is basically the approach an individual follows while leading other people. Usually, the leadership style a leader selects depends on his behaviour, nature, thought process, and perception he has regarding his subordinates or team members. Some of the leadership styles are explained in detail further (Figure 12.1).

Autocratic Style (Do What I Say)

In autocratic style, the leader decides and instructs the team and the subordinates to follow him and implement his decisions. Employees play no role in decision-making. The followers of this style believe that close supervision is essential to get the work done from subordinates. This style can be most appropriate when the leader is competent as it saves time spent in decision-making through the two-way communication process.

The major disadvantage of this style is that the employees do not get a chance in decision-making and sometimes feel demotivated.

Adolf Hitler and Colonel Gaddafi are examples of the autocratic leaders.

Participative Style (Let Us Work Together)

It consists of three sub-types as follows:

- **Consultative:** In this style, leaders take in opinions from the group members before coming to the final decision. At the same time, these leaders make it very clear that final decision would be made by them.
- **Consensual:** These leaders believe in motivating the group members to discuss on the issue and then arrive at a conclusion. These types of leaders assign more weightage to the group opinion in comparison to the consultative leaders. They arrive at a decision that echoes unanimity of group members. This style leads to delay in decision-making process.

Figure 12.1 Leadership Styles

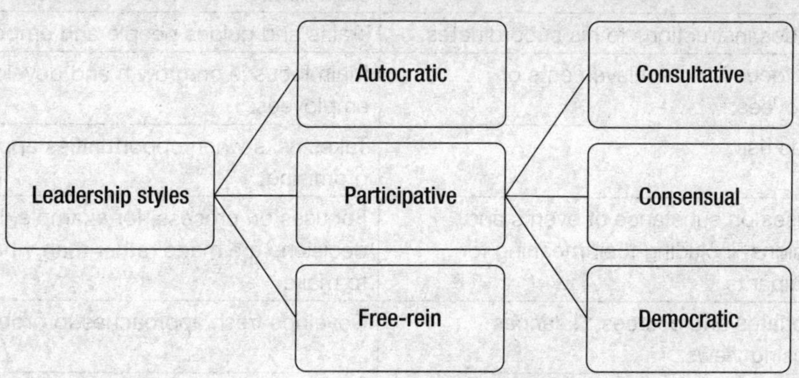

- **Democratic:** In this style, each group member votes before the leader takes any decision. Here, the entire authority lies with the group. The role of the leader is more or less like a coordinator.

The participative style can be advantageous because

- it leads to motivation and satisfaction of the group members,
- group members feel that their views are valued,
- it enhances sense of responsibility,
- it increases morale and self-confidence, and
- it lowers resistance to change.

This style can be successful only when group members are competent enough to take a decision. The prime demerit of this style is that it is time consuming and might lead to delay in decision-making.

Free-rein Style (I Go and You Work)

It is also known as laissez-faire. It is a laidback leadership style wherein the leader gives entire freedom to the group members to identify the goals and objectives, take decisions, and resolve issues. Here, the leader plays the role of a consultant and guide. This style proves to be effective when the members of the group are highly competent, experienced, skilled, educated, self-motivated, and responsible. For example, free-rein style of leadership occurs in research and development sections of industry.

Difference between Leader and Manager

The points of difference between a leader and a manager are as stated in Table 12.1.

Table 12.1 Difference between Manager and Leader

No.	*Manager*	*Leader*
1	An officially designated authority.	An authoritative individual.
2	Responsible for controlling and supervision of subordinates.	Responsible for building trust and confidence among followers
3	Receives and follows directions.	Provides a vision to believe in and strategic alignment.
4	Provides instructions to his subordinates.	Trains and guides people and empowers them.
5	Main focus is on achievements of employees.	Main focus is on growth and development of employees.
6	Avoids risk.	Takes risks when opportunities appear promising.
7	Focuses on substance of events and decisions, including their meaning for participants.	Focuses on process, for example, how decisions are made rather than what decisions to make.
8	Negotiates and coerces. Balances opposing views.	Develops fresh approaches to problems.

Leadership Models and Theories

Likert's Management System

Dr Rensis Likert developed four systems of management in the 1960s. He charted these systems to explain the association, participation, and roles of supervisors and subordinates in industrial settings. According to Likert, the style of management has a huge impact on the efficiency of the organization. The four systems developed by Likert are as discussed further.

Exploitative Authoritative

In this style, all the decisions are taken by the superiors and the subordinates have to abide by these decisions. This system makes use of negative motivational techniques. Without knowing the problems faced by the employees in the lower level of hierarchy, the decisions of the top management are just imposed on them.

Benevolent Authoritative

Unlike exploitative authoritative, benevolent authoritative style uses positive motivational techniques like rewards. Here, the top management feels responsible but the lower level does not. In this system, there is more of downward communication and very little upward communication.

Consultative

In this style of the management system, subordinates are motivated by offering rewards and a little involvement in the decision-making process. The opinions and ideas of the lower-level management are viewed positively and can be considered in the process of decision-making. Yet participation of subordinates is incomplete and key decisions are still made by senior management. There is greater level of upward communication in this style as compared with exploitative authority and benevolent authoritative style.

Participative

This is a system in which superiors have complete confidence and trust upon their subordinates. The subordinates are motivated by offering them monetary rewards. In this system, individuals at all the levels of management feel responsible towards the organizational goals. Among all the four systems of management developed by Likert, this one has the highest level of communication among superiors and subordinates. Also, this is the system wherein participation of lower levels of management in the process of decision-making is the highest.

According to Likert, the participative system of management is most effective if the organization wants to achieve higher level of effectiveness.

Managerial Grid: Blake and Mouton

Robert R. Blake and Jane Mouton developed a behavioural leadership model in 1964, which is known as managerial grid or leadership grid. Managerial grid is a graphical representation of two behavioural dimensions of a leader:

- **Concern for people (Y-axis):** This is the extent to which a leader accommodates the needs and interests of the team members and gives them priority while making a decision about best means to accomplish a task.

Figure 12.2 A Graphical Representation of the Managerial Grid

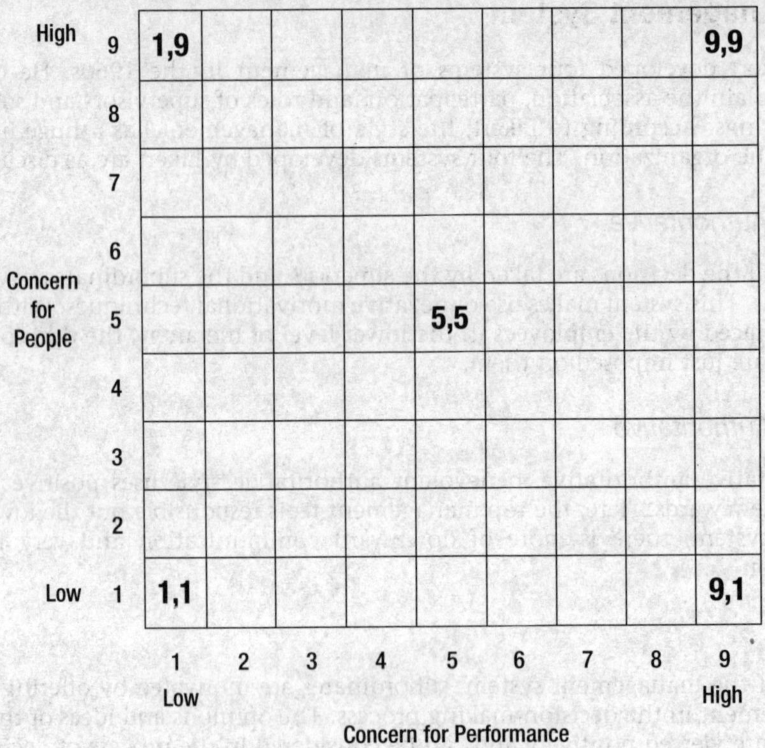

- **Concern for production (X-axis):** This is the extent to which a leader lays emphasis on tight schedules and high productivity while making a decision about best means to accomplish a task.

The scale of grid ranges from 1 (low) to 9 (high), thus forming 81 positions (Figure 12.2). The grid identifies five basic styles of leadership. These are explained further.

Impoverished Management (Avoid and Escape) (1,1)

Leaders with this style are considered to be ineffective since they have low concern for people as well as production. This type of leader is concerned only about preserving their job and seniority and does not want to be responsible for any mistakes. This causes the decisions to be less innovative and may also lead to dissatisfaction and disharmony.

Dictatorial (Produce or Perish) (9,1)

This style is based on McGregor's theory X. Leaders following this style believe that HR employed in the organization is just a means to an end. They consider the needs of the employees to be secondary and believe that organizational efficiency can result by following strict rules and work procedures.

Country Club (Yield and Comply) (1,9)

Leaders with this style have high concern for people and low concern for production. Leaders following this style pay more attention to the needs and comforts of their team members with an assumption that this would motivate the employees to perform better. The consequence of this could be friendly environment, which may not necessarily be productive.

Team Management (Contribute and Commit) (9,9)

According to Blake and Mouton, this is the most effective style. The leaders following this style have high concern both for people and production. It is based on McGregor's theory Y. The leader believes that enablement, commitment, faith, and respect play a major role in developing team atmosphere that will lead to not only satisfaction and motivation of team members but also higher production.

Middle of the Road (Balance and Compromise) (5,5)

In this style, the leader tries to maintain a balance between both the dimensions, that is, the concern for people and production. They hope to achieve suitable performance but do not realize that they are compromising on each of the dimensions up to a certain extent.

The managerial grid enables the managers/leaders to know where they stand in regard to the concern for people and the concern for production. Thus, it helps them to identify and analyse their leadership style. The drawback of this model is that it overlooks the internal and external environmental conditions and also does not take into account other aspects of leadership.

Situational Leadership Model (Hersey and Blanchard)

The situational leadership theory is a leadership theory developed by Paul Hersey, Professor, and Ken Blanchard, a management guru and author. These leadership models were developed in the late 1970s or the early 1980s. Situational leadership theory states that there is no single 'best' style of leadership. Effective leadership is all about setting high expectations and working towards it with the team and group of people they are leading. Effective leadership not only varies with the person or group that is being led but also depends on the task, job, or function that needs to be completed.

The Hersey–Blanchard situational leadership model rests on two elementary concepts (Figure 12.3):

- Leadership style
- Individual's or group's maturity level.

Choosing the Right Leadership Style for the Right People

The theory states that instead of using just one method, successful leaders should change their management styles based on the maturity of the people and the tasks accorded. Using this theory, leaders should be able to handle tasks and relationship with people accordingly.

Leadership Styles

According to Hersey and Blanchard, there are four main leadership styles:

- **Telling:** Leaders are more authoritative in their leadership styles and tell their people what to do and how to do it.
- **Selling:** Leaders provide more information and direction to get people on board.
- **Participating:** The leader works with the team and shares decision-making responsibilities.
- **Delegating:** Leaders pass most of the responsibility onto the group. The leaders still monitor progress, but they are less involved in decisions.

Figure 12.3 Hersey–Blanchard Situational Leadership Model

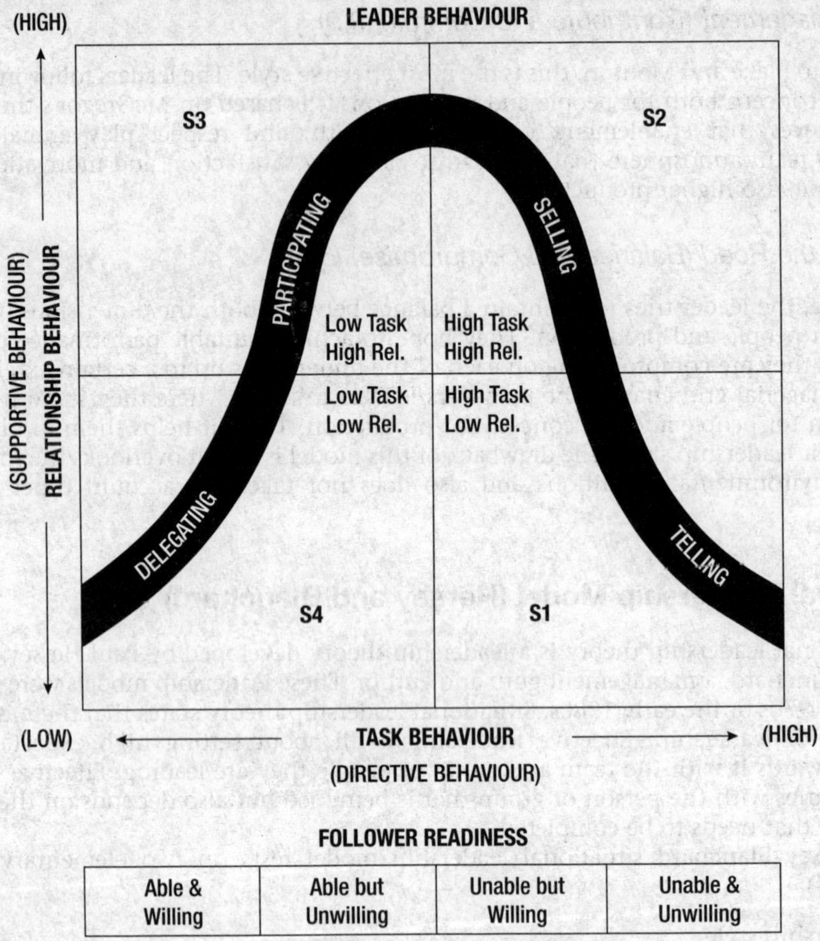

Basically, Styles 1 and 2 are focused on getting the task done and Styles 3 and 4 are more concerned with developing team members' abilities to work independently.

Maturity Levels

According to Hersey and Blanchard, leadership styles the maturity levels are broken down across four different levels:

- **M1:** People at this level of maturity are at the bottom level of the scale, lack knowledge, skills, or confidence to work on their own, and they need to be pushed to take up the responsibility of the task.
- **M2:** At this level, followers lack appropriate skills, but are desirous to work on the task until successful completion.
- **M3:** They have more skills, readiness than the M2 group, but lack of confidence in their abilities.
- **M4:** The group is able to work on its own. Members of the group have high confidence and strong skills, and they're dedicated to the task.

Table 12.2 Leadership Style and Maturity Level

Leadership Style	*Maturity Level*
Telling or directing	M1: Low maturity
Selling or ensuring conviction	M2: Medium maturity, low skill set
Collaborative	M3: Medium maturity, high skill set
Delegating	M4: High maturity

The Hersey–Blanchard model maps each leadership style to each maturity level as shown in Table 12.2.

To use this model, reflect on the maturity of individuals within your team. Table 12.2 shows which leadership style Hersey and Blanchard advise for people with that level of maturity.

EXAMPLE

You are about to leave for an extended holiday, and your tasks will be handled by an experienced colleague. He is very familiar with your responsibilities and excited to do the job.

Instead of trusting his knowledge and skills to do the work, you spend hours creating a detailed list of tasks for which he will be responsible and give full instruction on how to do them.

What is the result? Your work gets done, but you have damaged the relationship with your co-worker by your lack of trust. He was an M4 in maturity and yet you used an S1 management style instead of an S4, which would have been more appropriate.

EXAMPLE

You have just been put in charge of leading a new team. It is your first time working with these people. As far as you can tell, they have some of the required skills to reach the department's goals, but not all of them. The good news is that they are excited and keen to do the work.

You guess they are at an M3 maturity level, so you use the matching an S3 leadership style. You train them through the project's goals, pushing, and teaching where required, but mostly leaving them to make their own decisions. As a result, their relationship with you is strengthened and the team is successful.

Leadership Style and the Work: Fielder

According to Fiedler, stress is a key determinant of leader effectiveness (Gujral, 2012), and a difference exists between stress related to the leader's superior and subordinate or the situation itself. Fiedler concludes that experience impairs performance under low-stress situations but contributes to performance under high-stress situations. Fiedler's recommendations for such situations lie in capitalizing on the leader's strengths.

Fiedler's situational contingency theory holds that group usefulness depends on a leader's style and the demand for that situation. Fiedler's contingency model is a dynamic model where the personal characteristics and motivation of the leader are said to interact with the current situation that the group faces.

The first major factor in Fiedler's theory is known as the leadership style. This is the consistent system of interaction that takes place between a leader and work group. According to Fiedler, an individual's leadership style depends upon his or her personality and is, thus, fixed. In order to classify leadership styles, Fiedler has developed an index called the least-preferred co-worker (LPC) scale.

The LPC scale asks a leader to describe one person with whom he or she works the least well with from past and present. From a scale of one through eight, leaders are asked to illustrate this person on a series of bipolar scales such as the following:

Unfriendly	1 2 3 4 5 6 7 8	Friendly
Uncooperative	1 2 3 4 5 6 7 8	Cooperative
Hostile	1 2 3 4 5 6 7 8	Supportive
Guarded	1 2 3 4 5 6 7 8	Open

The response to these scales are summed and averaged. A high LPC score suggests human relations orientation, while a low LPC score depicts task orientation. Fiedler's logic is that satisfaction is derived in case of high LPC score because of interpersonal relationship and low scores denote more task satisfaction. This method reveals an individual's emotional result to people with whom he or she cannot work. In the first case, these leaders see that good interpersonal relations as a requirement for task accomplishment and in the second case they are more concerned with successful task accomplishment and worry about interpersonal relations later. For example, Papiya was elected president for a cultural committee on which she had no control. The committee is tasked with instituting a new policy that will ask the various music and dance groups to pay a registration fee for the forthcoming cultural event, and this is the first time that such decision has been made. The question is how she is going to implement this policy with a committee that she has no way of rewarding or punishing as a way of motivating the members. The LPC measure of Papiya is 98, which shows that, according to our text, she is motivated by relationships.

There are three factors to the contingency model: leader–member relations, task structure, and positional power. The leader–member relation factor for Papiya is good, the task structure defines that this is the first time when groups have to pay a fee and the task has clarity but no precedence, hence structuring is low, and the power factor is weak as the case states that she has no power to reward or punish the committee. The points collated by her are respectively 1, 5, 8. Based on Papiya's relationship motivation, she scored high on the relationship aspect and scored low on areas that detract from relationships. It is believed that she will use the relationship strength to further build the trust with the committee members and motivate them to be successful in the implementation of the new fee policy irrespective of being able to exude and control the members.

The second major factor in Fiedler's theory is known as environmental or situational variable. Fiedler then extends his analysis by focusing on three key situational factors: leader–member, task structure, and position power.

Each factor is defined as follows:

- **Leader–member relations:** Employee's acceptability for the leader.
- **Task structure:** Detailed job description of the subordinate.
- **Position power:** Formal authority possessed by a leader in the organization.

Table 12.3 Leadership Management Style

	Very Favourable		***Intermediate***				***Very Unfavourable***	
Leader-Member Relations	Good	Good	Good	Good	Poor	Poor	Poor	Poor
Task Structure	High		Low		High		Low	
Leader Position Power	Strong	Weak	Strong	Weak	Strong	Weak	Strong	Weak
Situations	I	II	III	IV	V	VI	VII	VIII

For leader–member relations, Fiedler maintains that the outcome of a good relationship is trust from subordinates. Fiedler explains that task structure is the second most important influential factor for a leader who correctly structures the task and specifies how a job is to be done in detail. Finally, as for position power, leaders who have the authority to employ, fire, and reward have more power than those who do not have these powers.

By classifying a group according to three variables, it is possible to identify eight different group situations or management styles, which are classified as either task orientated or relationship orientated.

According to Fiedler, a task-oriented style of leadership is more effective than a relationship-oriented style. The task-oriented leaders who get things accomplished prove to be the most successful. Blue-collar workers generally want to know exactly what they are supposed to do and hence the tasks are usually highly structured. Here, the leader–member relation can be made strong (Table 12.3).

The considerate style of leadership seems to be appropriate when the environmental or certain situation is moderately favourable or certain, for example, when

- leader–member relations are good
- the task is unstructured, and
- position power is weak.

For example, research scientists do not like superiors to structure the task for them.
Fiedler's theory gives some interesting conclusions:

- Candidates for leadership positions should be evaluated using the LPC scale.
- If a leader is sought for a particular leadership position, a leader with the appropriate LPC profile should be chosen, that is, task orientated for very favourable or very unfavourable situations and relationship orientated for moderate situations.

Fiedler's other observations were as follows:

- Only the leader performs better in some situations, but not all situations.
- Selection of situations can match his/her leadership style and hence anybody can be a leader.
- Finally, effectiveness of a leader can be improved by increasing or decreasing a leader's position power, changing the organization of a task, or influencing leader–member relations, an organization can alter a state to better fit a leader's style.

Limitations of Fiedler's theory:

- Absence of situational variables, like training and experience, has an impact in a leader's effectiveness.
- Uncertainties about LPC score.

Path–Goal Approach

The path–goal theory is a leadership theory developed by Robert House, an Ohio State University graduate, in 1971 and revised in 1996. The theory states that a leader's action directly correlates to the approval, keenness, and performance of her/his team member. The revised version also argues that the leader follows the path that appropriately complements subordinates' abilities and compensates for deficiencies. First, the theory was inspired by the work of Martin G. Evans (1970) and also influenced by the expectancy theory of motivation, developed by Victor Vroom in 1964.

According to this theory, a manager's job is to aid the team members in accomplishing goals and to offer the direction and support needed to align departmental goals to organizational goals.

A leader's behaviour is acceptable to subordinates when the leader offers coaching, directions, and rewards to the employees. Various behaviours of a leader are as follows:

- The directive path–goal clarifying leader behaviour refers to situations where the leader tracks the followers' progress and tells them how to perform their tasks. This behaviour has the most positive effect when the subordinates' role and task demands are uncertain and satisfying.
- The achievement-oriented leader behaviour refers to situations where the leader sets high-stake goals for employees, expects them to perform at a high scale, and shows self-assurance in their capacity to meet this standard.
- The participative leader behaviour involves leaders consulting the group and asking for their suggestion before making a decision.
- The supportive leader behaviour is directed towards showing concern for the group's psychological well-being where work leads to stress.

Path–goal theory assumes two variables, environment and group characteristics, that depict the leader behaviour–outcome relationship. Environmental factors determine the type of leader behaviour based on maximization of group outcomes. Group characteristics are the focus of control, experience, and perceived ability. Research demonstrates that employee performance and satisfaction rely on a leader's ability to overcome their shortfalls and carry out the goal attainment successfully. According to Northouse, the theory is useful because it reminds leaders that their main task as a leader is to help subordinates define and reach their goals in an efficient manner. Also, the theory justifies that fluidity be observed while choosing a leadership style. For example, a store manager might reward an employee's excellent sales performance with a promotion that assigns more responsibilities and rewards the employee both financially and professionally, or he can a create employee-training programme to help workers hone their sales skills, or clarify employees' expectations with regard to their duties and achievements, or have an open door policy to learn about employee grievances and tailor on-the-job training based on employees' experience and abilities. This prevents redundant training and makes effective use of employees' time.

Theories on Leadership Traits

Leadership theories revolve around the characteristics of successful and unsuccessful leaders, and the leaders are rated based on these characteristics to assess the probability of their success or failure.

Experts relying on this approach conducted study across the following dimensions:

- Physiological (appearance, weight, and height)
- Demographic (age, education, and background)
- Character (confidence, nature, and assertiveness)
- Intellect (knowledge, decisiveness, and judgemental)

- Work aspect (accomplishment initiative and perseverance)
- Communal characteristics (cooperation)

Successful leaders have interests, abilities, and personality traits that are different from those of the less-effective leaders. Through research conducted in the last three decades of the 20th century, a set of core traits of successful leaders have been identified. These traits are not responsible solely to identify whether a person will be a successful leader or not, but they are essentially seen as preconditions that endow people with leadership potential.

The core traits identified, among others, are:

- **Achievement drive:** High level of effort, ambition, energy, and initiative.
- **Leadership motivation:** An intense desire to lead others to reach shared goals.
- **Honesty and integrity:** Trustworthy, reliable, and open.
- **Self-confidence:** Belief in one's self, ideas, and ability.
- **Cognitive ability:** Capable of exercising good judgment, strong analytical abilities, and conceptually skilled.
- **Knowledge of business:** Knowledge of the industry and other technical matters.
- **Emotional maturity:** Adjusts well and does not suffer from severe psychological disorders.
- **Others:** Charisma, creativity, and flexibility.

Strengths/Advantages of Trait Theory

- It is a naturally pleasing theory.
- It is valid as a lot of research has validated the foundation and basis of the theory.
- It serves as a yardstick against which the leadership traits of an individual can be assessed.
- It gives a detailed knowledge and understanding of the leader element in the leadership process.

Limitations of the Trait Theory

- There is bound to be some subjective judgment in determining who is regarded as a 'good' or 'successful' leader.
- The list of possible traits tends to be very long. More than 100 different traits of successful leaders in various leadership positions have been identified. These descriptions are simply generalities.
- There is also a disagreement over which traits are the most important for an effective leader
- The model attempts to relate physical traits, such as height and weight, to effective leadership. Most of these factors relate to situational factors. For example, a minimum weight and height might be necessary to perform the tasks efficiently in a military leadership position. In business organizations, these are not the requirements to be an effective leader.
- The theory is very complex.

Trait Theory and Its Implications

The trait theory is characterized by the following:

- Information on leadership is constructive.
- It is applicable to people across all levels of the organization.
- Leaders can use the information from trait theory to be better leaders.
- Leaders get a detailed understanding of their own identity and personality and their effect on others in the organization.
- This theory helps managers inculcate leadership qualities.

Behavioural Theories

Behavioural theory encourages participative decision-making and emphasizes on people and collaboration with respect to leadership styles. It also helps in aligning individual and group objectives and focuses majorly on the behaviour of the leaders on two aspects: the task aspect and aspect of relationship.

What Is Behavioural Theory of Leadership?

Behavioural theory of leadership describes the behaviour of leaders and focuses on making of a leader, than ascertaining that leaders are born. Behavioural theories of leadership are classified as such because they focus on the study of specific behaviours of a leader. As per the study conducted by behavioural theorists, leadership influences and leadership success can be concluded from the behaviour of the leader.

Behavioural theory concentrates on the action plan set by the leader, rather than on what qualities they possess, and the attention focuses more on the styles of leadership.

Advantages of Behavioural Theory

- It encourages values of leadership styles with focus on collaboration.
- It promotes participative decision-making and team development.
- It helps managers evaluate their own style and its impact on their team, which affects the team's contribution towards organizational goals.
- A balance is achieved by the managers while they use different leadership styles with a focus on the concern for their team and its productivity. This theory helps managers find the right balance between different styles of leadership and decide how to behave as a leader, depending on concerns for people and for productivity.

Criticism/Arguments Against Behavioural Theory of Leadership

- The theory provides very less guidance on effective leadership in different situations.
- Researches carried out by various experts were different each time, leading to a number of inconsistencies.
- Leadership styles adopted were dependent on situations, environment they were working on, and the people they are working with.
- Today, no leadership style is right for managers which works under every circumstance.

Contingency Theories

Leader Member Exchange Theory

Vertical Dyad Linkage Theory

The first study of exchange theory is known as vertical dyad linkage (VDL) theory, which defines the nature of the relationship between managers and team members (dyadic relationships). The leader establishes a relationship with each of his team members, which influences their accountability, decision-making, and performance. This theory focuses on establishing positive relations between the leader and subordinates contributing to organizational success.

In-group and out-group

A leader's behaviour changes when he interacts with an individual. The quality of this relationship between the two is based on trust, loyalty, sustenance, respect, and obligation, and hence the relationship varies. Groups are further divided into subgroups: in-group and out-group. In-groups are groups of people who work well with the leader and out-groups are groups which represent the comfort level of the leader who works with the groups.

In-group

In-groups are favoured by the leader since they have greater role, responsibility, and commitment to the team's goals and are dependable with greater access to organizational resources. The in-group consists of highly competent and trustworthy followers. The members in this group receive considerable care, information, opportunities, and training, are highly confident and committed as well, and are very much inclined towards taking up a challenging job and successfully executing it.

Out-group

Relationships based on the formal defined roles are called the out-group. The members who are not in the 'in-group' fall into the 'out-group'. Members who show or emanate mistrust are put in the out-group. These individuals receive fewer valued resources from their managers. They are less like-minded compared with the leader, have limited work, do not advocate/confront challenging situations, and have, therefore, limited opportunities.

Relationship Stages

The various stages of relationship between manager and his team comprise role taking, role making, and routinization.

- **Role-taking:** This is the phase when the members join the team and their skills and abilities are assessed by the leaders before allocation of roles and responsibilities.
- **Role-making:** In the second phase, after a role is created for the members, they start working harder and with more commitment, fulfilling managers' expectations. Trust building is very important in this stage, and any negation to that would result in the member being demoted to the out-group. Work-related factors govern the thought process of managers in keeping the member in the in-group or out-group.
- **Routinization:** In the last phase, stability is attained and processes have more structure, which result in ongoing social interchange between the leader and the member. In-group team members work hard to maintain good relations with their managers by sustaining faith, esteem, sympathy, endurance, perseverance, fairness, and thoughtfulness. They are good at seeing the vantage point of other people, especially their leader. Hostility, irony, and being self-centric are abilities seen in the out-group as they may start to show aversion or disbelief in their managers.

Leader–Member Exchange Theory and Organizational Effectiveness

This theory directly promotes organizational effectiveness as a summation of leaders, members, groups, and organizational success. Amongst the in-groups considered to be of high standards, qualitative exchange of information, effective task execution, and greater performance result in less employee turnover, with quick promotions and high organizational productivity.

Vroom–Yetton Contingency Model

The Vroom–Yetton contingency model consists of a theory proposed by Victor Vroom, Phillip Yetton, and Arthur Jago, which states that the best style of leadership is dependent on the current environment or situation. Experts suggest that there are five different styles of leadership, ranging from autocratic to group-based styles under the normative decision-making model formulated by the group. These styles are crafted based on the organizational situation, environment, and level of involvement (Figure 12.4).

Figure 12.4 Vroom–Yetton Contingency Model

Autocratic type 1 (A1)	• Leaders make their own decision based on the information available.
Autocratic type 2 (A2)	• Information is collected by leaders from their followers but the decision-making lies with the leader in general.
Consultative type 1 (C1)	• Leader shares problems with the in-group members individually and takes in their views and opinions individually, not in group, and then using the various options available, makes his own decisions. Here followers do not meet and discuss possibilities, rather their contribution is to only put in their suggestions.
Consultative type 2 (C2)	• Unlike C1, members meet each other to discuss their ideas and alternatives, but again it is upon the leader who takes the decision alone, which may or may not reflect the members' thought process.
Group based (GII)	• Involves implementing ideas and opinions of the members or followers through brainstorming and group decision tends to be the final.

Vroom and Yetton designed seven questions to judge members' contribution to the decision-making and the questions are based on quality of decision taken, effort expended to make the decision and acceptance of the decision, and answer in 'yes' or 'no' were expected by the three experts.

- Is there a quality requirement? Is the nature of the solution critical? Are there technical or rational grounds for selecting among possible solutions?
- Do I have sufficient information to make a high-quality decision?
- Is the problem structured? Are the alternative courses of action and methods for their evaluation known?
- Is acceptance of the decision by subordinates critical to its implementation?
- If I were to make the decision by myself, is it reasonably certain that it would be accepted by my subordinates?
- Do subordinates share the organizational goals to be obtained in solving this problem?
- Is conflict among subordinates likely in obtaining the preferred solution?

The Vroom, Yetton and Jago model requires decision trees to be implemented to find the best decision alternative as represented in Figure 12.5.

Figure 12.5 Decision Tree to Be Implemented in the Vroom, Yetton and Jago Model

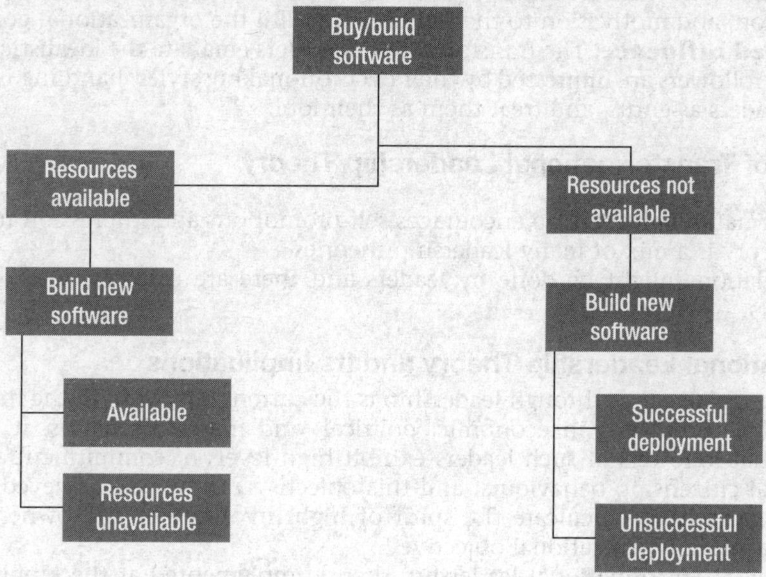

Transformational Leadership Theory

Transformational leadership theory aims at creating a high-performance workforce and special emphasis is given to the elevation of motivation level amongst the members in the team, which is considered to be essentially the task of the leader and transformation leadership theory evolved from this necessity. It has been seen that transformational leaders are generally spirited and zealous, actively involved in processes, and try to take out the best in every member within the group.

Transformational Leadership

Introduced by presidential biographer James MacGregor Burns, transformational leadership revolves around the mutual contribution of leaders and followers to advance to the next level of moral and motivation. Transformational leaders motivate followers to change outlook, insight, and impetus to work towards common goals.

Later, researcher Bernard M. Bass came up with Bass' transformational leadership theory. According to Bass, transformational leadership has four components (Figure 12.6):

Figure 12.6 Components of Transformational Leadership

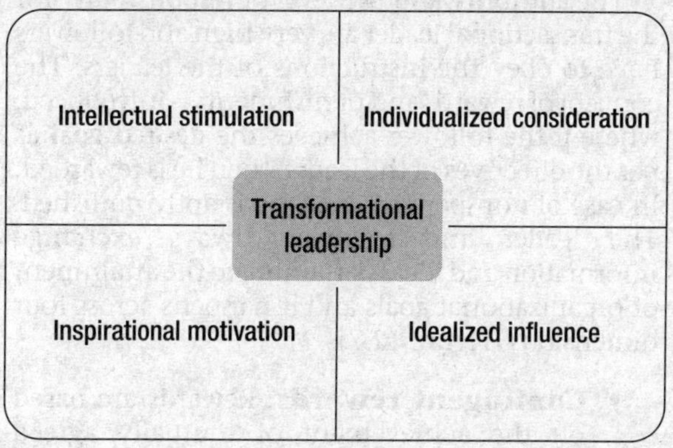

- **Intellectual stimulation:** Here, leaders encourage followers to come up with new ideas and explore new ways and opportunities.
- **Individualized consideration:** Transformational leadership also allows the members for free flow of

information exchange and ideas between leaders and members so that leaders can offer direct credit of the one-off assistance of each follower.

- **Inspirational motivation:** Transformational leaders communicate passion, dedication, and motivation to the followers to fulfil the organizational goals.
- **Idealized influence:** The transformational leaders emanate the idealistic view of them and the followers are impressed by their decision-making styles, handling issues, worship these leaders as gurus, and treat them as their idol.

Criticisms of Transformational Leadership Theory

- Transformational leadership encourages self-promotions and impression management.
- This theory is a mix of many leadership theories.
- Manipulations might be done by leaders and there are chances of losses accrued by followers.

Transformational Leadership Theory and Its Implications

Transforming organization through leadership is the current buzzword in the industry, and in times of global turbulence in economic, political, and market scenarios, it is very much mandatory that followers of such leaders exhibit high levels of commitment and engage in organizational citizenship behaviours, and this objective can be best achieved if the leaders take up the initiative to inculcate the spirit of high involvement and ownership amongst followers to achieve organizational objective.

For example, transformational leadership theory implemented at the Lippincott Nursing Centre encourages nurse managers who are effective communicators to meet with the nursing staff so that complaints and recommendations are discussed. Further, the nurse manager who communicates effectively will allow staff members to voice their worries and have reverence for employees by patiently listening to them. Also, the nurse managers should be inspirational, trustworthy, and work on effective stakeholder engagement by promoting teamwork and collaboration, which can give rise to new ways of service delivery at the centre, ensuring its positive impact on the patients.

Transactional Leadership Theory

Max Weber in 1947 first introduced the transactional style of leadership followed by Bernard Bass in 1981. This style focuses on the function of management, that is, controlling, organizing, and short-term planning. Transactional leadership theory was used by McCarthy and De Gaulle. Coaches of sports teams are a good example of appropriate transactional leadership.

The authority and the level of responsibility for the transactional leader are very high and followers have to obey the instructions of the leaders. The concept of rewards and punishments is introduced, where if the follower achieves the desired goal as per the directives of the leader, then he is rewarded. In case of non-performance, he is aptly punished. The leader and follower always exchange information and ideas pertaining to the attainment of organizational goals and it happens across four dimensions (Figure 12.7).

Figure 12.7 Dimensions of Transformational Leadership

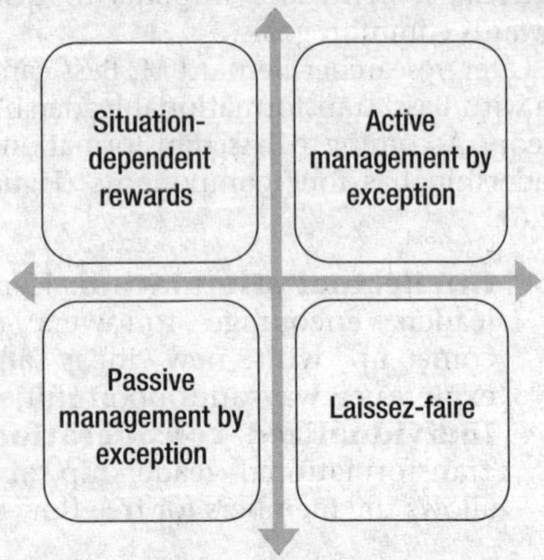

- **Contingent rewards:** Rewards are based on the achievement of mutually agreed goals by making available necessary resources. They set SMART (specific, measurable, attainable, realistic, and timely) goals for their members.

- **Active management by exception:** Transactional leaders actively monitor the work and performance of their members, see if there exists divergence from set of standards rules, and take remedial action to prevent errors.
- **Passive management by exception:** Transactional leaders' intervention happens when expectations are not met or when quality of tasks deviates from the standards defined. They may even use punishment for unacceptable performance.
- **Laissez-faire:** Opportunities are given in multi-fold to members wherein leaders themselves start avoiding making decisions on their own and, in due course, the group starts lacking direction.

Assumptions of Transactional Theory

- Employee motivation happens through rewards and punishment.
- There is a strict superior subordinate relationship.
- The leaders monitor the performance of the subordinates and control is exercised to get the work done from them.

Implications of Transactional Theory

- High level of emphasis on the short-term goals, standard rules, and procedures.
- Not much importance is given to team members' creativity and generation of ideas.
- Style of leadership works well for simple organizational problems.
- Transaction leaders go to lengths for cutting costs and improving productivity.
- Transactional leaders are highly focussed on professional achievements from organizational context and do not share emotional bonds with followers or members.
- Transaction between leader and member is through monetary benefits.

The transactional style of leadership is not adequate enough for developing the maximum leadership potential and if exercised heavily, it might lead to the formation of an environment infiltrated by position, power, perk, and politics.

Leadership Development

We often regard the success of a team or an organization to its leaders. However, the focus of developing leadership is now changing from just an individual to the entire organization. Today, leadership development is referred to as developing the quality of leadership among individuals as well as organization as a whole. The increasing importance of leadership has forced the modern-day organizations to focus on the leadership aspect in a more serious and mature manner. Organizations have now realized that for the long-term sustainable growth and development, leadership qualities need to be fostered. The organization which focuses on leadership development should promote the following:

- **Initiative thinking:** Whenever feasible, the subordinates should be given an opportunity to take independent decisions. Creative thinking should not only be appreciated but also taken into consideration. Opportunities to explore creative ideas should be introduced.
- **Personal skills development:** A training and development programme to refine skills and personalities, attitude, and overall professional grooming is mandatory. Job rotations can also play a crucial role in this regard.
- **Encouraging a challenging project:** Taking up challenging opportunities is also promoted in the case of leadership development.

CASE: LINKING BUSINESS STRATEGY TO LEADERSHIP STRATEGY

A business drives when there are leaders at all levels, and each and every individual is trained, coached, and aligned to the organizational objective. High-performing companies build execution into the culture.

EXAMPLE

1. UPS has outperformed its competitors for many years with continuous transformations happening in terms of promoting leadership culture of customer service and security and entrepreneurship.
2. Jack Welch, Chairman and CEO of General Electric, during his tenure increased the market value of the firm from approximately $12 billion to a colossal $505 with a market capitalization that was only exceeded by Microsoft. Strategic acquisitions under his leadership helped General Electric climb to its peak, with 10% or more earnings growth for many quarters, of which the most lucrative of Welch's acquisitions was $6.4 billion paid for Radio Corporation of America which owned National Basketball Association. Jack Welch built execution into culture.
3. IBM went through a major transformation when it shifted from 'technology selling' to 'delivering high-value services' by building a consulting mindset, driving innovation and inventiveness into the management team.

High-performers Develop Leaders at All Levels

Nowadays companies develop leaders bottom up where every individual is thought to be a leader and undertakes responsibility and makes decisions which supports the business motives. A very prominent organization who does that is Accenture, where every manager is made to believe that they should work to make Accenture a better organization every day. Senior executives 'serve' the needs of line leaders, like an inverse pyramid.

Summary

This chapter focuses on the importance of leadership from organizational perspectives and how great leaders make and break organizations. At the same time, it describes the various leadership models and theories and also the implications of using the modern and the traditional approaches to leadership styles and theories. The ultimate objective of this chapter is to inculcate amongst the enthusiasts the spirit of doing something innovative and creative and leading a group in accomplishing the holistic tasks which can facilitate the industry and the society as well.

Exercise

Objective Questions

1. Leadership is the ability of a ______ to induce subordinates (followers) to work with confidence and zeal.

- HR
- Manager
- Chief operating officer
- All of the above

2. In which leadership style, employees play no role in decision-making?

- Autocratic style
- Participative style
- Free-rein style
- None of the above

3. Which type of leadership style has lower resistance to change?

- Free-rein style
- Participative style
- Autocratic style
- None of the above

4. In which type of leadership, leaders take in opinions from the group members before coming to the final decision?

- Autocratic style
- Participative style
- Free-rein style
- None of the above

5. A _____ helps in building cordial relations among his team members which in turn helps in easy coordination.

- HR
- Manager
- Chief operating officer
- Leader

6. ________ is the one in which the leader decides and instructs and the subordinates follow and implement.

- Autocratic style
- Consultative style
- Democratic style
- Free-rein style

7. In which style of leadership, employees do not get a chance in decision-making and sometimes may be demotivated?

- Autocratic style
- Consultative style
- Democratic style
- Free-rein style

8. In which style of leadership, entire authority lies with the group?

- Autocratic style
- Consultative style
- Democratic style
- Free-rein style

9. Leader receives and follows directions.
   - True
   - False

10. _______ is a key determinant of leader effectiveness.
   - Change
   - Stress
   - Motivation
   - None of the above

11. Which of these theory states that a leader's action directly correlates to the approval, keenness, and performance of his/her team member?
   - Situational leadership
   - Path–goal
   - Managerial grid
   - None of the above

12. _______ encourages participative decision-making and emphasizes on people and collaboration with respect to leadership styles.
   - Situational leadership theory
   - Path–goal theory
   - Trait theory
   - Behavioural theory

13. The participative leader behaviour is not directed towards showing concern for the group's psychological well-being where work leads to stress.
   - True
   - False

14. In which of these, leaders encourage followers to come up with new ideas and explore new ways and opportunities.
   - Intellectual stimulation
   - Individualized consideration
   - Inspirational motivation
   - Idealized influence

15. In which of these theory, the authority and the level of responsibility for the transactional leader are very high and followers have to obey the instructions of the leaders.
   - Trait theory
   - Transactional leadership theory
   - Leader–member exchange theory
   - Behavioural theory

CASE STUDY

Pragstamin Private Limited is a manufacturing company of automotive parts. It has remarkable footprints in the market. Customers say that they want to do more business with Pragstamin. Shareholders believe that Pragstamin is one of the best investments.

Mr Amar was appointed as the new general manager. Before being promoted to general manager, he was executive in the company. He had five years of experience in total. He has completed his MBA in Production and he considers himself as a high flier. He was very enthusiastic about being promoted. However, because of young age, he lacked adequate experience and therefore was still considered as an executive by his subordinates.

These production units were primarily based into two regions: North America and Europe, the Middle East, and Africa (EMEA). Each of these locations was headed by a manager. Managers of these two regions reported to Mr Amar and they had over 16 years of experience with an average age of 47 years. These manages had been with the company for a very long time. Since Mr Amar had very less experience, they were against the decision of making him general manager had inculcated a hesitancy and suspicion among them.

Mr Amar started holding bi-weekly new meetings with these managers. In the meeting, he noticed that the managers were hesitant to speak to him. To act upon, he made some changes in the operating procedures so that efficiency is increased and announced this change in one of the bi-weekly meetings. He kept a close eye on the behaviour of the managers in the next meeting. He noticed that the managers were still not opened to him, and the problem still continued.

After three months, Mr Amar started receiving emails from the top management about the fall in the business. These complaints mentioned that the company has started losing the business from their core customers, and this has resulted into a huge loss for the company because of not continuing with its promise of high quality. He continued to receive emails from the top management and was becoming frustrated. One day, he walked down to the production unit and wanted to talk to the floor-operating manager for production. The manager, who reported to him for that division, was out of office. Later, the floor-operating manager was informed about the visit. The manager immediately called upon a virtual meeting with managers of other locations who directly reported to Mr Amar. In the meeting, upon knowing about the visit, the other manager commented, 'Mr Amar is incompetent and too young and dictated in the bi-weekly meetings. He shows no confidence in them and so they are fed up of this situation'. Hearing this, the other replied, 'we don't have a choice because Mr Amar has been regarded highly by the top management and, therefore, we should start looking for other job opportunities'. The other manager reluctantly agreed and ended up the meeting.

Questions

1. What actions would have been taken to avoid the problem?
2. What style of leadership does Mr Amar has? What are the pros and cons of this style in this situation?
3. What solution can you propose to solve the problem as a leader?

Critical Thinking Questions

1. Leadership is situational. Comment.
2. Imagine that you are appointed as a leader of a project and you are preparing for the first meeting, identify important actions you could take to help to set a positive influence on the team members.
3. Leader brings changes into peoples' life at work. Comment.

Chapter at a Glance

Leadership

Leadership is the activity of influencing people to strive willingly for mutual objectives.

(Continued)

(Continued)

Effective leadership can foster organizations in several ways, like coming up with innovative strategies, helping reduce resistance to change, finding creative ways of doing things, and so on.

Importance of Leadership

- Clarity and communication
- Motivation
- Change management
- Planning
- Employee relations
- Crisis management

Leadership Traits

- Sympathy
- Steadiness
- Uprightness
- Direction
- Communication
- Flexibility
- Faith and belief
- Complexity resolution
- Strategic action
- Innovation

Leadership Styles

Autocratic Style (Do What I say)

Leader decides and instructs and the subordinates follow and implement. The employees play no role in decision-making.

Participative Style (Let Us Work Together)

- **Consultative:** In this style, leaders take in opinions from the group members before coming to the final decision.
- **Consensual:** These leaders believe in motivating the group members to discuss on the issue and then arrive at a conclusion. These types of leaders assign more weightage to the group opinion in comparison to the consultative leaders.
- **Democratic:** In this style, each of the group members votes before the leader takes any decision. Here the entire authority lies with the group.

Free-rein Style (I Go and You Work)

The leader gives entire freedom to the group members to identify the goals and objectives, take decisions, and resolve issues.

Leadership Models and Theories

Likert's Management System

In this style, the management has a huge impact on the efficiency of the organization. The four systems developed by Likert are as follows:

- Exploitative authoritative
- Benevolent authoritative
- Consultative
- Participative

Managerial Grid

Managerial grid is a graphical representation of two behavioural dimensions of a leader.

- **Concern for people (Y-axis):** Leader accommodates the needs and interests of the team members and gives them priority while making a decision about best means to accomplish a task.
- **Concern for production (X-axis):** Leader lays emphasis on tight schedules and high productivity while making a decision about best means to accomplish a task.

The grid identifies five basic styles of leadership:

- Impoverished management: avoid and escape
- Dictatorial: produce or perish
- Country club: yield and comply
- Team management: contribute and commit
- Middle of the road: balance and compromise·

Situational Leadership Model

Situational leadership theory states that there is no single 'best' style of leadership. Effective leadership is all about setting high expectations and working towards it with the team and group of people they are leading.

Leadership Style and the Work

Fiedler's situational contingency theory holds that group usefulness depends on a leader's style and the demand for that situation. Fiedler's contingency model is a dynamic model where the personal characteristics and motivation of the leader are said to interact with the current situation that the group faces.

Limitations of Fiedler's Theory

- Absence of situational variables
- Uncertainties about LPC Score

(Continued)

(Continued)

Path–Goal Approach

In this approach, a leader's action directly correlates to the approval, keenness, and performance of his/her team members.

The various types of leader's behaviour are depicted as follows:

- The directive path–goal clarifying leader behaviour refers to situations where the leader tracks the follower's progress and tells them how to perform their tasks.
- The achievement-oriented leader behaviour refers to situations where the leader sets high-stake goals for employees, expects them to perform at a high scale.
- The participative leader behaviour involves leaders consulting the group and asking for their suggestion before making a decision.
- The supportive leader behaviour is directed towards showing concern for the group's psychological well-being where work leads to stress.

Trait Theory

Leadership theories revolve around the characteristics of successful and unsuccessful leaders, and the leaders are rated based on these characteristics to assess the probability of their success or failure.

Strengths/Advantages of Trait Theory

- It is naturally pleasing theory.
- Research has validated the foundation and basis of the theory.
- It serves as a yardstick against which the leadership traits of an individual can be assessed.
- It gives a detailed knowledge and understanding of the leader element in the leadership process.

Limitations of the Trait Theory

- Bound to be some subjective judgment.
- List of possible traits tends to be very long.
- Disagreement over which traits are the most important for an effective leader.
- Attempts to relate physical traits, such as height and weight, to effective leadership. Most of these factors relate to situational factors.
- Very complex theory.

Behavioural Theories

Behavioural theory of leadership describes the behaviour of leaders and focuses on making of the leader than ascertaining that leaders are born.

Advantages of Behavioural Theory

- It encourages values of leadership styles with focus on collaboration.
- It promotes participative decision-making and team development.
- It helps managers to evaluate their own style which affects the team's contribution towards organizational goals.
- Also, it helps managers to find the right balance between different styles of leadership.

Contingency Theories

Leader–Member Exchange Theory

This theory focuses on establishing positive relations between the leader and subordinate contributing to organizational success.

- In-group and out-group
- Relationship stages
  - Role-taking
  - Role-making
  - Routinization

Decision Theory/Leader Participation Model

This theory states that the best style of leadership is dependent on the current environment or situation. Experts suggest that there are five different styles of leadership ranging from autocratic to group-based styles under the normative decision-making model formulated by the group.

Transformational Leadership

Transformational leaders motivate followers to change outlook, insight, and impetus to work towards common goals.

Transformational leadership has four components:

- Intellectual stimulation
- Individualized consideration
- Inspirational motivation
- Idealized influence

Transactional Leadership Theory

In this theory, the authority and level of responsibility for the transactional leader are very high and followers have to obey the instructions of the leaders.

The leader and follower always exchange information and ideas pertaining to the attainment of organizational goals and it happens across four dimensions.

- Contingent rewards
- Active management by exception
- Passive management by exception
- Laissez-faire

Leadership Development

Leadership development is referred to as developing the quality of leadership among individuals as well as organization as a whole. The organization which focuses on leadership development should promote the following:

- Initiative thinking
- Personal skills development
- Encouraging a challenging project

CHAPTER 13

Motivation

Learning Objectives

- To understand motivation, its nature, and process with reference to organizational requirements.
- To enrich one's knowledge on types of motivation and to get a fair idea on theories of motivation and evaluate their applicability in today's organization.
- To understand the metrics of motivation and the mathematical deductions based on which employee motivations and outcomes from the motivation can be derived.
- To study equity theory and its applicability to various businesses.
- To understand the importance of employee motivation which has to be incorporated through various schemes at the organizational level for retention and growth.

An Opening Vignette

READY IT wanted a considerable increase in sales of its product Fastsol GIS App. So the management decided to engage and motivate the sales and marketing teams with an incentive. Employees who achieved their goals won 5% of salary as their incentive. All the employees then were engaged in further upheaval of sales in that quarter. Around 98% of the employees signed up for their 'Track-and-locate' feature campaign. The company's sales jumped 13% over the quarter.

India Inc. workers availed long leaves after every two years. They also got long service awards in terms of employee bonus after five years of service. For a project which earned a profit of more than 25% employee performance summed up to 5% of the profit.

At Shimadza Scientific Instruments (Eldersburg, Maryland), outstanding performers are 'promoted' to special assistant to the president for two weeks. 'It is a great ego trip,' says Louis Ratmann, Administration Manager, 'plus the improved understanding of the business demands are worth it.'

At Apple Computer, employees were loaned a computer just two months after joining the company. Their programme called 'Loan to Own' would then give the employees a machine after completion of a year's service. On one Christmas, all employees received a solar-powered calculator and the next year they received FM radio with headphones.

The above are some examples of employee motivation...

Introduction

Motivation is a driving force that creates an urge to take action to achieve our desired goals. There is always a motivating force behind anything we do and it is the intensity of our motivation which determines how well and how fast we succeed at obtaining what we wish to achieve.

Definitions

> *Motivation is the willingness of an individual to respond to organizational requirements in the short run.*
>
> Hodge and Johnson

> *Motivation is a reported urge or tension to move in a given direction or to achieve a certain goal.*
>
> Shartle

> *Motivation refers to the degree of readiness of an organism to pursue some destined goal and implies the determination of the nature and locus of the forces including the degree of readiness.*
>
> Encyclopedia of Management

> *Motivation is the process of attempting to influence others to do your will through possibility of gain of reward.*
>
> Flippo

> *Motivation is an ordered way of explaining why a person elects to channel his energies in one direction rather than in another.*
>
> Owen

Process of Motivation (Cycle of Motivation)

The motivation process starts with a need, an individual's perception of a deficiency that triggers behaviour or drive that is intended at a goal. For example, an employee might feel the need for promotion, recognition, appreciation, challenging work environment, and so on. In order to satisfy these needs, the employee might decide on a particular course of action. If the employee's selected option leads to desired outcome, he/she might feel motivated by the reward to act in a similar manner in the future. However, if an individual's action does not result in the expected reward, he/she is unlikely to repeat the behaviour. Thus, we can say that the reward plays a role of feedback mechanism to facilitate an individual to assess the consequences of the behaviour when considering futures' action.

Motives are believed to be cyclical in nature, they are aroused, they motivate certain behaviour that leads to a goal and subsequently they are shut off. The behaviour that is associated with drive state is called 'instrumental behaviour', because it is instrumental in satisfying a need.

Stages of Motivational Cycle

The process of motivation begins with a drive. The term 'need' is often used to refer to the driving state. A drive is created when an individual feels the need for something that he/she lacks and this creates tension in the individual. This tension in turn creates a driving state in an individual. This state urges an individual to behave in particular manner such that the need can be satisfied.

The second stage of the motivational cycle is the instrumental behaviour. It is instigated by the tension caused due to driving state. When instrumental behaviour leads to achievement of goal, the need is satisfied, which leads to a temporary period of relief. This is the third stage of the motivational cycle (Figure 13.1).

Figure 13.1 Cycle of Motivation

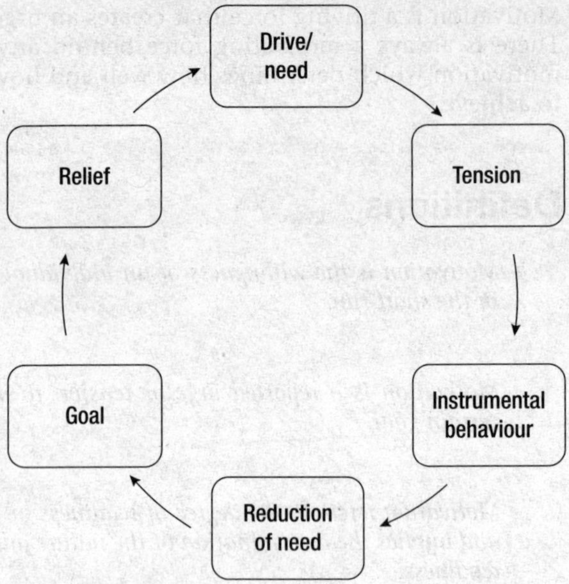

Nature of Motivation

The nature of motivation is explained below:

- **A psychological concept:** Every individual needs to be motivated in order to get the work done from him. But before motivating the individual, it is very essential to understand his psychology so that appropriate motivational technique can be used to create individual's interest in the assigned work. If lessons are taught in a playful manner, a child can be made to concentrate on lessons at school, which instantaneously arouses his interest.
- **Continuous process:** Every employee working in the organization may have different needs and wants, which are not constant and keep on changing. Similarly, the needs of the organization (goals and objectives) also keep on changing. Accordingly, the manager has to keep on motivating the subordinates to achieve these changing needs. Thus, we can say that motivation is a continuous process. For example, in the opening vignette we have discussed that for sales to go up, the organization wanted extra hours of effort from the employees and in return gave 5% compensation in salary for those who could achieve the target.
- **Considers whole individual:** An individual has different needs, which are all interrelated. Thus, the individual as a whole is to be considered for motivation and not as a part.
- **It may be financial or non-financial:** Depending on the employee to be motivated, the company can use either financial or non-financial motivation. Financial motivation includes hike in salary/wages, allowances, bonus, and so on. Non-financial motivation includes increase in responsibility, recognition, participation in the process of decision-making, and so on.
- **It may be positive or negative:** Positive motivation includes rewards for encouraging employees to perform better, for example, promotion, a hike in salary, and so on.

Negative motivation includes an element of fear. Negative motivation makes individuals perform better as they fear being punished if performance is not as per the expectation. For example, demotion, penalties, and so on.

Importance

> **CASE STUDY**
>
> Tata Steel has a course called 'Aspire Knowledge *Manthan*', which facilitates knowledge sharing among supervisors and workers. Its objective is to motivate workers to perform better and enhance their capabilities. Another Tata company, TCS, has a job rotation policy that exposes its employees to new responsibilities, functions, or geographies on a regular basis. Cognizant has introduced the concept of gamification to reduce employee turnover and absenteeism.

The following points explain the importance of motivation:

- **Effective utilization of resources:** The human resources employed in the organization are provided with financial as well as physical resources to achieve the organizational goals. All these resources involve a cost, and thus it is essential that these resources are utilized effectively. Motivation enables the employees to convert physical/financial resources to products/services. This is how motivation helps in effective utilization of resources.
- **Achievement of organizational goals:** Every organization exists to achieve some pre-determined goals and objectives. Thus, it becomes necessary that all the individuals working in the organization are motivated to put in their efforts towards achieving these organizational goals.
- **Improves efficiency of employees:** The work performance does not solely depend on the ability of the employee but also on his willingness to work. Willingness is of no use unless it is converted into action. Motivation creates willingness as well as encourages the employees to initiate actions that help achieve the organizational goals.
- **Reduced employee turnover and absenteeism:** Motivation creates a willingness to work and to perform better. The employees would be satisfied with their own performance and the rewards/appreciation they would get from the organization. This satisfaction further leads to reduced employee turnover and absenteeism.
- **Cordial organizational relations:** A good motivation system can be developed by offering improved working conditions and framing effective incentive plans. Existence of a good motivation system will lead to job satisfaction. This will create an environment of confidence among the employer and the employees. Thus, there would be no or very few conflicts, which would in turn lead to cordial organizational relations.

Types of Motivation

Some of the major types of motivation are as explained below:

- **Intrinsic motivation:** It refers to the motivation that arises from inside of an individual rather than from any external rewards, like monetary incentives or promotion. It basically talks about the motivation that develops from internal rewards (like sense of responsibility, achievement, and so on) or reinforcers (like guilty conscience and so on).

For example, an intrinsically motivated individual may work towards finding solutions to operate in a difficult situation because the challenge of finding the way out develops a sense of achievement within that individual.

A real-world example of intrinsic motivation which drives competence is the learning app Duolingo which in order to keep users occupied uses progress visualization (known as skill trees) to show users their advancement in the lessons. As users become better, they earn experience points that are used to unlock the next level.

Duolingo users possess four 'lives', losing one each time they make a mistake in a program module. Lose all four and you have to start over again. Duolingo currently boasts of 25 million users.

- **Extrinsic motivation:** It refers to the incentives that are external to the individuals like monetary benefits, promotions, and so on. It basically talks about the motivation that develops from external rewards (praise, award, and so on) or reinforcers (like policies and procedures, disciplinary actions, and so on).

For example, a word of appreciation or a hike in salary encourages a person to perform better.

- **Financial motivation:** It means encouraging the employees to perform better by offering the monetary incentives. Monetary incentives increase the purchasing power of an individual and lead to satisfaction since people can satisfy their material needs. Offering monetary incentives proves to be a potentially good option when the workers have to be motivated but is not a very good option when it comes to motivating people at higher levels.

For example, bonus, increment in salary, profit sharing, and so on.

- **Non-financial motivation:** Apart from the monetary incentives, there are several non-monetary incentives that can help in motivating the employees.

For example, job security, recognition, job enrichment, delegation of authority, promotions, and participation in decision-making.

- **Positive motivation:** According to Flipps, 'Positive motivation is the process of attempting to influence the psychological needs of the employees. Positive motivation is based on an optimistic approach'.

For example, salary hike, perks, promotions, recognition, and praise.

- **Negative motivation:** Negative motivation is the process of attempting to influence others to do at your will through the possibility of punishment. It involves using negative incentives in threatening the employees to complete the given task.

For example, demotion, dismissal, transfer, fine, and penalties.

Theories of Motivation

The theories of motivation are classified largely into content and process theories. Content theories deal with an individual's needs and goals and are focused on the factors that motivate an individual. Different theories of motivation that were developed with a 'content' perspective include; Maslow's hierarchy of needs, McClelland's learned needs theory, Alderfer's existence, relatedness, and growth (ERG) theory, Herzberg's two-factor theory, self-determination theory, and temporal motivation theory (TMT).

However, process theories deal with the 'process' of motivation and are concerned with the way in which motivation occurs. Different theories developed with the process approach include equity theory by Adams, expectancy theory by Porter and Lawler, and expectancy theory of motivation by Vroom.

Content Theories of Motivation

CASE STUDY

This is an example of the conceptual model of Maslow's theory applied to a real situation. There was a manufacturing plant in which most of the managers possessed degrees in engineering, finance and pharmacy. These mangers had very little or no training regarding human behaviour. Maslow's model acted as a blueprint and helped them to address the problems of lower productivity issues of lost productivity and unhappy labourers. With the help of this model, managers could identify not only the reasons behind the employees' behaviour but also the actions necessary to change the undesired behaviour.

One day a consultant presented Maslow's theory to the management team of a manufacturing unit. Maslow's hierarchy of needs was used to identify the needs of labours. From the study it was revealed that the labours had a decreased regard towards the traditional techniques of management and that the needs of employees had changed over the years, which in turn was causing unrest among the labours. It was noticed that the older employees were on a lower level of Maslow's scale (physiological and safety needs). But, when the newer generation of employees entered the unit, the management started facing resistance since the new workers had a higher level of education as compared to the older employees. The newer employees no longer sought satisfaction of their lower level survival needs. The newer generation had needs that correspond to the higher level needs of Maslow's hierarchy for example; recognition and personal growth. The consultant then revealed the findings of his study to the management of the firm. These finding helped the management team to solve the problems and settle the unrest.

Content theory or need theories are considered to be earliest theories associated with the concept of motivation. It outlines 'what' motivates an individual, which means it helps to identify the individual necessities and requirements that motivate a person. Each of these theories is explained in detail below.

Maslow's Hierarchy of Needs

In 1943, Abraham Maslow proposed a theory 'Maslow's Hierarchy of Needs', in a paper titled 'A Theory of Human Motivation'. To describe the array of human motivation, Maslow used the terms physiological, safety, belongingness and love, esteem, and self-actualization (Figure 13.2).

Maslow's hierarchy of needs is usually depicted in the form of pyramid that has

Figure 13.2 Maslow's Hierarchy of Needs

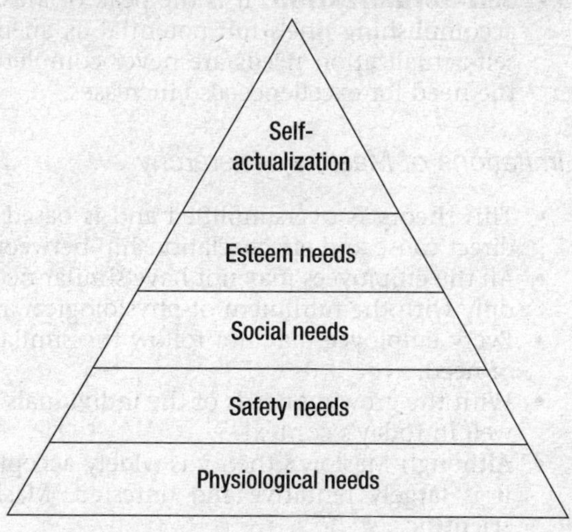

Table 13.1 Examples of Maslow's Five Basic Needs

Need	*Examples*
Self-actualization	Justice, wisdom, truth, and so on
Esteem	Self-respect, independence, self-confidence, and so on
Social	Love, affection, care, belongingness, friendship, and so on
Security	Job security, health security, and so on
Physiological	Air, water, food, shelter, sexual instinct, and so on

five layers, most basic needs being at the bottom. The first four layers are known as 'deficiency needs' or 'd-needs'. According to Maslow if basic needs are not met, the individual will not have a strong craving for the higher level needs. The five layers are explained in detail (Table 13.1):

- **Physiological needs:** If these needs are not fulfilled, the human body cannot function properly and going further human survival also becomes impossible. Thus, these needs are considered to be most vital and must be fulfilled first.
- **Safety needs:** Once the physiological needs are satisfied, the safety needs start dominating the behavioural aspect of an individual. Safety needs include
    - Physical safety
    - Economic safety
    - Environmental safety
    - Emotional safety
- **Social needs:** The next layer of pyramid portrays the social needs of an individual. Social needs are related to relational aspects and involve a sense of belongingness. Social needs include
    - Need for love
    - Need for belonging
- **Esteem needs:** After a person experiences a sense of belongingness, the desire to feel valued develops. Esteem needs may be either internal or external. Internal esteem needs include confidence, self-respect, freedom, and so on. External esteem needs consist of social status, recognition, and so on.
- **Self-actualization:** It is the peak of Maslow's hierarchy of needs. It is the journey of accomplishing one's full potential as an individual. Unlike the other level needs, the self-actualization needs are never completely satisfied; with the psychological growth, the need for excellence also increases.

Limitations of Maslow's Hierarchy

- This theory is oversimplified and is based on only human needs. It fails to reflect the direct cause and effect relationship between need and behaviour.
- All the employees may not have similar needs. Most of the employees may be contented only with the fulfilment of physiological and security needs.
- Every employee may not follow the similar pattern as suggested by Maslow's hierarchy of need.
- With the growing needs of the individuals the assumptions of this theory may not hold well in today's context.
- Although Maslow's theory is widely accepted, there is very little evidence to support it. It is largely tentative and untested. Maslow's writings are more philosophical than scientific.

- To Maslow's theory another dimension was added by Herzberg that was the degree of dissatisfaction in employees. Herzberg listed these factors as supervision problems, company policy, and relationship with peers and seniors, working conditions, salary, and security.
- Satisfaction and dissatisfaction do not form a continuum; hence, to improve productivity and attitudes, managers must identify and attend to both and not make false deduction that increase in satisfaction leads to a decrease in dissatisfaction.
- Tesco uses elements of Herzberg's theory to evaluate satisfaction and dissatisfaction level amongst its employees. The company motivates the individuals by involving employees in decision-making to the point that staff can also voice their input on pay rises, and so on. It is said that Tesco workers even get a chance to give their choices when bistro menus are designed, which gives them a sense of satisfaction.
- From a study conducted by the University of Malaysia it was found that the major factors determining job satisfaction for staff members were salary, policy, and administration and the factors which caused dissatisfaction were lack of personal growth and achievement in the professional front. Below we discuss the tenets of Herzberg two-factor theory.

Herzberg's Two-factor Theory

This theory was developed by Frederick Herzberg, a psychologist. The two-factor theory is also known as Herzberg's motivation-hygiene theory or dual-factor theory. This theory is based on the analysis done by Herzberg after interviewing 203 accountants and engineers in Pittsburgh, Pennsylvania.

The theory determines that some specific factors lead to job satisfaction, while there are other job factors that prevent dissatisfaction. According to Herzberg, the contrast of 'satisfaction' is 'no satisfaction' and the contrast of 'dissatisfaction' is 'no dissatisfaction'.

Herzberg classified the job factors into hygiene factors and motivating factors and suggested a two-step approach to understanding employee motivation and satisfaction (Figure 13.3).

- **Hygiene factors:** These factors do not actually act as motivation, but, if absent result in demotivation, like
  - working conditions
  - job security
  - fringe benefits
  - company policies, and so on

Figure 13.3 Herzberg's Two-step Approach

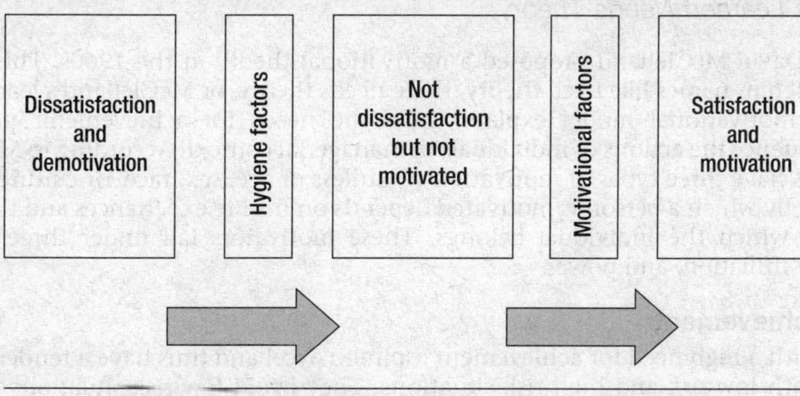

- **Motivational factors:** The presence of these factors creates a positive job satisfaction, like
    - Recognition
    - Responsibility
    - Status
    - Personal growth, and so on

Limitations of Two-factor Theory

- It does not take into consideration the situational variables.
- The theory assumes that greater satisfaction leads to greater productivity.
- The theory ignores blue-collar workers.
- No comprehensive measure of satisfaction was used. An employee may find his job acceptable regardless of the fact that he may dislike a portion of his job.
- The two-factor theory is not free from bias as it is largely based on the reaction of the respondents. For example, an individual might blame external factors, such as salary structure, company policies, and peer relationship for dissatisfaction. On the other hand, he might give credit to oneself for the satisfaction factor at work.

Next, we move on to discuss learned theory of needs by McClellands starting with an example. The theory will bring in clarity on various types of motivational indicators for different categories of employees.

CASE STUDY

An employee in the IT department of an organization created an application which could accurately post advertisements of internal jobs based on an employee's preference. The top management of the organization directed the senior manager of the IT department to applaud the employee's effort for the excellent application made.

So, the employee during the staff meeting was congratulated for his achievement in front of the team but he became extremely embarrassed with this so called hullabaloo.

What Did Actually Go Wrong?

It is said that employees respond to feedback and praises in different ways. David McClelland's human motivation theory gives way of identifying people's motivating drivers. In this case, according to McClelland's theory, the team member's motivational driver was affiliation, which meant that he never wanted to stand out in a crowd so either a private feedback or a personal email would have been apt in this situation. The succeeding section explains learned theory more elaborately.

McClelland's Learned Needs Theory

Psychologist David McClelland proposed a motivational theory in the 1960s. This theory is known by different names like need theory, three needs theory, or McClelland's learned needs theory. This motivational model explains how the needs for achievement, power, and affiliation influence the actions of individuals in managerial context. According to McClelland, all individuals have three types of motivation regardless of age, sex, race, or culture. The type of motivation by which a person is motivated depends on his life experiences and the opinion of culture to which the individual belongs. These motivators fall under three categories achievement, affiliation, and power.

Need for Achievement

Individuals with a high need for achievement aspire to excel and thus have a tendency to stay away from both low-risk and high-risk situations. They avoid low-risk situations since they believe that success achieved easily is not worth. According to achievers, high-risk projects are outcome of luck rather than ones efforts. Achievers expect regular feedback with an intention to keep an eye on the progress of their achievements. Generally, these kinds of individuals prefer either to work alone or with other high achievers. They take calculated risks to achieve their goals.

Need for Affiliation

Individuals having high need for affiliation call for sound associations with other people and feel the need to be accepted by other people. Due to their tendency to be liked by others they often go along with their group. They believe in collaborating with other group members rather than competing with them. They have a tendency to conform to the norms of their work group. Individuals having a high need for affiliation prefer tasks that provide noteworthy personal interaction.

Need for Power

An individual's need for power may be of two types personal or institutional. Those with a need for personal power wish to direct others. Such a need can be perceived negatively by other group members. Individuals with a need for institutional power wish to direct the efforts of others to achieve the goals of the institution. Individuals desiring high need for institutional power are likely to be more effective than those with a high need for personal power (Figure 13.4).

Implications for Management

Individuals possessing different needs need to be motivated differently. Those having a high need for achievement must be given challenging tasks with achievable goals. A person with high need for affiliation can prove to be a good group performer, thus can perform best in-group tasks, whereas those with high need for power must be given an opportunity to lead or manage others.

Alderfer's ERG Theory

Alderfer refined Maslow's hierarchy of needs theory to synchronization in an article titled 'An Empirical Test of a New Theory of Human Need' in the year 1969 (https://www.mindtools.

Figure 13.4 McClelland's Learned Needs Theory

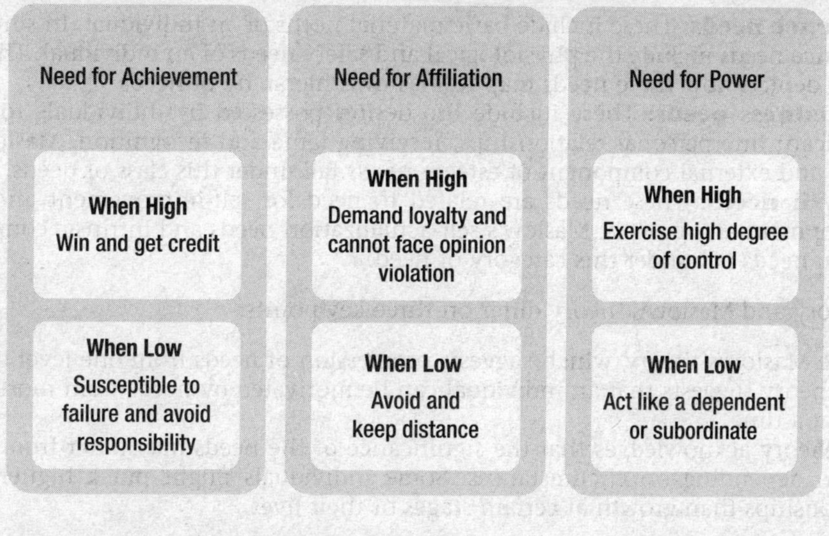

Figure 13.5 Relation Between Maslow's Hierarchy of Needs and ERG Theory

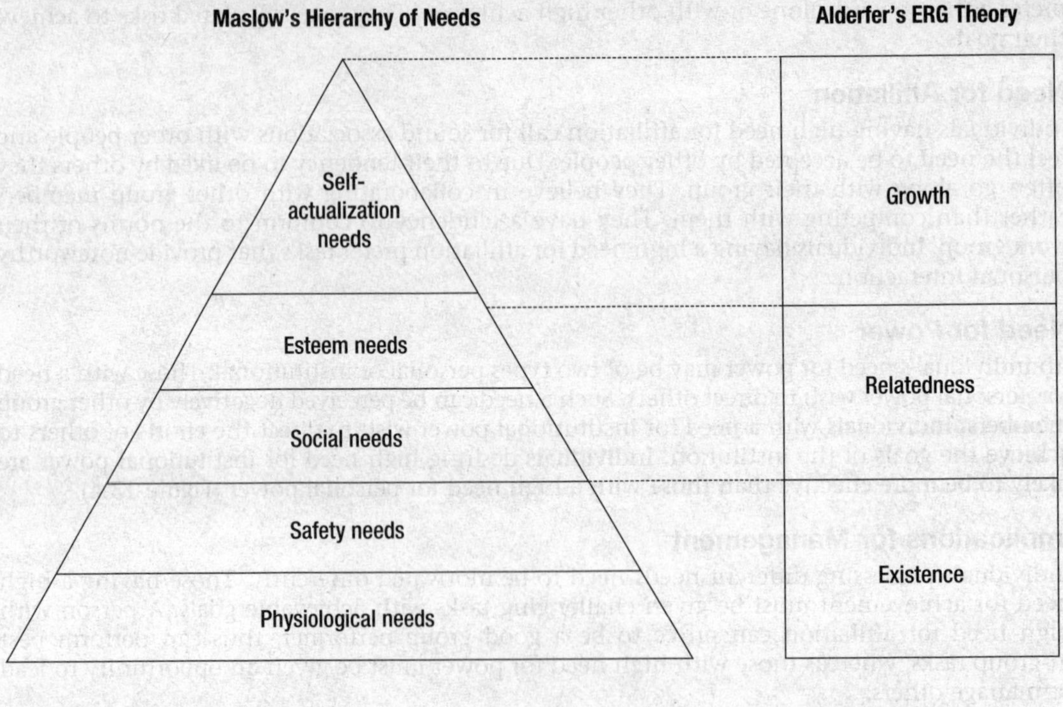

com/pages/article/newTMM_78.htm, accessed on 26 February 2016). His theory is called ERG theory of motivation. He compressed Maslow's hierarchy of needs into three simpler classes of needs namely Existence, Relatedness and Growth. For example, if an individual is working and needs the financial security in order to improve other costs and expenses, they might be in the 'existence' needs of the model. For an employee who prospers on interpersonal connection and acknowledgement from others, their needs are in the 'relatedness' sector. Finally, the needs for reflective 'growth' indicate that an individual has reached a level where they desire to grow personally in the sphere of professional development and enhancement (Figure 13.5).

- **Existence needs:** These include basic material needs of an individual. In simple words existence needs include the physiological and safety needs of an individual. The diagram below depicts how these needs map to Maslow's hierarchy of needs.
- **Relatedness needs:** These include the desires possessed by individuals to maintain significant interpersonal relationships, receiving fame and recognition. Maslow's social needs and external component of esteem needs fall under this class of needs.
- **Growth needs:** These needs are related to need for self-improvement and personal development and growth. Maslow's self-actualization needs and intrinsic component of esteem needs fall under this category of need.

ERG theory and Maslow's theory differ on three key points:

- Unlike Maslow's theory, which suggests progression of needs from one level to another, ERG theory suggests that an individual can be motivated by needs from more than one level at a time.
- ERG theory acknowledges that the significance of the needs may differ from person to person depending on circumstances. Some individuals might put a higher value on relationships than growth at certain stages of their lives.

- It has a 'frustration-regression' element. This means that that if the needs at one of the higher levels remain unsatisfied, individuals become frustrated and pursue lower-level needs again.

Self-determination Theory

The self-determination theory of motivation was developed by psychologists Edward Deci and Richard Ryan. According to this theory, people are driven by a need to grow and achieve fulfilment. The basic assumption of self-determination theory is that individuals are actively directed towards growth. Acquiring mastery over challenges and taking in new experiences are necessary for developing a cohesive sense of self.

Although people are often motivated by extrinsic motivation factors like money, prizes, and praise, self-determination theory focuses mainly on intrinsic motivation factors like a desire to gain knowledge or autonomy.

For example self-determination theory applied for the education sector is used primarily for promoting an interest for learning amongst the students, valuing their education, and being confident of their own capabilities which result in high-quality learning, understanding, and personal growth.

Self-determination theory acknowledges three basic psychological needs that must be fulfilled in order to promote well-being and health; these needs can be applied universally. However, some may be more prominent as compared with others at certain times and will be expressed differently based on experience, time, or culture.

- **Competence:** Try to control the outcome and experience mastery.
- **Relatedness:** It is the universal desire to interact, be connected to, and experience a sensc of belongingness.
- **Autonomy:** It is the universal urge to have control on onc's own behaviours and goals.

According to Ryan and Deci, when people understand these three things, they become self-determined and feel intrinsically motivated to pursue the things that interest them.

In order to fulfil these needs, it is necessary to realize that the psychological growth described by self-determination theory does not occur automatically.

Although individuals might be directed towards such growth, it requires unremitting sustenance. According to Deci and Ryan, social support is the key. Through our relationships and interactions with others, we can either foster or ruin well-being and personal growth.

Other factors that can help or hinder the three elements needed for growth are explained below.

According to Deci, giving individuals extrinsic rewards for already intrinsically motivated behaviour can undermine autonomy. As the behaviour becomes progressively more controlled by the external rewards, individuals begin to develop a feeling of less control on their own behaviour and intrinsic motivation diminishes.

Deci also suggests that presenting unexpected positive encouragement and feedback on an individual's performance can add to intrinsic motivation as this kind of feedback helps individuals to feel more competent (Figure 13.6).

Figure 13.6 Self-determination Theory

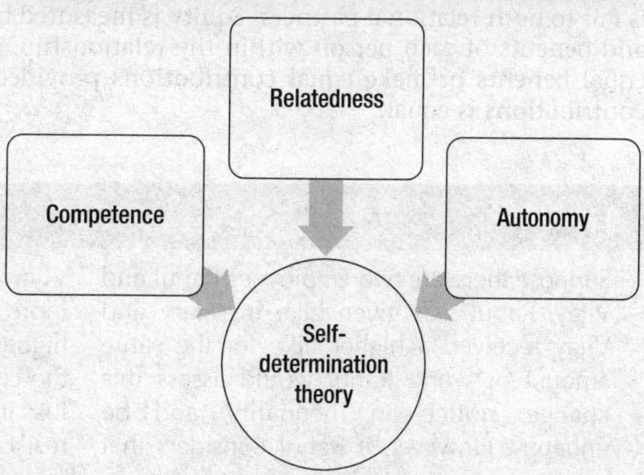

Temporal Motivation Theory

Piers Steel and Cornelius J. Konig (2006) developed an integrative motivational theory known as TMT. This theory emphasizes 'time' as a crucial motivational factor and focuses on the impact of deadlines on the allocation of attention to particular tasks. According to this theory, the perceived worth or benefit of an activity increases exponentially as a deadline nears. TMT is particularly useful for understanding human behaviours like procrastination and goal setting.

The theory suggests that an individual's motivation for a task can be derived using the following formula:

$$\text{Motivation} = (\text{Expectancy} \times \text{Value})/1+ (\text{Impulsiveness} \times \text{Delay})$$

where motivation is the desire for a particular outcome; expectancy is the probability of success; value is the reward linked to the outcome; impulsiveness is individual's sensitivity to delay; and delay is the time to realization.

Process Theories of Motivation

Process theory is a commonly used form of scientific research study in which events or occurrences are said to be the result of certain input states leading to a certain outcome (output) state, following a set process (source: https://en.wikipedia.org/wiki/Process_theory, accessed on 3 March 2016).

Process theory proposes that if an outcome is to be duplicated the process that originally created it also needs to be duplicated and that there are certain constant essential conditions to achieve the outcome. The process theories provide an explanation for 'how' something happens.

Equity Theory by Adams

John Stacey Adams, a workplace and behavioural psychologist, developed equity theory of motivation in 1963. He asserted that employees seek to maintain equity between the inputs that they bring to a job and the outcomes that they receive from it against the perceived inputs and outcomes of others (Adams, 1965). The belief is that individuals value fair treatment and this is what causes them to be motivated to keep the fairness maintained within the relationships of their colleagues and the organization. The structure of equity at the workplace depends on the ratio of inputs to outcomes. Inputs are the contributions made by the employees towards the organization.

According to equity theory, an individual who perceives himself as either undervalued or overvalued will experience distress, and that this distress leads to efforts to restore equity within the relationship. The focus of this theory is to identify if the distribution of resources is fair to both relational partners. Equity is measured by comparing the ratios of contributions and benefits of each person within the relationship. It is not necessary that the partners get equal benefits or make equal contributions provided the ratio between these benefits and contributions is equal.

EXAMPLE

Suppose there are two employees Rahul and Vijay. Rahul was given hike in salary and Vijay received a higher hike for the same amount of work. Rahul would assess this change, notice an inequality, and be unhappy. However, if Rahul considers that Vijay was given more responsibility hence more work, and had hence received a higher hike in salary then Rahul may assess the change and conclude that there was no loss in equality status, and hence would not resist the change.

An individual will believe that he is treated fairly if he perceives the ratio of his inputs to his outcomes is equal to those around him. This can be illustrated by the following equation:

$$\frac{\text{Individual's outcomes}}{\text{individual's own inputs}} = \frac{\text{relational partner's outcomes}}{\text{relational partners inputs}}$$

- **Inputs:** Inputs are defined as each participant's contributions to the relational exchange and are viewed as entitling him/her to rewards or costs. The inputs that a participant contributes to a relationship can be either assets (entitling him/her to rewards) or liabilities (entitling him/her to costs). Individual traits, such as boorishness and cruelty, are seen as liabilities entitling the possessor to costs (Walster, Traupmann, & Walster, 1978). Inputs typically include the following:
    - Effort
    - Time
    - Determination
    - Enthusiasm
    - Loyalty
    - Adaptability
    - Flexibility
    - Commitment
    - Tolerance
    - Skill
    - Personal sacrifice
    - Support from co-workers and colleagues
    - Education
    - Experience
    - Hard Work
    - Ability
    - Trust in superiors
- **Outcomes:** Outcomes are defined as the positive and negative consequences that an individual perceives a participant has incurred as a consequence of his/her relationship with another. Generally when the ratio of inputs to outcomes is close, employees are satisfied with their job. Outcomes can be both tangible and intangible. Typical outcomes include the following:
    - Job security
    - Salary
    - Expenses
    - Recognition
    - Responsibility
    - Sense of achievement
    - Praise
    - Employee benefit
    - Reputation

If people do not receive the above as per market standards, then their motivation levels decrease and they seek for change in every professional aspect.

Propositions of Equity Theory

- Individuals try to capitalize on their results (where results are rewards minus the expenses).
- Groups can capitalize on joint rewards by developing systems for justifiably distributing rewards and expenses among its members. A system of equity develops within groups, and members try to convince other members to agree and adhere to these systems. The only way groups can persuade members to justifiably behave is by showing the advantages of

behaving equitably. Thus, groups will generally compensate members who treat others justifiably and generally raise costs for those members who treat others inequitably.

- Individuals tend to get highly disturbed if they find themselves in inequitable relationships. According to equity theory, a person who gets 'too much' and the person who gets 'too little' feel distressed by an equal measure where the measure can be guilt or shame, anger or humiliation.
- Individuals who perceive that they are in an inequitable relationship attempt to eliminate their distress by restoring equity. The greater the inequity, the more distress people feel and the more they try to restore equity (Walster et al., 1978).

Three Primary Equity Theory Assumptions Applied to Most Businesses

The three primary assumptions are as follows:

- Employees expect a return in proportion to their contribution, referred to as the 'equity norm'.
- Employees determine the equitable returns on the basis of efforts expended and outcomes achieved in proportion to their co-workers. This perception is known as 'social comparison'.
- Employees who recognize as being in an inequitable condition will establish inequity either by distorting their efforts and/or outcomes otherwise known as cognitive distortion and this they do by directly altering inputs/outputs, or by leaving the organization (Carrell & Dittrich, 1978).

Implications for Managers

Equity theory has several repercussions for business leaders:

- People weigh the totals of their contributions and rewards. This means the mother of an infant may settle for lower monetary reward in return for more flexible working hours.
- Different employees might attach different perspectives to the contributions and results. For example, two or more employees having equal experience and skills and contributing for the same work and for the same pay may have varied insights into equality of the deal.
- Employees also adjust to purchasing power and local market conditions. Thus, a car driver living in a small town in India may accept lower compensation than a driver living in metros such as Mumbai, Hyderabad, Bangalore, and so on.
- Although it may be acceptable for more senior-level employees to receive a higher pay, there are boundaries to the equilibrium in the scales of equity and employees can find disproportionate executive pay discouraging.
- Staff's perception on contributions and results may be incorrect, and observations need to be managed effectively.
- An employee who thinks he is getting overpaid may also adjust the values that he attributes to his own personal inputs and might internalize a sense of supremacy, which can actually decrease his efforts.

Expectancy Theory of Motivation

Victor Vroom from the Yale School of Management proposed an expectancy theory in 1964. Vroom emphasizes on outcomes and results, and not on needs unlike Maslow and Herzberg.

The theory states that the intensity of a tendency to perform in a particular manner is dependent on the intensity of an expectation that the performance will be followed by a certain outcome and on the appeal of the outcome for the individual.

The expectancy theory states that employees' motivation is an outcome to what extent the employee wants to get rewarded (valence), that the added efforts will lead to expected performance (expectancy), and that the expected performance will finally lead to the reward (instrumentality). In brief, valence is the importance for the employee about the expected outcome. It is just the expected and not the actual satisfaction that an employee expects to receive after achieving the goals.

Expectancy is the belief that better efforts will result in better performance. Expectancy is influenced by factors such as possession of appropriate skills and capabilities for performing at the job, availability of correct resources, availability of crucial information, and getting the required support for completing the job.

Instrumentality is the trust that if an individual performs well in the organization, then an effective outcome exists. Instrumentality is affected by factors such as trust in the individuals who choose who receives what outcome and lucidity of association between performance and outcomes. Thus, the expectancy theory concentrates on the following three relationships:

- **Effort–performance relationship:** What is the probability that the individual's effort be recognized in his performance appraisal?
- **Performance–reward relationship:** It indicates that how much the employee believes that he will get a fair performance appraisal and the organizational rewards.
- **Rewards–personal goals relationship:** It is said that rewards encourage employees to work towards their personal goals. Vroom stated that motivational force can be calculated using the formula given below:

$$\text{Motivational Force} = \text{Expectancy} \times \text{Instrumentality} \times \text{Valence}$$

EXAMPLE

Consider the sales target to be achieved for a particular product, as stated in the opening vignette, for the company READY IT. For sales and marketing teams, to get a 5% salary rise on achieving sales target was an attractive option (valence 0.9 and expectancy 0.9) and they were highly optimistic that it would work out based on their previous attempts. By applying the formula, we see that the motivational force is very strong.

$$\text{Motivational Force} = 0.9 \times 0.9 = 0.81.$$

The range for the various components of motivation is shown in Table 13.2.

According to Vroom, employees consciously decide whether to perform a job. This decision completely depends on the employee's motivation level (Figure 13.7), which instead depends on three factors of expectancy, valence, and instrumentality.

Table 13.2 Expectancy Theory: Components of Motivation and Their Range

Component	*Range*	*Range Definition*
Expectancy	0 to 1	0 = perform unsuccessfully 1 = perform successfully
Instrumentality	0 to 1	0 = outcome independent of performance 1 = outcome dependent on performance
Valence	−1 to +1	− = avoidance of outcome 0 = indifference + = satisfactory outcome

Figure 13.7 Expectancy Theory of Motivation

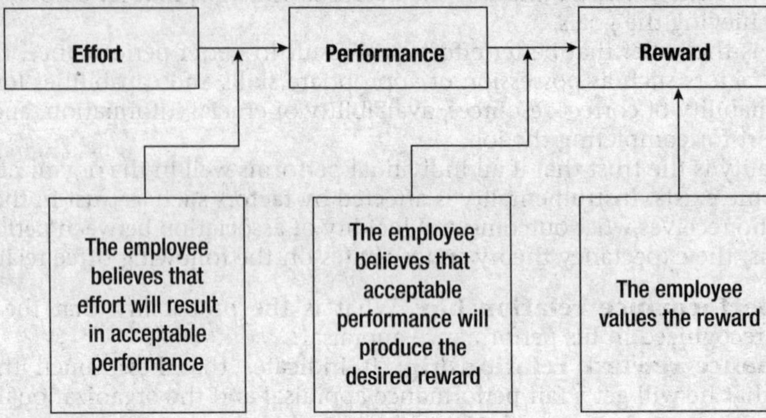

Advantages of Expectancy Theory

It is based on a self-interested individual who expects to gain maximum satisfaction and in turn minimize dissatisfaction.

- This theory focuses upon the expectations and perception; the real and actual is trivial.
- It highlights rewards or pay-offs or the other related aspects.
- It focuses on psychological indulgence where the final notion of employee is to achieve.
- Extreme benefits and least discomfort.

Limitations of Expectancy Theory

The expectancy theory seems to be idealistic as very few individuals attain high degree of correlation between performance and rewards.

The application and implementation of this theory is limited as reward is not directly correlated with performance in many organizations. It is relevant with other parameters as well, such as position, effort, responsibility, education, and so on.

Implications of the Expectancy Theory

Managers can synchronize the expected outcomes to the desired performance levels.

Managers must ensure that the employees achieve their aimed performance levels in a simplistic manner.

On the basis of performance evaluation, deserving employees must be rewarded for their exceptional performance.

The reward system must be free from partial and biased decisions, ultimately making it fair in an organization.

Organizations must evolve into designing dynamic and challenging tasks for the employees. Employees' motivation level should be persistently evaluated and analysed through various techniques, such as questionnaire, personal interviews, and so on.

Goal-setting Theory of Motivation

The goal-setting theory of motivation was introduced by American psychologist Edwin Locke. In his theory, he stated the essential linkage of the setting of goals to the task performance. His theory states that higher and better task performances are a result of contribution of complex and challenging goals along with appropriate feedback. In other words, goals display and give path to an employee about what needs to be done and how much efforts are required to do it. The important features of the goal-setting theory are as follows:

- The willingness to work towards achieving a particular goal is the root of job motivation. Clear, specific, and complex goals are greater motivating factors than simple, general, and unclear goals.
- Specific and clear goals lead to greater result and best performance. Non-messed, easily measurable, and clear goals along with deadline for completion avoid misunderstanding.
- Goals set should be realistic as well as challenging. It provides assurance that one can gain a certain amount of pride and success on achieving them, which sets him up for success of the next goal. The higher the complexity and realism in the goal, the more intense is the success and higher is the enthusiasm for obtaining it.
- Feedback on outputs gives direction to the employee behaviour and contributes to better performance than an absence of feedback. Feedback is means of getting focus, making specifications, and regulating goal complexities. It is very useful in getting employees to work with more dynamism and leads to greater job satisfaction.
- The participation of employees in goals is not always desirable.
- Goal-setting plays an important role in making a goal acceptable and it leads to more involvement.

Goal-setting theory has certain eventualities such as

- **Self-efficiency:** Self-efficiency is one's belief and faith that he has capability of doing task. Higher level of self-efficiency ensures the greater involvement of efforts by an individual when doing complex tasks. The lower the level of self-efficiency, the less is involvement of efforts by the individual.
- **Goal commitment:** This theory assumes that the individual is involved in the goal and will not leave the goal. The varied factors on which the goal commitment is dependent upon are the following:
    - Goals are made open, known, and broadcasted.
    - Goals should be self-implied and not assigned by another individual.
    - Goals made by an individual should possess the consistency and vision of organizational goals.

Advantages of Goal-setting Theory

- The theory is a kind of mechanism which can raise the incentives of employees to get work done with increasing speed along with steady effectiveness.
- Goal setting raises performance levels not only by producing increasing motivation and efforts, but also through increasing and improving the quality of feedback.

Limitations of Goal-setting Theory

- At times organizational goals and managerial goals do not match. And ultimately it has hampering effect on performance if it is used to spread incompatible action drift.
- Setting of difficult and complex goals leads to danger zone.
- Employee with lack of skills and competency to perform work to be done for goal affects success of goal setting and performance goes down.
- There is no strong justification or evidence to prove that goal-setting theory by Locke is responsible for improving job satisfaction.

Theory X and Theory Y of Motivation

Human behaviour, like perception, has two contradictory aspects: pessimistic (negative) behaviour of the employee and optimistic (positive) one, former called as theory X and the latter theory Y.

Table 13.3 Theory X and Theory Y of Motivation

Theory X (Pessimistic Views)	*Theory Y (Optimistic Views)*
Attitude negative: Do not like work and find it boring	**Attitude positive:** Like work and take interest in learning
Direction: To be forced to take effort	**Direction:** To take effort by oneself
Responsibility/ownership: Avoided	**Responsibility/ownership:** Self imposed
Motivation: Material gains lead to motivation only	**Motivation:** Self-motivated under healthy environment
Creativity: Not encouraged by self and others	**Creativity:** Encouraged by self and others

It was initiated in 1960 by Douglas McGregor. According to McGregor, theory X and theory Y are based on certain assumptions featured in Table 13.3.

Assumptions: Theory X

- On an average, employees resist work and will try avoiding it whenever possible.
- Employees emphasize on job security being less ambitious.
- For the dislike of employee towards his work, he must be mandated with protocols and warned with punishment so as to achieve desired goals and targets.
- The managers adopt a more dictatorial style.
- Employees do not easily accept change.
- Employees usually dislike responsibilities.
- An average employee always expects a formal guidance.

Assumptions: Theory Y

- Employees can perceive work normal and utilize physical and mental efforts in an inherent manner in their jobs.
- Employees may not always need to be threatened by external control, but a sense of self-direction and self-motivation exists if they are committed to achieve organizational objectives.
- Rewards at job are motivating and lead to more loyal employees.
- An employee can learn to identify and uphold the responsibility and sometimes to obtain the same.
- The employees may explore their skills and competencies.
- Their logical capabilities, if completely utilized, may lead to having a resourceful and worth employee for identifying and resolving multiple issues rising in and out in the organization.

Thus, we can say that theory X presents a pessimistic view of employees' nature and behaviour at work, while theory Y presents an optimistic view of the employees' nature and behaviour at work.

McGregor states that theory Y is comparatively valid implementing than theory X. Hence, he has encouraged team building, responsible and brain storming jobs, and a joint participation in the decision-making process of the organization

Implications of Theory X and Theory Y

- Employees being the most valuable assets of the organization, theory X is very less preferred today. Theory X leads to exercising tight control and supervision. It indicates the reluctance of the employees towards the organizational changes and hence does not encourage innovation and creativity.

- A plethora of organizations today are using theory Y. As theory Y implies that managers should encourage an optimistic work environment, providing opportunities to employees for taking initiative and being self-motivated. Employees should be given equal importance and opportunities towards the contribution to organizational enhancement.
- Theory Y expresses a distributed sense of power, teamwork, and participative decision-making in an organization. Theory Y elaborates on how an employee can make noteworthy contributions to an organization. It synchronizes and harmonizes employee's needs and aspirations with organizational needs and aspirations.
- This chapter summarizes on the need and importance of motivation and clarifies the theories of motivation laid down by management gurus.

CASE STUDY ON MOTIVATION

Shekhar Jaiswal joined ISIC Computers after some years at CITTI as he thought that the company would offer better career prospects, since it was a bigger company than CITTI. Although Shekhar had spent some of his best years there, he realized that to grow further in his field, he would have to join a bigger company, and preferably face some good clients on an international platform and he was sure he would excel in his own position.

Shekhar joined as a senior programmer at ISIC and was immediately put on client's side operations and there was more than a slim chance that he would be sent to the United States or the UK on a project. Shekhar was very excited about his new job.

He joined Radhika's team handling the US clients and had met Radhika during the orientation sessions. His team members seemed warm and friendly, and comfortable with their work. Shekhar in his Initial days hardly had time to interact with his boss, so out of curiosity wanting to know more about his boss, he asked his team members one day about her, to which they replied that Radhika was a non-interfering type of a person and let them carry on the way they wanted.

At CITTI, Shekhar had a very dynamic and considerate boss who was like a mentor for him and his entire team. The boss strongly believed in discourse, discussion and dialogue and would set up frequent brain storming session and let the team discover ideas, if any, through discussion and experience.

He rarely held an individual member of his team responsible for failure or success, which later Shekhar found was not the case with Radhika. In his first week at work, he found the atmosphere at the office a bit dull. However, he was quite excited. His team had been assigned a new project and was facing a few glitches with the new software but he had some solutions with him.

He wanted to discuss these on top priority with Radhika and was confident that Radhika would be happy to hear the solutions but this did not come true as Radhika showed no interest in hearing him, the day they all sat for a meeting to resolve the issues. Instead, she gave solutions which she thought were right and thought it was a waste of time asking the team for better ideas.

Shekhar felt his heart sink but again stood up thinking that he could bring some changes in the environment but Radhika was not someone who could be so easily handled. While she was efficient at what she did and extremely intelligent, she had no time for her subordinates and whenever schedules and deadlines were not met she would just put the blame on them.

Shekhar's motivation levels went down steadily and he started losing interest in work. Slowly his performance suffered and from being someone with substantial potential, Shekhar was now in danger of losing his sharpness.

Questions for Discussion

1. What, according to you, were the reasons for Shekhar's disillusionment? Answer the question using Maslow's hierarchy of needs.

Model answer: Referring to Maslow's hierarchy of needs, Shekhar's social needs were not satisfied. He received love, affection, recognition, independence in his former organization, which substantiates Maslow's hierarchy of security, social, and esteem needs, and his former boss was very adept in motivating him from within (intrinsic motivation) by making him realize in self that he bore substantial responsibility and ownership for his tasks. Shekhar had achieved targets in his former company and was rated as a top performer with high potential and had even reached the stage of self-actualization, where he would compare his past performances to his current ones but the current company environment did not allow him to do so and he was strongly missing the support of his boss. The contribution of his previous boss had worked wonders energizing his motivation levels.

2. What should Sekhar do to resolve his situation? What can a team leader do to ensure high levels of motivation among his/her team members?

Model answer: There are possible solution options for Shekhar to adopt. First is to motivate oneself intrinsically and then to set one's own goal and work towards it as has been stated under the goal-setting theory of motivation.

He should also form a team of his own at QUITO collating all team members working on his project and then distribute responsibilities informally to make them feel good for the ownership of tasks allocated and resolve all the minor issues cropping up with his team, instead of taking them every time to Radhika. This would be apt for him because of his experiential years as a team lead at his previous workplace. It will make the team also feel that they have somebody who could guide and mentor them and give both Sekhar and his team, the confidence of working together. Motivation could also be derived from the team mates by conducting special interactive sessions where business ideas would flow, get challenged, be appreciated by colleagues, and so on.

A team leader should use both the intrinsic and extrinsic methods of motivation, should see that as per Maslow's hierarchy the resources needs are met and guide them to adopt the goal-setting theory of motivation.

Summary

The chapter takes the reader through the nature, process, and types of motivation and gives him a fair idea on motivation theories and metrics of motivation, and their applicability from organizational perspectives. It provides an insight on the importance of employee motivation and the aspects of implementation in relation to inducing higher level of motivation amongst employees for organizational benefit, productivity, and increased employee retention.

Exercise

Objective Questions

1. Motivation is

   - psychological concept
   - continuous process
   - positive or negative
   - all of the above

2. Intrinsic motivation refers to the motivation that arises from inside of an individual rather than from any external rewards.

   - True
   - False

3. ______ is a kind of mechanism which can raise the incentives of employees to get work done with increasing speed along with steady effectiveness.

   - Theory X and Y
   - Expectancy theory
   - Goal-setting theory
   - None of the above

4. Two-factor theory was given by

   - Frederick Herzberg
   - David McClelland
   - Clayton Alderfer
   - None of the above

5. ______ is the belief that better efforts will result in better performance

   - Expectancy
   - Outcome
   - Competency
   - Instrumentality

6. According to McGregor, under theory Y creativity is not encouraged by self and others.

   - True
   - False

7. ________ are related to relational aspects and involve a sense of belongingness.

   - Safety needs
   - Social needs
   - Esteem needs
   - Self-actualization

8. Integrative motivational theory is also called TMT

   - True
   - False

9. Which of these has a 'frustration-regression' element?

   - Safety needs
   - Social needs
   - Growth needs
   - Self-actualization

10. Job security, health security, and so on come under

    - Security needs
    - Social needs
    - Esteem needs
    - Self-actualization

CASE STUDY

Jennifer Vas used to work in Zenich Solutions and joined Trigen Solutions in March as a programmer. Jennifer was career-aspirant. Zenich Solutions is a relatively small company. Jenifer considered that Zenich offer more opportunities as it was growing rapidly compared to Trigen Solutions. She enjoyed working at Zenich, but she believed that it was Trigen which could provide her more opportunities because it was a bigger company and she might get a chance to work on international projects as well. She was sure about doing her best at the new company, as the way she had proven herself at her old job.

Jennifer got promoted as a senior programmer with a good hike at Trigen. There was a chance of her to be sent to the UK on a project.

During the orientation sessions, she met Alan whom she was supposed to directly report to. Alan and his other colleagues gave a warm welcome to her for joining their team. She introduced herself and exchanged numbers.

Out of curiosity, to know more about her boss, she asked Ankita, one of her new colleagues. Ankita answered, 'Alan did not interfere with their work. She tries to avoid interrupting in their work.' Jennifer was surprised to hear this.

At Zenich, Jennifer reported to Vaibhav and had looked up to him whenever she wanted guidance. Vaibhav made sure that Jennifer always learns from experiences and always encouraged to bring new ideas at the table. She remembered telling her colleagues at Zenich that an ideal boss is one who does not interfere with his/her subordinate's work.

Jennifer believed that even Alan seems to be of non-interfering type. During her first week as new role in the office, and she found the atmosphere to be dull, but was also excited. Her team was assigned a new project and she was working under that project. Working for this project, she was facing few hurdles in the new software. She tried hard to solve the problem and tried to come up with several possible solutions. She then thought of asking help from Alan and his team by mentioning all the possible solutions that she tried. She started daydreaming about all the praise that she would be getting in the effort put into the project. Next morning, when Alan walked into the office, Jennifer was ready to get into his cabin. Alan asked Jennifer to come into the cabin after 10minutes.

When she went inside the cabin, Alan was completely blank and asked Jennifer to introduce her. Jennifer introduced herself. Later he asked, 'Why did you want to meet me?' Jennifer replied by mentioning about the problems they were facing. But before she could even finish, he told her that he has got very pack schedule and so he would send an email having solution to implement it by the team. Jennifer was disheartened. She came out of the cabin and went to her team members to know what ideas could come up from them. She discussed all the solutions that she could think of, and waited for others to suggest ideas. Nobody was interested. After few minutes, Rakesh, another colleague replied, 'there is no point in discussing because Alan would give the best solution and we will have to do whatever he says'.

Jennifer was disappointed. As the time passed by, Jennifer realized that Alan was complete opposite to her previous boss.

Gradually she started losing the interest in her work and was not at all learning new things. She felt that her career was going nowhere. Her performance was going nowhere.

Questions

1. According to you what are the reasons of disappointment for Jennifer. Answer the question using Maslow's theory
2. How does the team leader or a manager play a role in employee's performance?
3. What should Jennifer do in order to solve the situation?

Critical Thinking Questions

1. How does motivation affect human behaviour and performance?
2. Discuss few strategies for motivating
3. Which factors affect individual performance?
4. How does job situation affect performance?

Chapter at a Glance

Introduction

Motivation is the process of attempting to influence others to do your will through possibility of gain of reward. Motivation is the driving force that creates an urge to take action to achieve our desired goals. There is always a motivating force behind anything we do and it is the intensity of our motivation which determines how well and how fast we succeed at obtaining what we wish to achieve.

Nature of Motivation

- A psychological concept
- Continuous process
- Considers whole individual
- It may be financial or non-financial
- It may be positive or negative

Importance of Motivation

- Effective utilization of resources
- Achievement of organizational goals
- Improves efficiency of employees
- Reduced employee turnover and absenteeism
- Cordial organizational relations

Types of Motivation

- Intrinsic motivation
- Extrinsic motivation
- Financial motivation
- Non-financial motivation
- Positive motivation
- Negative motivation

Theories of Motivation

Maslow's Hierarchy of Needs

- Physiological needs
- Safety needs
- Social needs
- Esteem needs
- Self-actualization

Limitations of Maslow's Hierarchy

- It is over simplified and is based only on human needs.
- All the employees may not have similar needs.

(Continued)

(Continued)

- Every employee may not follow the similar pattern
- With the growing needs of the individuals the assumptions of this theory may not hold good in today's
- Context.
- Maslow's writings are more philosophical than scientific.

Herzberg's Two-factor Theory

Herzberg suggested a two-step approach to understanding employee motivation and satisfaction.

- **Hygiene factors:** These are basically the factors that do not actually act as motivation, but their absence results in demotivation.
- **Motivational factors:** The presence of these factors creates a positive job satisfaction.

Expectancy Theory of Motivation

The theory states that the intensity of a tendency to perform in a particular manner is dependent on the intensity of an expectation that the performance will be followed by a certain outcome and on the appeal of the outcome for the individual.

Advantages of Expectancy Theory

- It is based on self-interest individual
- This theory focuses upon the expectations and perception.
- It emphasizes on rewards or pay-offs or the other related aspects.
- It focuses on psychological extravagance

Limitations of Expectancy Theory

- seems to be idealistic
- application and implementation of this theory is limited

Goal-setting Theory of Motivation

It states that goals display and give path to an employee about what needs to be done and how much efforts are required to do it.

Goal-setting theory has certain eventualities such as

- self-efficiency
- goal commitment

Advantages of Goal-setting Theory

- Goal-setting theory is a kind of mechanism that can help raise incentives for employees to get work done very fast along with steady effectiveness.
- Goal setting leads to better performance by increasing motivation and efforts, but also through increasing and improving the feedback quality.

Limitations of Goal-setting Theory

- It hampers performance if it is used to spread incompatible action drift.
- Very complex and uneasy goal leads to danger zone.
- Employee with lack of skills and competency to perform work to be done for goal affects success of the goal-setting and performance goes down.
- There is no strong reason or evidence to prove that goal-setting theory improves job satisfaction.

McClelland's Learned Needs Theory

This motivational model explains how the needs for achievement, power, and affiliation influence the actions of individuals in managerial context. These motivators fall under three categories achievement, affiliation or power.

Alderfer's ERG Theory

Alderfer refined Maslow's hierarchy of needs theory to synchronization with his research

Self-determination Theory

The self-determination theory of motivation was developed by psychologists Edward Deci and Richard Ryan. According to this theory people are driven by a need to grow and achieve fulfilment. The basic assumption of self-determination theory is that individuals are activity directed towards growth.

TMT

Piers Steel and Cornelius J. Konig developed an integrative motivational theory developed known as TMT. This theory emphasizes 'time' as a crucial motivational factor and focuses on the impact of deadlines on the allocation of attention to particular tasks.

Expectancy Theory of Motivation

The theory states that the intensity of a tendency to perform in a particular manner is dependent on the intensity of an expectation that the performance will be followed by a certain outcome and on the appeal of the outcome for the individual.

Goal-setting Theory of Motivation

This theory states that higher and better task performances are a result of contribution of complex and challenging goals along with appropriate feedback.

(Continued)

(Continued)

Theory X and Theory Y of Motivation

Assumptions: Theory X

- On an average employee resist work and will try avoiding it whenever possible.
- Employees emphasize on job security being less ambitious.
- For the dislike of employee towards his work, he must be mandated with protocols and warned with punishment so as to achieve desired goals and targets. The managers adopt a more dictatorial style.
- Employees do not easily accept change.
- Employees usually dislike responsibilities.
- An average employee always expects a formal guidance.

Assumptions: Theory Y

- Employees can perceive work normal.
- Employees may not always need to be threatened by external control.
- Rewards at job are motivating leading to more loyal employees.
- An employee can learn to identify and uphold the responsibility and sometimes to obtain the same.
- The employees may explore their skills and competencies.
- Their logical capabilities if completely utilized may lead to having a resourceful and worth employee for identifying and resolving multiple issues rising in and out of the organization.

CHAPTER 14

Conflict Management

Learning Objectives

- Getting a detailed view of the process of conflict and the various conflict-resolution strategies from the organizational perspectives.
- Understanding the traditional and modern views on conflict and the various levels of conflict, such as interpersonal and intrapersonal conflicts, intergroup and intragroup conflicts, and their impact on the organization's strategic and operational activities.
- Getting insight into perspectives on transaction analysis since human interventions occur frequently in the everyday operations of the organization.
- Understanding the various conflict-management styles and their effectiveness from organizational perspective using an exemplary approach.

An Opening Vignette

Rebuilding Trust and Communication

The scenario relates to a company in the small- and medium-sized enterprises (SME) category in the service domain. The conflict between the members arose due to lack of communication and distrust building slowly over a period of time, resulting in dysfunctional conflict with gossip and rumours at every corner of the office about the improper task allocation, departmental goal variation, resource constraint, and so on, which left the team and team members in a state of unaddressed conflict. Therefore, to manage the conflict, several team-building sessions were conducted by a conflict management expert hired outside the organization, and a report of the same was given to the top management, and the stakeholders, consisting of a five-member team with a manager, customers, and the top management team.

During the team-building session, the expert encouraged the team to read *The Five Dysfunctions of a Team* by Patrick Lencioni (2012), which led to non-productivity within the company and this comprised the following:

- Absence of trust, for which the remedy was to build trust.
- Fearing conflict, for which it was required to efficiently manage conflict.

- Lack of consistency and commitment, for which focus and accomplishment of goals were remedial solutions for an individual.
- Avoidance of ownership and not focusing on results, for which the solution was to own up the responsibility and be result oriented.

The team then started seeing the facts as they were and stopped working on assumptions any more. They started viewing conflict as a base for improving productivity and performance. They set target for the team, and each one promised to expend his/her effort to achieve the same. Then they set to work out in the areas of their weakness where conflict was not properly managed and came up with the following findings:

- They found that most of the time the team, in its earlier phases, had made negative assumptions solely because of a lack of transparency in communication and the absence of a methodical communication flow.
- They learned how each person wanted to be intimated in communication and conflict.
- The team started meeting frequently to resolve important issues, which they were avoiding to discuss because some of the team members did not follow the collaborative style of conflict resolution and wanted to force the team to believe their individual perspectives. They started making extensive plans for the crucial issues inclusive of risk management policies prior to implementation of a plan.
- They started exuding ownerships for various tasks even if they confronted problems and complexities for which the solutions were designed in a collaborative manner, minimizing the chances of conflict evolution.
- The team, in due course, learned to respect each other, to solve problems more innovatively, and to lessen stress and tension in a very open manner. Overall, they started a collaborative mechanism of identifying issues, hearing each individual's perspective, narrowing down a hybrid feasible solution with high degree of transparency in communication, and ingraining in them a culture to see conflict in a positive note.

Introduction

Conflicts which are a common occurrence in organizations arise when the goals, needs, requirements, opinions, and areas of interest of the concerned individual(s) interfere with one another. Conflicts might occur between team members, amongst the various functional units, or members of a functional unit, department, organization, and customer, boss, and subordinate, and can also occur when organizational needs and personal needs are not aligned. Conflict, if intensified, might lead to non-productive results, which should be resolved to achieve better quality products or services. Therefore, conflict management is integral to a team which wants to deliver and perform well. Conflict management addresses solvable conflicts by learning to manage conflicts, which can decrease non-productive escalation. Conflict management involves acquiring skills to resolve conflicts and to be aware of various conflict modes and establishing a structure for management of conflict. Often a conflict leads to progress; hence, it is important to apply various conflict-resolution techniques.

Definitions

Conflict is a process that begins when one party perceives that another party has negatively affected, or is about to negatively affects, something that the first party cares about.

K.W. Thomas

Conflict is a struggle between incompatible or opposing needs, wishes, ideas and interests of people.

Chung and Meggison

Conflicts are communicative interactions among people who are interdependent and who perceive that their interests are incompatible, inconsistent, or in tension.

Conrad

Traditional Versus Modern View of Conflict: Functional and Dysfunctional Conflict

In early days, conflict was perceived in a negative way and the most appropriate approach to manage the conflict was to avoid it. The other view was that conflicts arise because people within a team or a group have a tendency to create trouble by bringing in negativity within the group. According to the traditional view, conflict is the result of reduced communication, dishonesty, and distrust between people, and the failure of managers to be receptive to the wants and desires of their employees.

The modern view of conflict is that conflict is a natural outcome, is unavoidable especially when conditions and situations are susceptible to change, and is functional if minimum level is attained. The modern view of conflict states that conflict between various bodies in the organization depends on organizational structure, variations in long- and short-term goals, insights, and employees values. According to the modern view, conflict contributes to organizational performance if prevalent minimally and detracts from organizational performance if it goes beyond control. In the modern era, controlled conflict is required for optimal organizational performance. Today, managements have come up with perspectives of conflict, as described below.

Functional Conflict

- This allows the groups pursue their goals and improves performance.
- Increases knowledge about persisting problems and provides solution for the same.
- With the onset of constructive conflict comes the concept of change, refinement, and rectification.
- Decisions are more robust because they pass through perspectives, visualizations, and so on of various people.
- It helps in the reduction of serious conflicts, which can affect performance of individuals or organizations.
- Conflicts or arguments can encourage people to find out new solutions.
- It enhances relationship and increases cohesiveness by learning more about each other.

Dysfunctional Conflict

- This conflict actually creates obstacles for the group performance within the organization.
- When a conflict arises between groups or individuals, it takes a lot of time to resolve differences in opinion and narrowing them down on a specific solution.
- Sometimes when the conflict is not under control, it disrupts the progress of the organization, conflict resolution does not happen, every member within the group does not remain aligned to the goals of the company or the project. As a result, the performance of the group and the organization decreases.

- Conflict, if not resolved, can lessen coordination and collaboration between members of the group and harmony and team spirit is lost.
- Due to conflict, the culmination of ideas originating from the group no longer exists, resulting in lower quality and productivity.
- Conflict also reduces team effectiveness.

For example, Joanna, heading a highway construction project in the East Coast, has faced vehement protests from the residents living along the highway in small villages. The villagers think it is an encroachment as it will lead to increase in pollution and noise levels. Discussions with residents have turned bitter, leading to a win–lose situation or a dysfunctional conflict.

Process of Conflict

The process of conflict comprises five stages (Figure 14.1).

Figure 14.1 Process of Conflict

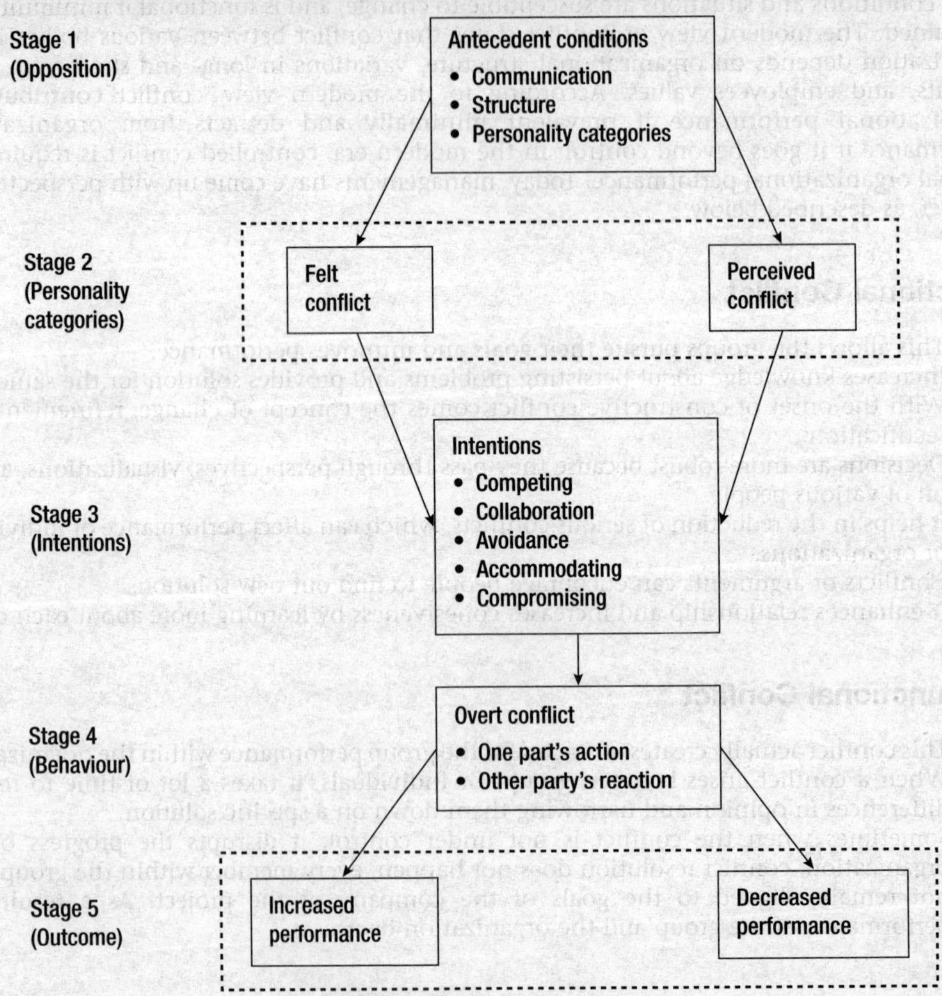

Opposition

The first stage in the process of conflict is the opposition stage, where an environment is created such that conflict can arise. For example, in an organization, there are a few recourses that need to be shared in common by the various departments. This could become the potential source of conflict. The disagreement arises due to (a) communication (b) structure, and (c) personality categories.

- **Communication:** Different jargons of speech or too much noise in the communication channel or even a gap in communication can give rise to conflict or are antecedents of conflict.
- **Structure:** Structure can refer to group or organizational structure and consists of variables such as size and task specialization, because large groups are mainly task-specific groups. The larger the group and younger the members, the more is the conflict between members and amongst the groups. Ambiguity in allocation of roles and responsibilities can also give rise to intergroup conflicts.
- **Personality categories:** Some personality types who prefer autocracy to a greater extent are sources of conflicts within the group. Also, because value realization differs from one personality type to the other, the amount of contribution towards achieving organizational goals also differs.

Cognition

This stage brings clarity on whether the conflict is felt or perceived between individuals and groups, and emotions play a crucial role in influencing perceptions. For example, while carrying out a quality assurance check for a large enterprise resource planning (ERP), it was found that the code did not pass through the testing phase after the development, rather it was deployed directly. This could pose a serious conflict between the marketer and the seller, because once the marketer starts to fall, it might disrupt its own brand value.

Intention

The purpose of a perceived or a felt conflict is identified at this stage. For example, managers of the marketer and the seller in the above-stated ERP, once they are in Customers Board of Management's review meeting, might feel open and not so pleasant confrontations on these issues and may prepare to state their pre-emptive measures mentally on the conflict.

- Competing: If an individual seeks to satisfy his/her own interest without considering people or groups who are party to the conflict, then it is said to be competing.
- Collaboration: If the parties to conflict try to resolve it by sorting out the problem and clarifying the differences, then they are said to be collaborative.
- Avoidance: It is an intention where a person either avoids the conflict or avoids the person with whom he has conflict.
- Accommodating: It is the intention wherein parties to conflict place opponents' interest above theirs.
- Compromising: It is an intention where each party to conflict can let go some of their points to narrow down to a resolution. Generally, intentions of people are ever changing.

Behaviour

Conflict is evident because there is external display of conflict using verbal and visual modes by the staff. For example, open discussions between the marketer and seller of the ERP about the various issues of the customer are verbally put forth, giving rise to conflict.

Outcomes

These are consequences which may be functional, in the sense that there was improvement in the performance of the group or organization, or dysfunctional. Functional conflict improves the quality of decisions, conjures up imagination and advancement, provides the medium through which tribulations can be settled and strain released, and promotes a situation of self-evaluation and transformation. Conflict is dysfunctional when there is breach in trust, and faith and leads to the obliteration of the group.

Levels of Conflict

Intrapersonal Conflict

Intrapersonal conflict refers to the internal conflict or frustration of a human being. This arises when numerous profiles within the self demand attention, which is not always justifiable to devote to, goals set by self which are not met, or some external social barriers which prohibit an individual to perform a task. For example, storekeepers keep fast-moving items and daily necessities at the end of the store and consumers are enticed to buy certain items which they might not even want and finally end up buying more items than their budget (Figure 14.2).

Another intrapersonal conflict is the goal conflict where attainment of one goal prevents the other goal from being attained. The major forms of goal conflict in existence are the following:

- **Approach–approach conflict:** For example, making a choice of an educational institution from a number of institutions, each offering some unique programs in addition to the regular course.
- **Approach–avoidance conflict:** For example, wanting to talk to a departmental head for allocation of a different project to the individual which has overseas opportunities, and then fearing that the proposal would not be fairly accepted by the head. This type of conflict becomes very difficult to resolve in scenarios like the following:
    - Independence versus dependence
    - Cooperation versus competition
    - Impulsive versus controlled expression
- **Avoidance**–Avoidance Conflict: For example, conflict between avoiding unwanted expenditures or cutting down on the budget.

The last intrapersonal conflict is the role conflict, where an individual needs to play several roles at the same time, but cannot afford to do so because of crunch in time and resource. For example, a boss has to suffer from a role conflict if he is firing an employee who is also a very

Figure 14.2 Intrapersonal Conflict

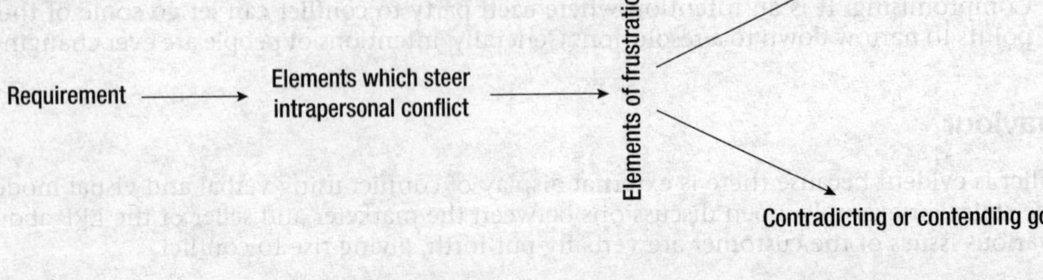

close acquaintance of his. Intra-individual conflict arises due to inconsistencies in a person's thought process or certain neurotic tendencies like keeping tight control over others or over the budget.

Interpersonal Conflict

Interpersonal conflict occurs between two individuals in an organization. Interpersonage conflict arises due to dissimilarities in insights, values, and ethics and no clear description of roles. The tools which can explain the occurrence of interpersonal conflict are transactional analysis, Johari Window, life position, and so on.

Transactional Analysis

Stages of communication between two or more people can correlate to the moves of the game. This concept was introduced by Eric Berne and made popular by Thomas Harris. The benefits of transactional analysis are as follows:

- Learning is very simple.
- It helps to improve interpersonal relationships in organizations.
- It encourages employees and increases productivity.
- It helps to improve communication amongst employees and clearly shows hidden cases, crossed and complementary transactions, and shows with clarity different ego states of an individual (child, adult, and parent) while a communication exists between two individuals.
- It improves clarity in problem analysis, reduces miscommunications amongst individuals, and explains vividly that a manager cannot always motivate his subordinate by assigning him the most complex task (otherwise known as boosting the adult ego state). Sometimes the manager should also act like a parent to his employees, thereby motivating them for better performance.
- This is highly valuable in educating in all business situations, where discrete communication is vital and know-how of people's process is worthwhile.

However, the limitation of transactional analysis is that the framework for assessing the outcome of a transactional analysis is neither very scientific nor can the ego states be quantitatively or qualitatively assessed.

Transactional analysis predominantly revolves around three ego states:

- **Parent ego state:** The person is authoritative, controlling, protective, and so on.
- **Adult ego state:** The person is balanced and mature.
- **Child ego state:** The person is dependent on others, like a child.

Transaction Types

Crossed transactions: When two people turn away from each other without further discourse or dialogue after they had a disagreement, it is a case of crossed transaction. Cross transactions are elements of discomfort in relationships, whether husband–wife, parent–child, and so on. If a friend says to another of his best buddies, 'Well, how you think I feel!', then the other one might feel sarcasm by the statement and choose not to respond (Figure 14.3).

Figure 14.3 Crossed Transaction

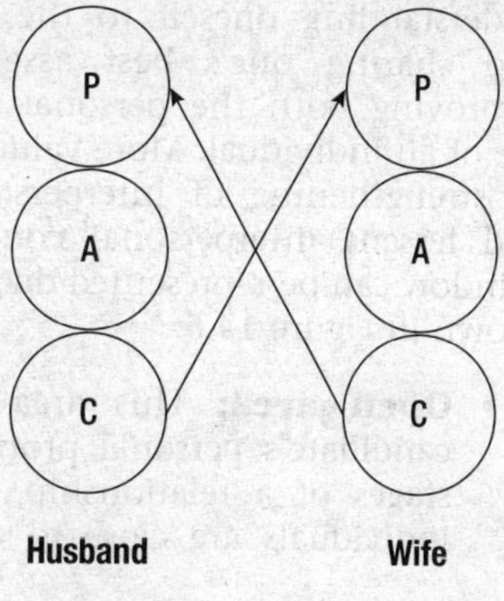

It is a transaction between two individuals, one representing the adult ego state and the other individual responding using a child ego state. Crossed transactions are a source of conflict.

Complementary transactions: It is a transaction between individuals when one person's ego state receives the appropriate response. An adult ego state gets an adult response and so on (Figure 14.4).

A complementary transaction can occur between any two ego states. For example, two people may transact adult–adult ego while solving a problem. If the response is the one that is sought for, then the transaction is complementary.

Figure 14.4 Complementary Transaction

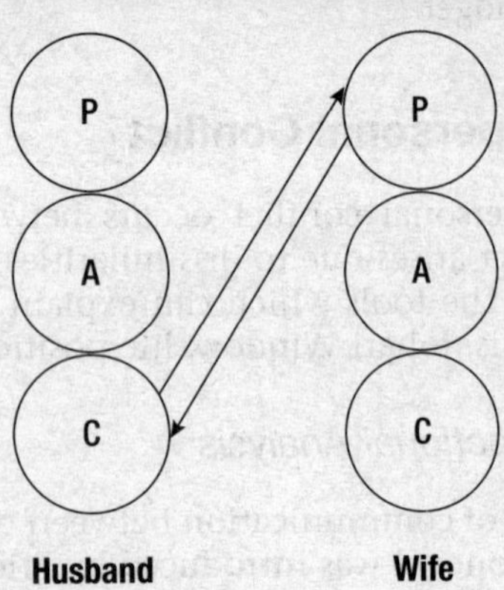

Ulterior transactions: Ulterior transactions are complex transactions and involve more than two ego states. In this communication, one has to read between the lines. If person A says to B, 'Since you are busy let's talk about it some other time'. Therefore, he is exuding both parent ego and adult ego, where he is being considerable about others' busy state and does not want an extended conversation at that point of time (Figure 14.5).

Figure 14.5 Ulterior Transaction

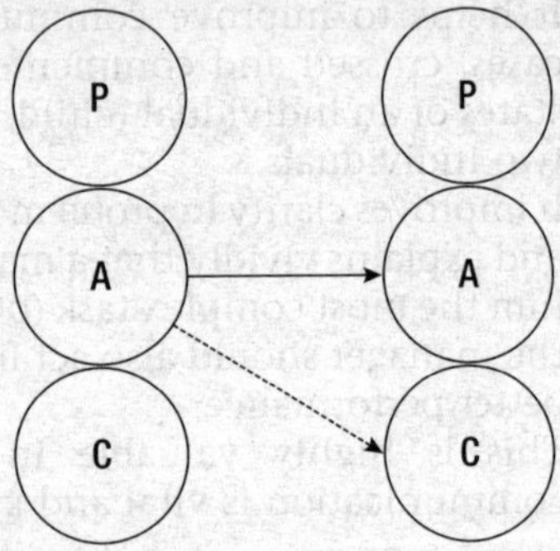

Johari Window

The next most commonly used tool is the Johari Window developed by Joseph Luft and Harry Ingham. The model is vital for representing interpersonal conflict and is based primarily on two concepts.

- The extent to which a person can self-assess himself/herself
- The extent to which the person is known to others

The concept of Johari Window is that understanding oneself to the minutest extent and sharing one's best assets can help in improving both the personal and professional life of an individual. More valued sharing results in strengthening of interpersonal relationship and lessens interpersonal conflict. The Johari Window can be represented diagrammatically, as shown in Figure 14.6:

Figure 14.6 Diagrammatic Representation of Johari Window

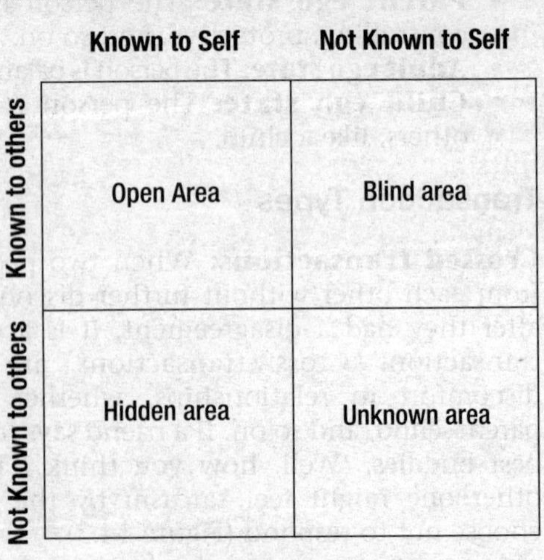

- **Open area:** This area correlates to a candidate's personal profile. In the initial stages of a relationship, because no two individuals are close to each other, their personal profiles are not known to each other. However, as the relationship grows, information sharing is high, compatibility amongst them increases, and conflict reduces.

- **Hidden self:** This area shrinks as the person shares more information with others. With more sharing comes more of trust and belief and less of conflict. However, this area is prone to more conflict.
- **Blind area:** This area contains information unknown to self and known to others. For example, movements in a person happening just out of sheer stress, such as stammering while explaining a presentation, or holding shifting from one foot to the next while standing to speak. Such habits, when pointed out by others, can reduce the blind area. The blind area can clearly depict a person's strength and weakness; the more a person is open to others' views, the more effective manager he can be.
- **Unknown area:** This is not the area which contains information not known to others nor does self, this area contains information which is deliberately suppressed. As a person grows, develops, and learns, this area goes on shrinking.

Life Positions

Life positions are a combination of positive and negative assessments of self and somebody else. These are used to justify other decisions about ourselves and others and to justify our behaviour. Four positions arise from the permutation (Figure 14.7).

Figure 14.7 Life Positions

Ok, Not Ok (Angry state)	OK, OK (Happy state)	**Positive**
Not OK, Not Ok (Hopeless state)	Not OK, OK (Helpless state)	**Negative**
Negative	**Positive**	

Intragroup Conflict

Intragroup conflict relates to the conflict between group members, leading to degradation in the performance of the group. It can also happen within a family-run business such as Tata and Birla. Intragroup conflict refers to the inappropriateness and incongruence among the members of a group, subgroups with regard to long- and short-term goals, policies, processes and methods, functions, or deeds of the group. In intragroup conflict, the majority of the members of a group or its subgroups must be involved.

Intergroup Conflict

Intergroup conflicts refer to the conflict between various groups of people, several units, or functionalities within the organization. Basically, intergroup conflicts occur due to several reasons as follows:

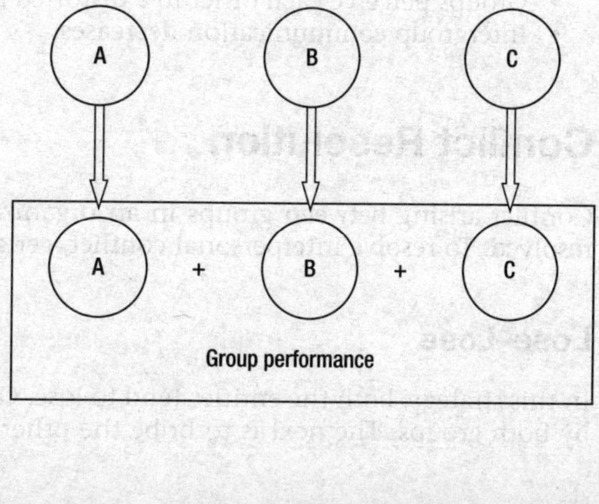

- **Task interdependence:** It is the interdependence between various functional units of an organization for information gathering or collaborative tasks performed by them. They can be represented as sequentially dependent; dependency is like a two-way handshake or in the form of pooling each team's resources to accomplish a particular task. Task interdependence can be of three types:

- **Pooled task interdependence:** Group performance is the sum of individual's contribution.
- **Sequential task interdependence:** There is interdependence on the sequence of tasks performed by the members.

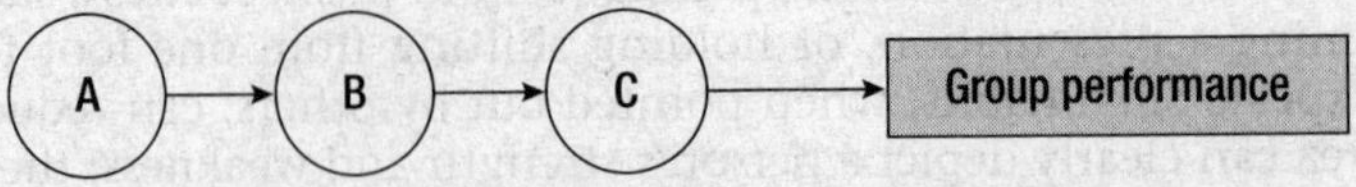

- Reciprocal task interdependence: Performance of a member executing a task directly affects the performance of other members executing the task in the same group.

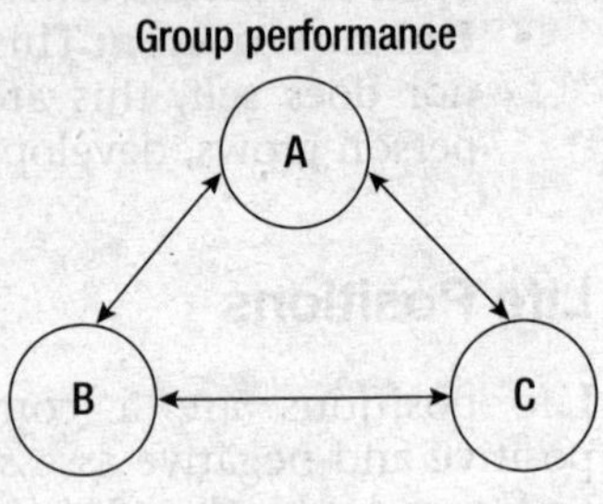

For all of the above scenarios, conflict arises when there is a mismatch between expectation and performance.

- Improper task allocation: This is another common cause of intergroup conflict when roles and responsibilities are not properly allocated to the respective groups.
- Interdepartmental goal variation: This can give rise to conflict. For example, the testing unit of a software developing organization might want to establish its goal at 0.3% defects per person per thousand lines of code, whereas the development unit might not want to adhere to that standard.
- Resource constraint: Various groups might fight for resources like manpower, money, material, infrastructure, or for intangible elements like authority, prestige, and status.
- Benefits or rewards: Conflict can occur amongst the group when there is a benefit or reward scheme operating across groups or units. So, the quality assurance department is rewarded for keeping product quality in sync with ISO standards, whereas the marketing department is rewarded for intelligent campaigning methods.
- Intrapersonage and interpersonage conflict: Both can give rise to intergroup conflict.

Scenario of Intergroup Conflict

Within the group

- Trust between members increases.
- Authoritative style of leadership persists within the group.
- Organizational hierarchy is not flexible.

Outside the group

- Groups perceive each other in a distorted manner and judge the other group irrationally.
- Intergroup communication decreases.

Conflict Resolution

Conflict arising between groups in an organization or within the groups or self need to be resolved. To resolve interpersonal conflict, certain approaches are used.

Lose–Lose

In this strategy, both the entities tend to lose. One of the solutions can be a compromise made by both groups. The next is to bribe the other party from carrying out further disputes. The third form is to bring an external entity or group that can mediate between the groups by giving honest judgments. The last approach is to use existing rules or regulations for resolution of the conflict.

Win–Lose

In this strategy, one entity wins and the other loses. For example, either the worker's union or the management of an organization wins. The conflict is mainly due to the difference in perspectives while looking at things; moreover, emphasis is on the solution approach rather than on the attainment of goals and objectives. Both the entities view issues from short-term perspectives and conflicts are more personalized.

Win–Win

Using this strategy, both the entities win, and the brainstorming of views and ideas to solve certain problems happen from positive perspective. To obtain a win–win situation for both the parties might not be realistic but should be set as an organizational goal for maximum outcome.

Transactional Analysis

To resolve interpersonage conflict, communication between two groups should resemble the communication between two adult ego states.

Changing People's Attitude and Behaviour

Interpersonal conflict can be resolved to quite an extent if the attitude and perception of people change.

Intragroup Conflict Resolution

To resolve intragroup conflict, the members of that group should recognize and honour the roles accorded to various members.

Intergroup Conflict Resolution

Certain strategies are used for resolving intergroup conflicts, as follows:

- **Problem-solving:** Problem-solving in collaboration is the most effective approach when both the groups try to identify the problem and resolve it using some solution strategies.
- **Organizational restructuring:** Intergroup conflict can be resolved if organizational restructuring is done so that roles and responsibilities are defined clearly and allocated to groups, and task interdependence between various units of the organization is reduced to lessen the level of conflict.
- **Alignment to common goals:** Both the groups can be aligned to a common goal wherein both the parties put in their efforts to achieve the goal, which in a way can reduce intergroup conflict. To work in unison when an organization faces bad weather is an example of a common goal of various organizational units.
- **Upgradation of resources:** If conflict arises due to constrained resources, then the best way would be to go in for resource upgradation and allocation of resources across various groups uniformly.

- **Not to let conflict happen:** For not so complex issues, the best way to resolve conflict is to withdraw from the phase of conflict. The withdrawal can happen either from both parties or from one of them.
- **Collating similarities amongst groups:** If similarities between groups are identified, then it becomes easier for groups to smoothen down on the conflicting issues and work with a renewed perspective.

Line and Staff Conflict Resolution

The following approaches to lessen conflict exist:

- Defining clear roles and responsibilities for line and staff.
- Role of staff managers is advising and line managers should follow suitable advice.
- Communication exchange between line and staff should be enhanced.
- Inferiority complex in line managers should not be allowed to develop.
- Both should have the freedom to approach top management if required.

Conflict Management Styles

It has been seen that bosses within the organization spend a lot of time resolving conflicts and issues. Therefore, there is need of managing conflicts in an appropriate manner, which will not only reduce time spent on the same but also help resolving them in an effective manner. To manage conflicts, one can use the following styles (Figure 14.8).

Competition or Application of Force

This style suggests that one party is the winner and the other is the loser. The advantage of this style is that the winner has very clear insight about the problem and the solution strategy, but at the same time the cons is that the other party's ego is hurt, which can boost up the enmity within groups and sometimes can even provoke worthy groups to withdraw from conflicts. This style is used when relationships are not important to a party and the party is aggressive as well as certain about its decision.

Figure 14.8 Conflict Management Styles

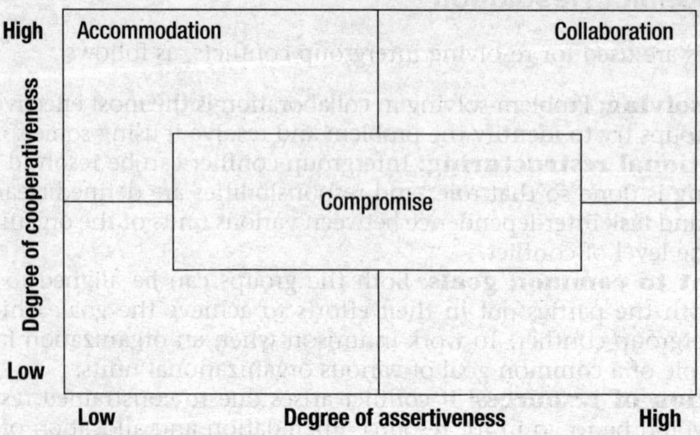

In certain instances, the individual strongly puts forth his/her concerns and worries irrespective of whether the other individual or group agrees to the same. Examples when aggression for instituting worries and concerns works are as follows:

- In situations when all other methods are ineffective.
- When a quick resolution is required and there is total justification in application of the force or pressure.

Advantages

- Rapid conflict resolution
- Increases self-respect when the other party examines the justification for applying force.

Disadvantages

- Relations with opponents may get strained.
- If imposition leads to uncontrolled authority taken up by individuals/groups who have imposed their opinion, it becomes very difficult for other individuals or groups to sustain.
- Taking this approach may require a lot of energy and is stressful for some.

Collaboration

This is also known as 'win–win' or 'problem solving'. In the collaborative style, both parties are the winner, which promotes good feelings amongst the parties, but this style takes a great deal of time and effort to bring both the parties to agree upon. This style is appropriate when consensus is important, when maintaining relationship is vital, time is not an important factor and merging both perspectives can bring out a good solution.

Collaboration involves two parties or individuals working in coalition towards a common goal or objective and get mutually benefited from the outcome. It takes into account the concerns of each group and finds solutions which satisfy both. Collaboration is appropriate when

- the parties agree to work as unit,
- the perspectives of various stakeholders are considered,
- presence of high level of trust,
- under conditions where decision-making is collaborative and needs consensus, or it is difficult for a single party or individual to take decision alone.

Advantages

- Problem solving gets easy, resulting in a win–win outcome.
- It promotes trust and respect and creates a framework for effective collaboration.
- Shared responsibility of the outcome.
- Since it is a collaborative effort, every individual/groups perspective is taken into account and relationships are maintained.
- The outcome of the conflict resolution is less stressful.

Disadvantages

- Commitment from all individuals or groups for the desired solution.
- It may require more effort and more time as conflict resolution happens in a collaborative style.

- This method is not appropriate when resolution demands instant decision-making.
- This should not be used in situations where relationship matters most because many a time the parties lose trust and faith at later times.

Compromise

This style is used when the chief concern is the attainment of goals and relationships. Both the parties sacrifice some of their goals to achieve a long-term goal in collaboration. This is used when an ideal solution cannot be perceived or all the parties are in equal power proposing their own solution. The style is used when both parties are satisfied by solutions which partially fulfil their perspectives. Appropriateness of this style can be explained better with the following:

- When goals have to be achieved in moderation.
- Ad hoc manner of issue resolution.
- To achieve realistic solutions on crucial issues.
- When parties do not know each other well or do not have high level of trust.
- When collaboration or forcing do not work.

Advantages

- Realistic and quick issue resolution.
- Ad hoc solutions provided while looking for the most optimal one.
- Lower degree of stress and tension.

Disadvantages

- It may result in a situation when both parties are not satisfied with the outcome (a lose–lose situation).
- It does not contribute to building trust in the long run.
- It may require close monitoring and control to ensure the agreements are met.

Avoidance

This style, which is known as withdrawing, helps to avoid conflicts and can be used when issue is not major or too much of conflict, has an impact on the relationship or when there is very little scope to fulfil a party's own needs, or when to reach to a solution can incur delay. The style adopted makes the person not address the conflict by putting in his views or opposing the other party's view. Situations when withdrawing may be appropriate are as follows:

- When issues are very inconsequential and there are other issues which require attention.
- Where dealing with the issue at a later stage might be beneficial.
- When it requires time to gather information and knowledge.
- When there is very little opportunity of getting appropriate solution from one's own perspective.
- Not well versed to handle conflicts.

Advantages

- Under conditions of force, one can postpone response to a later date until a favourable circumstance is established to voice one's own concern.
- Avoidance incorporates low level of stress approach.
- Better preparedness by gathering information over time to handle issues.

Disadvantages

- Showing no opposition can affirm to be an agreement in some cases.
- May have negative effect on the party that was relying on the action taken by that individual or group.

Accommodation

This style, otherwise known as smoothing, actually makes party overlook its own goals and accommodate its opponent's views and ideas. This strategy only helps in improving relationships and harmony and time is a constrained variable for resolving issues. Smoothing is keeping in priority the other people's concern and is appropriate under the following conditions:

- When it is required to provide temporary relief or buy time.
- When the issue is listed at low priority.
- When mistakes are accepted and continuous competition is not favourable for long-term relationships.

Advantages

- It encourages resolution of prioritized issues.
- It gives opportunity to speculate issues from various perspectives.

Disadvantages

- The opponent might take advantage of the accommodating style of the other; hence, a balance has to be maintained between when to accommodate and when not to do so.
- It may negatively affect the individual's confidence in response to aggressive opponents and some parties may not accept the concept of accommodating too often.
- It is difficult to transform to a win–win solution in the future.

CONFLICT MANAGEMENT: A CASE STUDY

The production unit of Company ABC is facing major conflict amongst its team members, who have divided themselves into two groups, and the coordinator of that unit has turned a blind eye to the same. The unit head now has to take a decision to either change the supervisor or intervene personally to resolve the issues since it was disrupting the unit's productivity.

The unit head thought that the best idea would be to assign responsibility to some other member who could mediate between the groups.

Therefore, a supervisor was appointed, who along with his professional load had to manage the unit's differences holistically.

Question: As per your speculation, what steps should be taken by the individual allocated to resolve the issue?
Model answer: Assumptions: The strategy taken depends on the conflict-resolution style of an individual, which can be as follows:

- Compete
- Collaborate
- Compromise
- Accommodate
- Avoid

(Continued)

(Continued)

The first coordinator avoided to resolve the problem. The second, if he himself is a collaborator, would like to establish a balance between two groups and would best suit a situation where maintaining relationship is vital for the success of the unit. If his style is the compromising type, then the best situation in which this strategy will work is when goals have to be attained and both the parties are at equal power to and can work towards it.

Let us assume that the coordinator who has been given the charge wants to use the collaborative style of management because he wants an optimum solution for both the teams without damaging relationships.

Solution: His strategy then would be to bring the teams together, which is possible only through regular team meetings and one-on-one meetings.

Every time during the team meetings, project issues were discussed and consensus was taken from both teams to agree on the resolution issues. The constraints for each and every project undertaken were discussed openly and actions for the same were seconded by an appropriate voting mechanism to bring a sense of togetherness with the team.

The one-on-one session between the coordinator and employees proved to be useful since employees were open to spill over their grievances. Even shy and introvert employees could voice their thoughts openly about their concerns and goals. In addition, the coordinator received some strong feedback on the strengths and weaknesses of the unit and solutions to eradicate the issues.

Some of the conflicts were a result of improper task allocation, as certain tasks were always given to the same staff due to resource constraints. Such type of conflict is referred to as intergroup conflict, and therefore the only solution for the coordinator was to shuffle responsibilities across groups and demand for more resources from the management.

As a result, team members were trained on new roles, which renewed their enthusiasm and helped with levelling out the playing field. People started working with a positive attitude.

The policies and procedures of the department were documented so that all were on the same platform while following them, resulting in a streamlined workflow and there was no redundancy in executing the steps.

Even the concept of work rotation helped in enhancing the knowledge of the entire unit since everybody in the team had idea about several tasks being performed, which balanced situations when employees were on leave.

Summary

The chapter takes the reader through various conflict-resolution and management styles and discusses the benefits and the caveat of various styles. It also sheds light on the conflict processes and levels of conflict as perceived within organizations by various experts and researchers hindering the decision-making, productivity, and profitability of the organization.

Exercise

Objective Questions

1. Which type of conflict lets the groups pursue their goals and improve the performance?
    - Intrapersonal conflict
    - Dysfunctional conflict
    - Functional conflict
    - Interpersonal conflict

2. Which type of conflict increases knowledge about what problem persists and solution for the stated problem?
    - Functional conflict
    - Dysfunctional conflict

- Intrapersonal conflict
- Interpersonal conflict

3. Which of these levels of conflict refers to the internal conflict or frustration a human being has?
   - Functional conflict
   - Dysfunctional conflict
   - Interpersonal conflict
   - Intrapersonal conflict
4. Interpersonage conflict arises due to dissimilarities in insights, values, ethics, and no clear description of roles.
   - True
   - False
5. ______ brings clarity on whether the conflict is felt or perceived between individuals and groups and emotions play a crucial role in influencing perceptions.
   - Opposition
   - Cognition
   - Outcomes
   - Structure
6. _______ is a tool to encourage employees of an organization and increase productivity
   - Transactional analysis
   - Johari Window
   - Life position
   - None of the above
7. Crossed transactions are not a source of conflict.
   - True
   - False
8. When two people turn away from each other, without further discourse or dialogue after they had a disagreement, it is said to be
   - Ulterior transactions
   - Complementary transactions
   - Crossed transactions
   - None of the above
9. Which area of the Johari Window can clearly depict a person's strength and weakness?
   - Open area
   - Hidden self
   - Blind area
   - Unknown area
10. Which area of the Johari Window contains information unknown to self and known to others?
    - Open area
    - Hidden self

- Blind area
- Unknown area

11. Task interdependence is the interdependence between various functional units of an organization for information gathering or the collaborative tasks performed by them.

    - True
    - False

12. Using which strategy of conflict resolution, both the entities win and the brainstorming of views and ideas to solve certain problems happen from positive perspective?

    - Lose–lose
    - Win–lose
    - Win–win
    - None of the above

13. Organizational restructuring can resolve

    - Intragroup conflict
    - Intergroup conflict
    - Intrapersonal conflict
    - Interpersonal conflict

14. Which style of conflict management suggests that one party is the winner and the other loser?

    - Competition or application of force
    - Collaboration
    - Avoidance
    - Compromise

15. Which style of conflict management provides realistic and quick issue resolution?

    - Competition or application of force
    - Collaboration
    - Avoidance
    - Compromise

CASE STUDY

Phantactic Textile Limited is into business of manufacturing of different types of yarns. It also carried out marketing of different types of yarns like syntactic yarn, cotton yarn, acrylic yarn, and many more. It is located in Jamshedpur, Madhya Pradesh, and has a good infrastructure. The company has grown considerably in both capabilities and experience and was nearing a handsome profit from the business. Top management team included the owner (managing director), chairman, technical director, and four vice presidents, each looking after finance and accounts, marketing, manufacturing, after marketing, and personnel and administration, respectively. These vice presidents have different executives working under them. A majority of the executives under them have done MBA from a top university.

The technical director was an expert in yarn dyeing and therefore used to concentrate more on the yarn quality, depending on the quality of dyeing. The production department was looked under the supervision of the factory manager who reported to one of the production vice presidents. Industrial relations was taken care by the personnel and administration vice president.

With the active support and cooperation of all the faculty members of business management of a nearby local university, Lenardial Management Association, a local affiliate of the All India Management Association, was formed. Many of the industrialists, managers, as well as large business organizations of the city became members of the association. The association became popular as it provided very good opportunity to the academics and the practitioners.

Dr Alan, one of the faculty members having behavioural science specialization of the management department of the university, was appointed as the secretary of the association for five years. The university encouraged visits to different universities as a part of its extension programme. After the visit, Dr Alan used to discuss the management problem with the different organizations.

Through informal sources, Dr Alan came to know that Phantactic Textile Limited does not have good industrial relations. Therefore, he thought this as an opportunity and decided to visit it as a courtesy call. During his visit, Dr Alan wanted to visit the factory. The vice president for personnel and administration was also the member of the association and therefore accompanied Dr Alan to the visit. During the visit, Dr Alan found that workers' behaviour was not amenable at all and they looked at both of them as uninvited guests. After the visit, the vice president and Dr Alan met and Dr Alan gave the vice president explained about poor industrial relations and lack of interest of the workers. On this, the vice president commented that there was nothing to worry and everything was all right. Dr Alan laughed along with the vice president but hinted that the matter should be given a thought.

After several months, in the morning some workers were having problems with the supervisor and a quarrel took place between them. The matter was settled down with the help of other workers of the factory. The supervisor left the factory immediately and met the factory manager, who coincidentally happened to be his relative. The factory manager came to the factory with the supervisor and called all the workers involved in the morning incident. There were a few other workers who joined as a mob along with the workers who were involved in the incident. Accusations and counter-accusations took place. The factory manager took out his personal pistol and fired, in which one worker died and a few workers were injured. As soon as this news spread, the workers stopped working and came out with iron rods which were used in the textile machines. They started hitting all the persons coming their way. They also killed the supervisor, the factory manager, and few more persons from the senior management. By this time, the police came and then the matter was resolved and a lockout was declared in the factory.

Next morning, on reading newspaper reports about the incident, Dr Alan was upset. Being the secretary of the association, he prepared a report condemning the incident and behaviour of the workers. He also approached the president of the association for the approval of the statement 'If the top management cannot understand their workers, then they deserve the treatment given by the workers and we should not support them.'

Questions

1. State the organizational climate that existed in Phantactic Textile Limited.
2. What if the conflict was brought forward? State the best and worst that could happen.
3. If you were the vice president of personnel and administration what actions would you have taken to stop the occurrence of the incident?

Critical Thinking Questions

1. Conflict is same as fight. Discuss.
2. Discuss pros and cons of conflict-resolution techniques in organizations.
3. Collaboration is one of the possible outcomes of a conflict situation. Discuss.

Chapter at a Glance

Conflict Management

Conflicts are communicative interactions among people who are interdependent and who perceive that their interests are incompatible, inconsistent, or in tension.

(Continued)

(Continued)

Traditional Versus Modern View of Conflict

- According to the traditional view, conflict is the result of reduced communication, dishonesty, and distrust between people, and the failure of managers to be receptive to the wants and desires of their employee.
- The modern view of conflict states that conflict between various bodies in the organization depends on organizational structure, variations in long- and short-term goals, insight, and employees' values.

Functional Conflict

- It allows the groups pursue their goals and improves the performance.
- It increases knowledge about a persisting problem and solution for the stated problem.
- It helps in the reduction of serious conflicts which can affect an individual's or an organization's performance.

Dysfunctional Conflict

- This conflict actually creates obstacles for the group performance within the organization.
- When a conflict arises between groups or individuals, it takes a lot of time to resolve differences of opinion and narrowing them down on a specific solution.
- Conflict, if not resolved, can lessen coordination and collaboration between members of the group and harmony and team spirit is lost.

Process of Conflict

- Opposition
  - The first stage in the process of conflict is the opposition stage where an environment is created such that conflict can arise.
  - Disagreement arises due to (a) communication, (b) structure, and (c) personality categories.
- Cognition
  - The stage brings clarity on whether the conflict is felt or perceived between individuals and groups and emotions play a crucial role in influencing perceptions.
- Intention
  - The purpose of a perceived or a felt conflict is identified at this stage.
  - The company prepares to state its pre-emptive measures on the conflict mentally by going for competing, collaboration, avoidance, accommodating, and compromising.
- Behaviour
  - There is external display of conflict using verbal and visual modes of visual or verbal displays put in by the staff.

Levels of Conflict

- Intrapersonal Conflict
  - This refers to the internal conflict or frustration of a human being.

- Intrapersonal conflict arises when numerous profiles within the self demand attention, which is not always justifiable to devote to, goals set by self which are not met or some external social barriers.
- The major forms of goal conflict in existence are the following:
  - Approach–approach conflict
  - Approach–avoidance conflict
  - Avoidance–avoidance conflict
  - Role conflict

- Interpersonal Conflict
  - Interpersonal conflict occurs between two individuals in an organization. Interpersonage conflict arises due to dissimilarities in insights, values and ethics, and no clear description of roles.
  - The tools which can explain the occurrence of interpersonal conflict are transactional analysis, Johari Window, life position, and so on
- Intragroup Conflict
  - Intragroup conflict relates to conflict between group members, leading to degradation in the performance of the group.
  - Intragroup conflict refers to the inappropriateness and incongruence among the members of a group, subgroups with regard to long- and short- term goals, policies, processes and methods, functions, or deeds of the group.
- Intergroup Conflict
  - Intergroup conflicts refer to the conflict between various groups of people, several units or functionalities within the organization.
  - Basically intergroup conflicts occur due to task interdependence (pooled task interdependence or sequential task interdependence).

Transactional Analysis

Stages of communication between two or more people can correlate to the moves of the game.

Transaction Types

- Crossed Transactions
  - When two people turn away from each other, without further discourse or dialogue after they had a disagreement is said to be just experienced a crossed transaction
  - Cross transactions are elements of discomfort in relationships be it husband-wife, parent-child, and so on.
- Complementary Transactions
  - It is a transaction between individuals when one person's ego state receives the appropriate response.
  - A complementary transaction can occur between any two ego states.
- Ulterior Transactions
  - It is a type of communication where one has to read between the lines. It is the complex types of transactions, which involves more than two ego states.

Johari Window

- This model is vital for representing interpersonal conflict and is based primarily on two concepts.
  - The extent to which a person can self-assess himself/herself.

(Continued)

(Continued)

- The extent to which the person is known to others.
- The Johari Window can be represented using the following four areas:
  - **Open area:** This area correlates with a candidate's personal profile. In the initial stages of a relationship, because two individuals are not close to each other, their personal profiles are not known to each other.
  - **Hidden self:** This area shrinks as a person shares more information with others.
  - **Blind area:** The area contains information unknown to the self and known to others.
  - **Unknown area:** This is not the area which contains information not known to others nor does self or this area contain information which is deliberately suppressed.

Conflict Resolution

To resolve interpersonal conflict, certain approaches are used:

- **Lose–lose:** In this strategy, both the entities tend to lose. One of the solutions can be a compromise made by both the groups.
- **Win–lose:** In this strategy, one entity wins and the other loses. For example, the worker's union wins or the management of an organization wins.
- **Win–win:** Using this strategy, both the entities win and the brainstorming of views and ideas to solve certain problems happen from positive perspective.

Conflict Management Styles

Competition or Application of Force

- In this style, one party is the winner and the other is the loser.
- This style is used when relationships are not important to a party and the party is aggressive as well as certain about its decision.
- Advantages:
  - Rapid conflict resolution.
  - It increases self-respect when the other party can see through the justification of applying force.
- Disadvantages:
  - Relation with opponent may get strained.
  - It may lead to uncontrolled authority.
  - It may require a lot of energy and is stressful for some.

Collaboration

- In the collaborative style both parties are the winner which promotes good feelings amongst the parties
- Collaboration involves two parties or individuals working in coalition towards a common goal or objective and get mutually benefited from the outcome.
- Collaboration is appropriate when the parties agree to work united, the perspectives of various stakeholders are considered and there is presence of high level of trust.
- Advantages:
  - Problem solving gets easy
  - Promotes trust and respect

- Shared responsibility of the outcome
- Every individual/groups perspective is taken into account and relationships are maintained.
- Less stressful
- Disadvantages:
  - It may require more effort and more time.
  - It is not appropriate when resolution demands instant decision-making.
  - Parties lose trust and faith at later times where relationship matters.

Compromise

- This style is used when chief concern is for attainment of goals and relationships. Both the parties sacrifice some of their goals to achieve a long-term goal in collaboration.
- This is used when an ideal solution cannot be perceived or all the parties are in equal power proposing their own solution.
- Advantages
  - Realistic and quick issue resolution.
  - Ad hoc solutions provided while looking for the most optimal one.
  - Lower degree of stress and tension.
- Disadvantages
  - Lose–lose situation.
  - It does not contribute to building trust in the long run.
  - It may require close monitoring and control.

Avoidance

- This style can be used when issue is not major, or too much of conflict has an impact on the relationship, or when there is very little scope to fulfil a party's own needs, or when to reach to a solution can incur delay.
- Advantages:
  - It incorporates low level of stress approach.
  - Better preparedness by gathering information.
- Disadvantages:
  - Showing no opposition can affirm to be an agreement.
  - It may have negative effect on the party who was relying on the action.

Accommodation

- This style helps in improving relationships and harmony and time is a constrained variable for resolving issues.
- Smoothing is keeping in priority other people's concern.
- Advantages:
  - Smoothing encourages resolution of prioritized issues.
  - Gives opportunity to speculate issues from various perspectives.
- Disadvantages:
  - Balance has to be maintained as when to accommodate and when not to do so as opponent.
  - party might take advantage.
  - It may negatively affect the individual's confidence.
  - It is difficult to transform to a win–win solution in the future.

CHAPTER 15

Organizational Development, Culture, and Change

Learning Objectives

- To create awareness amongst the readers about the goals and importance of organizational development and also about the principles of practice for organization development.
- To get insight into the various models of organizational development and types of organizational interventions using an exemplary approach.
- To get an in-depth view of organizational culture taking into consideration its importance from the perspective of organization's growth, creating a culture within an organization, the types of organizational culture and their characteristics, and how an organizational culture is built from stories, heroes and artefacts, work climate, rituals and ceremonies, language, and customs.
- A major portion of the text aims at discussing the changes in organizational culture, the forces leading to the change, resistance shown for the change implemented, which gives the reader a broad horizon to understand the concept of organizational development, which strongly recommends that a culture should evolve in every organization based on which employees working can identify themselves and work towards the specified goals. It also stresses on the need for adaptability to changes within organization so that there is increased chance of sustenance with changing market and business scenarios.

An Opening Vignette

Company ABC is a manufacturing firm of home appliances. Approximately 65% of the employees are located outside of South America, and the company has a rich and high multicultural mix of employees. The central goal of the company for their appliances is 'to be in every home and everywhere.' The company believed, because of having diversity, it is able to utilize all employee's strength to increase the profit, productivity and performance of the company.

The company made an effort to create culture of inclusion by:

- **Building awareness:** It began by building various business cases for diversity and change in marketplace of consumers.

- **Building competency:** It developed tools to effectively manage a global workforce and build more employee engagement.
- **Implementing best practices:** It began by incorporating diversified strategy for new employees and developed an educational curriculum that helps the managers to effectively manage a multicultural workforce throughout the organization.

Introduction to Organizational Development

Organizational development is a consciously designed endeavour to add to an association's efficacy. Vasudevan defined organizational development as endorsing organizational promptness to meet change. Organizational development is further said to be a universal learning and development strategy of an organization which aims at continuous change in viewpoints, outlook, principles, and standards of the existing organization to absorb complex tools and technologies, with recession and growth in market opportunities and business world.

Definitions of Organizational Development

Organization development is an effort (1) planned, (2) organization-wide, and (3) managed from the top, to (4) increase organization effectiveness and health through (5) planned interventions in the organization's "processes," using behavioural-science knowledge.

Richard Beckhard

Organization development is a system wide application of behavioural science knowledge to the planned development and reinforcement of organizational strategies, structure, and processes for improving an organization's effectiveness.

Thomas Cummings and Christopher Worley

Organization development is a long-term effort, led and supported by top management, to improve an organization's visioning, empowerment, learning, and problem-solving processes, through an on-going, collaborative management of organization culture—with special emphasis on the culture of intact work teams and other team configurations—utilizing the consultant-facilitator role and the theory and technology applied behavioural science, including action research.

Wendell French and Cecil Bell

Organization development is the attempt to influence the members of an organization to expend their candidness with each other about their views of the organization and their experience in it and greater responsibility for their own actions and organization members.

Nelson

A planned process of change in an organisation's culture through the utilization of behavioural science technology, research and theory.

Burke

Nature of Organizational Development

An organization consists of people, process, equipments, and machineries, and these entities change with time. Skills and attitudes of people need to be refined, equipments and machineries need to be changed, processes and procedures need transformation, and to make these changes happen by taking appropriate measures is the responsibility of the organization which can be named as organizational development. Organizational development is an ongoing, methodical, and continuous process.

To bring in development within an organization, goals have to be planned, with strong focus and intention and sound analytics, which can ensure organizational development. Organizational development is interdisciplinary and draws on sociology, psychology, and various motivational theories. Organizational development is a growing field that is responsive to many news approaches. For example, WW Bakers organizational climate, an important constituent of organizational development, became negative, as sales for cake products were declining and managers were under huge pressure as profit margins were going down. On the other hand, products, such as patties and rolls, made by them were achieving a new high. The employees were excited to have another chance at success. The organizational culture, an important constituent of organizational development, was very friendly at WW Bakers, and employees nurtured a culture of friendship and alliance which the top management thought should go in for a total transformation if the company wanted to expand and enlarge across global boundaries.

Characteristics of Organizational Development

The characteristics of current organizational development are as follows:

- It is a well-managed process and depends on extensive data gathering and planned with future expectations with a pronounced vision.
- It is integrated and has a problem-oriented approach, which affects the solutions.
- It also reflects a systems approach wherein the organization is viewed as a system, and system includes employee, employer, and technology.
- It depends on practical implementations of various organizational approaches in the analysis form.
- It involves the distinct role of a person who makes progress easier to ensure that changes are real.
- It involves learning principles that individuals as well as all employees of organization should have approach to work together and relearn at all levels in order to effect fundamental changes.
- It consists of a structured approach to detecting organizational problems and opportunities and then applying expertise to them.
- It is based on solid research and involves application of knowledge of behavioural science to the problems faced by the organization.
- It emphasizes on the fact that if organization has to change, then individuals also have to change.
- It aims to improve individuals and organization's professional health.
- It focuses more on problem solving.

Goals of Organizational Development

The goals of organizational development vary based on situations, and some of the most common goals are as follows:

- Goal of organizational development is to align the employee's mission with organization's mission, and workers should work in incision to achieve the goals.

- Goal of organizational development is again to motivate workers to solve the problems related to the enterprise, which in return also gives the workers the necessary exposure and experience and aids them in improving their performance.
- The process of planning for any task or planning to achieve the organizational goal is very crucial for an organization, and it requires active participation from the workers.
- Organizational development works towards developing a communication channel between the workers and the management, and an effective communication channel is mandatory to develop trust, cooperation, and strengthening the ties for the growth of the organization.
- Organizational development promotes conducive atmosphere for workers and makes them self-motivated to work for profitability and productivity and growth of the business enterprise.
- Organizational development enables workers to adapt to internal and external changes to the organization, which indirectly increases the work efficiency of the workers and also of the organization.
- Organizational development aims at building trust and confidence, which in turn makes workers feel that their contributions for the organization are significant and hence the management has started believing in him, which in turn renders more of cooperation from that individual and others as well, and this goes a long way in enhancing organizational performance.

Importance of Organizational Development

Organizational development aims at improving productivity and is very much required with respect to problem solving and decision-making, and implementing organizational development requires a capitalization of time and money.

Organizational Change

The process of organizational development seeks areas where change is required and an in-depth analysis of the change is done and put up in the change management plan. The plan then elaborates on the ways in which changes can be done and the impact the changes will have on the company operations. It also outlines who all will be affected by the change and how a smooth transition can be ensured while implementing the change. All this is possible because of organizational development.

Growth

Effective organizational development directly impacts business growth. Based on financial and sales growth and keeping in line customer demands, an organization's growth is perceived and uses human and material resources such as workforce and the distribution channels to lodge future growth.

Work Processes

Companies need to indulge in organizational development in order to grow and keeping their processes standardized, efficient, and accurate. Appropriate quality control measures are taken to attain company standards. Evaluators analyse the existing work processes and try to refine the processes as per company standards by crafting out plans and proposals which abide by the standard norms.

Product Innovation

With reference to innovation of products, organizational development assists in getting innovative strategies of competitors and analysis on the same, technology required for product development, the customers' preferences and demands, the market segment, manufacturing potential, and patents and trademarks on making of a new product.

Organizational Development: Principles of Practice

The practitioners of organizational development are guided by the following core values and beliefs which are put into practice:

- **To respect** the perspectives of every individual.
- **Collaboration**—wok together to achieve a particular goal.
- **Authenticity**—entrusting people to stick to sound beliefs and goals.
- **Self-awareness**—committed to developing self-awareness and interpersonal skills within the organization.
- **Empowerment**—to allocate sense of authority to every individual simultaneously and providing them support in order to improve productivity and raise employee morale.
- **Democracy and social justice**—it implies if employees feel that the organization's surge towards success is primarily because of their contribution, then definitely for all organizational initiatives, they would be supportive. Hence, the perception of democracy and practice of democracy should prevail amongst the employees.

Support from Other Disciplines

Organizational development draws its support from theories which include the applied behavioural and physical sciences.

Systems Focused

Systems-focused approach relies heavily on open systems theory and techniques to understand communities and organizations. Therefore, a change made in an area of the system always results in changes in other areas as well, and organization being a system change in one process, standard, schedule, and services will bring in a change in other components.

Action Research

A distinguishing organizational development feature is the continuity in the research undertaken, wherein planned action must be constantly scrutinized and policies revised as intrusions unfurl.

Process Focused

Organizational development is process focused, and management consultants are more worried with 'what' instead of 'why'.

Data Driven

Organizational development involves the investigation and evaluation of the internal and external surroundings in order to unearth authentic information and craft a basis for change and promise to the accomplishment of a more sound state of the organization.

Action Research Model of Organizational Development

Wendell L. French and Cecil Bell defined organizational development at one point as 'organization improvement through action research'. Conceptualized by Kurt Lewin and later elaborated and expanded by other behavioural scientists, Lewin believed that the motivation to change was strongly related to action: The employees who are active in decisions affecting them, they are more likely to adopt new ways. Rational social management, as per Lewin, proceeds in a series of steps, each of which is composed of a loop constituting of planning, action, and fact-finding about the result of action (Figure 15.1).

The change in process from Lewin's perspective involves following three steps:

- **Unfreezing:** A problem in the existing process might lead the individual or group to believe that there is a requirement for change.
- **Changing:** New behavioural models are explored and then tested.
- **Refreezing:** If the new behavioural model after an evaluation deems to be fit, then it is adopted.

Figure 15.1 consolidates the steps and processes involved in planned change through action research, which includes initial investigation, collection of data/information, and feedback of output received. Here, the client and the change agent work together. Action research is

Figure 15.1 System Model of Action Research Process

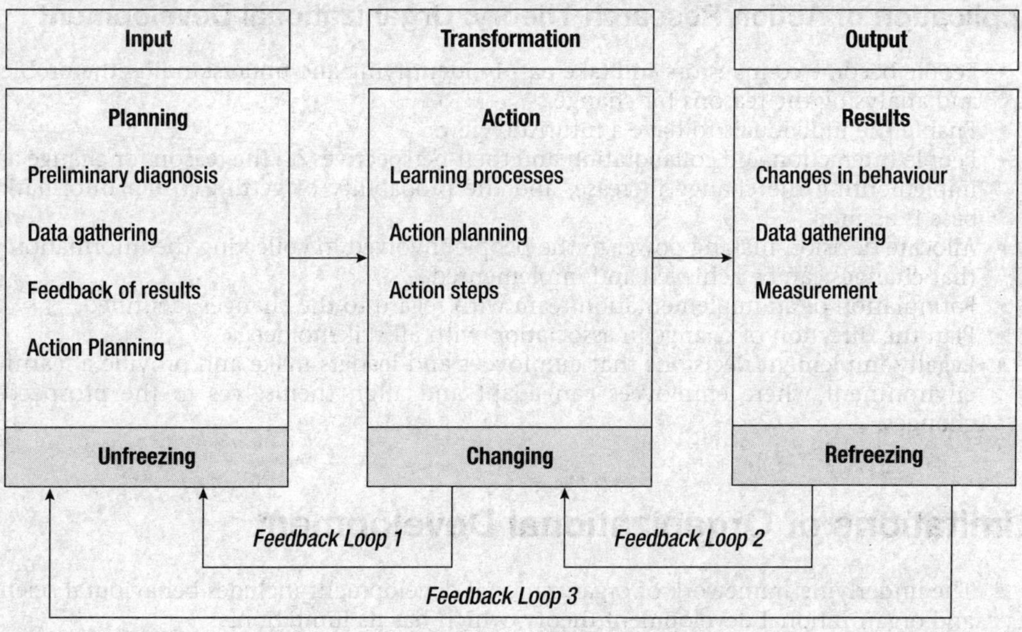

depicted as a cyclical process of change. The systems theory states that this is the input phase where the client system identifies the need for change and becomes aware that an external agent is required to bring in the changes and initiates a dialogue with the consultant to diagnose the problem.

The next stage of action research is the transformation phase. This stage includes activities related to the learning processes and planning and implementing the behavioural changes in the client organization. In Figure 15.1, every stage is associated with feedback, and hence if the feedback at the second phase is not justifiable, then it would mean to alter the plan to make the learning better aligned to the organizational objective. Here, there is a regular interaction between the client and the consultant for more accurate transformations.

The third stage of action is the result phase, which includes monitoring actual changes in behaviour resulting from the implementation of the changes. This phase includes data collection from the client system so that improvements can be understood and minor adjustments in learning activities can be made via the feedback loop as shown in Figure 15.1, whereas major ones will have to be undertaken from the initial phase. This model is similar to Lewin's three-step process of unfreezing, changing, and freezing.

Characteristics of Action Research Theory

- It is problem centric, client centric, and action orientation.
- It is characterized by problem identification and problem-solving process.
- There is a very close interaction between the client and the change agent wherein they go through the stages of identifying and ranking problems, to understand their causal effect, and formulating plans to tackle them.
- Since the action research theory is based on research methodologies, it constitutes data gathering, hypotheses formulation, testing hypotheses, and evaluating outcomes.
- Action research is supported by a mechanism for sustaining and improving the efficiency of the client's system where the system is powered by tools for self-analysis and renewal.

Application of Action Research Theory: Organizational Development

- People become co-investors and take part in identifying and understanding the problem and analysing the reasons for change.
- Enable the individuals to have a futuristic view.
- People interaction and collaboration and their perspectives on the reason for change and implementing the change increase, and the probability of getting a rich information base is assured.
- Allocate decision-making power to the people involved in collecting the information so that changes can be achieved and implemented.
- Formulation of an implementation team with regard to the changes identified.
- Plan the direction of change in association with all stakeholders.
- Legally implement decisions that employees and leaders make and provide a learning environment where employees can adapt and align themselves to the prospective changes.

Limitations of Organizational Development

- The underlying framework of organizational development includes behavioural science and organizational development theory, which has its limitations.

- Limitations of organizational development accrue to its inability to challenge a complacent person's motivation.
- Organizational development implementations are circumstantial, and mostly research and development organizations are not impacted by organizational development.

General Process of Organizational Development

The organizational development process is based on the action research model, which begins with an identified problem or need for change followed by analysis of what change is required and how it has to be done, collecting information to evaluate the involvement and implications of change, and tracking the status of progress in a cyclical approach till the attainment of the result.

The phases (shown in Figure 15.2) of organizational development are as follows:

Problem Identification

The identification of the problem in relation to growth and utilization of resources, which has a direct impact on the vital statistics of the organization, calls for a change or else the top leadership strata of the organization want to bring a total transformation in the organization.

Analysis

Once the problem is identified or the decision is made to change the current execution scenario, the next step is to analyse the existing conditions, the causal scenario, the avenues which require change, and what sort of changes need to be done. This analysis is done using the techniques of documentation reviews, taking feedback from focus groups, interviewing, or conducting an extensive survey. For a very impartial assessment, the assessment could be done by members external to the organization. The analysis done constitutes the following:

- **Structural analysis:** Alignment of different units of the organization to organizational goals.

Figure 15.2 Process of Organizational Development

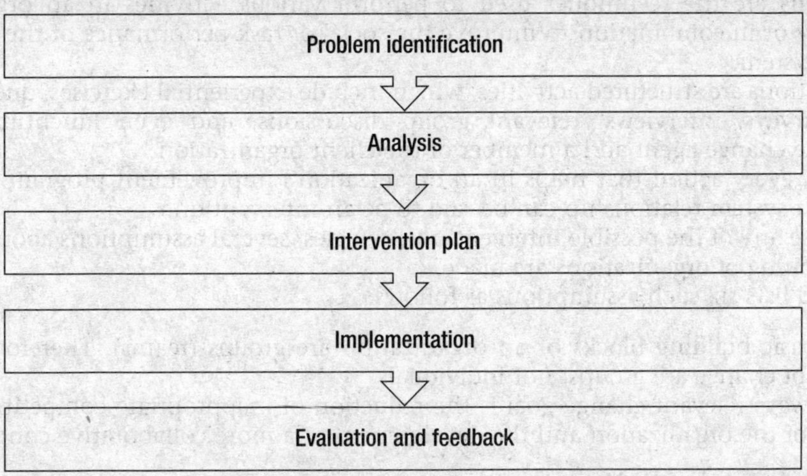

- **Process analysis:** It correlates to decision-making, group dynamics, communication, and conflict management within the organization.
- **Function and domain analysis:** Function analysis relates to the performance of certain variables, results, and outcomes, and domain analysis reflects upon the area of the organization subjected to analysis.

Plan an Intervention

The intervention will depend directly on the changed goals, and they could be of the form of skill based or process training and development or collaborations in the management teams across the units to achieve the changed goals.

Implementation

After the planning for the change and collecting the required data for change, the execution of implementation plan is initiated.

Evaluation and Feedback

For example, if the intervention were process training for individual employees or for certain units of the organization, data have to be accumulated to track changes in knowledge and competencies.

Based on evaluation and feedback, the leadership body or the stakeholders can decide whether the process has to end or whether to follow another cycle of intervention or involvement.

For example, Coca Cola undertook organizational development or transformation that would better suit the North American market by establishing two big units—Coca-Cola North America and Coca-Cola Refreshments—and went on to consolidate the leadership of its global operations as Coca-Cola International and Coca-Cola Americas to enhance their focus on execution and accelerate the refranchising of their bottling system in their flagship market.

Organizational Development Interventions

Interventions are the techniques used to perform various activities in an organized way individually or in combination to improve the social or task performance of the members of the client system.

Interventions are structured activities, which include experiential exercises, questionnaires, attitude surveys, interviews, relevant group discussions, and even lunchtime meetings between the change agent and a member of the client organization.

In short, every action that helps in an organization's improvement program in a change agent–client system relationship can be said to be an intervention.

To choose any of the possible intervention strategies, several assumptions about the nature and functioning of organizations are made.

Beckhard lists six such assumptions as follows:

- The basic building blocks of an organization are groups (teams). Therefore, the basic units of change are groups, not individuals.
- An always relevant change goal is the reduction of inappropriate competition between parts of the organization and the development of a more collaborative condition.

- Decision-making in a healthy organization is located where the information sources are, rather than in a particular role or level of hierarchy.
- Organizations, subunits of organizations, and individuals continuously manage their affairs against goals. Controls are interim measurements, not the basis of managerial strategy.
- One goal of a healthy organization is to develop generally open communication, mutual trust, and confidence between and across levels.
- People support what they help create. People affected by a change must be allowed active participation and a sense of ownership in the planning and conduct of the change.

Types of Organizational Development Interventions

Large-scale interventions

Large-scale interventions involve a whole system working simultaneously to achieve a particular set of goals.

These interventions are highly structured as all the activities are planned beforehand. Each level of the organization participates for the implementation of planned activities for the long-term support.

Cummings and Worley (2001) describe the three-step process involved in any large-scale intervention as follows:

- The preparation of the large-group meeting.
- Conducting the meeting.
- Following on meeting outcomes.

Some other examples include appreciative inquiry summit, future search, open space, and real-time strategic change.

Strategic Interventions

These interventions link the internal functioning of the organization to the larger environment and transform the organization to keep pace with changing conditions. Strategic intervention helps organizations to understand its current status and to develop more strategies, such as cost-cutting to diversifying into innovating new products or alteration in the services as per the changing market scenarios, to compete with other organizations.

Kormanik (2005), under the umbrella of strategic interventions, includes mission/vision/purpose, strategic planning and goal setting, visioning/scenario planning, benchmarking, SWOT, communication audit/strategy, values clarification and commitment, climate survey, and culture change.

Techno-structural Interventions

Techno-structural interventions rely on a deficit-based approach, and the idea is to find problems to solve.

These interventions focus on the technology and structure for the development and are rooted in the fields of engineering, sociology, and psychology, combined with socio-technical systems and job analysis and design.

Kormanik (2005), under the umbrella of techno-structural interventions, includes organizational structure, organization systems, business process redesign, space and physical settings, socio-technical systems, change management, job design/enrichment, competency-based management, knowledge management, and organizational learning.

For example, ABC Co Ltd. decided to divide the project work across three subunits—planning, design, and development—and coordinated the work of these departments using a very efficient communication channel. Later, the manager made decisions about how to deliver the services to client and how to link people to tasks, an example of techno-structural interventions.

Management and Leadership Development Interventions

These interventions aim to develop the quality and effectiveness of the leaders.

Kormanik (2005), under the umbrella of management and leadership development interventions, includes executive and professional development, mentoring, coaching, action learning, action science, MBO, succession planning, 360-degree feedback, participative management, and technical/skills training.

A research study conducted by the Corporate Leadership Council (2001) revealed that organizations are focusing on the following five actions to increase their leadership bench strength:

- Redefining the leadership profiles to better respond to current business needs.
- Targeting future leadership needs.
- Ensuring top-management accountability for leadership development.
- Creating a continuous development culture.
- Customizing the development opportunities to the leaders' needs.

Team Development and Group Processes Interventions

Team development and group processes interventions aim at improving various aspects related to group performance and also the interdependency among the group members.

According to Robbins (1994), team building is applicable where group activities are interdependent. The main objective of these interventions is to improve the coordination among the team members, which will result in a better performance.

Individual/Interpersonal Process Interventions

These interventions are the most personalized of all, and probably the most widely used by organizations. Individual/interpersonal process aims at the development of specific skills of every individual in the organization.

The most common examples of this type of interventions are learning strategies, life transitions, mentoring, and interpersonal communications among other.

Definitions of Organizational Culture

> *The set of the set of beliefs, values, and norms, together with symbols like dramatized events and personalities that represents the unique character of an organization, and provides the context for action in it and by it.*
>
> Gareth Morgan

> *A pattern of shared basic assumptions that the group learned as it solved its problems that has worked well enough to be considered valid and is passed on to new members as the correct way to perceive, think, and feel in relation to those problems.*
>
> Edgar Schein

Organizational culture refers to the pattern of beliefs, values and learned ways of coping with experience that have developed during the course of an organization's history, and which tend to be manifested in its material arrangements and in the behaviours of its members.

Andrew Brown

Organizational Culture

Organizational culture revolves around organization's prospects, knowledge, viewpoint, and principles that bind it and is expressed in its execution process, exchange of information with the outside world, and future prospects. It is dependent on shared feelings, values, traditions, and explicit and implicit rules. Organization culture is also termed as corporate culture, which includes the following:

- Process of conducting the business, the conduct of employees, customers, and other stakeholders.
- The approach to decision-making and innovation of ideas.
- The power and authority allocated across the levels and the information flow through the hierarchy.
- The commitment level of employees and the approach to attain the objective.
- Impact on organization's performance, process, and productivity and focus on improving customer service, product quality, production methods, safety and security, marketing and advertising strategies, and product innovation.
- Variation in culture from organization to organization.

Subculture and Counter-culture

An organization might have culture within its own culture known as subculture. For example, people working on the support desk may have a different culture, which induces openness and human interaction or intervention, than people working in the production unit, which emphasizes innovation and management. A culture that evolves within different units and subunits or geographic boundaries is called a subculture. Mostly, subculture is attuned to the work environment and conditions.

Counter-culture of an organization or a subunit within an organization comprises values, beliefs, and traditions which are in direct opposition to the actual culture. For example, a unit within the organization may adopt frequently changing strategies which are at par with the current market, whereas another unit might be less flexible in adapting to the changes which can later be perceived as a threat, and this counter-culture needs to be eliminated.

Strong Versus Weak Culture

Strong culture helps organization operate smoothly with less friction amongst the subordinates or peers with very solid execution methodology and with very less amendments required, whereas the counter sequence is envisaged in a company having weak culture and greater control to be exercised in such situations.

Research carried out in organizations makes the fact evident that organizations with strong culture make employees align with the culture very quickly, and service sector organizations tend to exhibit that sort of culture. The benefits derived from developing strong and prolific cultures are as follows:

- To work towards company's vision, mission, and objectives.
- Employees are highly inspired and exude trust.
- Increased solidity amongst various units and subunits of the organization.
- Promoting reliability with proper control within the company.
- Making organization more efficient by implementing sound execution concepts.
- For example, Infosys as a company has a very strong organizational culture.

The deficiencies are as follows:

- Company which has a strong culture provokes the concept of groupthink since the employees believe that what they think and do is correct. The concept of groupthink is dealt extensively in the chapter of group and group dynamics.

Characteristics of Organizational Culture

The seven characteristics of organizational culture are as follows:

Innovation

Companies who adopt a culture which promotes exploring new ideas and avenues encourage employees to take risks, whereas those who do not undertake risks do not focus much on the area of innovations and explorations.

Detailing

Detailing refers to the accuracy with which employees are expected to work and organizations which stress on the same expect employees to work with precision than organizations which focus much less on the aspect of detailing.

Result and Outcome

Companies that focus on meeting the desired outcome attach importance on this trait of organizational culture. For example, a company directs its marketing executives to do aggressive marketing so that the sale of their product achieves a significant high within a very short span.

Employee Centric

Companies that have employee-centric culture place a great deal of importance on how their decisions will affect the people in their organizations. In such companies, the culture is to treat employees with respect and dignity.

Teamwork

Companies that organize work activities around teams place strong emphasis on this characteristic of organizational culture. People who are employed in such companies have very good relations with their peers and manager.

Competitive Edge

Companies with an aggressive culture place a strong emphasis on being the market leader and outperforming the competition at all costs.

Stability

A company whose culture focuses majorly on stability are rule-oriented, predictable, and officious in nature. They provide consistent output and operate best in non-changing market conditions.

Organizational Culture and Its Functions

Culture Endorses Code of Conduct

An organization with strong culture sets acceptable behavioural norms and code of conduct to achieve good business outcomes.

Culture Facilitates Recognition

Organization's name and fame are not only based on the products or services they sell but also on the culture they adopt and the recognition they receive from adopting good culture.

Culture Provides Self-satisfaction

Employees associated with organizations which have strong culture are deemed to be satisfied employees.

Culture Provides Opportunity to Set the Standards of Performance

An organization with strong culture enables employees to get a chance to set the performance standards. They try to achieve the standards. It becomes a tool depending on which organizations develop and prosper.

Culture within Organizations Mentor Employees

Organizational culture acts as a motivator that forms a base for employee guidance and control.

Organizational Culture Also Helps in Attainment of Goals

A robust culture directs the stance and conduct of the employees towards the accomplishment of goals.

Culture Orients People towards Development

Organizational culture develops implicit rules which make people oriented towards self-development and discipline.

Culture Inculcates Positive Attitude

Culture inculcates positive attitude and good behavioural norms amongst employees.

Conflict Reduction

A common culture promotes steadiness in observation and reduction in conflict because every employee is aligned to the culture of the organization.

Coordination and Control

Organizational culture promotes steadiness of viewpoint and also facilitates processes of coordination and control.

Uncertainty Reduction

Adopting the cultural mindframe simplifies the work methods and helps in selecting alternatives easily and initiating actions in response to the alternatives.

Motivation

A consistent and unified culture motivates employee so that he develops his identity, fosters belief and loyalty, and performs to his potential

Competitive Advantage

Strong culture improves the organization's chances of being successful in the marketplace.

Types of Organizational Culture

Normative culture

In such an organizational culture, the standards and procedures are defined before, and the rules and regulations are set accordingly. The employees are bound by norms and stick to the policies and there is no attempt to break the rules. For example, Accenture has normative organizational culture where standards and procedures are already set.

Pragmatic Culture

Customer satisfaction is the main motto of the organization in realistic environment, and most of the companies follow this culture. In a pragmatic culture, customer is treated as God. Customer satisfaction is the main motive of the employees in order to get more business deals. Mostly all service-based companies follow pragmatic culture.

Academy Culture

The organization which tries to follow this type of culture has highly skilled employee base. The role and authority are distributed according to the technical qualification and education background, appropriate training programs are conducted in an academy, and association of employees with the organization is of long duration. Example can be of premiere management institutes across India.

Baseball Team Culture

In complete contrast to the pragmatic culture, a baseball team culture considers the employees as the most precious asset of the organization. These employees in due course exhibit indifference to their organization and ad agencies, event management firms and financial institutions are followers of this culture.

Club Culture

Organizations have highly skilled professionals and are very choosy about the employees they induct with regard to their specialization, educational qualification, and areas of inclination. The organization follows the process of promotions and appraisals on a regular note. Some examples include military organizations and legal firms.

Organization-centric Culture

In this culture, profit of the organization is more important. If the organization is not able to perform well, then it terminates the employee.

Performance-based Culture

In such type of culture, performance of an individual is important. The employee is under continuous observation, and based on performance, person can be rewarded. For example, loan disbursement firms and premiere car companies.

Process Culture

All the procedures of the company are very much important. They are already established. Reviews do not matter in such organizations. Employee should work according to the already establish procedure. For example, IBM follows a process culture.

Levels of Organizational Culture

Organizational culture consists of three interrelated levels, of which some are visible and some are intuitive consisting of assumptions, values, and artefacts. The three levels of organization culture as portrayed by Schein in Figure 15.3 are as follows:

Artefacts

Architecture, furniture, and dress code, all denote organizational artefacts immediately recognized by other culture people.

Figure 15.3 Levels of Organizational Culture

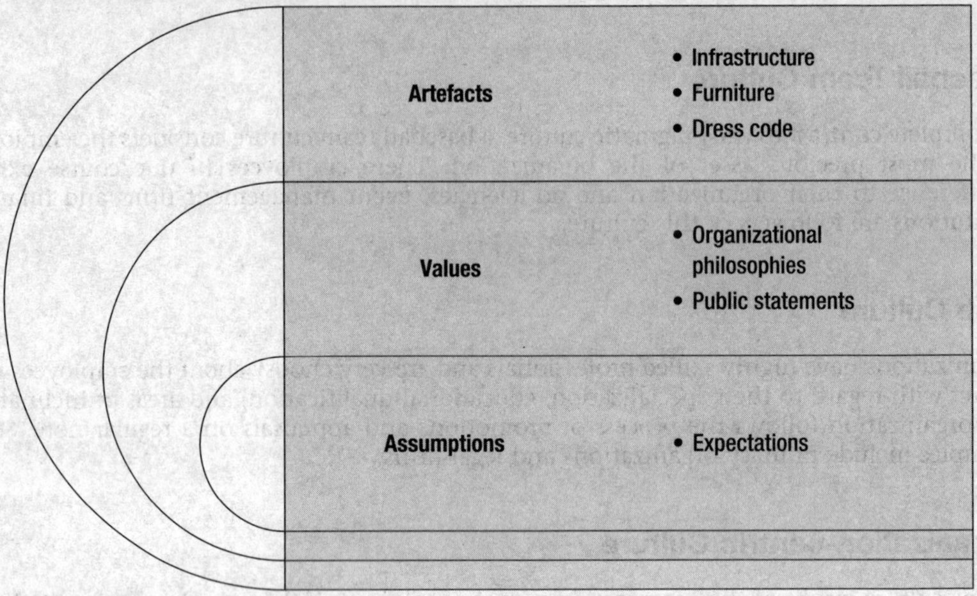

Values

Espoused values are the organization's stated values which are inculcated amongst the members to project organizations' values not only to others but also to themselves. This is often expressed in official philosophies and public statements of identity.

Assumptions

Shared assumptions are deeply rooted and so well incorporated in the office dynamic that they are hard to identify from within. For example, a basic assumption on satisfied employees in an organization might be translated into values, such as consensus, transparency, and tolerance in relationships for which the artefacts might be conference rooms equipped with modern amenities, company lawns and courts, and frequent company picnics where the employees get to interact with each other irrespective of the unit they are working in. Organizational cultural is best depicted through its physical infrastructure, employee interactions, company policies, and reward systems. For example, the company culture cannot be understood only by taking a note of the outside appearance of the infrastructure since more lies beneath it, which is the level of interaction amongst the employees, their choices, beliefs, and perspectives on the dos and don'ts of the behavioural norms.

Dimensions of Organizational Culture

The organization culture as defined by Geert Hofstede, social psychologist and authority on global and organizational cultures, consists of six dimensions:

Means Versus Goal Oriented

The two aspects differ in how and what: for example, a means-oriented culture focuses on how work is to be done and avoids approaches which undertake risks, whereas a goal-oriented culture aims at finding what work is to be done and involves risk-taking approaches. In such cases, outcome is also mandatory. From the perspective of organizational effectiveness, goal-oriented culture is very effective.

Internally Versus Externally Driven

Internally driven employees are those who think that they know what is best for the customer, whereas externally employees focus on customers' requirements and wants. As Steve Jobs once said, 'A lot of times, people don't know what they want until you show it to them'.

Easy-going Versus Strict Work Discipline

As the very term suggests that work discipline refers to the structured method in which the work is executed, and if some control is exercised, then there is more of imposition on employees to get it done in a methodical manner with focus on productivity and efficiency, whereas in an easy-going culture, the approach to work is informal, slack, unpredictable, and these factors steer fair amount of innovation.

Local Versus Professional

In an organizational culture, which is of local type, employees identify with their managers and the members of the team where risk taking is low because of social obligations, whereas in a company with a professional culture, employees identify with their work, which has low level of predictability since work needs to be finished.

Open Versus Closed System

In an open system, new employees are welcome with open arms and people fit well in those open systems, but in closed ones, the adaptability to accept and align by employees both internal and external to the system is constrained, and employee satisfaction is also less.

Employee Versus Work Centred

Organizational culture which is employee centric keeps the employees satisfied and happy even at the expense of productivity and profitability, but in a work-centred environment, focus is on work performance, and the leaders have extremely low level of sympathy where employees' personal problem is concerned.

Creating Organizational Culture

Creating organizational culture involves developing the identity of the organization, creating organizational values and sound traditions, and adopting management best practices. The prerequisite to creating or refining organizational culture is through a four-step process:

- **Acquire:** First, knowledge, facts, skills, processes, and concepts are acquired.
- **Embed:** All the above acquisitions are then embedded in the learning and practices followed by the organization.
- **Integrate:** The various refined subprocesses within the processes are then integrated and then put for the next step.
- **Test:** At this stage, the refined concepts are then tested and then implemented.

Organizational Culture and Its Sustenance

The key entities which play a role in sustaining organization's culture are the following:

- **Selection practices:** Selection practices adopted for hiring individuals with the right skill sets, knowledge, and abilities to perform the tasks successfully and have organizational values embedded in self. These are also characterized by potential task force who wants to work with the organization and are very much interested in knowing its history and culture (Brown, 1998). Also, the selection process is a mechanism to choose individuals who adopt and align to the organizational culture (Martins & Martins, 2003).
- **Socialization process:** It is the process in which a new employee is made to adapt to the organizational culture prior to joining the organization otherwise termed as pre-arrival. Encounter process actually makes the employee understand the difference between expectations and realities followed by metamorphosis wherein the employee masters the skills required for the job and takes up new roles and responsibilities.
- **Stage of incorporation or rejection:** This is the final stage with regard to the sustainability factor of the organization culture where incorporation leads to acceptance of members by the workgroups and alignment to organizational culture by members and rejection leads to loss of values, goals, and assumptions which might lead to identity crisis amongst the members of the organization, a theory formulated by Scheins, Brown, and Martin.

Organizational Culture and Its Elements

The elements of organizational culture consist of stories, rituals, ceremonies, languages, and customs, some of which are discussed below. It is through these that the culture has evolved and has been learned.

Stories

Stories in the form of laying the stones of foundation, challenges faced in the initial years by founders and leaders, and how these issues were dealt with in the context of the organization form the base of the culture the organization carries today, and employees of the organization tend to relate to the past based on the current scenarios, and this gradually evolves as an organizational culture.

Rituals and Ceremonies

Rituals are organizational events conducted when someone is accorded a promotion or in case of events like superannuation, resignation, project success, clinching deals, festivals, where the employees gather to celebrate in some form or the other based on the event and the circumstance. These all combine to sustain culture of the organization along with a few add-ons, such as working for stipulated hours of the day, learning professional etiquettes, and reinforcing organizational values. Ceremonies include national holidays or event like award-giving ceremonies where major contributors to the organization are facilitated.

Language and Customs

A company's culture is often associated by language and customs where there are slogans, expressions, and sayings basically to motivate employees to achieve desired objectives or to ingrain in them the core ethics and values and focus of the company. For example, some very-often-heard sayings that 'Transformation of customer satisfaction to delight' can enthuse employees to follow that culture. Even customers can appreciate the service deliveries by sending in gifts or greetings.

Symbols and Symbolic Action

Symbols and symbolic actions remind employees of the organizations ethics and values and focus on clothing and office décor, whereas status symbols signify usage of the right behaviour with others as per the superiority and the individual's status and position. There may be many symbols around an organization highlighting products, services, and cultural etiquettes from around the world.

Beliefs, Assumptions, and Attitudes

Sharing of beliefs is a common culture across the employees in an organization and can make them not see through the dangers. Attitudes can be positive or negative wherein members very positively adapt to changing scenarios in situations where they show positive traits and always show resistance in case of the negative attitude leading to a flexible or a constrained culture.

Rules, Norms, and Ethics

The norms and ethics of organizational culture are ingrained in artefacts, symbols, stories, and so on, and to sustain culture, employees might abide by them.

Mission and Values

Organization's mission statement is the underlying base on which future course of action is planned. For example, to be a globally respected corporation that provides best-of-breed business solutions, leveraging technology, delivered by best-in-class people is Infosys's mission in relation to consulting and IT services. As for values, if employees are treated as important assets, then the organizational policies should provide them the necessary support. Shared values are strong motivators and provide a competitive edge.

Climate and Habits

The climate of an organization is basically decided by the top management before it reaches the other level employees, and this constitutes whether the climate is conducive for employees to do whatever they want or pursue their dreams in relation to the organizational context and whether they are also able to spend quality time with family and so on. People of an organization develop habits which are portrayed by the top leaders of the organization, so a lot depends on the steering committee of the organization to pave the way for a corporate culture within the organization.

Heroes and Artefacts

Heroes are basically the founder members of the organization or people having special accomplishments who have taken the organization through exponential growth or have helped the organizations to diversify in other areas as well.

Ethical Organizational Culture—Sustainability Issue

When we use the term organization culture, we are actually referring to the following aspects as shown in Figure 15.4.

To create and sustain an ethical organizational culture which is further a strenuous task, people need to align themselves to the organizations values and ethics which need to be discussed and communicated continuously across the levels, ensuring that leaders and staff members are aligned to those values and living the principles. An ethical organizational culture ensures the continuity in decision-making, trust building, and consistency and commitment in operating under difficult situations and challenging conditions when information is unclear and vague.

Figure 15.4 Ethics and Organizational Culture

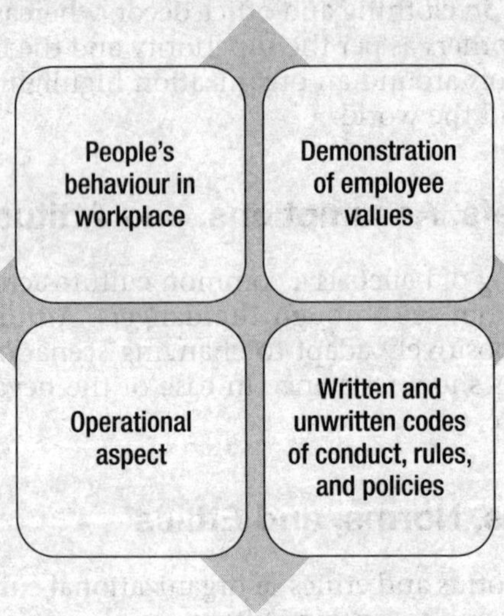

Changing Organizational Culture

Change management comprises three aspects of change instituted within the organizational culture: adapting to change, controlling change, and effecting change. This incorporates defining and implementing changes, procedures, and technologies to deal with changing business scenarios. From the IT perspective, change management refers to information updates with relation to hardware, software, and tools for which employees need to adapt themselves by building new structures and mechanisms to implement change. Change management is an important part of project management where a plan is designed to implement the changes.

Sometimes, culture of organizations needs to be changed, especially when it becomes unhealthy or weak or when it acts as an obstacle in implementing a new plan or strategy.

- The behavioural approach emphasizes the surface level of culture and the pattern of behaviours that employee exhibits.

- The competing value approach seeks to access an organization's culture in terms how it resolves dilemma.
- The competing value approach provides clan culture adhocracy, culture, hierarchical culture, and market culture.

Guidelines for Changing Organizational Culture

- **Formulate a Clear Strategic Vision:** Organization should have clear vision of its long-term goals and about a new strategy they will be implementing.
- **Display Top-management Commitment:** The top-level of management should be committed to their values and beliefs, which give positive image to managers and workers to follow and abide the values.
- **Model Culture at the Highest Levels:** Seniors executives are free to communicate and express the values to the employees of organization.
- Restructure the organization to support the new culture.
- The organizational structure should be redesigned or re-engineered with the changing time, and the workers should be able to adapt to the changes made in organizational structure.
- Select and socialize newcomers and terminate deviants.
- People need to be selected and terminated in terms of their consequences. This especially develops key leadership positions, where actions of people significantly promote new values and actions.
- Develop ethical and legal sensitivity.

Culture change may arise conflicts, but the top management should able to convey and provide assistance to employees to adapt keeping in mind the ethical and legal norms.

Nature of Change

Organizational change is the process by which organizations move from their present state to some desired future state to increase their effectiveness.

Characteristics of Change

- It is a process and is not any event that has occurred.
- It is normal and constant in nature.
- Directive change is implemented by top to down in management hierarchy.
- Participative change involves everyone or those who are directly or indirectly affected by change.
- It is interdependent on organizational culture.

Process of Change

Figure 15.5 shows the process of change as follows:

Stage 1: Unfreezing

- Unfreezing means that old ideas and practices need to be cast aside, so that new ideas can be learned.

Figure 15.5 Process of Change

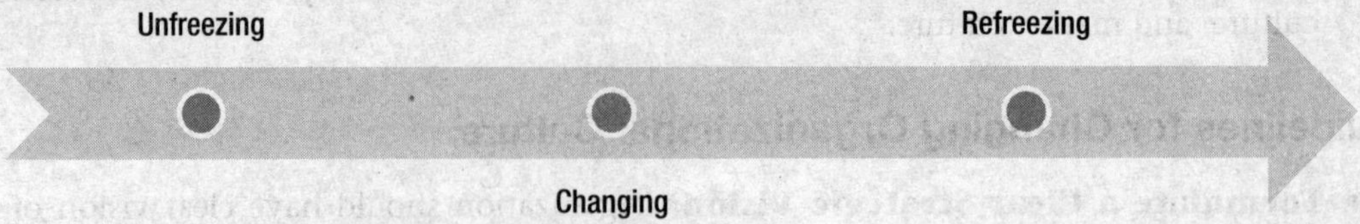

- It basically means to have an open mind and flexibility to accept new changes.
- It is basically the breaking of current comfort zone and getting ready for a change. Therefore, a manager must help employees clear their minds of old roles and procedures.

The unfreezing stage is probably one of the most important stage to understand the world in which we live today. With so many changes in government rules policies and processes, organizations have to discard old ways of working and introduce new operational procedures.

Stage 2: Change or Transition

- Changing is a step in which new ideas and practices are learnt.
- This process involves helping an employee think reason and perform in a variety of new ways.
- It can be a time of confusion, disorientation, overload, and despair. Patience is very important in this point.
- There should be hope, discovery, and excitement to overcome all chaos and enter a new mode of development. Big transitions to mobile-based services have been incorporated across IT and ITES organizations.

Stage 3: Refreezing

- Refreezing means that what has been learned is integrated into actual practice.
- The new practices are incorporated into the employee's routine behaviour.
- Successful on-the-job practice then must be the ultimate goal of the refreezing step. In this step, emphasis is on stabilizing the work process after rapid change transition.
- Organizational change is the process through which an organization moves from the present state to an improved state. Change is vital for organization's survival.
- Change management comprises three elements: evolution of the firm, its management and organization, and the people who work for it.
- External and internal forces change in organization.

Forces Responsible for Change in Organizations

Changes brought forth from outside the organization are due to external causes, and those from within the organization are called internal causes.

External Forces

The external causes which are instrumental in bringing the changes in the organization are as follows:

Demographic Characteristics

Diversity management is mandatory for organizations operating across the globe to ensure consistent contribution and commitment from employees.

Social and Political Pressures

With respect to social pressures, managers may need to adjust their style to accommodate changing employee values which consist of employees' needs and priorities.

Political events can also create substantial changes. For example, the collapse of the Berlin Wall created many new business opportunities, and at that time in India, the Bharatiya Janata Party (BJP) government has major plans for expansion across various business verticals.

Globalization

It has made organization rethink its boundary as the level of competition has risen. The organization has to rethink in the most efficient way to utilize its resources more efficiently and by making people think from global perspectives so that global markets could be captured, and organization has to develop people to become global citizens by capturing new global markets in terms of products, services, and demographics.

Economics

Adaptability is very important in changing business scenarios, such as low supply and high demand or high supply and low demand or low-cost product lines or more efficient operational paradigms which can change the entire financial scenario.

Competition

Changes can also happen through mergers, acquisitions, or launching of new products or services which can give a competitive edge to the other players in the market, so a company has to strive continuously and enforce change with the rapidly changing market. If a change is not successful, leading to weak financials of the companies, then also adaptability to such business situations is extremely essential.

Technology

Technological changes are a constant menace, and embracing new technologies requires adaptability. When media went digital, many companies quickly found ways to stay competitive while many failed in this endeavour.

Legislation

New laws and legislation can dramatically change operations for companies like the concept of value added tax, service tax to be paid by companies consistently to the government, or the individuals/group who has set up an organization/company of his own has to abide by the Indian Company Act, and any new rule formulated under this act.

Internal Forces

Internal forces consist of employee changes to social amendments to operational challenges.

Problem of Manpower

Symptoms of such problems are absenteeism and attrition which should be addressed by the organization by using innovative job designs, minimizing role conflicts, removing bias, distributing employee workload, minimizing stress, and so on. These problems arise from employee's perceptions of the treatment they receive at workplace and the alignment of individual and organization needs and desires.

Crisis

A crisis also effectuates change in organization, especially like employee strikes which may lead management to take appropriate actions. Also, exit of people from leadership roles is a type of crisis that the company has to face. A much-publicized crisis of Exxon's oil spill from the tanker brought about many changes in Exxon's environmental policies.

Employee Expectations

Expectations from new employees of the company can be different from the expectations from the older ones, as they have been inducted because of their additional skills and experience. But, this has its disadvantage that these employees expect more from the company such as balance between career and family and as a result facilitate dependents from company perspectives.

Work Environment

Work climate should be conducive and motivating for employees, and organizations who perform layoffs frequently do not exude such type of work climate and employees because of constant fear of being laid off fail to be productive.

Reduction of Impact

Declining impact causes companies to formulate change strategies, such as that some companies that experience its quarterly loss consecutively within a fiscal year are motivated to incorporate strategies, such as layoffs and massive cost-cutting programs, whereas others view the loss as symptomatic of an underlying problem and try to find out the cause of the problem.

Management Change

New CEOs or other executive board members can significantly affect strategy and business culture. Understanding consequences of changing new upper management is crucial to making a good decision on best fit.

Organizational Restructuring

Organizations restructuring to adapt to new business situations in terms of new product lines or service deliveries or global expansion require hierarchy and communication channels to be reintegrated and trainings to be imparted to adapt them well to the new processes.

Innovation from External and Internal Source

Capitalizing on a new idea by organization's top management will require reallocation of resources, branding, and hiring.

Resistance to Change

People often resist change when the individuals feel that their freedom is threatened and give a negative reaction to the same. Some of the major reasons for resisting change are as follows:

Lack of Proper Communication

News of a change spreads through the chain of command, which is sometimes highly skewed giving incorrect information to the next-level employees, and this can therefore cause resistance to change.

Self-ego

Employees having personal agenda act on their own self-interest, instead of the organization's interest, and hence resist change.

Feeling Excluded

Employees who are decision makers, when they hear of a sudden change, are offended for not having been considered to take decisions and resist to change.

Lack of Reliance/Trust

Lack of reliance or trust can make members of the organization violent and create negativity amongst them which can ultimately lead to resistance to change.

Mastering Skills/Training Needs

Having to work with a new technology can bring resistance amongst employees unless organizations set up trainings for employees prior to working with new technology.

Fear of the Unknown

Change is always accompanied by uncertainty and is evidenced by a story from the past that when computerization/automation first came in India, the people from an esteemed organization were reluctant to change to computerized processes since they were very comfortable in their own arena and were not willing to learn something new and implement it.

Fear of Loss

Change may lead to employees losing their jobs or reducing manpower when machines can achieve intelligence like man and work with minimal errors. Computer systems experts, for example, may feel threatened when they feel their expertise is eroded by the installation of a more user-friendly information system. Computerizing the customer service function at Southwestern Bell threatened the independence of the service representatives.

Fear of Failure

Some employees fear changes because they fear that they will fail. In many cases, a change has led to failure. In one large library that was undergoing a major automation effort, employees had their doubts as to whether the vendor could really deliver the state-of-the-art system that was promised. In this case, the implementation never became a reality and the employees' fears were well founded

Change in Interpersonal Relationships

Employees may resist change that threatens to limit interpersonal relationships amongst their peer, boss, or subordinates. For example, with the onset of automation, the men at the assembly line of a factory feared that they would have minimum interaction amongst their colleagues in exchanging important information on manual assembling of their product since every task in assembling would be performed by the machines under the direction of a single supervisor at that point, thus decreasing interaction amongst the human resources and also the need for them.

Personality Conflicts

If a person acting as a change agent emanates negative reactions from the employees, then the employees might resist the change because the change agent who appears insensitive to employee concerns and feelings may meet considerable resistance, because employees perceive that their needs are not being taken into account. For example, while implementing a critical incident management plan in a nursing institution, the chief staffing officer faced a lot of resistance from the senior nursing staff when he set the ratio of 1:1, that is, one-nurse-to-one-patient system shiftwise as they felt that they were being subjected to handle critical care incidents alone without more of staff support and for 70% of their time in a month.

Politics

Organizational change may bring in change in the balance of power, and groups or individuals who hold authority under the current scenario feel intimidated by losing these political benefits in times of change. For example, with rapid digitization's and launch of smart city concepts across the Indian subcontinent, an initiative by the BJP government, the stake holders of many organizations are fearing that control now will be increasingly government centric and they will be losing monopoly in their operations and executions.

Cultural Assumptions and Values

Sometimes cultural assumptions and values can be impediments to change, particularly if the assumptions forming the basis of change are unknown to employees. For IBM introduction, the concept of business process management in its work culture offered stiff resistance from the IBM employees during the initial years.

Managing Resistance to Change

The traditional view of resistance to change is thought to be as an attempt from the employees to hinder some aspect which requires that the attempt to resist has to be overcome by the management. But the modern approaches suggest that it is a form of feedback which has to be taken into consideration and can be used to effectively manage the change. Three key strategies which are instrumental in managing the resistance to change are as follows:

- Communication.
- Involvement.
- Sympathy and support.

Employees should be communicated of the change and the reason why the change is being implemented. Communication about impending change is essential if employees are to adjust effectively. The details of the change should be provided, but equally important is the rationale behind the change. Providing the correct information at the right time and providing clarity on the consequences of change are the key to successful change implementation. Educating employees on new work procedures is often helpful. For example, when employees are trained on new tools and technologies, they derive a new-found confidence level once they start operating applications based on these technologies, so educating people on processes, tools, technologies, equipment, and machineries helps ease out inhibitions and fear. Also, employee participation or involvement during change implementation is highly essential. Even a very simple case of a retail outlet shifting to a different location should actively involve customer service staff to notify customers about the change of address before and after the change, and the customer service staff should also be made aware as to why a change is being sought. Similarly, the financial institutions, such a securities and banking, employees are kept updated about the change in product plans and services, and they in turn update the customers of the new product and service offerings.

Do Change Management Right the First Time

Much of the conflict can be shunned from if effectual change management is applied in an organization from the very beginning. Considering it, the following change management activities can be taken into account:

- Implement an appropriate change management plan.
- Involvement of senior-level management is mandatory.
- Advocacy by middle-level management.
- Communications that describe the need for change, the change impact, and the employee benefits.

Expecting Resistance

Even if a solution is an improvement to a problem and offers resistance, human beings tend to get very comfortable with their current status quo.

A second aspect of expecting resistance is when a certain project is getting started, one should be specific about where resistance is likely to come from and the likely objections, and then the management can confront it accordingly. So the possible areas from where resistance can be due are as follows:

- Employees who are working with the current tactic.
- People who helped create the current way of doing work.
- Employees fearing more work due to change.
- Employees who proposed the alternative solution to bring in change.

Formal Address

Phase 1: Preparing for Change

During the creation of the change management plan, the resistance points are envisaged and tactics are derived to confront resistance.

Phase 2: Managing Change

Once the change management plan is drafted, in phase 2, the plan is executed by focusing on individuals through their own change process and addressing the obstacles for making the change successfully.

Phase 3: Implementing Change

The deviation report is derived at this stage and is seen to what percentages have the individuals aligned themselves to the new workflows and processes. Evaluating the report allows the management to identify gaps and react to resistance that may still be occurring.

Identify the Root Causes

The root causes to resistance are evident, such as complaining, not attending meetings, not providing information or resources, or not adopting the change. Effective resistance management requires identification of the root causes of resistance, understanding why an individual is showing resistance, and so on. The root cause also could be the following:

- **For employees:** Lack of awareness of why the change was being made.
- **For managers:** Lack of getting managers involved in designing the change and change management plan.

Engage appropriate resistance managers

The resistance managers in an organization are the senior leaders wherein they can moderate resistance by making a convincing case for the need for change and by showcasing their commitment to a change because the lower levels of management and employees look up to their senior leaders. Managers and supervisors should be keen on adopting change so that their employees follow suit (Table 15.1).

Reducing Resistance to Change

Approach	*Condition Where It Is Implemented*	*Advantages*	*Disadvantages*
Communicating and training	Lack of information and analysis	People if convinced support to implement the change	Extremely time consuming when there are many people
Involvement	Where the employees have substantial authority to be involved	People involvement results in successful change implementation with additional inputs or perspectives from them for greater effectiveness of change	Those involved if they suggest changes that are inappropriate to the situation, then their involvement will lead to wastage of time and effort
Facilitation and support	Situations where there is less tolerance to changing conditions	No other mechanism to facilitate change	Can be time consuming, costly, and susceptible to failure
Discuss the change and agree on the implementation points—a form of negotiation	This method is adopted in situations where there are agreements made with the employee/ employees for change implementations	The form of negotiation and implementation reduces resistance to change	Can be too expensive if other to negotiate for compliance

Approach	*Condition Where It Is Implemented*	*Advantages*	*Disadvantages*
Manipulation and co-optation	The inability to implement any other strategy	Relatively quick and easy in case of high degree of resistance	Manipulation if felt by employees or people in later period might have negative consequences
Explicit and implicit force	Initiators of change possess considerable power	It is fast paced and quickly implemented	Can be risky if it seeks people's displeasure for initiators

CASE STUDIES

Kodak

Eastman Kodak Company was found by George Eastman in the year 1880. The company had at first started making photographic plates and eventually switched to photo films, and it became so user-friendly that it became a possession of every household in a four-year tenure. The founder's philosophy was

- Low-cost production.
- Global distribution.
- Phenomenal promotioning.
- Growth through research and development.

The company started diversifying into new product lines, such as cameras, medical imaging, and graphical arts. And the company worked across the following segments:

- Health group constituting medical films, digital products, such as x-rays, and hardware supplies,
- Digital and film imaging, such as camera rolls and cameras, and photo finishing services and supplies.
- Graphic communication segment such as inkjet printers.
- Initially, it did very well for a span of four to five years and then went into decline because of failed strat egies, such as failure to innovate consistently, ignoring the current customer trend, and having a contented cultural attitude within the company.

Pre-emptive measures which should have been adopted by KODAK then are as follows.

- Creating small business units as per the three segments.
- licensing the brand/technology.
- Not bring the digital into prominence.

ABCL

ABCL came into existence in the late 1980s. Earlier, its main business was of sawmilling and later started producing veneers. By diversifying into new business area, certain changes had to be incorporated as follows:

- Changes in organizational business strategy.
- Changes in organizational structure.
- Changes in organizational culture.
- Changes in technology.
- Changes in organizational workflow.

(Continued)

(Continued)

Employees resisted change due to the following reasons:

- Allocation of new roles and responsibilities.
- Redundancy of doing the job again.
- Addition of extra responsibilities.
- Fear of whether the responsibility taken will bring success or not.

The changes were in the form of strikes, and the consequence was that production got delayed and suspended, and employees were reimbursed for no work done.

The change resistance could be better managed by properly educating employees, effectively communicating with them and providing them enough warmth and support as motivation, and letting them have absolute trust on the organizations culture even after a change is incorporated.

Summary

The chapter summarizes on the development of organization, the various models used over the years which have contributed successfully towards the organizations development reinforcing a culture within the organization which employees can correlate to and gather motivation to work for improved productivity and business. With the development of organization and sustaining a culture within the organization, the chapter stresses the need to adapt to the ever-changing political, economic, social, cultural, and market scenarios by various business organizations.

Exercise

Objective Questions

1. Phases of organizational development are
   - Problem identification, analysis, plan an intervention, implementation, evaluation and feedback
   - Problem identification, analysis, implementation, evaluation and feedback
   - Problem identification, plan an Intervention, analysis, implementation, evaluation and feedback
   - None of the above
2. __________ contribute to align the organization with its environment.
   - Large-scale interventions
   - Techno-structural interventions
   - Strategic interventions
   - Group processes interventions
3. Interpersonal process interventions do not aim at improving organizational performance by developing specific skills of individuals.
   - True
   - False

4. A culture that emerges within different departments, branches, or geographic locations is called

   - Counter-culture
   - Subculture
   - Strong culture
   - None of the above

5. In weak culture, there is little alignment with organizational values, and control must be exercised through extensive procedures and bureaucracy.

   - True
   - False

6. Which characteristic of organizational culture dictates the degree to which employees are expected to be accurate in their work?

   - Innovation
   - Emphasis on people
   - Emphasis on outcome
   - Attention to detail

7. Which of the following is true?

   - Culture promotes code of conduct
   - Culture facilitates recognition
   - Culture provides self-satisfaction
   - All of the above

8. In pragmatic culture, more weightage is given to clients and the external parties.

   - True
   - False

9. In which type of organizational culture, the individuals always have an upper edge and they do not bother much about their organization?

   - Normative culture
   - Academy culture
   - Baseball team culture
   - Performance-based culture

10. A goal-oriented culture places importance on how work is to be done and emphasis on avoiding risk, and means-oriented culture identifies with what work is to be done.

    - True
    - False

11. In an open system, newcomers are not welcomed easily, and in closed system, newcomers have to prove themselves.

    - True
    - False

12. Creating organizational culture includes following four processes.

    - Acquire—Embed—Integrate—Test
    - Embed—Acquire—Integrate—Test

- Embed—Integrate—Acquire—Test
- None of the above

13. In ________ , a new employee is made to adapt to the organization culture prior to joining the organization otherwise termed as pre-arrival.

- Selection practices
- Socialization process
- Incorporation stage
- None of the above

14. ________ are the physical things that are found that have particular symbolism for a culture.

- Rituals
- Mission and values
- Artefacts
- None of the above

15. _______ is a systematic approach to dealing with change both from the perspective of an organization and the individual.

- Change management
- Organizational culture
- Pragmatic culture
- Organizational change

16. ________ is the process by which organizations move from their present state to some desired future state to increase their effectiveness.

- Change management
- Organizational culture
- Pragmatic culture
- Organizational change

17. Refreezing means that what has been learned is integrated into actual practice.

- True
- False

18. Change often brings

- Fear of losing the jobs
- Lack of reliance
- Substantial uncertainty
- None of the above

19. _________ is an important part of project management.

- Change management
- Organizational culture
- Pragmatic culture
- Organizational change

20. In which type of organizational culture, the profit of the organization is more important?

- Normative culture
- Process culture
- Organization-centric culture
- Performance-based culture

CASE STUDY

Ravisti Industrial Limited powers the business worldwide by manufacturing and supplying industrial products. The major market that company deals with is from the United States. For supporting this core manufacturing division, there is an IT department to provide the services.

Mr Mitesh has several years of experience in various roles in his career. He is young, passionate and believed in results. He has recently completed his Master of Business Administration having specialization in Personnel Management from the United States. He has joined as a COO in IT department for the Mumbai Location. The office timing when he joined was from 9.30 to 6.30 pm He felt that as the company gets most of its business from the United States, the job timings should be from 11.30 to 8.30 pm so that more services could be offered. He announced the change of timing officially and also gave the reason for changing the timing.

There was no reaction for the first week. Later, Mr Mitesh received a memorandum for the old office timings to be restored or have different shift timings for different people. Mr Mitesh did not yield to the demand. However, he was convinced that a step should be taken to build cooperative spirit among his employees via an informal get-together. He started with a scheme where a monthly dinner was planned for all the employees at the office, and all the employees would bring their home-made dishes. They were also encouraged to bring their wives and children along for the dinner. The scheme was announced by sending an email to all the employees. Also, the suggestions were welcomed to make the scheme successful.

No suggestions were received on two monthly dinners. On one occasion, when the dinner party was nearing, Mr Mitesh heard a conversation between two employees.

One of the employee said to another: 'What are you bringing for the coming dinner party. I would be bringing Nachos'. The other replied, 'I would be bringing Biryani', and both of them laughed.

Mr Mitesh felt that nobody was concerned about the suggestion for the dinner party.

Questions

1. Assess the positive and negative consequences of change being implemented for the work timings.
2. What are the possible reasons for employees not supporting the actions of Mr Mitesh?
3. Suggest how should Mr Mitesh proceed in this situation?

Critical Thinking Questions

1. What are the factors where organizations and people resist to change?
2. Identify the roles of change agents in organizations.

How the changes can be incorporated in an organization in the best possible manner?

Chapter at a Glance

Organization development is the attempt to influence the members of an organization to expend their candidness with each other about their views of the organization and their experience in it and greater responsibility for their own actions and organization members.

Characteristics of Organization Development

- Well-managed process.
- Integrated and has a problem-oriented approach.

(Continued)

(Continued)

- Reflects a systems approach.
- Depends on practical implementations.
- Involves the distinct role of a person who makes progress easier to ensure that changes are real.
- Involves learning principles.
- Systematic approach to the planned change.
- Involves the application of our knowledge of behavioural science.
- Recognizes the reciprocal relationship between individuals and organizations.
- Goal oriented.
- Designed to solve problems.

Importance of Organization Development

- Organizational change.
- Growth.
- Work processes.
- Product innovation.

Action Research Model of Organization Development

- Unfreezing.
- Changing.
- Refreezing.

Limitations of Organization Development

- It is based on behavioural science which has its limitations and so has organization development theory.
- Inability to challenge a complacent person's motivation.
- For research and development, organizations are not impacted by organizational development.

Process of Organization Development

- Problem identification.
- Analysis.
- Plan an intervention.
- Implementation.
- Evaluation and feedback.

Types of Organization Development Interventions

- **Large-scale interventions:** This involves a full-size group of stakeholders, working toward the definition of a future state.
- **Strategic interventions:** This helps organizations to gain a better understanding of their current state and environment that allow them to better target strategies for competing or collaborating with other organizations.

- **Techno-structural interventions:** This focuses on improving the organizational effectiveness and human development by focusing on technology and structure.
- **Management and leadership development interventions:** These types of organization development interventions aim to improve organizational performance by increasing effectiveness of formal and informal leaders.
- **Team development and group processes interventions:** The important objective of team-building interventions relies on improving interdependency of team members.
- **Individual/interpersonal process:** This aims at improving organizational performance by developing specific skills of individuals.

Organizational Culture

- Organizational culture refers to the pattern of beliefs, values, and learned ways of coping with experience that have developed during the course of an organization's history.
- Subculture—A culture that emerges within different departments, branches, or geographic locations is called a subculture.
- Counter-culture—It is defined as shared values and beliefs that are in direct opposition to the values of the broader organizational culture, and counter-cultures are often shaped around a charismatic leader.
- Strong and weak culture—Strong culture is said to exist where staff respond to stimulus because of their alignment to organizational values. Weak culture is where there is little alignment with organizational values, and control must be exercised through extensive procedures and bureaucracy.

Characteristics of Organizational Culture

- Innovation.
- Attention to detail.
- Emphasis on outcome.
- Emphasis on people.
- Teamwork.
- Aggressiveness.
- Stability.

Functions of Organizational Culture

- Culture promotes code of conduct
- Culture facilitates recognition.
- Culture provides self-satisfaction.
- Culture provides opportunity to set the standards of performance.
- Culture guides and controls the employees.
- Culture directs employee behaviour towards goal achievement.
- Culture makes people development oriented.
- Culture develops positive attitude.

(Continued)

(Continued)

Types of Organizational Culture

- **Normative culture:** In such a culture, the norms and procedures of the organization are predefined, and the rules and regulations are set as per the existing guidelines.
- **Pragmatic culture:** More weightage is given to clients and the external parties.
- **Academy culture:** The organization which tries to follow this type of culture has highly skilled employee base.
- **Baseball team culture:** In such a culture, the individuals always have an upper edge and they do not bother much about their organization.
- **Organization-centric culture:** In this, profit of the organization is more important.
- **Performance-based culture:** In such type of culture, performance of individual is important.
- **Process culture:** All the procedures of the company are very much important, and they are already established.

Change Management

Change management is a systematic approach to dealing with change both from the perspective of an organization and the individual.

Characteristics of Change

- It is a process and is not any event that has occurred.
- It is normal and constant in nature.
- Directive change is implemented by top to down in management hierarchy.
- Participative change involves everyone or those who are directly or indirectly affected by change.

Process of Change

- **Stage 1: Unfreezing:** Unfreezing means that old ideas and practices need to be cast aside, so that new ideas can be learned.
- **Stage 2: Change or transition:** This process involves helping an employee think reason and perform in a variety of new ways.
- **Stage 3: Refreezing:** This means that what has been learned is integrated into actual practice.

Forces for Change in Organization

- External causes
  - Demographic characteristics.
  - Social and political pressures.
  - Globalization.
  - Economics.

    - Competition.
    - Technology.
    - Legislation.
- Internal forces
    - HR problems/prospects.
    - Crisis.
    - Employee expectations.
    - Work climate.
    - Reduced effectiveness.
    - Management change.
    - Organizational restructuring.
    - Intrapreneurship.

Resistance to Change

- Lack of proper communication.
- Self-ego.
- Feeling excluded.
- Lack of reliance/trust.
- Mastering skills/training needs.
- Fear of the unknown.
- Fear of loss.
- Fear of failure.
- Disruption of interpersonal conflicts.
- Personality conflicts.
- Politics.
- Cultural assumptions and values.

Managing Resistance to Change

- Do change management right the first time.
- Expect it.
- Formal address.
- Phase 1: Preparing for change.
- Phase 2: Managing change.
- Phase 3: Implementing change.
- Identify the root causes.

CHAPTER 16

Stress Management

Learning Objectives

- Getting an overview of stress, its types, and signs and symptoms with special focus on organizational stress.
- Getting insight on the causes of stress and methodologies adopted to handle stress.
- Having clarity on how performance is affected by stress and how organizations can conduct stress management sessions for improving the efficiency of employees.

An Opening Vignette

Managing Stress

The employees of Company ABC were afflicted to high levels of stress due to increased work pressure, unrealistic schedules, and environmental constraints and for some self-inflicted imbalance in work–life aspect.

Problem Scenario

The company wanted to implement measures for dealing with stress amongst its employees. A survey by an expert showed that employees had an inclination to avail more leaves than necessary during the project delivery period due to work-related stress, even some could not maintain a healthy work–life balance.

Objective

The company wanted to introduce certain benefit schemes to enthuse the employees and decrease their stress levels. For this purpose, they conducted a detailed survey across all units and all levels.

Steps Taken by the Company

- Introducing stress risk assessment methodologies and policy formulation dictating appropriate stress management standards and circulation of these to all units.
- Introducing stress-relieving sessions such as regular yoga classes, laughter sessions, weekly team dinners, quarterly outings, and so on.
- Increasing peer-to-peer and boss–subordinate interactive sessions.
- Including stress management training sessions for all compromising on stress definitions, stress points, targets aimed at reducing stress cases, the company's legal obligation to health and safety legislations, and so on.
- Advising managers to initiate effective time management across teams, ensure healthy working patterns through increased communication and collaboration, initiate smooth transitions amongst the members of the team, and promote proper exercise, diet, and sleeping rules for them and self as well.
- Weekly visits by stress management consultants for expert suggestions and ideas of how to de-stress.
- Starting up with a gymnasium and indoor play area for employees to stay fit.
- Proper task allocation to avoid work overloading.
- Having taken these steps, it was found that within the span of a quarter, employee stress came down from 37% to 17% within the organization. The productivity rose from 42% to 58% and overall employee satisfaction increased to a whopping 79%. The top- and middle-level management was satisfied to have combated stress for a long time.

Introduction

The term 'stress' has been derived from the Latin word 'stringer', which means to draw tight. It is a multifarious phenomenon. It is an emotion that arises when we face a particular situation. It may differ from individual to individual. In other words, a situation or circumstance might be a challenge for one individual, whereas for the other it might be a stressor. This basically depends on the experience, personality, and the environment in which the individual operates. The ever-changing situations that an individual has to face cause stress. Thus, today stress has become a part of our daily life, which has a large impact on all the activities we perform. Hence, managing stress effectively is very essential and important.

Definitions

Stress is a feeling experienced when a person thinks that, the demands exceed the personal and social resources the individual is able to mobilize.

Richard S. Lazarus

Stress is the psychological, physiological and behavioral response by an individual when they perceive a lack of equilibrium between the demands placed upon them and their ability to meet those demands, which, over a period of time, leads to ill-health.

S. Palmer

Stress can be considered as any factor, acting internally or externally that makes it difficult to adapt and that induces increased effort on the part of the person to maintain a state of equilibrium both internally and with the external environment.

Humphrey

Stress is caused by a multitude of demands (stressors), such as an inadequate fit between what we need and what we are capable of, and what our environment offers and what it demands of us.

Levi

Non-specific response of the body to any demand for change.

Hans Selye

Understanding Stress

Today, life is full of worries, targets, frustrations, and burdens. For a number of people, stress is so common that it has become a part of everyday life.

The term stress was coined by Hans Selye in 1936 (http://www.stress.org/about/hans-selye-birth-of-stress/, accessed on 26 February 2016). He stated that 'stress is not bad always'. In small doses, stress not only helps an individual perform under pressure but also motivates to give best performance. This kind of stress is called 'eustress' (good stress). However, when stress exists for a larger span of time, places constant demands, and causes problems, then it is called 'distress' (bad stress). He presented 'general adaptation syndrome', which states people react in a similar way when exposed to stressors. A stressor is defined as something that causes stress.

Figure 16.1 represents three stages of the general adaption syndrome.

General Adaptation Syndrome

- **Stage 1 (Alarm reaction):** A stressor leads the body to use its alarm reaction. Any cause of worry or excitement that further causes emotional or physical changes can be called a stressor and that leads the body to start alarm reaction. For adult people, stressors can be vacation plans, family conflicts, work responsibilities, bills, and so on. Physical changes start occurring when the body starts its alarm reaction to a stressor. This may cause an increase in the heart rate and other physical changes.
- **Stage 2 (Resistance):** After the alarm reaction, the body adjusts itself and enters the second stage of general adaptation syndrome. This stage is called the stage of resistance

Figure 16.1 General Adaptation Syndrome

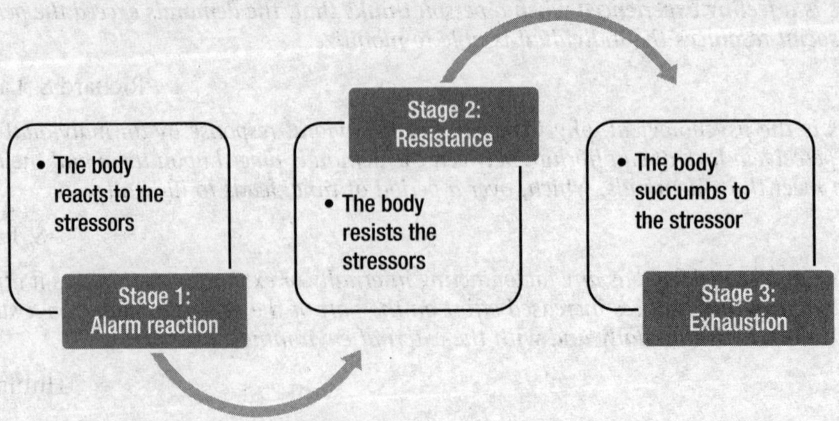

as the immune system resists or fights the stressor. Also, in case of illness, antibodies are sent to fight, and in case of physical stressors such as doing heavy exercises, the heart rate goes up accordingly in order to supply more blood and oxygen to the body. In most of the cases, the resistance of the body is enough to overcome the stressor and return to normal state.

- **Stage 3 (Exhaustion):** In extreme cases, the body enters the third stage of the syndrome, that is, the stage of exhaustion when the body is unable to resist. To overcome and to help resist and overcome the stressor, various medical treatments are necessary. If the stress is to the extent that even the body and medicine cannot fight against the disease then death can occur.

Relation between Stress and Performance Level

The relationship between stress and performance was described by Robert Yerkes and John Dodson in 1908. The Yerkes–Dodson law states that up to a certain level stress is beneficial as it motivates an individual to perform. The usefulness can also be reflected in the health and well-being of an individual.

Certain amount of stress is necessary to succeed. This is seen in various events in life like sports, academics, and so on. The level of performance increases with the increase in the level of stress; however, this happens only to a certain point. On the other hand, when the level of stress increases beyond this level, the performance starts diminishing and affects the health and well-being of a person. All stressful experiences are not harmful as there are basically two kinds of stress. The term *eustress* is used to describe 'positive stress'. It helps you meet challenges and do the best and makes life more enjoyable. Various situations like riding a roller coaster, successfully competing in an activity, passing a driving test, playing in the school band, and meeting new people are some examples that produce *eustress*. On the other

Figure 16.2 Stress and Performance

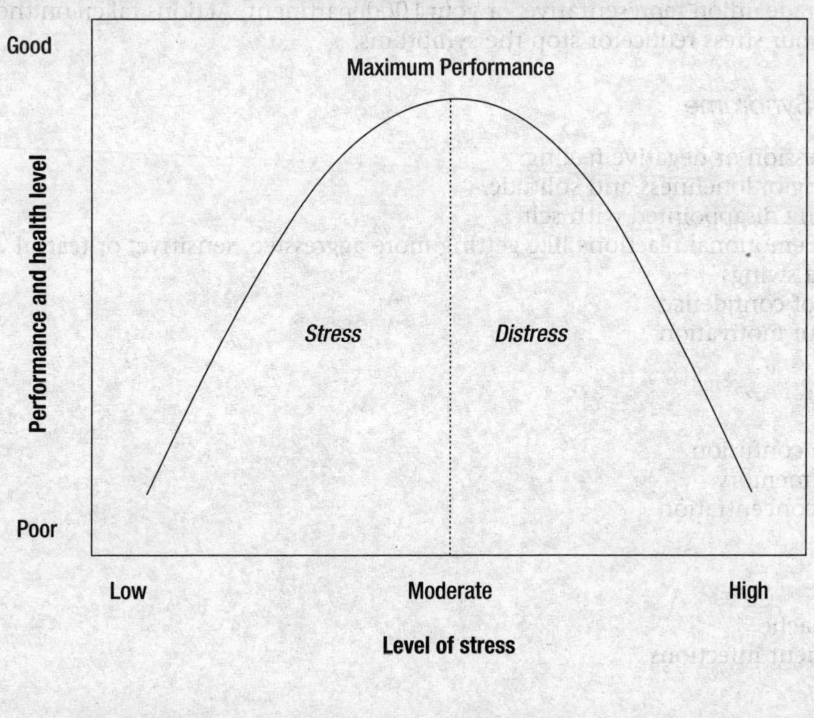

hand, there are unpleasant situations that cause 'negative stress' called as distress. Distress includes the situations that cause worry, sorrow, anger, or pain.

There are many occasions where a situation is a stress for one person but for other person it is distress. For example, an outgoing person always likes to participate in extracurricular activities at college or attend social events, but, at the same time, for a shy person this would be a situation of stress. There can be situations where you experience stress or you experience distress for a similar experience at different times. For example, if an individual is well prepared for the upcoming test, then the test would be situation of less stress, whereas if the same individual is not prepared for the test then it is a situation of distress. The experience of low level of stress may help you to deal with more stressful situations in the future. For example, physical activity may be a stressor, but regular physical activity helps you to stay healthy, happy, and fit and you would be able to handle the stress more easily. This is shown in Figure 16.2.

Signs and Symptoms of Stress

Stress can lead to various changes in the life of a person who is experiencing it. It is seen many a time that people are experiencing stress at work and it can be prevented if required actions are taken at the earlier stages.

Everyone looks out for changes in the behaviour of a group or a person so as to identify if there is any potential issue or stress-related problem so that positive actions are taken as early as possible; this can be a critical matter for the line manager.

Stress can be seen in different ways. Some of the signs are mentioned below. Managers may need to manage the staff showing few of these signs in a different manner.

Signs of Stress in Individuals

If you are suffering from most of the following symptoms, it may be possible that there are effects of stress on you. If work aspects are leading to these symptoms, speak to your line manager, trade union representative, or your HR department. Actions taken on the early stages may ease your stress reduce or stop the symptoms.

Sensitive Syndrome

- Depression or negative feeling
- Feeling of loneliness and solitude
- Getting disappointed with self
- More emotional reactions like getting more aggressive, sensitive, or tearful
- Mood swings
- Loss of confidence
- Loss of motivation

Mental

- More confusion
- Poor memory
- Less concentration

Physical

- Headache
- Frequent infections

- Muscle beat
- Breathlessness

Changes in Normal Behaviour

- Changes in eating habits
- Arriving late or taking more time to do things
- Changes in sleep pattern
- Mood swings that affect the behaviour
- Increased drinking, drug intake, and smoking

Signs of Stress in Groups

Stress can be found at workplace too and can be contagious. We have often seen that low job satisfaction is discussed among the employees. If stress in the organization is not noted and acted upon by the management at an early stage, then team dynamics may destroy, hampering the social and cultural synergies that exist in the organization.

Managers play a different and unique role when it comes to dealing with workplace stress. They would be responsible for assigning tasks, maintaining peace, and cherishing social customs that direct the work group.

Managers should consistently discuss about job satisfaction and professional and personal health with their subordinates. Some other common signs include

- conflict and sickness
- increase in staff turnover
- more absence due to sickness
- poor performance
- difficulty faced in attracting new staff
- increased stress reports
- increase in the number of compliances and grievances
- customer complaints or dissatisfaction

Types of Stress

There are three types of stress: acute, episodic acute, and chronic. Each type possesses typical features, indicators, period, and treatment methods. Because of these variations, it becomes difficult and challenging to manage stress. Each type of stress is explained in detail below (see Figure 16.3).

Acute Stress

Among all the forms of stress, acute stress is most commonly experienced since this occurs due to day-to-day demands and pressures faced by every individual. Acute stress in small amount creates a stimulation but causes fatigue when goes beyond a certain level. For example, riding a motor boat might be exciting for some time but when the activity is stretched over hours, it might be tiring. Acute stress exists for a short span and may occur due to burden of work, abiding by the deadlines, trivial accident, and so on. Some of the common symptoms include:

- **Emotional Distress:** irritability, anxiety, depression, and anger.
- **Physical Problems:** muscular problems, headaches, dizziness, and so on.

Acute stress is very common and can occur in anybody's life and is easy to manage and treat.

Figure 16.3 Types of Stress

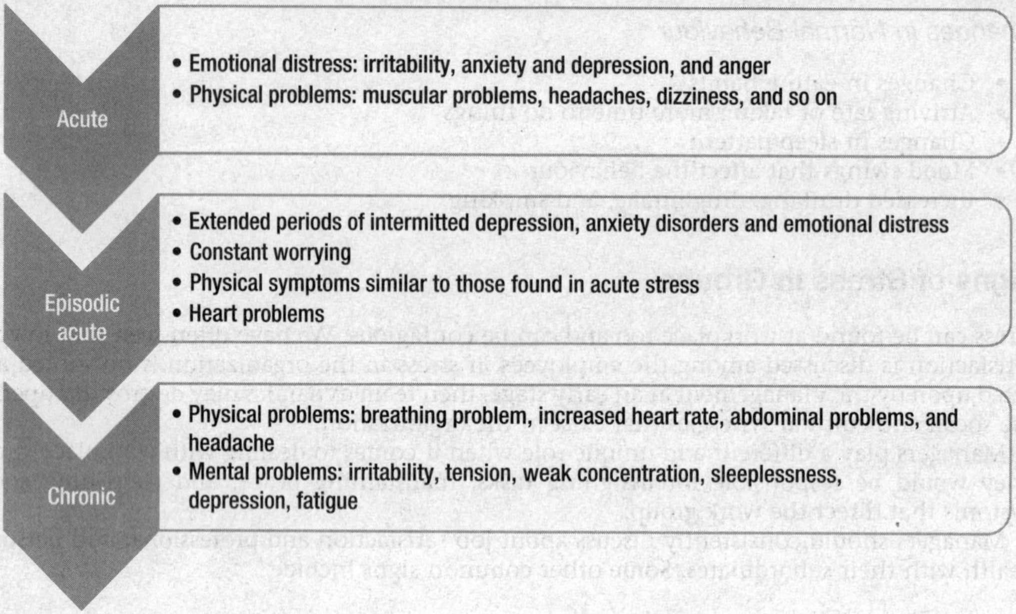

Episodic Acute Stress

When acute stress is experienced frequently, it is termed as episodic stress. This stress is typically noticed among individuals who create self-inflicted, impractical, or unreasonable demands which get all messed up and bring a lot of stress in their effort to achieve these goals. Episodic stress is generally seen in people with 'type A' personality, who are exceedingly competitive, aggressive, and demanding. The symptoms of episodic stress include

- extended periods of intermitted depression, anxiety disorders, and emotional distress.
- constant worrying.
- physical symptoms similar to those found in acute stress.
- heart problems.

Chronic Stress

Chronic stress contrasts with acute stress. Acute stress is exciting and thrilling, whereas chronic stress is harmful and unhealthy. This stress occurs due to long-term exposure to stressors. Chronic stress can occur as a result of some traumatic events, unhappy marital life, prolonged illness, problems in relationships, job dissatisfaction, and so on. Stress arising out of such situations seems to be never ending and life threatening, as there are chances of a person committing suicide or becoming violent. Severe illnesses like stroke, heart attack, depression, and post-traumatic disorder can initiate due to chronic stress. The symptoms of chronic stress include:

- **Physical problems:** Breathing problems, increased heart rate, abdominal problems, headache, and so on.
- **Mental problems:** Irritability, tension, weak concentration, sleeplessness, depression, and fatigue.

Chronic stress arises when an individual does not find a way to get rid of the problematic situation. It is the stress of pounding burdens and pressures for seemingly endless periods of time.

Causes of Stress

Stress can be categorized as organizational and non-organizational stress. The following are the causes or sources of organizational and non-organizational stress.

Causes of Organizational Stress

- **Role ambiguity:** It exists when an individual working in the organization is not clear about his roles and responsibilities. This causes confusion and the individual is not able to understand what work is he supposed to do, which leads to stress.
- **Role conflict:** Many a time an individual working in an organization is required to play more than one role. The stress situation arises when an employee has to play roles wherein the demands are conflicting. For example, due to the bad financial conditions of the company, the head of labour union, Rajesh, is asked to give a list of non-performing individuals so that they can be terminated. Here, Rajesh has to play two roles that have conflicting demands.
- **Negligible management support:** When there is no support from the top management, then it becomes very difficult for the teams to perform and remain productive and stress and frustration level amongst employees increases. For example, when a company wanted to restructure its supply chain to maximize returns on investment by digitizing decision-making, by putting data from Oracle data warehouse, then it faced a lot of cost pressures and challenges from some members from the board which delayed the implementation for some months and inadvertently caused stress amongst the rest.
- **Time pressure:** Even tight deadlines can be a cause of organizational stress amongst the individuals and the team involved in projects.
- **Less interest in participation:** Organizational stress can occur when employees are not motivated to participate in decision-making or follow a creative approach in their work.
- **No sense of belongingness:** A sense of belonging is the one as portrayed in the example as follows: when Tina puts on her QUITO name tag, she feels like she is representing the high value that QUITO places on customer service. When Tina goes the extra mile to assist a customer, she feels like her efforts match the goals of everyone who works at QUITO, absence of which might not lead Tina to work to her fullest capacity and in due course can be a cause of stress.
- **Less opportunities:** If the organization does not provide enough opportunities to grow or perform it can indirectly affect the employees' enthusiasm and effort expended, leading to negativity and stress.
- **Working conditions:** Improper working conditions like insufficient lighting and ventilation, too much noise and dust, unhygienic sanitation facilities, and so on act as major stressors.
- **Work underload or overload:** Both the situations, underload or overload of work, lead to stress. When the employee is underloaded, he might experience boredom or sometimes a decrease in self-confidence, which causes frustration and stress. On the other hand, work overload might cause excessive pressure on the individual, which in turn takes the form of stress.
- **Conflicts at workplace:** It is the difference in attitudes, values, perception, and beliefs of the individuals that lead to conflicts at workplace. The conflicts may be interpersonal or intergroup. These types of conflicts are potential source of stress.

- **Shift working:** Often adjustments in shift timings lead to health and family problems. Working in shifts is a popular and most common source of stress among people working in rotating shifts.
- **Lack of recognition:** Recognition of the work done is a major motivator. However, lack of recognition may lead to dissatisfaction and stress.
- **Organizational changes:** Adapting to and managing change causes stress among the people. Some of the examples are transfer and introduction of new technology or policy.
- **Lack of power:** In a workplace, the status of a person also affects the level of stress. Employees of all categories in a workplace get affected by the stress, though not at the same level. However, the lower-level employees, who have less control over their jobs, are more likely to experience stress than employees at higher level. This indicates that authority is an important factor complicating the work stress environment.
- **Social interactions and stress:** Bullying in the workplace can be a threat to an employee's overall and professional or personal image or status. Workplace bullying can involve threats to an employee's professional or personal image or status, deliberate isolation, or giving an employee excess work.
- **Destabilization:** Destabilization is another type of workplace bullying, where an employee is not given credit for their work or is assigned meaningless tasks. This can create a negative effect in the work ethic of the employees and their contribution to the organization.

Causes of Non-organizational Stress

Non-organizational stress incurred by an individual during his lifetime arises due to high expectations in life, followed by the fact that they are not met in due course or some unforeseen mishaps, highly hectic schedules, and demands from family members which are not met timely or are not possible to be met.

Following are the causes or sources of stress:

- **Basic needs:** Unavailability or insufficiency of basic needs like food, water, shelter, air, and clothing are major sources of stress.
- **Sudden undesirable changes in life:** Sudden undesirable changes in life like transfer to a new location, death of near one, and loss of job can cause immense stress to an individual.
- **High expectations:** Unrealistic expectations, that is, higher than those that an individual can actually achieve, can cause frustration, which ultimately lead to stress.
- **Too busy schedule:** When an individual has a very busy schedule and he/she cannot spare time for the family, relaxation, hobbies for a long stretch of time, these become potential sources of stress.
- **Home demands:** Relationships, children, and family, which are hard to ignore, are some of the reasons for stress. *The Academy of Management Journal* states that this constitutes 'an individual's lack of personal resources needed to fulfil commitments, obligations, or requirements' (Robert et al., 2009).
- **Personal demands:** Personal demands are brought on by the person when an individual takes on too many responsibilities from work or any other place.

Managing Stress

Stress should not be ignored, but it has to be managed. Both individuals and organizations can take necessary actions to manage stress. Some of the tips to manage stress are as follows:

- **Communicate with friends and family:** Friends and family members are the people who care for you and are ready to listen to your problems. They are the ones who understand you and can suggest some way to overcome your stress.
- **Regular exercise:** Regular physical exercise helps reduce stress to a very good extent, which will prevent you from falling into bad stress zone. Endorphins are the natural painkillers and mood-elevating chemicals in our body. Aerobics helps in releasing endorphins. Doing regular exercise and mediation to relax muscles and mind are two effective ways of managing stress.
- **Meditation:** Meditation focuses on slowing down your mind and clearing it of unimportant matter or things. There are various techniques for meditation; however, all the techniques revolve around the same aim of grabbing your mind's focus on a particular thing.
  Techniques can vary greatly, but they all centre around attempting to focus your mind on 'one thing'. This one thing can be your breathing. It can also be an object, a chant, or a phrase, or even a positive thought (Stein, 2003).
- **Managing time:** Planning and prioritizing activities to be carried out in advance lead to reduction in the level of stress. Thus, managing time can prove to be a good effort in managing stress. Therefore, it is necessary to avoid taking new responsibilities or activities if you find it unable to give them the time required.
- **Healthy diet and sleep:** Having healthy diet plays a crucial role in managing stress. Thus, an individual should carefully follow the diet plan. Good health practices such as getting a good amount of sleep and good nutrition help an individual remain in good stress zone. It is like energizing yourself before physical exercise rather than waiting until you die out of thirst. Adequate amount of sleep is a must to do best of what a human being can and handle stress.
  According to research, lack of sleep makes an individual more prone to illness and reduces focus. It has been suggested by health experts that most adults should get at least 7 to 9 hours of sleep in a day.
- **Leisure/hobbies:** Hobbies are a very good way to manage stress. Hobbies help an individual forget problems and relax the mind. Leisure time helps reduce stress as it slows down your mind, which helps you be calmer and better. It helps recharge the body and the mind.
- **Eliminate stressors in environment:** One of the potential sources of stress is poor working conditions, like insufficient lighting, poor ventilation, and so on. Efforts taken to improve the working condition will be helpful in reducing stress.
- **Avoid excessive alcohol:** The intake of alcohol and substance containing caffeine should be restricted to reduce stress.
- **Visit doctor:** If the stress continues to persist in spite of putting in efforts to manage or reduce it, it is advisable to visit a doctor and undergo proper treatment.
- **Identify the stressor:** Identify the reason for stress. For example, if anger is the reason for stress, then try to identify the reason for the anger.
- **Accept things that cannot be changed:** All the problems cannot be solved in the same way as the way you have planned or intended, but still that problem can be solved in a more successful manner. For example, an individual is asked to trim the bushes. He starts trimming the bushes and finds that he is not able to trim correctly. That individual cannot change the bushes that have already been trimmed, but can deal with this stress by realizing that all people tend to make mistakes. An individual can learn from the mistakes and get better insights for doing the job better next time.
- **Positive thinking:** One has to be positive in all aspects. For example, thinking that an individual will get a hit in the softball game instead of getting tensed about the strike out, one could make an effort to perceive a stressor as a challenge rather than thinking it as a problem.

EXAMPLE

Companies That Are Using Meditation as a Stress Management Technique

- **Apple:** Meditation had been promoted at Apple by Steve Jobs since a long time. Jobs had maintained a lifelong relationship with many monks and also had taken part in many retreats. Some believe that the main reason behind his success was the mental control he had gained from meditation. Jobs wanted to pass on his love for meditation to others in the workplace, allowing employees of the tech giant to take 30 minutes each day to meditate at work, providing classes on meditation and yoga on-site and offering the use of a meditation room.
- **Nike:** Nike's motto 'just do it' applies to meditation as well, it seems. This company is also one of many big businesses that incorporate meditation practices into their workplace. Employees are provided with access to relaxation rooms, where they can take some rest, pray, or, of course, meditate. In addition to these quiet rooms, employees can also take part in meditation and yoga classes without leaving the office.
- **Google:** Even when you are working in a company like Google, things can get a bit stressful on the job. Chade-Meng Tan, who is one of Google's original software engineers and now head of personal growth, has been working hard to bring meditation to workplace.

  Tan initiated a programme called 'Search Inside Yourself' at Google in 2007. This programme helped more than 500 employees in improving emotional intelligence, breathe mindfully, and listen to co-workers. The company offers various meditation space and meditation courses for their mental health and wellbeing.
- **Home Box Office:** For turning the viewers into couch potatoes, the employees of HBO have to work really hard and therefore it provides them a wealth of resources to help them stay healthy both mentally and physically. The company offers free yoga classes, meditation classes, and gyms for the same. The promotion of meditation and mindful exercise helped inspire their newly hit show *'Enlightened'.*
- **Procter and Gamble:** P&G's CEO A.G. Lafley believes, 'You cannot out-work a problem, you have to out-meditate it'. He has his own meditation practices and thinks it will help his employees as well. The company offers various fitness programmes that include meditation for the employees.

CASE STUDY: MANAGING STRESS AND FINDING NEW WAYS OF SUSTENANCE

An educational institution running a particular course is finding it very difficult to sustain in this competitive environment as year on year it is observing that student enrolments are decreasing due to better alternatives available for the student community. The head of the institution is facing a tough challenge as to what measures they should take to come out of this scenario. The impact of fewer enrolments has traversed deep down to the lowest-grade staff and every individual is concerned about his/her job. But, the entire team is trying to handle the stress levels through establishing and enhancing student connect across the west, central, and east zones by starting various initiatives such as scholarships to the bright and the poor, inducting working students and encouraging them to work while they do the course, and facilitating with paid jobs and training right from the students induction into the institute and are optimistic that they will manage to handle stress and ensure business continuity in these troubled times.

Summary

This chapter summarizes human interventions or leans towards the psychological perspectives involved in doing businesses, since the operations are handled by human beings, who differ in their thought processes, attitudes, and behaviour towards other individuals or groups irrespective of whether they are working as teams or as individuals. Whichever business process requires human interventions, it has been seen that many psychological instances, such as stress, dissatisfaction, and demotivation, surface for which resolution strategies are fabricated to efficiently manage them as a measure to ensure business continuity, and such resolutions are discussed in the chapter.

Exercise

Objective Questions

1. ______ is a feeling experienced when a person thinks that the demands exceed the personal and social resources the individual is able to mobilize.
    - Conflict
    - Stress
    - Want
    - None of these
2. A stressor leads the body to use its alarm reaction.
    - True
    - False
3. Unpleasant situations that cause negative stress are called
    - *Eustress*
    - Harm
    - Distress
    - None of these
4. Mood swings is which kind of sign of stress
    - Sensitive syndrome
    - Physical
    - Mental
    - None of these
5. Stress is not contagious
    - True
    - False
6. Which type of stress occurs due to the day-to-day demands and pressures faced by every individual?
    - Acute
    - Chronic
    - Episodic acute
    - None of these

7. When acute stress is experienced frequently, it is termed

   - Acute
   - Episodic acute
   - Chronic
   - None of these

8. Hobbies are a very good way to manage stress.

   - True
   - False

9. Less concentration is which kind of sign of stress

   - Physical
   - Sensitive syndrome
   - Mental
   - None of these

10. ________ focuses on slowing your mind down and clearing it of unimportant matter or things.

    - Regular exercise
    - Excessive alcohol
    - Meditation
    - None of these

CASE STUDY

Infobridge Private Limited is a product development company. It started with two employees and has now grown to 275 employees. This huge growth occurred because of its innovative product development and it is still growing rapidly.

Alan Gay had joined as a managing director in 2009 and started managing its operations. Despite the economic crises in 2010, the company made profits and the credit was given to the managing director. Later in 2012, the company found that it has started going into losses. On investigating, it was found that many employees are on leave for sickness, a few of them are complaining about the sleeping problem, and some of them have upset stomachs. The employees were forced to work overtime and were expected to help each other.

The managing director then hired John Stewart to assess this problem and take necessary actions. On analysing, John realized that there is a strong correlation between the organization and the employee. The top management met and discussed the problem. To have more clear insights into this matter, a one-day workshop was organized for the top management. They conducted few games where the top management was involved into spontaneous movements of their body. They were asked to touch a body part which they found to be very firm. Aggressively, Alan touched the back of his body. This was quite obvious as he carries all the responsibilities on his back for all the operational matters of the organization. The workshop clearly revealed the problems because of which employees were on leave and could not be productive. In another meeting they discussed about the problems that arose in the organization with all the possibilities of intervention. After a long discussion, it was decided that three departments would be established, each separate from the other on professional basis. Three leaders were appointed to look after these departments independently. They also decided to have a rest policy where employees can spend few minutes as a coffee break at 3.30 pm.

To measure the efforts put by the management in order to overcome from losses and regain profit levels, they chose few parameters like decreasing the number or sick leaves, increasing profit levels, physical symptoms, and increasing work satisfaction.

Six months later, the outcomes were evaluated. The profit levels started to grow again and the number of sick leaves was dropped to minimum. A questionnaire was carried to assess the work satisfaction. Stress management was proved to be successful within six months.

Questions

1. What type of job stress is found in this situation?
2. How did the stress affect the organization?
3. What other stress management strategies could have been implemented?

Critical thinking Questions

1. Give an example of a work situation that really stressed you to the maximum.
2. What are the most effective stress strategies to cope up with?
3. What is your word to work under stressful situations that will push you to excel?

Chapter at a Glance

Introduction

Stress is a feeling experienced when a person thinks that the demands exceed his personal and social resources.

Signs and Symptoms of Stress

Signs of Stress in Individuals

Sensitive Syndrome

- Depression or negative feeling
- Feeling of loneliness, solitude
- Getting disappointed with self
- More emotional reactions like getting more aggressive, sensitive, or tearful
- Mood swings
- Loss of confidence
- Loss of motivation

Mental

- More confusion
- Poor memory
- Less concentration

Physical

- Headache problem
- Frequent infections
- Muscle beat
- Breathlessness

(Continued)

(Continued)

Changes in Normal Behaviour

- Changes in eating habits
- Arriving late or taking more time to do things
- Changes in sleep pattern
- Mood swings that affect the behaviour
- Increased drinking, drug intake, and smoking

Signs of Stress in Group

- Stress can be found at workplace too and can be contagious.
- Example: job satisfaction.
- If the organization is not able to note and act upon stress at an early stage, this may be detrimental to team dynamics.

Types of Stress

Acute Stress

- This occurs due to the day-to-day demands and pressures faced by every individual.
- Acute stress in small amount creates a stimulation but causes fatigue when goes beyond a certain level.
- For example, riding a motor boat might be exciting for some time but when the activity is stretched over hours it might be tiring.
- Acute stress exists for a short time and may occur due to burden of work, abiding by the deadlines, trivial accident, and so on.

Episodic Acute Stress

- When acute stress is experienced frequently, it is termed episodic stress.
- This stress is typically noticed among individuals who create self-inflicted, impractical, or unreasonable demands which get all messed up and bring a lot of stress in their effort to achieve these goals.
- Episodic stress is generally seen among the 'type A' personality people who are exceedingly competitive, aggressive, and demanding.

Chronic Stress

- This stress occurs due to long-term exposure to stressors.
- It can also occur because of some traumatic events, unhappy marital life, prolonged illness, problems in relationships, job dissatisfaction, and so on.
- Severe illnesses like stroke, heart attack, depression, and post-traumatic disorder can initiate due to chronic stress.

Causes of Stress

Stress can be categorized as organizational and non-organizational stress, which are caused by the following:

Causes of Organizational Stress

- **Role ambiguity:** It exists when an individual working in the organization is not clear about his roles and responsibilities.
- **Role conflict:** Many a time an individual working in the organization is required to play more than one role. The stress situation arises when he/she plays roles wherein the demands are conflicting.
- **Negligible management support:** When there is no support from the top management, it becomes very difficult for the teams to perform and remain productive and, therefore, stress and frustration level amongst employees increases.
- **Time pressure:** Even tight deadlines can be a cause of organizational stress amongst the individuals and the team involved in projects.
- **Less interest in participation:** Organizational stress can occur when employees are not motivated to participate in decision-making or following a creative approach in their work.
- No sense of belongingness.
- **Less opportunities:** If the organization does not provide enough opportunities to grow or perform, it indirectly affects employees' enthusiasm and effort, leading to negativity and stress.
- **Working conditions:** Improper working conditions like insufficient lighting and ventilation, too much noise and dust, unhygienic sanitation facilities, and so on act as major stressors.
- **Work underload or overload:** When the employee is underloaded he might experience boredom or sometimes a decrease in self-confidence, leading to frustration and stress. On the other hand, work overload might cause excessive pressure on the individual, which in turn takes form of stress.
- **Conflicts at workplace:** It is the difference in attitudes, values, perception, and beliefs of the individuals that lead to conflicts at workplace.
- **Shift working:** Often, adjustments to the shift timing lead to health and family problems.
- **Lack of recognition:** Recognition of the work done is a major motivator. However, lack of recognition may lead to dissatisfaction and stress.
- **Organizational changes:** Adapting and managing change causes stress among the people.
- **Lack of power:** In a workplace, the status of a person also affects the level of stress. Employees of all categories in a workplace get affected by stress, though not at the same level.
- **Social interactions and stress:** Bullying in the workplace can be a threat to an employee's overall and professional or personal image or status.

Causes of Non-organizational Stress

Non-organizational stress incurred by an individual during his lifetime arises due to high expectations in life followed by the fact that they are not possible to satisfy.

- **Basic needs:** Unavailability or insufficiency of basic needs like food, water, shelter, air, and clothing are major sources of stress.
- **Sudden undesirable changes in life:** Sudden undesirable changes in life like transfer to a new location, death of near one, and loss of job can cause immense stress to an individual.

(Continued)

(Continued)

- **High expectations:** Expectations that are higher than those that an individual can actually achieve can cause frustration, which ultimately lead to stress.
- **Too busy schedule:** When an individual has a very busy schedule he/she cannot spare time for family, relaxation, and hobbies, which in a longer stretch become a potential source of stress.
- **Home demands:** Relationships, children, and family, which could not be ignored, are some reasons for stress.
- **Personal demands:** Personal demands are brought on by the person when an individual takes on too many responsibilities from work or any other place.

Managing Stress

Stress should not be ignored, but it has to be managed. Both individuals and organizations can take necessary actions to manage stress. Some of the tips to manage stress are as mentioned below:

- **Communicate with friends and family:** Friends and family members are the people who care for you and are ready to listen to your problems. They understand you and can suggest some way to overcome your stress.
- **Regular exercise:** Regular physical exercise helps reduce stress to a very good extent, which will prevent you from falling into bad stress zone.
- **Meditation:** Meditation focuses on slowing down your mind and clearing it of unimportant matter or things.
- **Managing time:** Planning and prioritizing activities in advance lead to reduction in the level of stress. Thus, managing time can prove to be a good effort in managing stress.
- **Healthy diet and sleep:** Having healthy diet plays a crucial role in managing stress. Good health practices such as getting a good sleep and good nutrition help an individual remain in good stress zone.
- **Leisure/hobbies:** Hobbies are a very good way to manage stress. Hobbies help an individual forget problems and relax the mind.
- **Eliminate stressors in environment:** One of the potential sources of stress is poor working conditions like insufficient lighting, poor ventilation, and so on.
- **Avoid excessive alcohol:** The intake of alcohol and substance containing caffeine should be restricted to reduce stress.
- **Visit doctor:** If stress continues to persist in spite of putting in efforts to manage or reduce, it is advisable to visit a doctor and undergo proper treatment.
- **Identify the stressor:** Identify the reason for stress. For example, if anger is the reason for stress, then try to identify what is the reason for anger.
- **Accept things that cannot be changed:** All the problems cannot be solved in the same way as the way you have planned or intended, but still that problem can be solved in a more successful manner.
- **Positive thinking:** One has to be positive in all aspects.

Bibliography

Anbuvela, K. 2007. *Principles of Management MG 1351*. New Delhi: Laxmi Publications.

Aswathappa, K. 2005. *Human Resource and Personnel Management*. New Delhi: Tata McGraw-Hill Education.

Avitsur, P.N., D.A. Padgett, and J.F. Sheridan. 2009. Social Interactions, Stress, and Immunity. *Immunology and Allergy Clinics of North America*, 29(2): 285–93.

Barnard, C. 1971. *The Functions of the Executive*. Boston, MA: Harvard University Press.

Bhat, A., and A. Kumar. 2008. *Management: Principles, Processes, and Practices*. New Delhi: Oxford University Press.

Brown, A.D. 1998. *Organisational Culture*. London: Financial Times.

Campbell, J.P., M.D. Dunnette, E.E. Lawler III, K.E. Weick. 1970. *Managerial Behavior, Performance, and Effectiveness*. New York: McGraw-Hill.

Cegarra, J.G. 2012. 13th European Conference on Knowledge Management, 6–7 September 2012, Cartagena, Spain.

Chandan, J.S. 1999. *Management Theory and Practice*. Noida: Vikas Publishing.

Cranwell-Ward, J., and A. Alyssa, 2005. *Organizational Stress*. Palgrave Macmillan.

Cummings, T.G. and C.G. Worley. *Organization Development and Change*. Cincinnati, OH: SouthWestern College Publishing.

Dayal, R., P. Zachariah, and K. Rajpal. 1996. *Management Principles and Practices*. New Delhi: Mittal Publications.

Deci, E. and R.M. Ryan. 1985. *Intrinsic Motivation and Self-Determination in Human Behavior*. New York: Kluwer Academic; Boston, MA: Plenum Publishers.

De Janasz, S., G. Wood, L. Gottschalk, and C. Suzanne. 2006. *Interpersonal Skills in Organisations*. Australia: McGraw-Hill.

Deb, T. 2006. *Strategic Approach to Human Resource Management*. New Delhi: Atlantic.

Fiedler, F.E. 1964. 'A Contingency Model of Leadership Effectiveness'. In *Advances in Experimental Social Psychology*, edited by L. Berkowitz. New York: Academic Press.

Fiedler, F.E. 1967. *A Theory of Leadership Effectiveness*. New York: McGraw-Hill.

Forsyth, D.R. 2014. *Group Dynamics*. Belmont, Canada: Wadsworth Cengage Learning.

Funkenstein, D.H., M.E. Drolette, and S.H. King. 1957. *Mastery of Stress*. Boston, MA: Harvard University Press.

Gujral, G.S. 2012. *Leadership Qualities for Effective Leaders*. New Delhi: Vij Books.

Hickman, Gill R. (Robinson). 2010. *Leading Organizations: Perspectives for a New Era*. SAGE Publications.

Hogg, M.A. and G.M. Vaughan. 2008. *Social Psychology*. London: Pearson; Prentice Hall.

Humphrey, J.H. 2002. *Teenagers Will Be Teenagers*. New York: Kroshka Books.

Karl, A. 1979. *Stress and the Manager*. Englewood Cliffs, NJ: Prentice-Hall.

Koontz H. 2010. *Essentials of Management*. New Delhi: Tata McGraw-Hill.

Kormanik, M.B. 2005. *White males in transition: Describing the experience of a stalled career*. Dissertation Abstracts International.

Kumar, A., and R. Sharma. 2000. *Principles of Business Management*. New Delhi: Atlantic.

Lencioni, P. 2012. *The Five Dysfunctions of a Team*. San Francisco, CA: Pfeiffer.

Lonbardo & Eichinger. 2001. *Corporate Leadership Council*. McCall.

Lussier, R., and C. Achua. 2009. *Leadership: Theory, Application, and Skill Development*. Boston, MA: Cengage Learning.

Martins, N. and E. Martins. 2003. Organisational Culture. In S.P. Robbins, A.T. Judge, A. Odendaal, and G. Roodt (Eds), *Organisational Behaviour: Global and South African Perspectives* (pp. 379–400). Cape Town: Pearson Education.

Maslow, H. 2013. *A Theory of Human Motivation*. Start Publishing LLC.

Mayo, E. 1933. *The Human Problems of an Industrial Civilization*. New York: Macmillan.

Mayo, G.E. 1941. *Critical Evaluations in Business and Management*. Volume 1, Management and Morale. Cambridge, MA: Harvard University Press.

McGrath, J.E. 1976. 'Stress and Behavior in Organizations'. In *Handbook of Industrial and Organizational Psychology*, edited by M.D. Dunnett. Chicago, IL: McNally College Publishing.

Murugan, M.S. 2008. *Management Principles and Practices*. New Age International Pvt Ltd Publishers.

Mustafa, A. 2013. *Organisational Behaviour*. Global Professional publishing Limited.

Northouse, P.G. 2012. *Leadership: Theory and Practice*. SAGE Publications.

O'Rourke, J., and S.D. Collins. 2005. *Module 5: Managing Conflict and Workplace Relationships*. Cengage.

Paul, D., J. Cadle and P. Thomas. 2012. *The Human Touch: Personal Skills for Professional Success*. London: British Computer Society.

Piers Steel and C.J. Konig. 2006. Integrating Theories of Motivation. *Academy of Management Review*, 31(4): 899–913.

Prasad, L.M. 2006. *Principles and Practice of Management*. Sultan Chand and Sons.

Quaddus M.A., L.L. Tung, W.M. Foo, L.-j. Poh, and C.M. Soon. 2000. Group Conflict and Conflict Management in a Decision Conferencing Environment in Singapore. In the Proceedings of the 33rd Hawaii International Conference on System Sciences.

Raines, S.S. 2013. *Conflict Management for Managers Resolving Workplace, Client, and Policy Disputes*. San Francisco, CA: Jossey-Bass.

Rawat H.S., and Singh Y.K. 2006. *Human Resources Management*. New Delhi: APH Publishing Corporation.

Robbins, S.P., R. Bergman, I. Stagg, and M. Coulter. 2009. *Management*. Australia: Pearson Education.

Robbins, S.P. 1994. *Organisational Behaviour: Concepts, Controversies and Applications*. Australia: Prentice Hall.

Sahu, R.K. 2010. *Group Dynamics and Team Building*. Excel Books.

Sengupta, N., M.S. Bhattacharya, and R.N. Sengupta. 2006. *Managing Change in Organizations*. New Delhi: Prentice- Hall.

Singh, K. 2009. *Organizational Behaviour: Text and Cases*. Pearson Education.

Stein, J. Just Say Om. *Time Magazine*, August 4, 2003.

Torrington, D., and S. Taylor. 2009. *Fundamentals of Human Resource Management: Managing People at Work*. Prentice Hall/Financial Times.

Katta, A.K. 2013.Training and Development Practices and Performance of SCCL. *International Journal of Pharmaceutical Sciences and Business Management*, 1(1): 82–103.

Tripathi, P.C. 2008. *Principles of Management*. New Delhi: Tata McGraw-Hill Education.

Williams, J.C. and G.P. Huber. 1986. *Human Behavior in Organizations*. Cincinnati, OH: South-Western Publishing.

Wyer, R.S., C.-y. Chiu, and Y.-y. Hong. 2009. *Understanding Culture: Theory, Research, and Application*. New York: Psychology Press.

Web Resources

https://en.wikipedia.org/wiki/Managerial_grid_model

http://essays.pw/essay/the-directing-and-controlling-accounting-essay-8456

http://www.managingstress.com/#!definitions-of-stress/c194k

http://www.webmd.com/balance/guide/tips-to-control-stress

https://explorable.com/three-different-kinds-of-stress

http://www.onlinemba.com/blog/10-big-companies-that-promote-employee-meditation/

http://managementstudyguide.com/management_functions.htm

http://www.yourarticlelibrary.com/recruitment/recruitment-process-5-steps-involved-in-recruitment-process-with-diagram/35261/

http://www.ijpsbm.com/

http://www.yourarticlelibrary.com/employees/training-methods-on-job-training-and-off-the-job-training-methods/5421/

http://www.statpac.org/walonick/leadership.htm

https://www.americanexpress.com/us/small-business/openforum/articles/leadership-styles-5-most-common-techniques-decoded/

http://managementhelp.org/groups/dynamics-theories.htm

http://grantspace.org/tools/knowledge-base/Nonprofit-Management/Sustainability/contingency-and-scenario-planning

http://www.bizjournals.com/tampabay/news/2015/06/16/meet-publixs-next-big-threat-lidl-the-german.html

http://www.business-standard.com/article/b2b-connect/bilcare-research-plans-capacity-expansion-in-germany-115090900683_1.html

http://www.myersbriggs.org/my-mbti-personality-type/mbti-basics/

http://www.medicinenet.com/stress_management_techniques

http://www.psychologydiscussion.net/conflicts/conflicts-notes-on-3-types-of-conflictspsychology/688

https://commons.wikimedia.org/wiki/File:Systems_Model_of_Action-Research_Process.jpg

http://www.managementstudyguide.com/herzbergs-theory-motivation.htm

http://managementocean.blogspot.in/2012/07/summary-introduction-and-foundations-of.html

http://psychologyconceptswithhrm.blogspot.in/

http://academlib.com/2814/management/models_organiational_behaviour

http://wikieducator.org/Organizational_Behavior

http://nptel.ac.in/courses/110105034/SM_Web/Module%20one-lec-1.2.3.pdf

http://www.newagepublishers.com/samplechapter/001395.pdf

https://blog.udemy.com/stages-of-conflict/

http://academlib.com/2866/management/stages_conflict_conflict_process

http://study.com/academy/lesson/what-is-the-conflict-process-definition-and-stages.html

http://www.edunote.info/2013/01/5-stages-of-conflict-process.html

http://www.fao.org/docrep/w7504e/w7504e07.htm

http://www.personalityexplorer.com/FREEResources/ConflictManagementTechniques.aspx

http://www.foundationcoalition.org/publications/brochures/conflict.pdf

http://hrweb.berkeley.edu/guides/managing-hr/interaction/conflict/resolving

http://armandojusto.blogspot.in/2009/04/organizational-development-od.html

Index